Women, Poverty, and Demographic Change

The International Union for the Scientific Study of Population Problems was set up in 1928, with Dr Raymond Pearl as President. At that time the Union's main purpose was to promote international scientific co-operation to study the various aspects of population problems, through national committees and through its members themselves. In 1947 the International Union for the Scientific Study of Population (IUSSP) was reconstituted into its present form.

It expanded its activities to:

- stimulate research on population
- develop interest in demographic matters among governments, national and international organizations, scientific bodies, and the general public
- foster relations between people involved in population studies
- disseminate scientific knowledge on population.

The principal ways through which the IUSSP currently achieves its aims are:

- organization of worldwide or regional conferences
- operations of Scientific Committees under the auspices of the Council
- organization of training courses
- publication of conference proceedings and committee reports.

Demography can be defined by its field of study and its analytical methods. Accordingly, it can be regarded as the scientific study of human populations primarily with respect to their size, their structure, and their development. For reasons which are related to the history of the discipline, the demographic method is essentially inductive: progress in knowledge results from the improvement of observation, the sophistication of measurement methods, and the search for regularities and stable factors leading to the formulation of explanatory models. In conclusion, the three objectives of demographic analysis are to describe, measure, and analyse.

International Studies in Demography is the outcome of an agreement concluded by the IUSSP and the Oxford University Press. The joint series reflects the broad range of the Union's activities; it is based on the seminars organized by the Union and important international meetings in the field of population and development. The Editorial Board of the series is comprised of:

John Cleland, UK   Henri Leridon, France
John Hobcraft, UK   Richard Smith, UK
Georges Tapinos, France

Women, Poverty, and Demographic Change

Edited by
Brígida García

OXFORD
UNIVERSITY PRESS

This book has been printed digitally and produced in a standard specification
in order to ensure its continuing availability

OXFORD
UNIVERSITY PRESS

Great Clarendon Street, Oxford OX2 6DP

Oxford University Press is a department of the University of Oxford.
It furthers the University's objective of excellence in research, scholarship,
and education by publishing worldwide in

Oxford New York

Auckland Bangkok Buenos Aires Cape Town Chennai
Dar es Salaam Delhi Hong Kong Istanbul Karachi Kolkata
Kuala Lumpur Madrid Melbourne Mexico City Mumbai Nairobi
São Paulo Shanghai Singapore Taipei Tokyo Toronto

with an associated company in Berlin

Oxford is a registered trade mark of Oxford University Press
in the UK and in certain other countries

Published in the United States
by Oxford University Press Inc., New York

© IUSSP 2000

ISBN 0-19-829486-7

Dedicated to the
Memory of
Bruno Remiche

Contents

viii   *Contents*

Contributors

ALAKA MALWADE BASU	Cornell University
DEBORAH S. DEGRAFF	Bowdoin College
SONALDE DESAI	University of Maryland, College Park
KATHARINE M. DONATO	Louisiana State University
BRÍGIDA GARCÍA	El Colegio de México
ROSA N. GELDSTEIN	Centro de Estudios de Población, Buenos Aires
PAVALAVALLI GOVINDASAMY	Macro International Inc., Calverton, Maryland
GRACIELA INFESTA DOMÍNGUEZ	Centro de Estudios de Población, Buenos Aires
SHAWN MALIA KANAIAUPUNI	University of Wisconsin, Madison
ANJU MALHOTRA	International Center for Research on Women
MARIO MONTEIRO	Nucleo de Estudos de Saude Coletiva, Rio de Janeiro
S. PHILIP MORGAN	Duke University
BHANU B. NIRAULA	Agricultural Project Service Center, Kathmandu
ORLANDINA DE OLIVEIRA	El Colegio de México
EDITH A. PANTELIDES	Centro de Estudios de Población, Buenos Aires
ZEBA SATHAR	The Population Council, Pakistan
SUSHEELA SINGH	The Alan Guttmacher Institute, New York
MICHAEL TAWANDA	University of Zimbabwe
HANIA ZLOTNIK	United Nations Population Division, New York

Preface

This book grew out of a seminar on 'Women, Poverty and Demographic Change' held in Oaxaca, Mexico, on 25–28 October 1994. The seminar was sponsored by the IUSSP Committee on Gender and Population (1990–1994), co-chaired by Shireen Jejeebhoy and Karen Oppenheim Mason, with Brígida García, An-Magritt Jensen, Paulina Makinwa-Adebusoye, and Catherine Pierce as regular members.

As a result of two previous seminars emphasizing family transformations in industrialized countries and women's position and demographic change in Sub-Saharan Africa, the Committee on Gender and Population decided to organize a seminar to explore the relation between women in poverty and demographic change in developing countries. World poverty has begun to elicit the increasing concern of the international community, although insufficient research and policy efforts have been directed towards explaining the different experience of poverty between men and women in relation to population issues. This constitutes the starting point for the various chapters in this book, which brings together research and experience from the developing nations of Asia, Africa, and Latin America.

In Part I, conceptual and methodological problems concerning the relation between women's position, poverty, and demographic change are critically analysed using numerous examples from several national contexts while at the same time cautioning against over-generalization. In Part II, changes in fertility and marriage, as well as abortion practices, are examined according to women's poverty status. The aim of this part is not only to establish the differences between poverty groups, but also to study cultural influences as well as women's attitudes and motives. Part III focuses on women's migration and participation in the labour force, as distinct from men's, and the extent to which these strategies may help to alleviate poverty. Finally, in Part IV women's behaviour concerning their health is critically analysed, together with the implications for policy design. The essays in this book provide important evidence indicating the ways in which women's condition, their poverty status, and demographic change are interrelated. From another perspective, the book shows how addressing women's position in society and the role of gender contributes to a better understanding of the relation between poverty and demographic change.

The publication of this book serves as an appropriate occasion to honour the memory of Bruno Remiche who, as Executive Secretary of the IUSSP, worked closely with the members of the first Committee on Gender and

Population in all its activities from the time of its inception in 1990. Bruno was an extremely generous and knowledgeable adviser and we also benefited from his skills as a fund-raiser, negotiator, organizer, and world traveller. He was also a loyal friend and enthusiastically supported the incorporation of the gender perspective into population studies; he will always be fondly remembered.

Finally we wish to thank the institutions and people who supported the organization of the seminar and participated in the various stages of the book's production. Special thanks are due to the Centre for Demographic and Urban Studies (CEDDU) of El Colegio de México and the State Population Council of Oaxaca. We are particularly grateful to the MacArthur Foundation for funding several activities organized by the Committee on Gender and Population. We are also indebted to Irene Grignac of the IUSSP, and Alma Barba and Coral Chamu of CEDDU, for their professional commitment, copy-editing, and administrative and secretarial support.

Brígida García

Introduction: Women, Poverty, and Demographic Change in Developing Countries

Brígida García

Global poverty is increasingly attracting the attention of the international community. Poverty has various important manifestations, including lack of income and productive resources sufficient to secure a sustainable livelihood; hunger, malnutrition, and ill-health; and lack of access to education, housing, and other basic services. Although there are many dimensions to poverty, global estimates of the world's poor are usually based on income levels.[1] It is generally assumed that below a certain level of income (termed the 'poverty line') individuals cannot obtain adequate nourishment, shelter, and health services.

According to some of these income estimates made by the World Bank—which uses US$1 per person per day as a minimum poverty line for consistent international comparisons—about 30 per cent of the population of the developing countries, or 1.3 billion individuals, were below the poverty line in 1993. This absolute number is forecast to remain approximately the same in the year 2000, even under the most favourable assumptions of economic growth (see World Bank 1990, 1993; Livi-Bacci 1994; Fourth World Conference on Women 1995).

The deep roots of poverty can be found in the unequal distribution of opportunities and resources, and also in the uneven access of different population groups to the benefits of progress. However, in many areas of the world, global impoverishment has been exacerbated by the transformations taking place in the current economic system. Trade deregulation and rapid technological change, as well as economic, fiscal, and social restructuring, have provided opportunities for some individuals, but in many cases have also intensified existing inequalities (see UNIFEM 1995).

The relationships between demographic change and poverty can be addressed in different ways. The most common approach is to study the ways in which poverty influences demographic outcomes, for example, by analysing the numbers and characteristics of the poor regarding fertility, mortality, age distribution, migration, and patterns of settlement. The next interesting possibility is to analyse the reverse relationship: that is, the extent to which demographic behaviours and phenomena may affect poverty. For example, emigration can affect the ability of individuals to escape from poverty, and sickness and orphanhood may determine the decline into poverty (see Livi-Bacci 1994).[2]

All of these different types of relationships have been addressed to some extent in the demographic literature, but without placing particular emphasis on the issue of gender. Nevertheless, it has been argued that women experience poverty in a different way than men do, and that they represent a disproportionate and increasing share of the world's poor. One of the main explanatory factors for women's over-representation in poverty is the increasing proportion of female workers in low-status occupations that offer very low income. Other important aspects are the greater propensity of female-headed households towards poverty, their increasing numbers, and the greater extent to which female heads bear the sole responsibility for meeting household needs. Women's relative disadvantage is usually exacerbated by their limited or non-existent access to education, training, decision-making, and economic resources (such as credit, technology, land ownership, and inheritance) as well as the segregation of the labour markets (see Buvinic and Lycette 1988; Feldman 1992; Lloyd 1993; Basu, Chapter 1 of this volume).

Many authors also point out that women in many parts of the world have been particularly affected by recent changes in economic policies which have resulted in declining standards of living; this situation has forced women to increase the number of hours spent in extra-domestic activities and household tasks. Available evidence demonstrates that in many developing countries women average more work hours per week than men when unpaid work and household activities are taken into account (see United Nations 1991; Fourth World Conference on Women 1995; Basu, Chapter 1 of this volume).

Given the rapidly growing numbers of women in poverty, and the lack of knowledge of how poverty and gender are related to demographic phenomena, the Gender and Population Committee of the International Union for the Scientific Study of Population (IUSSP) decided as one of its priorities to hold a Seminar on the topic of 'Women, Poverty, and Demographic Change'. The Seminar was held in Oaxaca, Mexico, in October 1994. This book contains a selection of the papers presented at that Seminar which analyse from a gender perspective the extent to which poverty affects, but may also be influenced in different ways by, demographic behaviour. The specific objectives of the book are: (1) to examine the ways in which women's experiences of poverty, to the extent that they are different from men's, lead to particular demographic outcomes; (2) to show the paths by which demographic events may determine women's ability to achieve well-being and escape from poverty; (3) to make explicit the specific circumstances that poor women face in trying to attain a healthy life for themselves and their children.

The organisation of the book closely follows these basic objectives. In Part I, 'Overview and Critical Issues', conceptual and operational aspects regarding the relationships between the position of women, poverty, and demographic change are addressed. In Part II, 'Nuptiality, Fertility, and

Abortion Practices by Poverty Status', various types of demographic behaviours are analysed for poor and non-poor women in different regional contexts of the developing world, using quantitative and qualitative methodological approaches. In Part III, 'Strategies to Alleviate Poverty: Women's Extra-domestic Work and Migration', the specific alternatives and limitations that women face in implementing work and migration strategies are closely examined. Finally, in the last part of the book, 'Health Care Behaviour in the Context of Poverty', poor women's health care behaviour as well as that of their families is analysed, showing the particular gender and socio-economic aspects which constrain the ability to lead a healthy life in some countries of the Third World.

The studies have been conducted in a variety of national and regional contexts in the developing world: Nepal, Pakistan, and Sri Lanka in Asia; Mali in West Africa; Egypt in North Africa; and Mexico, Brazil, and Argentina in Latin America. There are also some chapters which look at women's poverty and demographic change from an international perspective.

The different investigations refer to the situation of poor women in comparison with the non-poor, but also address the comparison between poor women and men, or take into account women's and men's relative socio-economic position in explaining demographic outcomes. The authors use a range of definitions of poverty, reflecting different positions regarding the ongoing debate between more restricted definitions of poverty and poor groups (mostly based on income and educational levels) and wider conceptions of poverty which incorporate dimensions of social interaction, discrimination, exclusion, decision-making power, and freedom of thought (see Sen 1981; Desai 1992; UNDP 1996).

Alaka Basu is the author who uses the widest definition of poverty. Besides exploring poverty indicators which are independent of sex (access to employment and income; education and information; health; nutrition; private property; common property; leisure; state and legal protection of rights), she also analyses other dimensions which take into account gender issues (decision-making authority and control over resources in the household; the extent to which public and private domains of life are demarcated; reproductive health and rights, including control over sexuality; marital and domestic stability, including domestic violence; and the level of physical security outside the home). In the same line of reasoning, authors such as Orlandina de Oliveira refer to *the quality of life* or the well-being of women, combining access to economic resources with the presence of instability and conflict in the family of origin (presence of alcoholism, irresponsibility, physical violence, family disintegration due to the parents' death or abandonment of the children), in contrast with love and respect, dialogue, family understanding and unity, responsibility, trust and equality.

Other authors define social class (poor/non-poor; low/middle/upper) in the classic sense of ownership of means of production and combine indicators of land value or land tenure status, ownership of cattle, business enterprise or petty shop. Also, different household or housing variables are used to define socio-economic status: construction materials used in houses, number of rooms, and ownership of consumer durables such as radios, bicycles, televisions, refrigerators, and others.[3]

Finally, some authors define poverty or socio-economic status based on single measures of income or occupational and educational status.[4] Those that use some measure of employment or occupation to refer indirectly to a person's socio-economic position consider that poor persons have few assets other than their labour; in that way, their occupational characteristics are a fundamental determinant of their economic situation (see Bilsborrow, DeGraff, and Anker 1992; Zlotnik, Chapter 8 of this volume).

In the next four sections of this introduction, the main concerns and findings of the different chapters in this book are synthesized, with the objective of pointing out each chapter's significance for particular fields of study. Attention is also given to methodological and design issues. The last section draws together the main conclusions in the book and its general contribution to the study of gender and population.

Overview and Critical Issues

In this part of the book, conceptual and analytical problems in defining the interrelationships between the situation of women, poverty, and demographic change are first examined critically by Alaka Basu, in her essay on 'Women, Poverty, and Demographic Change: Some Possible Interrelationships over Time and Space'. This chapter is an overview of the literature which offers numerous examples as well as important notes of caution. In the second study included in this part, 'Gender Inequality in Two Nepali Settings' by Bhanu Niraula and Philip Morgan, the authors are also mainly concerned with conceptual and measurement problems regarding the notion of women's autonomy in poor settings, as this is considered to be one of the key dimensions of gender-stratification systems that influences demographic change. Niraula and Morgan's chapter is based on research conducted in two villages in Nepal which explores the connections between social, demographic, and economic characteristics (age, education, employment) and women's autonomy. Their investigation is one of the few available that combines direct measurement of women's autonomy at the individual level with a study design that compares communities differing in gender systems (see Mason 1995).

In Chapter 1, Basu first calls our attention to several different indicators of poverty and to the range of situations in which poor women live. Given the vast extent of potential indicators, her main proposition is that the relations between the position of women, poverty, and demographic change can be similarly varied. She expresses scepticism about universal generalizations, which can be invalid and irrelevant for policy purposes. Her key thesis is to take 'context' into account, where context refers to the larger settings in which many of these interrelations are played out: a combination of cultural, household, and individual-level forces that can drastically change over time and space.

Basu explores various aspects of the relationships between gender and poverty. She finds conclusive evidence of the widespread and disproportionate impact of poverty on women, but also notes a broad range of situations in which the poor woman may be better off than her richer sister in terms of decision-making power and freedom of movement. A second concern is demographic change and poverty from a gender perspective. She points out unexpected interrelationships and also shows how they vary over time and space in different cultural contexts. According to Basu, the evidence is least conclusive on the matter of poverty and fertility; the usual understanding is that the poor have more children than do the non-poor, but the evidence is not unambiguous on this matter, in part because of the role played by intermediary variables such as fecundity and spousal separation.

Finally, Basu considers how female poverty is related to demographic change and behaviour. Again, she argues that there are conflicting results here. For example, poor women often have lower levels of education and higher rates of economic activity, variables which usually have opposite effects on fertility. The net effect then depends on the strength of influence of each factor.

Basu's overall approach is undoubtedly controversial and thought-provoking. In her conclusions she acknowledges that her paper has taken the safe way out by exhibiting a vast canvas of possibilities and by critically examining a few key interrelationships, instead of arriving at solid generalizations. She succeeds, however, in raising important questions regarding the variables of interest and how they are interrelated in specific regions of the world and moments in time, questions that other chapters of the book contribute to answering.

As was noted above, the changing education and economic activities of poor women can lead to a modification of reproductive patterns. It is important to acknowledge, however, that these variables can sometimes be conceptually distant from the dimensions of gender-stratification systems which are often hypothesized to influence demographic change (for instance, women's autonomy, women's empowerment, women's control over resources; see Mason 1995). Niraula and Morgan are interested precisely in exploring further the connection between characteristics such as age, education, and employment, and women's autonomy in poor settings. They conceptualize women's autonomy as women's freedom of movement and as women having input in household decision-making.[5]

Their results are mostly consistent with their hypotheses and hold across settings. That is, older women, better-educated women, women who are spouses of the household head, and poorer women have greater autonomy (the greater autonomy of poor women is explained by the fact that in the Nepali cultural setting, these women are relatively less subject to household seclusion). Results for the employment of the wife are the major exception, as the authors had expected that wage work would increase women's power by providing them with direct access to resources. Their results add to the evidence that the effects of wage work are strongly context-specific. Whether wage work increases women's status very likely depends on the type of work available, the structure of work routines, and the degree of control women have over the wages they earn.

Nuptiality, Fertility, and Abortion Practices by Poverty Status

Three chapters are included in Part II of the book: 'Quality of Life and Marital Experiences in Mexico' by Orlandina de Oliveira; 'Adolescent Women in Buenos Aires: The Influence of Social Class and Gender Images on Repro-ductive Behaviour', by Edith A. Pantelides, Graciela Infesta Domínguez, and Rosa N. Geldstein; and 'Levels of Childbearing, Contraception, and Abortion in Brazil: Differentials by Poverty Status', by Susheela Singh and Mario Mon-teiro. These authors analyse different types of demographic behaviours and outcomes for poor and non-poor women in three Latin American countries. In some cases their aim is not only to establish the existence of differences between social groups, but to study cultural influences as well as women's attitudes and motives regarding nuptiality and fertility outcomes in poor and non-poor groups. Additionally, the chapter by Singh and Monteiro draws together scattered evidence on abortion practices by income levels in Brazil.

It is sometimes claimed that the evidence gathered from comparing demographic characteristics of poor and non-poor groups systematically indicates that poor groups have higher fertility, mortality, and family size than the more privileged sectors of society. As was mentioned above, however, some authors argue that this is not always the case (see Livi-Bacci 1995; Basu, Chapter 1 of this volume). That there can be more than one type of relation-ship indicates the usefulness of investigations that compare poor and non-poor groups, particularly in under-researched sub-areas such as abortion and sexuality (Singh and Monteiro, Chapter 5 of this volume), or of studies that contribute to our understanding of the subjective dimensions of women's demographic behaviour in poor and non-poor groups through qualitative analysis (Chapters 3 and 4 in this volume). Regardless of methodology or focus, analysing the demographic characteristics of the poor in comparison with the non-poor is a preliminary way of understanding poverty and a necessary first step to the formulation of policies and the planning of interventions (Livi-Bacci 1994).

In Chapter 3, Oliveira analyses the marital experiences of a small group of women in Mexico, classifying different types of families according to the availability of economic resources and the presence of conflicts during their childhood and adolescence. Her findings indicate that the availability of economic resources is the most important aspect to take into account in analysing perceptions of married life and the meaning of marriage. Nevertheless, family background is also important to understanding women's age at marriage and their motivations for marrying.

Women from poor families face more problems in married life than do non-poor women (violence, alcoholism, lack of economic support on the part of the spouses, restrictions on their movement outside the home, and so on).[6] Also, reasons for marrying for these women focus more on economic support, companionship, and motherhood, while for non-poor women it is the search for understanding that counts. Additionally, it is very important to consider the internal dynamics of the family of origin—together with the availability of economic resources—in order to understand fully the age at first conjugal union and the motives for marrying. In extreme cases, women from poor, unstable, and conflict-ridden families are more prone to early unions and to marrying in order to escape from family problems than are women from non-poor, stable, and less conflicted families, who marry later and tend to marry for love.

Chapter 4, by Pantelides, Domínguez, and Geldstein, concerning adolescent women in Buenos Aires, Argentina, explores the relationship between gender images, sexual initiation, and contraceptive use in two social classes (lower class and upper middle class as defined by mother's and father's occupational and educational status). The concept of gender images refers to the set of different subjective representations that both males and females have of their relative positions and roles, involving different degrees of autonomy and power. According to the authors, this concept may help us simultaneously to grasp aspects frequently related to adolescent fertility such as self-esteem, achievement orientation, perception of alternative opportunities, and sense of self-control.

For Pantelides, Domínguez, and Geldstein, traditional gender images encompass a wide range of beliefs about men being the providers and more interested in sex, in contrast to women being the mothers and housekeepers, and incomplete human beings if they do not bear children. Their findings for a small group of adolescent women indicate that there is a positive relationship between traditional gender images and risky contraceptive behaviour (having unprotected intercourse), but that this association holds only for the lower class.[7] That is, those women with more traditional responses regarding gender images in the lower class show higher frequencies of unprotected first intercourse and also tend to answer more frequently that their partner is the one who should take care of contraception.

Finally, the aim of the chapter by Singh and Monteiro (Chapter 5) is to bring together the somewhat scattered information that is available on poverty levels among women of reproductive age in Brazil in relation to women's reproductive behaviour (fertility levels, contraceptive use, and abortion).[8]

According to these authors, family size in Brazil continues to be higher among poor women, as it was in the past, even before the fertility decline began. The estimates of the level of induced abortion for income sub-groups developed in this chapter suggest that the lowest income group of women is less likely to terminate a pregnancy by abortion than are better-off groups. These estimates, however, do not provide a definitive answer to the question whether the abortion rate (the number of abortions per 100 women per year) differs according to poverty status. Depending on the pattern of under-reporting that is assumed, the authors obtain conflicting results. Nevertheless, circumstantial evidence from income-status differences in contraceptive use (which are very small) compared to differences in fertility (which are relatively large) suggests that higher-income women probably have a higher abortion rate.

Strategies to Alleviate Poverty: Women's Extra-Domestic Work and Migration

Women's market work

Chapters 6 and 7 ('Daughters and Wives: Marital Status, Poverty, and Young Women's Employment in Sri Lanka' by Anju Malhotra and Deborah S. DeGraff; 'Class and Gender in Rural Pakistan: Differentials in Economic Activity' by Zeba Sathar and Sonalde Desai) contribute to our understanding of the relationships between poverty and women's market work and how they operate in different national and economic settings. Both chapters focus on South Asia; Malhotra and DeGraff study the Kalutara district of Sri Lanka while Sathar and Desai analyse the case of rural areas in Pakistan.

Market work and territorial mobility are frequently considered possible ways in which poverty can be alleviated. In particular, it has increasingly been found that women's economic contributions to poor households are distinctive from men's and make a difference in welfare, particularly because women's earnings and extent of contributions are central to ensuring the family and children's nutritional well-being (see Buvinic and Lycette 1988).

With regard to differences according to social groups, in many countries poor women are more likely to participate in the labour market than are the non-poor because of economic need. There is also evidence, however, that a negative or even curvilinear relationship between socio-economic status and women's employment exists in some settings for various reasons. Poor women may lack the training and skills needed to obtain jobs, their daily domestic burdens may be very time-consuming, and better-off women may have access to domestic help and therefore be in a better position to enter the labour market (see Malhotra and DeGraff's chapter, and García and Oliveira 1994 for evidence on Mexico, a country where middle-class women generally have skills and domestic help that greatly facilitate their labour market participation).

Malhotra and DeGraff address the issue of women's market work in different social classes in Sri Lanka, a society where the position of women has been relatively favourable, and where late entry into marriage, as well as women's access to education, has been important. One of their main interests is the role played by marital status in shaping women's market work in different social classes. Because marriage is central to women's lives in most Asian societies, they assume that freedoms and restrictions, as well as the expected contributions to household survival strategies, would be perceived differently by unmarried daughters as compared to wives.

Malhotra and DeGraff's findings show a different interplay between socio-economic position and marital status in determining women's employment.[9] In Sri Lanka, poverty promotes women's market work, regardless of marital status. In that sense, women's employment is part of a household survival strategy among the poor, as evidenced by the greater propensity of poor working women, both single and married, to contribute their earnings to the household. However, this is not the case among wealthier women. Here clear differences by marital status were found. Upper-class status leads to a greater likelihood of employment among young married women, but not among young single women. It seems that married women aspire or are expected to contribute to maintaining or improving the household's status, and in that way employment is not merely poverty-driven among the group of married women; in contrast, the labour force participation of unmarried daughters appears to be more oriented towards personal fulfilment. This goes along with the idea that unmarried daughters in Sri Lanka are more often viewed as receiving care, and as such their role is not strongly prescribed by family obligations and responsibilities.

Sathar and Desai compare women's (and men's) market work (agricultural, non-agricultural; wage, on own farm, on own business) in different social classes in rural Pakistan. Central to their paper is the issue of men's and women's differential experience of poverty. They analyse gender differences in employment across households, as well as the interdependence between employment of men and women within the same household.[10]

Their findings suggest that women from almost all classes do work, but the burden of long hours of work is more prevalent among the poorest groups, that is, sharecroppers and those in households that do not own land, livestock, or a business. Regarding the differences between women's and men's experiences of poverty, they conclude that the burden of poverty is borne disproportionately by women. Men and women are equally restricted in their access to productive agricultural resources, but a large proportion of men manage to find work in the non-agricultural sector. For women, there are few opportunities available for better-remunerated work outside of agriculture because of their lack of educational skills. Thus, although men and women are equally affected by the nature of the rural economy, women are limited in their ability to cope with its negative consequences due to gender inequality and cultural norms circumscribing their physical movements.

Women's Migration

The first chapter on this topic (Chapter 8, by Hania Zlotnik), analyses the relationship between women's participation in migratory flows and poverty alleviation, an economic perspective in the study of migration frequently considered only for the case of men. The other two chapters, by Katharine Donato and Shawn Kanaiaupuni (Chapter 9) and Michael Tawanda (Chapter 10), explore the determinants of women's migration in poor contexts, including their economic and social position relative to men and to different household members. These authors show the importance of taking into consideration gender and social issues, as well as more traditional economic factors, in explaining women's and men's migration.

Migration has generally been viewed as a process through which individuals can obtain better economic opportunities and earn higher wages. From that perspective, it is also pertinent to enquire to what extent it can be a means of alleviating or combating poverty. The relationship between migration, improved employment, and poverty alleviation has, however, been mostly explored for men (Todaro 1976; Zlotnik, this volume). Zlotnik provides a comprehensive analysis for the case of women. She studies the relationship between female migration, female labour force participation, and occupational status, and their potential for reducing or alleviating poverty, for various countries of the developing world.

Zlotnik points out that comparable data on migration and employment at an international level come mostly from population censuses and are relatively scarce. A careful analysis of these data suggests the following pattern, however. At low levels of development, when agricultural work prevails, women who migrate and are economically active do not have many options besides engaging in agricultural activities. In this case, the potential effect of migration on poverty is likely to be small. At a later stage of development, the concentration of resources in cities improves the well-being of a part of the population, which then becomes able to hire domestic workers. In those cases, many migrant women who are economically active leave agricultural work for domestic service, which can provide some alleviation from poverty because of the opportunity to earn an income and gain independence within the family.

In yet more advanced countries, women's employment in the production sector tends to rise. To the extent that manufacturing jobs provide an alternative to domestic service for unskilled women, migration to secure these jobs may contribute to poverty alleviation. Yet, the lack of promotion prospects for unskilled women in sectors such as manufacturing and domestic services is not conducive to the long-term improvement of their economic status. An important group studied by Zlotnik is foreign domestic workers. The evidence indicates that their migration has a positive impact in combating poverty, although this impact may be short-lived because the restrictions that female migrant workers face while abroad prevent any sustained improvement of their economic gains.

The chapter by Zlotnik offers a useful background for the study of Mexican female international migration by Donato and Kanaiaupuni, and the analysis of African migration from rural areas in Mali by Tawanda.

Donato and Kanaiaupuni are well aware that a persistent finding in international migration research is that individuals move in search of economic opportunity. They argue, however, that adding gender makes the relationship more complex. Women's economic and social position relative to men's can be a crucial determinant of female migration. For example, women's decision-making autonomy, or perhaps their ability to place their own welfare above that of their families, may influence their migration. Also, women's employment prospects relative to men's, or their differential access to the resources available from migrant networks, may influence whether they decide to migrate (see Lim 1993).[11]

Donato and Kanaiaupuni use two indicators of women's status relative to men's, based on sex-specific migration prevalence and labour force activity rates. Their findings lead to the conclusion that these relative dimensions of women's status are significant in shaping their migration flows. At the community level, the predominance of men in US migration lowers the chances for women to migrate, as they are probably left with increased family responsibilities. This can be attributed to the fact that Mexican women have not been able to place their own needs above those of other family members. Moreover, growing employment opportunities for women in their communities of origin, relative to that of men, also depress women's territorial mobility. This chapter then shows specific ways in which women's status, relative to that of men's, can influence their migration patterns. The results provide a basis for future work on gender, migration, and poverty.

In the last chapter of Part III, Tawanda is also interested in exploring the effects of social dynamics as they differ from the economic determinants of rural outmigration. He argues that besides gender differences, the central aspect to take into consideration in explaining rural population retention or outmigration is the degree of subordination of both men and women to the head of the household or patriarch. Patriarchy is defined as a social system in which rights and obligations are distributed along the axes of generation, age, and gender; patriarchs are conceptualized as being interested in the continuity of the social order upon which their power and status are based.

Tawanda studies the Kayes Region of Mali in West Africa, and utilizes multi-level longitudinal data collected during the period 1983–9, as part of two migration surveys conducted in the Senegal River Valley.[12] His results provide support for the hypothesis that subordination has a positive effect on rural–rural migration. Highly subordinate females were also more likely to engage in international migration than were their male counterparts. In general, the findings are consistent with the general proposition that household social factors (subordination to the patriarch, co-residence of patriarch's kin, ethnicity) play a critical role in population distribution.

Health Care Behaviour in the Context of Poverty

The investigations included in the final part of the book (Chapters 11 and 12, by Pavalavalli Govindasamy and Sonalde Desai, respectively) are devoted to the analysis of the specific circumstances that women—as distinct from men—face in trying to attain a healthy life for themselves and their children. Survival, the ability to lead a healthy life, and generational reproduction are often conceptualized as some of the basic capabilities of a human being. As noted earlier, it is often argued that an individual in poverty does not have the necessary resources to guarantee a minimum level of well-being on these dimensions, and is also unable to interact socially, gain knowledge, or exercise freedom of thought (see Sen 1981; Desai 1992).

The study of maternal health and the utilization of maternal health services are important points of departure for understanding women's general health-seeking behaviour. These phenomena have been identified as important components of many international strategies targeted at both the alleviation of poverty and the improvement of women's status. In Chapter 11, Govindasamy is interested in the question of why utilization of health services in Egypt is relatively low, given that availability of these services is high and physical distance is not a barrier. She contemplates the possible effect of socio-economic factors, cultural influences on women's position, and religious factors on the utilization of such health services as receiving tetanus toxoid and pre-natal care from a health professional, having an institutional delivery, and receiving delivery care from a health professional.[13]

Govindasamy's findings confirm that Egyptian women who are in an advantageous position regarding education and paid employment are more likely to utilize maternal health care services than are their less advantaged counterparts; younger and low-parity women are also more likely to utilize these services. Religion, specifically being of Islamic faith, was not found to be a significant factor for utilization, a finding which Govindasamy believes requires further research. Finally, particularly interesting is the fact that the statistical analysis supports the conclusion that direct measures of women's position—and also their perception of this position—exert an independent and strong influence on their health-seeking behaviour. The most important variables in this respect were having a say in the household budget and reproductive decision-making and being able to express opinions in general.

Women who are in a more privileged position, particularly those who have more education, have also been found to be more successful in guaranteeing their children's survival in many different cultural and socio-economic contexts. Desai offers an evaluation of the empirical evidence regarding the frequently established relationship between maternal education and child health, and the evolution of health policies based on this line of research. She argues that although the majority of studies in this area show a positive but weak relationship between maternal education and child health, it is difficult to conclude from these studies that this relationship is causal. From her point of view, over-emphasizing the linkage between maternal education and child health and survival has a variety of negative implications from a policy perspective, particularly for poor women. This stress on the individual behaviour of women tends to create unrealistic expectations for mothers and can result in increased demands on their time. Mothers are seen as all-powerful actors determining children's survival, with the implication that uneducated women are somehow failing in their responsibilities.

The belief that increased maternal education results in improvements in child health and survival has provided a strong impetus for advocating investments in women's education. Desai maintains that there can be little doubt about the importance of women's education for the economy, society, and women themselves, but she is concerned about the emphasis on investment in women's education as the central core of health policies in developing countries. Her main point is that by vesting the responsibility for maintaining child health in mothers, the burden on women may be increased—and can harm children as well—particularly when the emphasis on individual behaviour is used to justify reductions in public health expenditures.

Main Conclusions

The essays in this volume provide importance evidence which is suggestive of how the condition of women, their poverty status, and demographic change are interrelated. One area of interest is the study of the demographic behaviour of poor women in comparison with the non-poor, as a way of learning how poverty influences different demographic phenomena. Although several regional contexts are taken into consideration, the evidence presented generally confirms that poor women have higher fertility, higher frequencies of unprotected first intercourse, and an earlier age at marriage than do non-poor women. Additionally, women from the lower socio-economic strata face more problems in their married life (violence, alcoholism, and lack of economic support on the part of the husbands), and exhibit a lower use of maternal health services. Finally, in the case of abortion, evidence indicates that lower-income women probably have a lower abortion rate than do wealthier women, at least in some countries.

Regarding the impact of demographic events on women's well-being, different chapters address the issue of migration and market work as strategies to alleviate women's poverty. It has been found that women from the poorer groups show high rates of labour force participation, and that this takes place in some contexts regardless of marital status. In some rural areas the burden of long hours of work is also more prevalent among the poorest groups. In spite of the growing importance of poor women's market work and territorial mobility in search of better economic conditions, the impact of these strategies on combating poverty is still limited. Employment options for poor and unskilled women are very restricted, especially in the earlier stages of the development process. Evidence from rural areas of very poor countries also shows that female wage work does not automatically lead to improvements in women's autonomy in the household. Even in more advanced countries, the lack of promotion prospects for women in sectors such as manufacturing and domestic service has limited long-term improvements in their economic status.

Finally, a highly relevant overall theme of most of the chapters in this book is the importance of addressing women's position in society or the gender context in analysing the relationship between poverty and demographic change. In the case of reproductive patterns, higher fertility levels among the poor are frequently attributed to socio-economic reasons such as the economic value of children or the search for security in old age. The authors of this book demonstrate the importance of looking at other dimensions, such as the centrality of motherhood in poor women's lives, the fact that many of these women believe that they are incomplete human beings if they do not bear children, and the belief that their partners are the ones who should take care of contraception. With respect to early nuptiality patterns or particular types of migratory movement, some chapters show the relevance of incorporating in explanations for these phenomena the subordinate role of women in their families of origin, as well as the conflicts that they face in these households.

Addressing the gender context is particularly relevant in explaining why poverty alleviation strategies such as market work and migration may have different conditioning factors as well as different results for men and women. In respect to extra-domestic work, some chapters of this book indicate that even when individuals from both sexes are equally restricted to the productive resources of a rural economy, women are more limited in their ability to cope with the negative consequences of this restriction because of gender inequality in educational skills and cultural norms regarding motherhood, marital status, and the limiting of physical movement. Female subordination to family interests can also limit either women's ability to leave their place of origin or the number of places to which they can migrate, thereby diminishing their possibilities for improving their standard of living. It is also pointed out that the predominance of men in migratory movements, and also the direction of male migratory flows, can restrict the possibilities for women to migrate. These findings may indicate that in many developing countries women have not yet been able to place their own needs above those of other family members.

Women's experiences as health-seekers and as procurers of family health are also different from men's. Individuals of either sex who are in a less advantageous socio-economic position may be less successful in guaranteeing their own as well as their family's survival. However, in the case of women, other factors related to their position in the gender-stratification system also play an important role in their health-seeking behaviour. In particular, women's autonomy in household decisions may exert an independent and strong influence on their ability to obtain maternal health care; additionally, the fact of being married to a relative may reinforce traditional patterns of health care use. Finally, it is relevant to note that cultural norms prevailing in many developing countries focus on women as procurers of family health. Public health measures which rest on that notion may unduly overburden women, particularly poor women.

To summarize, the authors of this book have taken a step forward in analysing specific demographic implications and conditioning factors of women's experience of poverty as different from men's. Their ideas, discussions, and findings illustrate the importance of incorporating the gender perspective into population studies.

Notes

I am very grateful for the very valuable comments and worthwhile suggestions made on previous drafts of this introduction by Karen Oppenheim Mason, Shireen Jejeebhoy, and Susan Parker. Their time and effort are deeply appreciated.

1. There are some recent and important exceptions to this widespread rule. In the Human Development Report of 1997 the United Nations Development Program (UNDP) estimates poverty on an international scale using an alternative measure (the Human Poverty Index) based on variables such as the estimated population that will die before age 40, adult illiteracy, access to health services and potable water, and the proportion of undernourished children under the age of 5 (UNDP 1997).

2. Livi-Bacci (1994) also mentions another important way to address the relationship between demography and poverty at the aggregate or population level. He refers to the examination of whether or not rapid population growth generates poverty through effects such as capital dilution and obstacles to investment and accumulation.

3. See the chapters in this volume by Niraula and Morgan, Malhotra and DeGraff, Sathar and Desai, Donato and Kanaiaupuni, Zlotnik, and Govindasamy.

4. See the chapters by Pantelides *et al.*, Singh and Monteiro, Zlotnik, and Tawanda.

5. Data for their study were collected using micro-demographic research methodology; most of the information analysed in their chapter comes from interviews with 665 ever-married women in the two villages. (See also Morgan and Niraula 1995, where the authors explore the association in these two villages between women's autonomy and fertility change).

6. It is important to point out that context also plays an important role in explaining the relationship between poverty and women's freedom of movement. In Mexico, unlike the case of Nepal analysed in Chapter 2, it is poorer women who face more restrictions on their freedom of movement.

7. Adolescent women in the upper middle class in Buenos Aires mostly hold non-traditional gender images and have protected intercourse.

8. The analysis of abortion and spontaneous foetal loss uses data on 'interrupted pregnancies' collected in 1989 in a national survey on health and nutrition, which also offered information on income levels.

9. Malhotra and DeGraff base their analysis on a survey of 1,460 women aged 18–33, interviewed in 1992.

10. The results of this study are drawn from a survey conducted in 1991, which comprises a national sample of both rural and urban areas. The paper utilizes information on 2,397 households in rural areas.

11. Donato and Kanaiaupuni's chapter is based on data from the Mexican Migration Project, which surveyed 24 Mexican communities during the winters of 1987–8 through 1991–2. Within each community, a simple random sample of 150–200 households was drawn. These samples were supplemented with a non-random survey of outmigrants located in US destination areas.

12. The Kayes study area is situated in the Malian portion of the Upper Senegal River Valley. The sample consists of 317 households with 2,863 persons of at least 7 years of age, located in 39 villages.

13. The data base is the second Egypt Demographic and Health Survey (EDHS), which included 9,864 interviews of ever-married women aged 15–49.

References

Bilsborrow, Richard E., DeGraff, Deborah, and Anker, Richard (1992), 'Poverty Monitoring and Rapid Assessment Surveys', unpub. MS, Geneva: International Labour Office.

Buvinic, Mayra, and Lycette, Margaret (1988), 'Women, Poverty and Development in the Third World', in John Lewis *et al.*, *Strengthening the Poor: What Have We Learned*, New Brunswick, NY and Oxford: Transactions Books, 149–62.

Desai, Meghnad (1992), 'Population and Poverty in Africa', *African Development Review*, 4: 63–78.

Feldman, Shelley (1992), 'Crises, Poverty and Gender Inequality: Current Themes and Issues', in Lourdes Benería and Shelley Feldman, *Unequal Burden*, Boulder, Colo. and Oxford: Westview Press, 1–25.

Fourth World Conference on Women (1995), *Beijing Declaration and Platform for Action*, Beijing: United Nations.

García, Brígida, and de Oliveira, Orlandina (1994), *Trabajo femenino y vida familiar en México*, Mexico City: El Colegio de México.

Livi-Bacci, Massimo (1994), *Poverty and Population*, Distinguished Lecture Series on Population and Development, Liège: IUSSP.

Lloyd, Cynthia (1993), *Household Structure and Poverty*, New York: The Population Council.

Mason, Karen Oppenheim (1995), *Gender and Demographic Change: What Do We Know?*, Liège: IUSSP.

Morgan, S. Philip, and Niraula, Bhanu B. (1995), 'Gender Inequality and Fertility in Two Nepali Villages', *Population and Development Review*, 21: 541–61.

Sen, Amartya (1992), *Inequality Reexamined*, Oxford: Oxford University Press.

Todaro, Michael (1976), *Internal Migration in Developing Countries*, Geneva: International Labour Office.

UNDP [United Nations Development Program] (1997) *Human Development Report 1997*, New York: United Nations.

UNIFEM [United Nations Development Fund for Women] (1995), *The Human Cost of Women's Poverty: Perspectives from Latin American and the Caribbean*, Mexico City: UNIFEM Regional Office for Mexico, Central America, Belize, Panama, Cuba, and the Dominican Republic.

United Nations (1991), *The World's Women: Trends and Statistics*, New York: United Nations.

World Bank (1990), *World Development Report 1990: Poverty*, Oxford: Oxford University Press.

World Bank (1993), *Implementing the World Bank's Strategy to Reduce Poverty*, Washington, DC: World Bank.

PART I

Overview and Critical Issues

1 Women, Poverty, and Demographic Change

Some Possible Interrelationships over Time and Space

Alaka Malwade Basu

I. Introduction

This chapter originally had a slightly different sub-title from the current one. This earlier sub-title was 'Some Interrelationships over Time and Space' and it was chosen to emphasize that this was going to be a general essay on a vast canvas; that is, it would not be a nit-picking description of the situation in one particular study situation. But as work on the chapter progressed, the sub-title took on an entirely new meaning. I discovered as I went through the literature that one cannot really talk about the interrelationships between poverty, the situation of women, and demographic change at any real level of generalization—one must always specify the study situation one is referring to in terms of both space and time. That is, not only do the nature of the inter-relationships vary with the physical location of the characters involved, these interrelationships are also in a highly dynamic state of flux and can change, sometimes drastically, over time.

This multiplicity of findings has resulted in a more conceptual piece on the possibilities rather than a laying out of numbers to support any particular argument. All the empirical evidence presented here is illustrative rather than absolute. And what I usually seek to illustrate is not any universal relation-ships between the three parameters of interest but the great variations in these relationships. Such a 'decentralization' is I think essential not only for greater academic rigour, but also to make the point that any policy prescriptions that are based on this evidence also need to be thus localized.

Particularly problematic is any attempt to develop a single description of the situation of poor women. The 'universal' woman is a myth that feminists rightly discarded long ago and that demographers must also now more openly recognize as non-existent. While gender confers a very important identity, individuals also subscribe to a number of other identities which greatly condition their female experience.

More importantly, one needs to be constantly aware that the same outcome can have different causes in different situations. A simple example is the interpretation one chooses to explain increasing levels of female labour force participation in poor households. While the pessimistic temptation usually is to ascribe this to the increasing impoverishment of poor households and a consequent 'push' of women into the labour force, there is also evidence that in many situations, the changing structure of employment opportunities 'pulls' women out of the home as it becomes increasingly economically worthwhile for them to join the labour force.

The key word is 'context'. And so important is the bearing that context has on larger relationships that in the next section I will find it worthwhile to include a short description and definition of the word to improve the understanding of the interrelationships discussed in subsequent sections.

The aim of this chapter is to develop a conceptual framework for analysing the interrelations between poverty, women, and demographic change, not with the implication that any one piece of research can empirically adhere to this framework, but to lay out a broad puzzle of which a single study can fill in only specific parts. In other words, this paper scans the existing literature to specify some of the ways in which the variables of interest *can* be related to one another rather than the ways in which they *are* related.

Even more importantly, I hope to demonstrate the need for caution in drawing simple conclusions; not only are generalizations unwise, even within a single study category, but also several things can happen at the same time so that it is not possible to unmask an unambiguous relationship between the variables of interest.

Two more general points. First, it is important to be constantly aware, even if this awareness is somewhat in the background, that poverty is an important analytical issue in itself. The current focus on women in poverty is not meant to downplay the tragic consequences of poverty in general irrespective of sex, age, or nationality. In a sense, this focus on women should instead highlight the question of household poverty in general because so much of the situation of women in poverty has profound implications for the situation of households and communities as a whole.

Secondly, one needs to be conscious of the two-way nature of many of the possible relations discussed. For example, while poverty may affect women more than men, as just mentioned, the situation of women may in turn influence poverty levels. Similarly, the poverty of women and their demographic behaviour are intertwined in ways which often make it difficult to disentangle cause and effect. As the cliché says, poverty leads to vicious circles.

Before moving on to the body of the subject, the next section (Section II) tries to define some of the key variables. It suggests a range of measures of poverty and of demographic change to simplify further analysis and to highlight the complex nature of possible interrelationships. In subsequent sections, I consider some of these possible relationships in two broad categories.

In Section III, 'Interrelationships between Gender and Poverty', two questions are analysed. First, does poverty hit women harder than men? And secondly, is the economically poor woman worse off than her richer sister in all other aspects of poverty as well? Section IIIa, 'Development and Women in Poverty', is a subsection of the topic of gender and poverty and goes beyond the static question of gender differences in existing poverty to consider the special disadvantage of women when general economic conditions change. It briefly considers the role of development in general and the role of development policies in particular in exacerbating or mitigating the situation of poor women.

In Section IV, 'Interrelationships between Female Poverty and Demographic Change/Behaviour', a modified intermediate-variables framework is adopted. Rather than ask if female poverty affects demographic outcomes, I look at possible links between specific female characteristics and demographic outcomes and then at links between female poverty and those female characteristics which turn out to be important for demographic behaviour. Conversely, I also look at the possible impact of demographic behaviour on the situation of women in ways which impinge on their poverty. This section cannot be completed without a broader look at 'Interrelationships between Poverty and Demographic Change/Behaviour' (Section IVa). The literature on this subject is vast, interdisciplinary, and contentious and I concentrate here on the possible links which involve women as mediators or victims of the relationship. The two broad questions in this section are: (1) do the poor (the poor in general, not just poor women as a special category) have different demographic outcomes from the better off?; (2) do demographic factors influence poverty?

II. Measurement Issues

Before plunging into a consideration of the ways in which the three variables of interest in this book—women, poverty, and demographic change—may be interrelated, one needs to specify what these terms mean in the debate. The main problem is that there is no one measure or definition of any of the variables (except women, I suppose, or at least women as a biological category). Not only does no single measure capture the essence of the parameter in any way, different measures may often move in completely different directions, making it impossible to specify net relationships. For example, it is quite plausible for women's health to worsen as their employment levels rise (the latter may in fact precipitate the former); in such cases, does one infer an increase or decrease in female poverty? Similarly, female autonomy in households may rise with the breakdown of the joint family, but their physical burden may increase (a variant of what historians refer to as the 'nuclear hardship hypothesis'). I therefore now briefly list some measures of demographic change and of poverty which are more relevant to the present debate. In particular, I try to identify the key features that define the poverty level of the poor woman as opposed to the poor individual or household in general.

Demographic Behaviour/Change

Any standard textbook of demography defines these indicators for us. Briefly, measures of demographic behaviour and demographic change are captured by measures of fertility, mortality, nuptiality, and migration. In turn, there are of course several measures of each of these factors and a fruitful discussion of the relationship of female poverty to demographic behaviour may well find that the relationship varies according to the kind of indicator studied. In the case of fertility and poverty in particular, one needs to be aware that family size is clearly not necessarily synonymous with fertility desires; natural fertility may be affected by a host of features associated with poverty. The relationship may become even more complicated when one tries to decompose these indicators of fertility and mortality, into their (usually biological) proximate determinants.

Poverty

How does one measure the poverty status of women? Income, or even expenditure, is now accepted as being but one indicator of poverty and not the primary one at that. If by 'poverty' one refers to deprivation, this is very imperfectly captured by the amount of money a household earns. But to be fair, income may imperfectly capture poverty both because it may understate as well as overstate the real level of deprivation. For example, it is quite plausible, and often the case, that income levels give us a worse picture about household socio-economic status in situations in which public services are good or some amount of domestic survival is provided by access to common property resources.

Poverty is even more imperfectly captured by household income when one is looking at the welfare levels of individuals within a household. In particular, poverty in women has several aspects which are exclusive to them.

The new mantra is 'the quality of life'. People's level of even purely physical welfare is now agreed to depend on a range of attributes and abilities, actual money being only one of these. The number and precise nature of these attributes and abilities varies according to the perceptions and objectives of the agency listing these. For present purposes, indicators of poverty may be classified into two groups: those that define the poverty level of any index individual and those that define the poverty level of women in particular; the latter group takes into account the ways in which women are uniquely disadvantaged in terms of access to a life of quality.

A possible list of indicators which define the quality of life of individuals regardless of sex would include the following:

1. Access to and level of employment or income; this is a vast arena, with several sub-areas, as I shall discuss briefly in the next section. In turn, this of course independently affects and is independently affected by the other indicators in this list.

2. Access to and level of education and information.
3. Health status.
4. Nutritional status.
5. Access to private property.
6. Access to common property resources.
7. Access to and extent of leisure.
8. Access to state and legal protection of rights.

On most of these indicators the poor, as defined by income, fare worse than the non-poor and the relevant question here is whether poor women in turn fare worse than poor men. In addition, one may separate out a set of indicators of poverty which are more specific to a female–female comparison (on which more shortly):

9. Decision-making authority and control over resources in the household.
10. The extent to which public and private domains of life are demarcated.
11. Reproductive rights, including control over sexuality.
12. Reproductive health.
13. Marital and domestic stability, including domestic violence.
14. The level of physical security outside the home.

Many of these indicators of poverty and deprivation are interconnected of course (for example, access to common property resources influences nutritional status and access to education affects employment), but (1) none of them is completely defined by another and (2) the interconnections are often in contrary directions; that is, in directions which do not have the same direction of impact on overall welfare.

This is a long list by any reckoning. It becomes even longer if one dares to demand that the extent of poverty should also be judged by indicators which are currently believed to be a legitimate concern only of affluent communities—such as the quality of the physical environment, the extent of political participation and freedom, and attention to human rights (this last measure may have much gender-specificity, crimes against women by the state or by other repressive bodies being qualitatively and quantitatively different from those against men). But, for reasons of convenience rather than of ideology, these indicators will remain outside the purview of this chapter. I also completely leave out of my discourse such measures as the sexual division of household tasks. This measure is so universally consistent across cultural and economic boundaries that seeking any pattern of variation will involve at best describing a few exotic tribes in which the men also grind corn.

This is also the place to digress briefly into a methodological clarification on the standard against which we measure the situation of poor women. Are we defining their special disadvantages relative to poor men? Or to non-poor women as well? I would give equal importance to both these levels of comparison because the latter situation does not yield only the obvious results expected from the difference in income between the two groups. Indeed, many of the results are unexpected, in that poor women do not necessarily fare worse than non-poor women on all counts. This is also why it is necessary to decompose the quality of life into its constituent parts, as mentioned earlier.

Finally, there is another level of comparison that an analysis of the situation of poor women would do well to take into account. This is the extent of gender inequality faced by poor women as compared to non-poor women, with respect to any or all of our indicators of a good life. That is, on several counts, while poor women may display worse absolute outcomes than non-poor women, these outcomes may be less discriminatory between the sexes in poor as compared to non-poor households. The question then is, what rankles more—the level of absolute disadvantage or the level of relative disadvantage? I would say that the answer to that need not be consistent for all the measures of disadvantage listed above. For example, poor women may well be willing, indeed even eager, to relinquish their freedom of physical movement for the secluded but more financially secure life of their richer sisters, even if this means that their men will enjoy much greater freedom than they will. The issue therefore is not only whether poor women fare worse than poor men. It is also whether poor women fare worse than non-poor women in absolute terms as well as in terms of their inequalities with men.

These are difficult empirical and ideological issues and highlight once again the central theme of this chapter—that any consideration of interrelationships and of the normative value of these interrelationships must be extremely sensitive to context. The word 'context', while it is not a part of the title of this paper, therefore deserves a brief definition as well.

Context

What does one mean by context? The word refers to the larger setting in which many of these interrelations are played out. This context can be artificially divided into several sub-contexts which modify, nullify, or even invert expected relationships. To use the social scientist's language, context can be conceived of as consisting of two mutually reinforcing forces—those that operate at the larger or macro-level, and those that involve agency and response at the level of the household or individual. In the former category, one could place a number of historical, institutional, and ecological features of a situation that go to make up the broad umbrella of what is called 'culture'. The nature of development processes and specific policies employed provide the macro-level modifications of this culture, while the micro-level context refers to individual or household or community ability and will exploit or manipulate this larger environment of constraint and opportunity. Not only does the combination of macro- and micro-level forces that define a context vary greatly over space, it can also change drastically over time, so that what is held good in one region at one time need not hold good at all in the same region at another time.

Particularly overpowering and often unexpected is the impact of technological change. Technological breakthroughs periodically throw spanners into the works, so that predictions about interrelationships have to be rewritten. The radical impact of the industrial and agricultural revolutions on rates of production and growth and their implications for Malthusian scenarios could not be foreseen even by experts very close to the scene (Wrigley 1988). In this century, contraceptive technology has turned out to be an easy alternative to the trying voluntary moral restraint previously believed to be necessary for birth control. And in recent years, new foetal technology appears to be providing a further incentive to limit births by allowing couples to manipulate both the number and sex composition of their offspring. It is therefore entirely conceivable that the bounds of human possibility will once again be extended to change the context greatly enough to make many of our present deliberations irrelevant. More pessimistically, it is also conceivable that negative developments can throw spanners into the works. Medical catastrophes are one such important possibility, as the pandemic of AIDS and the relatively minor scares of resurgences such as plague in India have recently demonstrated.

III. Poverty and Gender

The previous section listed some of the practical concomitants of poverty. The first question then is this: when a household or community is poor, are its women poorer than its men (even though, as is usually the case, women's total contribution to the household is equal to or even greater than that of men)? That is, are women over-represented among the poor and are gender relations more unequal among the poor? There is a vast and emphatically unanimous literature on the first of these issues and it would be inefficient to attempt a general review of this literature here (for an analytical review of the subject, see Quibria 1993). What I shall attempt instead is to point out some of the methodological problems in this area of study and then illustrate the relatively greater poverty of women on a few specific counts. The main conclusion is once more that there are many dimensions to poverty and that the relative disadvantage of women is more severe on some matters than on others and also varies according to the larger context. I then move on to a brief illustration of the thesis that a comparison of relative welfare levels of poor and non-poor women can sometimes yield unexpected results. The question of whether women pay a greater price when poverty levels increase in a society is considered in the next section.

A major problem with much of the general writing on poverty and gender is a tendency to infer motives from outcomes. The use of female employment as an indicator of female welfare provides the most classic example of falling into this trap, which often leads to contradictory conclusions. The literature is replete with generalizations about the unacceptably low levels of labour force participation by poor women at the same time that it insists that most female employment is driven by poverty. How then does one interpret rising or falling levels of employment among poor women? Without reference to the larger context, it would be unwise to make any sweeping statements about the implications of trends in female employment, statements that are not at all uncommon, as reference to the publications of a number of international organizations will reveal. Even if one goes a step further and laments the relatively poor access of women to *wage* labour, should one then applaud the finding that in recent years there seems to have been a clear rise in female wage employment in many parts of the developing world? Does the finding that in the 1980s in Latin America and the Caribbean 62 per cent of working women earned wages compared to 56 per cent of men (United Nations 1991) mean that in this region poor women get a better deal than poor men? If one goes even one step further and specifies that the issue is really the concentration of female workers in the informal sector, the policy implication is not necessarily that female employment opportunities in the formal sector need to be drastically increased. For many poor women it is a toss-up as to whether they benefit from or prefer the often illusory protection provided by regular employment (most employers being quite adept at bypassing any labour laws), given the more stringent demands such employment also makes on their time and flexibility.

Much more useful than demonstrating that poor women have higher or lower employment levels than poor men are empirical demonstrations of the hypothesis that when poor women are employed, they are more likely than poor men to be employed in low-status occupations, to receive lower wages even for equal work, and to be concentrated in the most monotonous and repetitive jobs. Even more crippling is the closing of avenues for advancement inherent in extension education, marketing, and credit policies which systematically exclude women. Given that poor men themselves fare badly enough on all these counts, the condition of poor working women can then be well imagined.

At the same time, at least on the employment front, it is not at all clear whether the more important issue is the gender differential or the grinding poverty itself. Once the poverty diminishes, many women may eschew employment itself, as the evidence in parts of South Asia suggests, thereby widening the gender differential on this score, but often voluntarily. One could of course get into a semantic discussion of what 'voluntary' action means to women who have been traditionally denied any decision-making authority on such matters. But it is worth bearing in mind that such discussion would also often include strong observer views on what is good for women and what they should be made to want (the example in Jeffery and Jeffery 1993 of young women who gladly abdicate decision-making authority on important household matters because that also absolves them of responsibility when things go wrong provides a sobering piece of counter-evidence).

The more productive and policy-relevant approach in attributing motives would be to search for the contextual factors which lead to such unexpected results as women withdrawing from the labour force when household economic conditions improve. Is it a 'supply' matter, in that no economic opportunities are available? Or is it to do with a culture that respects the homebound woman more? Or could it also sometimes be that most people consider regular employment a drag (and there is no doubt that most lower-level jobs are not very inspiring) and it is the men who need to be pitied for being tied to stereotypes that require them to be the main breadwinners? If one is sufficiently convinced that paid work (as opposed to control over economic resources, which is not at all the same thing) is the only way to improve the status of poor women, then such a separation of underlying contextual factors could go a long way toward designing policies that more effectively draw women into the labour force and also do them good in the process.

I think my main point is that one must not *begin* with the conviction that women invariably get the worse end of the stick in *all* dimensions of the quality of life. Such an approach, which is unfortunately very common in the feminist literature on the subject (and not just the popular literature), has two serious drawbacks: (1) it makes the problem less tractable by failing to separate the important from the trivial or even the non-existent; (2) more importantly, it leads to paradoxical conclusions which reduce the credibility of much that is real and important.

And there is no doubt that there is much that is real and important. In particular, there is much to be said and done about the greater poverty of female-headed households, a poverty that has implications for much more than the welfare of these female heads themselves. (In the long-overdue but now burgeoning literature on this subject, see in particular Lloyd 1933; Mencher and Okongwu 1933.) But I want to illustrate the unambiguous gender difference in poverty with a much simpler example, which is not sufficiently considered in the literature although it has so many wider ramifications for women and for poverty. This is indicator number 7 in my list in the previous section: access to leisure.

Leisure may seem to be a strange thing to worry about for poor households given their intense preoccupation with day-to-day survival. But there is no doubt that some access to leisure enhances the quality of life not only of the leisured individual but also of his or her associates. Women have traditionally not had the kind of access to leisure that produces good artists and musicians, of course, but the gender difference in this indicator of welfare is also very sharp when one looks at very simple forms of leisure such as a chance to relax. Poor women seem to be the worst-affected in this regard in both absolute terms and in terms of their difference from poor men. Empirically this is of course very difficult to demonstrate on any large scale. The conventional method would be to net out the time spent on 'economically productive' activities and allocate the rest to leisure. But we all now know that economically productive activity is difficult enough to measure, so much of it not being paid for.

In addition, there is all the unpaid work that goes into social reproduction and the running of a domestic unit, work that is infinitely more tedious and intensive in poor households. The only method of analysis which can take such activities into account is one that relies on measuring the allocation of time to various activities by different individuals. This is naturally a difficult undertaking and not surprisingly, there are not many time-allocation studies around and the ones that exist are beset with methodological and comparison problems. But they all seem to end up with a few common findings:

1. The typical poor woman has a very long working day with very little time to herself and usually no space to herself either (see, for example, some of the descriptions in Jacobson 1993).

2. The typical poor woman spends an undue amount of time on activities of which the non-poor woman is not even aware. The collection of fuel, fodder, and water are the activities most commonly mentioned in this connection. For example, various micro-studies in India record daily fuel collection times ranging from forty-five minutes to five hours.

3. Much household work in poor families is extremely labour-intensive and repetitive. All the investment in labour-saving technology world-wide seems to have concentrated on labour-saving outside the home (especially in industry) and labour-saving in rich households.

4. Even the notion of leisure is alien to many poor women. Viewed in this way it is not surprising that many of the women in a survey in Kerala in India (Saradamoni 1977) mentioned washing clothes and cleaning the house when asked what they did in their free time.

5. The parallel situation is very different for men, even poor men. Consider some of the estimates. In several parts of the developing world, women average 12 to 13 hours more work per week than men when unpaid work and household activities are taken into account (United Nations 1991). The even more unfair part is that when there is a narrowing of this gap by men taking on some of these household responsibilities, it is the most relaxing and enjoyable ones that they first allocate to themselves. All over the world (including the developed countries), shopping seems to be the major male input into household activities. Quite apart from depriving poor women in developing countries in particular of an important source of interaction with the outside world, this appropriation also strengthens male control over the spending of financial resources.

Leisure is of course not a clearly defined activity; it can very often be combined with work (gossiping with neighbours while peeling potatoes, for instance). To the extent that this is so, it is true that statistics may overstate women's work burden. But all indications are that the bulk of the misstatement is in the direction of understating the female workload.

So much for an illustration of the poor woman–poor man comparison. What about the relative poverty comparison between poor women and non-poor women? At an obvious level, especially if one defines poverty by income and other material goods, of course the latter fare better. But if we accept the broader notion of poverty discussed in the last section, indicators 10–13 in the list there are relevant for female–female comparisons and do not necessarily place the non-poor woman at an advantage.

I illustrate this with a peculiarly South Asian (and perhaps Middle Eastern as well) example—the inside–outside dichotomy. This term refers to the usually symbolic but often also real demarcation of the private space from the public space. The latter is considered to be the legitimate domain of a restricted class of people, usually male but also females of certain categories—the very young, the old, and most importantly, the poor. Such a cultural demarcation confines many better-off women to their immediate surroundings and restricts sharply their interaction with the world of men. Much of their interaction with the real world is through what has been called 'mediated access' (World Bank 1991). As to why more direct interaction should be desirable in the first place, I think this does not need addressing here, except to say that it does also affect other indicators of female welfare—for example, women's access to employment, their ability to use public services, their ability to migrate for a better life, and their ability to manage in times of crisis when male providers are missing for whatever reason, be it death, desertion, or incapacitation. Indeed, direct interaction enables poor women to be the deserters themselves in many difficult situations which non-poor women would have to grin and bear. But the context is again important here. My example refers to South Asia and the Middle East. In other parts of the world, Latin America and the Caribbean in particular, poor women are relatively more handicapped than non-poor women even in areas such as physical mobility.

For the same reason, perhaps poor women are better off on another measure of welfare as well—their control over their sexuality. On the other hand, there is no doubt that their lower level of resources and harder lives in general make them worse off on the measure of reproductive health. On the fourth measure—exposure to domestic violence—the evidence is at best ambivalent. The secrecy and social approval surrounding much domestic violence make it difficult to generalize but there is some evidence that when it does appear to be greater among the poor, this may be at least partly a reflection of the refusal or inability of the non-poor to talk about or report it (United Nations 1991). At the same time, perhaps the poor do pay a higher price in greater marital instability, both in terms of voluntary marital disruption and (especially) marital disruption which is circumstantial and triggered by poverty—spousal separation because men migrate to support the family, for example. The only trouble is that such involuntary separation also has its costs—not just in terms of an incomplete conjugal relationship, but perhaps more so as a contributor to female poverty as the pressure to send money home declines (Lloyd 1993).

IIIA. Economic Policy, Poverty, and Gender

This section should more correctly be concerned with the processes of economic development in general and their impact on poverty. Not all development processes are the outcome of conscious policy; and in any case policy itself is ever-changing, often very ineffective, and dictated by political considerations rather than by informed thought. It is also thrown out of gear by a number of exogenous events, technological change and international pressure being just two such invincible forces.

It would be foolhardy to join the ideological debate among economists about the best paths to economic growth. The tenacity of both sides of the participants in these debates is proof of the inconclusiveness of the arguments on either side as much as of the stubbornness of the discussants. But a related question, whether growth ought to be a central objective at all, has acquired a slightly larger consensus, with the gradual receptivity of traditional economics to the idea that trickle-down effects can be too slow and that social development and decreased inequalities are important components of economic development. Feminist economics has been a major determinant of this shift (see Beneria 1995) and has indirectly served to draw attention to several disadvantaged categories, something it is now also trying to do more directly (see, for example, Folbre 1994).

The impact of development policies and processes on poor women may be easier to deduce intuitively or empirically than their impact on poverty per se. Although the complicating factors are large, we do now have some notion or agreement about some of the indicators of worsening female poverty based on some of the measures discussed in Section II; declining access to common property resources, for example. Worsening health facilities is another; so are increasing exposure to domestic or outside violence.

Taking such objective indicators of female welfare into account, what is the evidence that past policies or natural development processes have been good or bad for women? This is again a wrongly framed question because policies and processes have many components, with different components having different impacts on the same indicator of welfare. One needs to comment on specific aspects of policy to draw any meaningful and relatively 'pure' conclusions. Nevertheless, there is general agreement today that most economic policies are not sufficiently 'engendered', a lack that is not only unfair to half the world's population, but is also self-defeating because gender sensitivity is in turn an investment in development in general (see, for example, UNDP 1995).

The recent structural adjustment programmes (SAPs) adopted by a host of developing countries to stabilize their economies and eventually foster development have sufficiently well-defined components for it to be feasible to attempt an evaluation of their potential impact on women's welfare. Actual impact is much harder to gauge because we do not have enough data to go by and because few of these SAP components have been in operation for long enough. Moreover, different places have used different mixes of the standard components of SAPs, so that allocating net impact to the various components is fraught with difficulties. I am not even going into the difficulties involved in *interpreting* intermediate impacts. For example, if wage employment opportunities for poor women have increased, as they reportedly have in many countries, what does this imply for women in poverty? Does it make them better off or worse off? Or—a more intractable difficulty—what do rising wages, greater employment, and very likely associated rising prices mean for those women too poor and unskilled to be absorbed into this new labour force? It is wiser to stick to more obvious measures of women's welfare such as nutritional status or access to credit.

What are the major components of structural adjustment programmes? Broadly, these include varying amounts of the following specific activities: the control of fiscal and balance of payments deficits, trade liberalization, and privatization. In Eastern Europe and formerly socialist economies, where the private sector has been virtually non-existent, the central tenet of SAPs has been privatization, including the setting up of private stock exchanges. In Latin American countries, where fiscal deficits have haemorrhaged uncontrollably, resulting in hyperinflation, the emphasis has been on the control of fiscal deficits and money supply. And in South Asian countries, such as India, where the economic reforms began in response to a crisis in the foreign exchange sector following the Gulf War of 1990–1, the bulk of the attention has been given to trade liberalization and the decontrol of foreign exchange.

Before going into the specific question of impact on the poor and on poor women, let us quickly review the main expectations that have been associated with SAPs and their general impacts—to the extent that these are known. The need to control the fiscal deficit is one of the least controversial features of an SAP, though, even here, the consensus breaks down as soon as we go into the components of a fiscal cutback. Economists with tunnel vision often care little about social welfare expenditures. These are also usually the soft targets, with no vocal lobby resisting their reduction. Hence, during an SAP the brunt of fiscal adjustment is often borne by welfare expenditures and one can see the greater negative impact on the poor in general and poor women in particular of such cuts in social investment, given that the poor depend more on these services (although it is true that they are appropriated more often by the non-poor).

The policy of privatization is controversial because of what may be called the problem of 'geographically transferred concern'. In Eastern Europe, privatization is indeed important if only because there is so little of it. But as a consequence of this importance, privatization has become a buzzword and has been talked about a lot even in other parts of the globe. In India for instance what many do not realize is that the size of her public sector is as small as in South Korea. India's problem has been one of excessive control of the private sector. Hence, India's primary need is not privatization but privatization of the private sector (Basu 1993).

But another kind of privatization has certainly accompanied economic policy in recent decades even in countries such as India that have relatively little government infrastructure to privatize. This is the privatization of natural resources that had traditionally belonged to communities but were taken over by the state, both colonial and post-colonial, without in most cases closing community access to them. But with increased privatization of these resources, their new owners have been markedly stricter about allowing public access to them and the impact has been directly greater on poor women who depend on the collection of free fuel, fodder, and food for their family's upkeep, and indirectly greater on this family upkeep.

Trade liberalization means that domestic sectors that have been protected until now will come under increased foreign competition and some may even face closure. This has led many to conclude that once trade is liberalized by economically weak countries, they will not be able to withstand foreign competition. Imports will flood into these countries, and at the same time these countries will not be able to export. This argument is fallacious if imports depend on exports. But if, as is often the case, they are tied to foreign invest-ment, loans, or aid, then of course the globalization of the economy can tie the hands of national governments quite tightly. Moreover, what does seem to be true is that with trade liberalization, existing industries may collapse and new ones arise, causing dislocation in labour and frictional unemployment. Since in most poor countries there is little provision of social welfare, such disruption may be particularly painful. This suggests what is in fact a central message of informed critiques of SAPs—that they must be accompanied by complementary programmes of social welfare, so that even if jobs are not protected, the jobless are; even though prices are not controlled, the poor are protected from frictional changes in prices.

Whatever the long-term benefits of current structural adjustment pro-grammes, there is evidence that at least some countries have not enjoyed any short-term benefits at all, with economic growth often being negative; on the situation in Sub-Saharan Africa, for example, see National Research Council (1993). One may argue (as has been done in the literature) that (1) these are only teething pains and/or (2) that these reversals are not in fact the result of the new policies but a continuation of the trends which necessitated the policies. But the more damning fact remains that this burden has been very unevenly distributed, so that the poorest groups in many countries experiencing these policies are demonstrably worse off according to many indicators (to its credit UNICEF was among the earliest to raise this possibility; see also Jolly and Cornia 1984 and Cornia, Jolly, and Stewart 1987). For example, real wages in the rural sector in India did definitely drop during the first two years of its structural adjustment programme (Chandramohan 1995). Latin America too in the 1980s witnessed a major casualization of the labour force, with a dramatic rise in underemployment (see, for example, Beneria 1992; McFarren 1992). Pakistan and Bangladesh seem to have displayed a similar worsening of the situation of the poor in the late 1980s (Islam 1994). Economic transformation in Eastern Europe and the former Soviet Union may be exacting similarly larger costs from the poor (Moghadam 1994).

However, it should be noted that in principle there is nothing *inevitable* about the deterioration in the social indicators of poverty summarized above. The East Asian countries are a living example of structural adjustment without increases in poverty (Islam 1994). The policy response called for from the East Asian example and as the evidence for increased hardship among the poor mounts in other countries has concentrated on demands for increased investments in the social sector (with a vocal but still less-heard radical movement questioning the legitimacy of structural adjustment policy itself). Which spending gets slashed seems to be largely a political matter, a conclusion buttressed by the ways in which several governments have been able to step up public social spending when political pressure has demanded this. This political pressure has tended to come from within the country and also from the very international agencies that first imposed structural adjustment programmes and then re-evaluated the impact of these programmes. In India, for example, since 1992, the government has doubled its investment in the different employment-guarantee schemes in rural areas, schemes which had faced major cuts in the first years of the programme. This renewed investment has—it appears—pushed the rural wage rate to levels above those that prevailed before adjustment began (Chandramohan 1995).

In addition to increased social expenditure on health and education, several writers have pointed to the need for more skills training to make workers able to enter the new occupations which they must now take up as the face of the economy changes (see, for example, Islam 1994; Beneria 1995). Once again, this seems to be a largely political decision that governments need to be pressurized into taking themselves or imposing upon the private sector (the latter attempt has not been very successful when tried in East Asia; see Islam 1994). And finally, as Feldman (1992) and Elson (1992) point out, the new economic policies could even be directed into a new politicization process whereby changing structures of hierarchy and opportunity are exploited by disadvantaged groups (and especially women) to their own advantage in the long run. The increasing labour force participation of women may be particularly powerful in this regard.

But until all these compensating events actually occur, has this deterioration in the lives of the poor, whatever its basis, made things even worse for poor women? Many would argue that it has, because the burden of making ends meet with declining household incomes has fallen disproportionately on women given their primary responsibility for household maintenance—leading to an even more strenuous domestic routine and to attempts to supplement family incomes through an increasing 'feminization' of the informal labour force. My earlier example of leisure becomes very apt in this context.

IV. Female Poverty and Demographic Change

A modified intermediate-variables approach may be the most useful way to understand the potential relationships between female poverty and demographic behaviour/change. This approach involves seeking links between specific characteristics of women and their demographic behaviour and then looking at interrelations between poverty and those female characteristics relevant for demographic behaviour. In turn, of course, there is a large, growing, and often inconclusive literature on the biological or semi-biological intermediate variables linking these female characteristics and demographic behaviour, but I shall pay only marginal attention to this link here.

But first, is it true that the poor have different demographic outcomes from the non-poor? The evidence is fairly consistent on absolute levels of mortality being worse, which in turn is consistent with what we know about the determinants of mortality. But in areas which exhibit a gender differential in mortality, the differential by income or socio-economic status in general is less consistent. Very often, the greater intra-household equality between men and women in poor households seems to get translated into lower gender differentials in physical welfare among other household members, children in particular, as well (see Basu 1989).

The evidence is the least conclusive on the matter of poverty and fertility. While the usual macro-understanding of the situation is that the poor breed the fastest, in actual fact the evidence on this matter is not unambiguous. To begin with, the relationship between poverty and fecundity is unclear; and if there is a relationship it must surely be in the direction of the poor being less fecund. Once again, the larger context of poverty appears to be paramount. For example, poverty which is related to wage labour and especially to mobile wage labour may reduce fertility because of greater spousal separation (see, for example, Cain 1985). On the other hand, poverty among the self-employed may increase the number of births, not only because natural fertility is now higher, but also because self-employment can find more uses for additional children. The confusion is even greater when it is 'wanted' fertility that one is referring to (it is true that excess or 'unwanted' fertility may be higher among the poor because of the greater costs of fertility control).

When the costs of contraception are not a major constraint (as is the case in most developing countries today), do the poor still have higher fertility than the non-poor? The evidence on this score is extremely messy, but the balance is if anything tilted in the opposite direction. This is especially the case when one abandons cross-sectional data and looks at the changes in fertility that seem to be associated with changes in poverty. The historical evidence does find a negative relationship between grain prices and marriages and births in pre-industrial Europe (see, for example, Lee 1981; Galloway 1988). In the contemporary world, similar relationships have been demonstrated between economic changes and marriages and births in Latin America (Hill and Palloni 1992) and between economic changes and marriages and first and second births in Sub-Saharan Africa (National Research Council 1993). (For both contemporary and historical evidence on this issue, see also Merrick 1985 and Wrigley 1996.)

At a cross-sectional level too, even if the general finding is of an inverse relationship between income and fertility, a relationship that has been explained in terms of various demand and need factors in the literature, it is not improbable that if one disaggregated the poor by income, the 'middle poor' would in fact have higher fertility than the 'poor poor' (Basu 1987).

To return to the question of female poverty and demographic behaviour, what female characteristics have been related most often to demographic behaviour? On the whole, a few characteristics crop up again and again in both the speculative and empirical literature on the subject. These characteristics themselves are not mutually independent—many of them influence and are influenced by one another—but they are also sufficiently strong predictors in themselves of demographic outcomes not mediated through one another. In listing these, I would place female education at the top, and then add economic activity, autonomy, knowledge, and attitudes.

All these characteristics in turn influence the willingness or *desire* to control fertility and mortality, as well as the *ability* to control fertility and mortality (including the biological ability—an especially important factor given the links between poverty and nutrition, poverty and infection, and poverty and marital instability). In addition, given the situation in many parts of the world, one should perhaps expand the phrase 'to control fertility and mortality' to read 'to control fertility and mortality in *any* direction'.

The task of the researcher then becomes to identify the relationship between low incomes and these relevant attributes of women in the specific cultural, institutional, and socio-economic context of her study area if she wants to postulate a relationship between female poverty and demographic behaviour/change. And once again, one can get conflicting results. For example, poor women are likely to be less educated, a factor driving their fertility upwards according to current theory. But they are also more likely to be in the labour force for reasons of poverty, a factor driving their fertility downwards according to current theory. The net result would then depend on the relative force of these conflicting effects and my own hunch is that among the very poor, the extreme shortage of resources that may be driving women into the labour force may win the day.

Putting all this together, is there any rationale for expecting structural adjustment programmes to affect demographic parameters? Health and mortality effects through effects on social expenditure such as on health services are easy to conceive and have been demonstrated; for example, child mortality did increase during the economic reversals in sub-Saharan Africa (National Research Council 1993; however, this study did not address the question whether the economic reversals were themselves an outcome of the new economic policies; see also Lockwood 1995). In addition, one may postulate a worsening of women's health as their physical burden increases and also as an indirect fallout of some of their attempts to seek an income; one can refer in particular to the large numbers of poor women reportedly being drawn into the commercial sex sector, with all its implications for the transmission of infections including HIV/AIDS.

What about a potential fertility impact? Even if one were to assume an effect of structural adjustment on poverty, as is being increasingly suggested, it would be difficult to make the jump to any particular effect on fertility, given the relative lack of consensus on the poverty–fertility link. One possible fertility-enhancing factor could well be the increased costs of fertility control if structural adjustment includes cuts in social expenditures such as health and family planning. But most governments either experience sufficient political and international pressure to maintain resources for fertility control even if health and education budgets falter, or receive international funding for family planning programmes (see Camp 1994; Gulhati and Bates 1994). If this happens and if it is also true that among the poor, increased poverty increases the relative costs of childbearing, then fertility may well decline with these economic transformations. The empirical record certainly suggests that fertility is falling all over the developing world (see, for example, the confirmatory evidence in the various demographic and health surveys of the late 1980s and early 1990s); it would now be worth testing to see if at least a part of this decline is motivated by increased hardship among the poorest sections of the population.

Finally, such an analysis would not be complete without an explicit recognition of the converse relationship—the impact of demographic processes on poverty and especially on women in poverty. Two levels of analysis are possible here: the impact of their own fertility on the poverty of women and the impact of wider population changes on the poverty of women. The two kinds of impact need not coincide. To illustrate just two of the possible contradictions, in a system of female inability to join the labour force and no state support for survival (an all too common combination of circumstances in the developing world), children, especially sons, represent an essential source of security and a buffer against further impoverishment through circumstances such as widowhood. On the other hand, the welfare of the household in general and of its children in particular may well be compromised by high fertility in poor families (see Lloyd 1994). At the same time, the pressure of increased population growth occasioned by women thus protecting themselves can erode natural resources and especially common property resources, of which poor women are the chief consumers (Jodha 1985), so that poor women now have to walk longer distances to collect fuel and water and work harder to earn the free food that they earlier foraged in the forests. Needless to say, these pressures are not eased by official policies which often reduce the access of women to common property in any case.

V. Concluding Remarks

This chapter has been littered with examples and with notes of caution rather than presenting a systematic and neatly bundled review of the interrelationships between poverty, women, and demographic behaviour and change. As I have already elaborated, such an overview is not possible without a plethora of 'ifs' and 'buts'. Indeed, one of the propositions of this chapter is that such an overview is not a good idea at all, both because it can end up saying very little and also because it can end up becoming irrelevant for policy because it makes invalid generalizations.

At the same time, if one is forced to state some general conclusions, mine would be of the following kind:

1. On the question of an interrelationship between poverty and gender, the evidence is on balance conclusive in the direction of a widespread disproportionate impact of poverty on women.
2. On the question of links between gender and demographic behaviour, relationships are often unexpected and also exhibit a fair amount of variation over time and space.
3. On the issue of demographic–economic interrelationships, there is scope for the greatest amount of disagreement, at both the micro- and macro-levels of analysis.

Given these hesitations, this chapter has taken the safe way out and concentrated on first presenting a vast canvas of possible interrelationships and then illustrating these possibilities by critically examining a few key interrelationships. Many of the interrelationships not discussed in any detail here are the subjects of later chapters in this book.

This is a revised version of the paper presented at the IUSSP Conference on Women, Poverty and Demographic Change. I am very grateful for the comments and suggestions made by participants in general and those by Rosa Maria Rubalcava and an anonymous referee in particular.

References

Basu, A. M. (1987), 'On the Possibility of a Poverty-Induced Fertility Transition: Birth Control by Assetless Workers in Kerala, India', *Development and Change*, 17: 265–82.
——(1989), 'Is Discrimination in Food Really Necessary for Explaining Sex Differentials in Childhood Mortality?', *Population Studies*, 43: 193–210.
Basu, K. (1993), *Economic Graffiti*, New Delhi: Oxford University Press.
Beneria, L. (1992), 'The Mexican Debt Crisis: Restructuring the Economy and the Household', in Beneria and Feldman (1992), 83–104.
——(1995), 'Towards a Greater Integration of Gender in Economics', *World Development*, 3: 1839–50.
——and Feldman, S. (eds.) (1992), *Unequal Burden: Economic Crises, Persistent Poverty and Women's Work*, Boulder, Colo.: Westview Press.
Cain, M. (1985), 'On the Relationship between Landholding and Fertility', *Population Studies*, 39: 5–15.
Camp, S. L. (1994), 'The Politics of US Population Assistance', in L. A. Mazur (ed.), *Beyond the Numbers: A Reader on Population, Consumption and the Environment*, Washington, DC: Island Press, 122–34.
Chandramohan, N. (1995), *Impact of Liberalization on the Rural Poor in India*, New Delhi: Business India, mimeo.
Cornia, G. A., Jolly, R., and Stewart, F. (eds.) (1987), *Adjustment with a Human Face: Protecting the Vulnerable and Promoting Growth*, Oxford: Clarendon Press.
Elson, D. (1992), 'From Survival Strategies to Transformation Strategies: Women's Needs and Structural Adjustment', in Beneria and Feldman (1992), 26–48.
Feldman, S. (1992), 'Crises, Poverty and Gender Inequality: Current Themes and Issues', in Beneria and Feldman (1992), 1–25.
Folbre, N. (1994), *Who Pays for the Kids? Gender and the Structures of Constraint*, London: Routledge.
Galloway, P. (1988), 'Basic Patterns in Annual Variations in Fertility, Nuptiality, Mortality and Prices in Pre-industrial Europe', *Population Studies*, 42: 275–303.
Gulhati, K., and Bates, L. M. (1994), 'Developing Countries and the International Population Debate: Politics and Pragmatism', in R. Cassen (ed.), *Population and Development: Old Debates, New Conclusions*, New Brunswick, NJ: Transaction Publishers, 47–77.
Hill, K. H., and Palloni, A. (1992), 'Demographic Responses to Economic Shocks: The Case of Latin America', paper presented at the IUSSP Conference on the Peopling of the Americas, Veracruz, Mexico.
Islam, R. (ed.) (1994), *Social Dimensions of Economic Reforms in Asia*, New Delhi: International Labor Organisation.
Jacobson, J. L. (1993), 'Closing the Gender Gap in Development', in L. R. Brown *et al.* (eds.), *State of the World*, New York: Norton and Company, 132–49.
Jeffery, R., and Jeffery, P. (1996), 'Jats and Sheikhs in Bijnor: Schooling, Women's Autonomy and Fertility Outcomes', in R. Jeffery and A. Basu (eds.), *Girls' Schooling, Women's Autonomy and Fertility Change in South Asia*, New Delhi: Sage Publishers, 150–83.
Jodha, N. S. (1985), 'Population Growth and the Decline of Common Property Resources in Rajasthan, India', *Population and Development Review*, 11: 265–314.

Jolly, R. and Cornia, G. A. (eds.) (1984), *The Impact of World Recession on Children*, Oxford: Pergamon Press.

Lee, R. D. (1981), 'Short-Term Variation: Vital Rates, Prices and Weather', in E. A. Wrigley and R. W. Schofield (eds.), *The Population History of England 1541–1871*, Cambridge, Mass.: Harvard University Press, 356–401.

Lloyd, C. B. (1993), *Household structure and poverty*, New York: Population Council.

——(1994), *Investing in the Next Generation: The Implications of High Fertility at the Level of the Family*, New York: Population Council.

Lockwood, M. (1995), 'Structure and Behavior in the Social Demography of Africa', *Population Development Review*, 21: 1–32.

McFarren, W. (1992), 'The Politics of Bolivia's Economic Crisis: Survival Strategies of Displaced Tin-Mining Households', in Beneria and Feldman (1992), 131–58.

Mencher, J. P., and Okongwu, A. (eds.) (1993), *Where Did All the Men Go? Female-Headed/Female-Supported Households in Cross-cultural Perspective*, Boulder, Colo.: Westview Press.

Merrick, T. W. (1985), *Recent Fertility Declines in Brazil, Colombia and Mexico*, The World Bank Population and Development Series No. 1, Washington, DC: World Bank.

Moghadam, V. (ed.) (1994), *Democratic Reform and the Position of Women in Transitional Economies*, Oxford: Clarendon Press.

National Research Council (1993), *Demographic Effects of Economic Reversals in Sub-Saharan Africa*, Washington, DC: National Academy Press.

Quibria, M. G. (1993), *Gender and Poverty: Issues and Policies*, Manila: Asian Development Bank.

Saradamoni, K. (1977), 'Labour Statistics: Wages, Earnings and Employment', in A. Bose, D. B. Gupta, and G. Raychauhuri (eds.), *Population Statistics in India*, New Delhi: Vikas, 179–87.

UNDP [United Nations Development Program] (1995), *Human Development Report 1995*, New York: United Nations.

United Nations (1991), *The World's Women: Trends and Statistics*, New York: United Nations.

World Bank (1991), *Gender and Poverty in India*, Washington, DC: World Bank.

Wrigley, E. A. (1988), 'The Limits to Growth: Malthus and the Classical Economists', *Population and Development Review*, 14(suppl.), 30–48.

——(1996), 'A Historical Perspective on Population and Resources', in B. Colombo, P. Demeny, and M. F. Perutz (eds.), *Resources and Population: Natural, Institutional and Demographic Dimensions of Development*, Oxford: Clarendon Press, 6–24.

2 Gender Inequality in Two Nepali Settings

Bhanu B. Niraula and S. Philip Morgan

Gender inequality has existed in most human societies. The nature and causes of gender inequality, changes in its severity, and the consequences of gendered inequality have been among the most debated and researched topics of the past two decades. We draw on this literature to help explain the dramatic differences we will document in women's status across two villages *and* within them. More specifically, we have conducted surveys in two Nepali villages. The first setting is in the central hills 75 kilometres south-west of Kathmandu; the second setting is in the plains (tarai), 200 kilometres south of Kathmandu very close to the Indian border.[1] The plains setting we study is considered a cultural extension of the Indian Gangetic plains (e.g., similar to the north Indian pattern described by Dyson and Moore 1983, and by Basu 1992). In this region, women have low status and autonomy compared to south India. Purdah (e.g., female seclusion) is practised in the plains and women are nearly invisible to an outside visitor. In the Nepali hills, where north Indian culture has joined with tribal and ethnic culture, this north Indian pattern is weakened. In the hill setting, women clearly defer to men and 'serve' them. But these women have much greater freedom of movement and converse freely with other villagers, including men.

Our work will demonstrate substantial variability in women's status and autonomy within settings. Which factors account for this variability? Are these factors the same across these two settings that vary greatly in the intensity of gender inequality? We are especially interested in multi-level theories that stress the import of social institutions that constrain women's autonomy (e.g., Blumberg 1984: 49). We will consider individual characteristics (the woman's age and education), a measure of household context (whether the woman is spouse or daughter-in-law of the household head), and a measure of social class (landholding per household member).

Women's Status and Its Determinants

Social inequality refers to differential possession of and access to wealth, power, and prestige. Stratification systems depend upon institutionalized behaviours that perpetuate social inequality. These generally accepted definitions seem to cause confusion primarily when discussing gender inequality. Perhaps, as the van de Walles (1993) point out, this is because no society wishes to acknowledge that its female members are systematically exploited or that their status is low. Mason (1984) argues that a root cause of the confusion lies in the multidimensional nature of women's status. She says, 'failure to recognize that women's power, prestige and wealth do not necessarily rise and fall together may explain several controversies in the demographic literature.' Mason uses purdah as an example: purdah may lower women's control of resources and thereby wealth and power; simultaneously, it may increase women's prestige.

Thus, we must resolve a crucial conceptual issue: which dimensions of women's status shall we focus on? There are many measures and dimensions used in previous research (see Whyte 1978; Mason 1984). We will focus on women's autonomy because we believe it to be a signal feature of gender stratification and because it is a key dimension influencing demographic outcomes (see Dyson and Moore 1983; Mason 1984). Autonomy refers to the 'ability—technical, social and psychological—to obtain information and use it as a basis for making decisions about one's private concerns and those of one's intimates' (Dyson and Moore 1983: 45). By limiting autonomy, persons' access to social rewards can be limited. For instance, Spain (1993: 137) argues that the 'physical separation of women and men . . . contributes to and perpetuates gender stratification by reducing women's access to socially valued knowledge' (emphasis in original). Furthermore, as we define it, autonomy parallels common definitions of power. That is, power 'is the ability to act or produce an effect' and/or to 'influence others' actions or thinking' (see, for instance, *Webster's* 1991). Thus we will operationalize measures of (1) women's freedom of movement and (2) women's role in household decision-making. Greater freedom of movement and a greater role in family decision-making imply greater autonomy. Greater autonomy, in turn, provides the resources and opportunity to pursue opportunities. Autonomy is antithetical to gender stratification.

A second decision we make is to consider variability in gendered experiences. Gender stratification is fundamentally different from that based on caste, class, or ethnicity. Because of their family and kin relationships with men, women are generally distributed across these other social hierarchies. One implication of this is that women's status is far from uniform and women's experiences with gendered inequality are diverse. Thus, thinking of women as a single oppressed set ignores substantial heterogeneity. At the least, Mason (1984) argues that one must simultaneously consider gender and class/caste hierarchies. A second implication of these comments is that there are clearly two referents for evaluating 'women's status'. First, one can compare women to men. Second, women can be compared to other women. We will use both referents in this paper.

What will influence women's autonomy, specifically autonomy as measured by freedom of movement and by influence on household decision-making?

Following Blumberg (1984), Cain (1993), and others (such as Chafetz 1990 and Collins and Coltrane 1991), we stress the import of social institutions, such as patriarchy, which constrain women's autonomy. Cain (1993: 47) defines patriarchal structure as 'the sum of institutional mechanisms that serve to limit women's economic autonomy relative to men's'. While both settings we study are patriarchal, the ecology and historical development of these areas have produced a more rigid form of patriarchy in the plains than in the hills—one personified by the practice of purdah in the plains setting. We discuss the settings in more detail below, but we maintain that the variability in women's autonomy between settings is due to patriarchal features of the social context. Controlling for individual characteristics, for instance, will not attenuate the differences across settings. The aggregate differences observed reflect differences in macro-features of the social context.

Striking differences at the aggregate level are not incompatible with variability within settings. Macro-structures can impinge disproportionately on subsets of women. Furthermore, there are additional structures within settings (i.e., caste/class, household structure, etc.) which can further condition autonomy. Of special interest to sociologists and demographers are factors that might operate consistently across settings. We will focus on five such factors.

1. The materialist approach of Blumberg (1984), Chafetz (1990), and Collins and Coltrane (1991) stresses the importance of women's control of resources. Wage work should increase women's autonomy by giving them direct access to economic resources.
2. Following Mason (1984), we acknowledged above the potential importance of a social class hierarchy, as well as a gender one. Land is the basis of wealth in these communities and thus best reflects class/caste distinctions. We expect that the landless and the poor will have greater freedom of movement and will exercise a greater role in household decision-making. Their greater freedom of movement may originate in the exigencies of poverty that do not allow them to follow the practices of the more wealthy. Poorer women may have greater decision-making roles because of their greater contribution to the household economy compared to women in more wealthy households (Balk 1994: 29). Specifically, both greater freedom of movement and more decision-making power may result from the greater likelihood that poor women will work for wages. Paid work is inconsistent with some traditional practices (like purdah) and provides women with an independent source of income.
3. Women's education is sometimes used as a general measure of 'women's status'. Like Mason (1984), we eschew such broad measures of multidimensional concepts. Given our focus on autonomy and the settings we study, we believe education may measure exposure to Western ideas (Caldwell 1982).

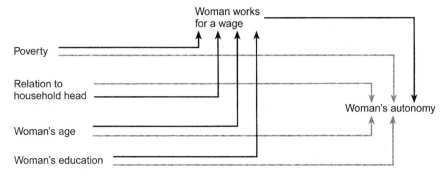

Fig. 2.1. Expected associations within each setting

4. Women who are daughters-in-law of the household head, as opposed to the spouse of the household head, will have less autonomy. Balk (1994: 28) argues that this is because the older generation works to maintain the status quo. Perhaps this is because in the agricultural, patriarchal household wealth flows to the senior generation (Caldwell 1982).

5. Finally, women's autonomy may vary over the life course (Mason 1984: 16–17). This claim is consistent with the one above in that, with age, women will become spouses of household heads instead of daughters-in-law. Further, with age women bear more children (and more sons), which may provide women with status and power.

We believe that the above arguments for within-setting effects are quite general and thus would be visible in many settings. But the evidence and arguments for context-dependency are strong. Blumberg (1984: 49) offers a general theory of context-dependency:

Since macrolevels influence microlevels more than the reverse, where women's relative economic power at the macrolevels (society; class; at times, community) is less than at the microlevel(s), the less favorable macrolevels will act as a 'discount rate' to reduce (but not eliminate) the extent to which women can exercise their relative economic power at the more micro level(s); that is, women's actual micro-power will be less than their potential power.

The gist of this general argument is that micro-level effects will be weakened in situations where patriarchy is most rigid. Other contextual arguments are specific to a particular setting. As an example, Mason (1984: 28–9) cites Jain's (1970) study of Indian overseas wage labourers. The power of men in this circumstance is so great that wives automatically turn over all income to men, thus relinquishing control of important material resources. The likelihood of context-specific effects leads us to test specifically for them.

Fig. 2.1 summarizes the expected associations. Note that wage work assumes a key role as a possible intervening variable. Specifically, wage work may mediate the influence of other variables' influence on women's autonomy.

Data Collection in the Settings

Data were collected in early 1993 using a micro-demographic research methodology, which has the components of both survey research and anthropological research (Caldwell and Hill 1988; Caldwell, Reddy, and Caldwell 1988; Axinn, Fricke, and Thornton 1991; Fricke, Thornton, and Dahal 1991). We supplemented the survey data with in-depth case studies, intensive interviews, observation, group discussion, and discourse with key informants. Three questionnaires were administered: a household questionnaire, a married woman questionnaire, and a husband questionnaire. Trained male and female interviewers were involved in interviewing husbands and wives respectively. In addition, roughly half of the team members involved in data collection were from the study area. The research team, including Bhanu Niraula, stayed in the village for the five-month study period. This strategy enabled the researchers to observe and better understand the day-to-day life of these rural people. In fact, villagers invited us to participate in various life-cycle rituals such as marriage and festivals. This methodology improved the quality of the survey data we collected and has deepened our understanding of the two settings.

Most data analysed in this chapter come from interviews with ever-married women aged 15–49. These selection criteria yielded 313 ever-married women in the hill setting, and 352 ever-married women in the plains setting.

Choosing the Two Settings

How does one select the villages for study? Smith (1989: 178) advocates purposive sampling with a 'controlled comparison' being one option. This method 'mirrors the basic principle of the quasi-experimental design—that objects under study be as alike as possible, differing only with respect to a single "test" variable'. This strategy follows from our desire to maximize variability in women's status to provide a strong test of the effect of women's status on fertility (Morgan and Niraula 1994). Such a strategy may seem straightforward, but its implementation is quite difficult. That is, one seldom finds a sharp contrast in women's status, for instance, when all other variables remain the same.

We were confident that a hill setting and a tarai (plains) setting would provide a sharp contrast in women's status. While we do not try to sort out the precise linkages here, the expected differences in women's status emerge from the ecological and historical peculiarities of these regions. To explain briefly, 'the hills' refer to the mountains that lie at the foot of the dramatic Himalayan range that runs across northern Nepal. This is the area of Nepal that has attracted the attention of most travellers and scholars. The tarai, in contrast, is a lowland plain at the foot of the mountains along the southern border of Nepal. This area has been little studied, perhaps, as suggested by Gaige (1975: p. xv), because 'it is hot, dusty, topographically undramatic and, until recently, malarious'.[2] The tarai long operated as a barrier between northern India and the hills of Nepal. The heavily forested, tropical, malarious tarai was sparsely populated until the 1860s. The hills were inhabited by many tribal groups, many influenced by Tibetan Buddhism. The Muslim invasions of India in the twelfth, thirteenth, and fourteenth centuries drove many north Indian Hindus through the tarai and into the hills. Here, they established a number of principalities. The culture and society that emerged in the hills is a less orthodox Hinduism incorporating aspects from tribal and Buddhist societies. By contrast, more recent Hindu migrants dominate the tarai settlements. These migrants arrived between 1860 and 1950 from the northern states of Uttar Pradesh and Bihar. Islam influenced Hinduism in these north Indian states; the practice of purdah is the most obvious example. Gaige (1975: 13) argues that the hill and tarai areas are culturally distinct. The tarai more closely resembles the north Indian, Gangetic plains area. Gaige says:

Their religious traditions, languages and the caste system, their food, style of clothes, forms of entertainment and even personal mannerisms are cultural characteristics they share with people who live across the Indian border in Uttar Pradesh and Bihar.

In contrast,

The more flexible social traditions of Hinduism as practiced in the hills result largely from the interaction between Hinduism and the less rigid social traditions of Tibetan Buddhism.

Associated with these differences are differences in women's freedom and autonomy. Others have noted these differences (Acharya and Bennett 1981), and they seemed obvious to us as we investigated potential study sites in the hills and the tarai.

As the discussion above suggests, the settings we chose differ in several important ways. We return to these in the next section. But within these regions, our search was aimed toward selecting villages that were economically and demographically comparable. The villages we chose are small-village settings that are primarily agricultural (see Table 2.1). Both have recently experienced substantial development inputs, such as schools and health posts. In both study sites, the government has introduced high-yielding varieties of wheat, paddy, and oilseeds. Also, the government has encouraged the use of chemical fertilizers to boost agricultural productivity. Agriculture is still seasonal, based on the monsoon. Farmer-managed irrigation schemes operate in both areas, but these efforts are more successful in the hills than in the

Table 2.1. Characteristics of villages selected and of the study, Nepal, 1993

Background characteristics	Benighat	Bagahi
Of villages selected		
Location	Hill	Plain
Economy		
Main occupation	Agriculture	Agriculture
Main crops	Maize, paddy, wheat	Paddy, wheat, pulses
Landless households (%)	12.8	18.8
Wives working for wage (%)	20.0	31.8
Husbands working for wage (%)	58.1	60.2
Per capita landholding (h)	0.115	0.111
Per capita income from land (rupees)	1,963	1,975
Demography		
Size of household	5.8	5.8
Median age of the population	18	19
Development Input		
Health post in the village	Yes	Yes
Secondary school in the village	Yes	Yes
Households having a radio (%)	46.0	23.3
Households having electricity (%)	—	24.6
Household having toilet (%)	31.0	4.5
Social		
School-aged population (6–15)	427	470
Population 6–15 not in school (%)	11.5	71.6
Boys not in school (%)	11.2	60.6
Girls not in school (%)	11.7	91.3
Wives having some education (%)	24.6	6.0
Husbands having some education (%)	75.0	44.0
Caste system	Yes, relatively simple and flexible	Yes, more complex and rigid
Of the Study		
Study population	1,798	2,028
Number of households	309	346
Number of women interviewed	313	352
Number of husbands interviewed	244	274

Source: Field work by the authors.

tarai. Farmers plant a variety of crops (instead of mono-cropping), which affects labour demand at various stages of crop cultivation. These innovations have increased crop yields, living standards, and work availability in both settings. The hill village we studied produces surplus vegetables and dairy products that find easy markets in Kathmandu. The plains village produces surplus food grains that are easily marketed in Birganj. Both economies are increasingly monetized and are linked to the forces of national and international trade.[3]

Description of the Two Settings

The first setting is located in a hilly region 75 kilometres south-west of Kathmandu.[4] This village fits many common stereotypes of Nepal. It sits next to a rapidly flowing river. Farming is done on terraced hills and on a plateau above the river. While marred by substantial deforestation, the hill setting is quite picturesque.

In the early 1970s a major highway was constructed, linking Kathmandu with northern India. This road passes through the village. The highway has had a major influence on economic development in the hills, including our study site. Settlers have come to our study area primarily because of job opportunities provided by the opening of this major highway. Some development efforts include livestock and dairy farming, intensive vegetable cultivation, and expansion of educational institutions. Yet even in 1993 this area was not electrified.

The second setting is located 200 kilometres south of Kathmandu in the tarai, near Birganj. Gaige's (1975: 10) generic description of tarai villages well describes the one we studied:

There are 6,258 nucleated villages in the tarai, most of them no more than several hundred mud and thatch huts clustered around large shady pipal, pakari or bagad trees. Occasionally one will find a two-story brick house built by a large landowner. The village water is drawn from open hand-dug wells, and villages' links with the outside world consist of rutted bullock-cart tracks, generally impassable during the monsoon season.

The plains setting is also near the major road connecting Kathmandu to northern India. A fair-weather road connects the study village with the main canal of the Narayani Irrigation Project. The road along the canal bank further connects the village with Birganj municipality. Transport becomes difficult in the rainy season when the fair-weather road, and the bridges and culverts, are washed away by the monsoon rains.

As in the hills setting, many forces of change are at work in the plains setting. Several industries have developed in neighbouring areas, and the government is carrying out various development programmes. A significant number of people from the plains setting commute to an industrial estate to work in factories, mostly in low-salaried jobs. But a few are well-educated and work as clerks and supervisors.

Both settings have primary and secondary schools in the village itself. The first primary school in the tarai setting was established nearly a decade earlier (around 1952) than in the hill setting. The opening of schools facilitated the expansion of education, mostly for boys. Even today, there are very few girls enrolled beyond primary level. As Table 2.1 shows, many more children attend school in the hills than in the tarai. Also, educational levels differ substantially between the two settings.

In both settings (like the rural areas of other developing economies), agriculture is the mainstay of the local economy. Land is still an important source of employment, income, and socio-economic status. Table 2.2 shows that in both villages, larger and more productive landholdings are owned and operated by the higher-caste families. However, land distribution is more skewed in the tarai than in the hills. Nineteen per cent of the households in the tarai are landless compared to 13 per cent in the hills. The land tenure system is almost identical in these settings. Most of the households are owner-cultivator in both settings. Because of absentee landlords, various forms of sharecropping are practised much more in the plains than in the hills. Patron–client relations are much more evident in the tarai than in the hills. In both settings very few respondents reported legal 'tenant-cultivator' status and also in both cases women's ownership of land is negligible, partly because the inheritance law of the country favours sons' over daughters' rights to ownership.

Table 2.3 shows the economic activities of women taken from the household roster.[5] Employment opportunities in the hills are much more diverse than in the plains. Since a major highway passes through the hill setting, business opportunities are growing. There are number of local offices such as a health post, a forest checkpost, an agricultural and livestock extension post, and a milk collection centre. Many people visit these places as they wait for buses to various destinations. These activities generate a clientele for tea/snack and other retail shops in the hill village. It is significant that most of the tea/snack and retail shops are actively managed and operated by women from varied caste-ethnic backgrounds. Women are also active participants in the cultivation and sale of vegetable crops. We have seen women loading baskets of vegetables in trucks to take them to market in Kathmandu. The Trishuli River, which passes through the study area, is a popular rafting destination. Rafting companies employ seasonal labour, mainly men from the area. Highway repair and maintenance work is another source of employment, mostly for men. Economic opportunities have broken the mould of caste-ethnic occupational norms: all caste groups are increasingly involved in business opportunities. For example, high-caste Brahmans own and operate the larger retail shops; such jobs were traditionally done by Newars (or Vaisya).

Table 2.2. Caste-ethnicity and economic status, Nepal, 1993 (landholdings in hectares)

Setting	Landholding		Per cent of		N
	Size (ha)	Value (rupees)	Land	Household	
A. Benighat (hill)					
Hindu Caste					
Higher caste					
Brahman	1.01	337,710	49.3	33.1	102
Chhetri	0.74	193,026	33.1	30.4	94
Service caste					
Untouchables	0.33	81,382	7.3	15.2	47
Hill ethnic groups					
(Gurungs, Ghale, etc.)	0.49	81,000	4.6	6.5	19
Newar	0.27	49,757	5.3	13.6	42
Others	0.20	35,000	0.3	1.3	5
Total	0.68	195,184	100.0	100.0	309
B. Bagahi (plain)					
Hindu Caste					
Higher caste					
Hill Brahman	3.32	480,555	11.67	2.6	9
Tarai Brahman	1.32	131,214	3.60	2.0	7
Middle caste					
Mahato	1.02	165,953	12.76	9.2	32
Yadav	0.14	11,800	0.20	1.2	4
Kurmi, Raut	0.73	85,000	18.00	18.2	63
Kanu, Teli, Saha	1.72	171,804	28.54	13.3	46
Thakur, Lohar	0.81	96,800	7.87	7.2	25
Sahani	0.22	17,981	4.06	13.9	48
Roy, Bhar	0.99	133,071	5.36	4.1	14
Lower caste					
Harijan, Ram, Darja	0.21	23,385	8.00	28.2	97
Total	0.74	90,455	100.00	100.0	346

Source: Field work by the authors.

Table 2.3.   Main and secondary occupation for females aged 11 and above based on household roster, Nepal, 1993

Occupation	Benighat (hill)		Bagahi (plain)	
	Main	Secondary	Main	Secondary
Agriculture	150	184	22	143
	(23.8)	(29.2)	(3.6)	(23.6)
Service	5	—	1	1
	(0.8)		(0.1)	(0.2)
Business[a]	45	23	1	1
	(7.1)	(3.6)	(0.2)	(0.2)
Agricultural labour	10	11	7	134
	(1.6)	(1.7)	(1.2)	(22.1)
Off-farm labour	3	—	3	—
	(0.5)		(0.5)	
Student	145	2	7	1
	(23.0)	(0.3)	(1.2)	(0.2)
Housework	253	234	524	14
	(40.1)	(37.1)	(86.6)	(2.3)
Traditional occupation	1	3	1	1
	(0.1)	(0.5)	(0.2)	(0.2)
Not working	19	174	39	310
	(3.0)	(27.6)	(6.4)	(51.2)
Total	631	631	605	605
	(100.0)	(100.0)	(100.0)	(100.0)

[a] Also includes tea/snack stall and general-provision shops.

Source: Field work by the authors.

People in the plains setting, and women in particular, have a more narrow range of employment opportunities. Although the nearby factories provide employment opportunities for males, we did not find a single female worker from our study village employed as a factory worker. Whatever employment opportunities exist for women are limited to wage earning in agriculture and such work is seasonal. Agricultural wage work is considered a low-status job and only women from the lower caste are involved in such activity. Even working their own land is considered to be a low-status job. Only older women work their own land: younger women are seldom allowed to work in the fields. As a result, nearly nine women out of ten reported 'housework' as their main occupation/activity. Note, however, that more women in the plains setting reported wage work as their second most important activity than did women in the hills. As noted earlier, most wage workers in the plains setting are landless, lower-caste women.

Because of disparities in employment opportunities across the settings, the wage rate is high in the hills compared to the plains. The expected wage in the hills during the peak season is 45 rupees (equivalent to US$1.00 per day per adult male), which is one-third higher than in the plains. Off-peak wage rates are negotiated and are often lower, especially for agricultural and domestic work. In the hills, because of the diversity of work and employment opportunities, there is always a demand for manual labour.[6]

There are differences in the caste system too.[7] Table 2.2 showed the caste-ethnic composition and size of landholdings, the single most important source of socio-economic status, income, and employment. In the hills, about 63 per cent of households are from the higher-caste Hindus (Brahman and Chhetri). Of the higher-caste Brahman and Chhetris, more than half are descendants of two clans: Kadel and Bisural. In fact, settlement clusters are named after these two groups. Both these settlements lie on an elevated land known as Tar on the banks of the Trishuli River. Of the remaining households (37 per cent), about 14 per cent are from the Newar community, a group that is neither a Hindu caste group nor a tribal group. About 6 per cent of the households belong to a Tibeto-Burman group that we categorize as a hill ethnic/tribal group. About 12 per cent are from the service-caste untouchables and the remainder are quite varied. However, due to the overwhelming majority and dominance of caste Hindus in our hill village, we see very few differences in the values and norms of non-caste groups.

The caste system in the plains is more rigid and more complex than in the hill setting. There are many more occupational groups in the plains than in the hills. And unlike the hills, the majority of households in the plains belong to the 'middle caste' group. Kurmi, a traditional farmer caste, accounts for 18 per cent, followed by the fisherman caste Sahani/Gorhi (14 per cent). Teli, a caste traditionally involved in the oil business, accounts for another 13 per cent of the households. However, the single largest plains group belongs to the lower caste: untouchables, known locally as Ram, Dom, and Harja. The hill caste Brahman (mostly Baral), despite their small number in the plains (2.6 per cent) are the richest and play an important role in the politics and development of the village.

The Gendered Division of Labour in the Hills and the Plains

Structural theories posit that rewards (power, status, and wealth) are linked to specific hierarchical statuses which are defined by their socio-economic niche (e.g., role). Rewards accrue to incumbents of these niches. Stratification systems maintain themselves by denying access to some or by hindering individuals in the pursuit of high status. Chafetz (1990: 28) argues that 'the more differentiated [specialized or segregated] the division of labour in the family, the greater the degree of [overall] gender differentiation.' Chafetz makes a similar claim about the division of 'productive labour', e.g., labour outside the household. In short, the 'more different the social roles performed by each sex, the more different the general roles performed by each sex, and this in turn creates the widespread perception that the sexes are indeed fundamentally different' (Chafetz 1990: 28). Or in the more recent terminology, by following gendered proscriptions people are 'doing gender'. From this perspective, the division of labour by sex is the backbone of systems of gender inequality.

In Table 2.4 we show wives' answers to a series of questions about responsibility for household tasks. (See Appendix 2.1 for the exact wording of the question and for the worksheet filled in by the interviewer.) We have ordered the items from tasks most often done in the hill setting by women to those most often done in the same setting by men. For instance, in the hill setting 309 wives reported that 'getting water' for the household was a woman's task (the wife's or her daughters'); only two wives reported that this task was done by men (the husband or sons). The odds that wives reported that females (as opposed to males) did this task are estimated as 154.5. In fact, the first six tasks are heavily feminine in both settings—usually done by women. For instance, women wash clothes (task 6) in over 20 households for each household where this task is done by men (odds = 21.1); in the plains setting the comparable odds are 57.3. The last column of Table 2.4 shows the odds ratio. This statistic measures the difference between settings in the extent to which tasks are feminine (or masculine). For five of the first six tasks the odds ratios are below 1.0; this indicates that the tasks are *less* feminine in the hills than in the plains (although only for item 6 is the difference statistically significant).

Items 7 (getting cooking fuel) and 8 (tending animals) are feminine tasks in the hills but are done by both men and women in the plains. Actually, item 7 is not very useful in the plains because most households there buy their cooking fuel and reported that 'no one' did this task.

Items 9 through 12 are clearly masculine. Moreover, the odds ratios indicate that these tasks are less masculine (or more feminine) in the hills than in the plains. For instance, item 10, 'Handles household money', is 3.54 times as likely to be done by men in the plains setting as in the hill setting.

Overall, we claim that there are three important observations to be gleaned from Table 2.4. First, almost all tasks are gendered—performed disproportionately by women or by men. Second, the rank ordering of tasks from feminine to masculine is very similar across settings. And third, the plains setting shows a sharper division of labour by gender than does the hill setting—five of the first six 'feminine' tasks are more feminine in the plains than in the hills. Likewise, all five of the more masculine tasks (items 9–13) are more masculine in the plains setting than in the hill setting.

In theory, the fact that men and women perform different tasks does not necessarily translate into gender inequality. These different tasks could be equally valued and rewarded. But in both of the settings we studied, as

Table 2.4. Division of household labour by sex, Nepal, 1993

Tasks	Benighat (1)	Rank (2)	Bagahi (3)	Rank (4)	Odds Ratio (1 ÷ 3)
1. Gets water					
N: F/M	309/2	1	337/4	3	
Odds: F ÷ M	(154.5)		(84.3)		1.83
2. Cooks meals					
N: F/M	306/6	2	349/3	2	
Odds: F ÷ M	(51.0)		(116.3)		0.44
3. Cares for the children					
N: F/M	197/4	3	258/1	1	
Odds: F ÷ M	(49.3)		(258.0)		0.19
4. Cleans up after meals					
N: F/M	305/12	4	347/5	4	
Odds: F ÷ M	(43.6)		(69.4)		0.62
5. Cleans the house					
N: F/M	300/12	5	345/7	6	
Odds: F ÷ M	(25.0)		(49.3)		0.507
6. Washes dishes					
N: F/M	296/14	6	344/6	5	
Odds: F ÷ M	(21.1)		(57.3)		0.37*
7. Gets cooking fuel					
N: F/M	255/12	7	50/36	7	
Odds: F ÷ M	(21.3)		(1.4)		15.29***
8. Tends animals					
N: F/M	206/32	8	149/108	8	
Odds: F ÷ M	(6.4)		(1.4)		4.66***
9. Does other agricultural work					
N: F/M	86/136	9	66/191	9	
Odds: F ÷ M	(0.63)		(5.3)		1.83**
10. Handles the household money					
N: F/M	86/227	10	34/318	10	
Odds: F ÷ M	(0.38)		(0.11)		3.54***
11. Buys food grains					
N: F/M	73/237	11	23/329	11	
Odds: F ÷ M	(0.31)		(0.07)		4.4***
12. Buys clothing					
N: F/M	80/233	12	28/324	12	
Odds: F ÷ M	(0.34)		(0.09)		4.0***
13. Works for income					
N: F/M	34/276	13	21/331	13	
Odds: F ÷ M	(0.12)		(0.06)		1.95**

* = Significant at the 0.05 level.
** = Significant at the 0.01 level.
*** = Significant at the 0.001 level.

Source: Field work by the authors.

elsewhere, a gendered division of labour translates into a male advantage. As Chafetz (1990: 46) says:

Because men constitute the primary extra domestic work force, the remaining tasks that must be accomplished—those involved in child rearing and family household maintenance—become the speciality of women. Women's first . . . priority has been to work in the domestic sphere. However this work produces no direct access to money or other material goods. Women may garden, create handicrafts, or provide services for nonfamilial members. In this way, they may earn money or produce material goods for sale or exchange. However, when they do these things, they are engaged in one of two types of work. To the extent that they produce goods for family consumption (food, clothes, or other handicrafts), they are not acquiring resources that can be exchanged with others outside the family. They are engaged in subsistence production, which garners few rewards and little social recognition in societies whose economies are structured around surplus production and exchange.

When husbands provide more valued and scarce [i.e., more irreplaceable] resources to the family than do wives, wives balance the exchange by offering deference to, or compliance with, the demands of their spouses. . . . Where women bring in no such resources, their deference and compliance are greatest.

In short, gender differentiation of tasks leads to differential power between husbands and wives. This differential power is reflected in lower autonomy for women. Given the greater differentiation of tasks in the plains setting one would expect that women's autonomy would be more restricted there than in the hills.

A key feature of autonomy is freedom of movement and association. The wives' questionnaire asked directly whether it was 'acceptable' for them to go alone to certain places. (See Appendix 2.2 for the exact wording of these questions.) Note that we did not ask men these questions because men's freedom of movement is universally recognized. Thus, all married men would respond 'yes' to these questions in both settings. The degree of gender inequality is indexed by the degree to which wives' responses diverge from 100 per cent.

As in Table 2.4, we order the items in Table 2.5 from those places where women in the hill setting are most likely to be able to go alone to those least likely. In the hill setting, almost all women can go to the local health centre (96.6 per cent). Their freedom of movement vis-à-vis the health centre is comparable to their husbands. In the plains setting, roughly three out of four women (78.8 per cent) say that going to the local health centre is acceptable. Thus, there is noticeable gender inequality in freedom of movement in the plains setting. Note that there is a health post within the village in each of the settings we have studied. Other destinations, like travel to the next village, are much less acceptable in both locales, suggesting substantially greater gender inequality. Thus, there are severe constraints on women's freedom of movement in both settings.

Table 2.5. Wives' responses to question on where it is acceptable for them to go alone, Nepal, 1993

Places wives can go alone	Benighat (1)	Rank (2)	Bagahi (3)	Rank (4)	Odds Ratio (1 ÷ 3)
1. Local health centre					
N: Yes/No	285/10	1	260/74	1	
Odds: Yes ÷ No	(28.50)		(3.51)		8.12**
2. Local market					
N: Yes/No	283/12	2	141/193	3	
Odds: Yes ÷ No	(23.58)		(0.71)		32.30**
3. Visit with relatives					
N: Yes/No	230/65	3	204/130	2	
Odds: Yes ÷ No	(3.54)		(1.57)		2.23**
4. Fields outside village					
N: Yes/No	151/144	4	65/269	4	
Odds: Yes ÷ No	(1.05)		(0.24)		4.25**
5. Community centre					
N: Yes/No	110/185	5	9/325	8	
Odds: Yes ÷ No	(0.59)		(0.03)		19.70**
6. Fair/Shrine/Mela					
N: Yes/No	82/213	6	33/301	5	
Odds: Yes ÷ No	(0.38)		(0.10)		3.45**
7. Next village					
N: Yes/No	71/224	7	14/320	6	
Odds: Yes ÷ No	(0.32)		(0.04)		7.80**
8. To a movie					
N: Yes/No	23/272	8	10/324	7	
Odds: Yes ÷ No	(0.08)		(0.03)		2.70**

** Significant at the 0.01 level.
Source: Field work by the authors.

In the rightmost column of Table 2.5 we change the referent from men to a comparison of women in these two settings. As in Table 2.4, the rank order of items is similar in the two settings. But the differences between settings are stark: the odds ratio in the rightmost column is greater than 1.0 and statistically significant for every item. For item 1, most women in each setting report that they can go to the local health centre alone. The odds ratio, 8.12, indicates that women in the hills are 8.12 times as likely as women in the plains setting to say it is acceptable for them to go there alone.

Another indicator of women's status is the influence of wives in household decision-making. As Dyson and Moore (1983: 45) say: 'equality of autonomy between the sexes ... implies equal decision-making ability with regard to personal affairs'. Our survey asked directly about decision-making. Our questions included the items shown in Table 2.6. We used the following preface:

Now I would like to find out who makes certain decisions in this household. For each decision I mention, please tell me whether you usually decide this *alone*, whether you and your husband reach a decision *together*, whether he decides this *alone*, whether some *other family member* makes this decision, or whether *no one* makes this decision.

Given our purposes here, Table 2.6 contrasts the 'wife alone' and the 'husband and wife together' responses with the 'husband alone' and a small number of 'other household member' responses. The first two responses represent a greater role in decision-making for women compared to the last two responses. The rank order of items is again very similar in the two settings. Generally, women claim that they decide alone or together with the husband whether to have more children, whether to take a sick son or daughter for treatment, whether or not to punish a child for misbehaviour, and the level of schooling for their children. Women are less likely to decide or jointly decide what food to buy, whether to sell or purchase major goods, and whether the wife should work. This is especially true in the plains setting—for items 8 to 10 the odds for the wife's role in decisions (WB ÷ O) are significantly greater in the hills than in the plains. Take item 10 for instance: wives in the hills are 4.12 times as likely to decide (or help decide) whether to sell or purchase major goods as are wives in the plains setting.

Note that it would be incorrect to say that the wives in the hills have more say in all decisions. In fact there is an interesting pattern of increasing odds ratios as one moves from item 1 to 10. For the first five items, the plains setting women are slightly (but not significantly) more likely to play a decision-making role. The greater role of the hill setting woman begins to emerge when the issue of controlling resources arises—schooling for children, whether the woman works, and purchases and sales of major goods.

Determinants of Women's Autonomy in the Hills and the Plains

Fig. 2.1 and the discussion that preceded it identified a set of possible determinants of women's autonomy. Table 2.7 presents descriptive information on the measures of factors shown in this figure. In both settings land is the main source of income and employment, and of wealth and socio-economic status. Thus, we use per capita value of land to produce three categories of socio-economic status: landless, poor, and non-poor.[8] As shown in Table 2.1, the average size of landholding per capita is almost equal in both settings: 0.12 hectares in the hills and 0.11 hectares in the tarai, which translates into 0.7 hectares per household in the hills compared to 0.6 hectares per household in the tarai. About 19 per cent of households in the tarai

Table 2.6. Who decides what to do in the household, Nepal, 1993

Decision (WB = Wife alone + Both together; HO = Husband alone + Others)	Benighat (1)	Rank (2)	Bagahi (3)	Rank (4)	Odds Ratio (1 ÷ 3)
1. Whether to avoid having another child					
N: WB/HO	264/49	1	311/41	1	
Odds: WB ÷ HO	(5.38)		(7.59)		0.71
2. Seek treatment for son					
N: WB/HO	262/51	2	303/49	3	
Odds: WB ÷ HO	(5.14)		(6.18)		0.83
3. Seek treatment for daughter					
N: WB/HO	261/52	3	295/57	5	
Odds: WB ÷ HO	(5.02)		(5.17)		0.97
4. Punishes a son for misbehaviour					
N: WB/HO	261/52	4	304/48	2	
Odds: WB ÷ HO	(5.02)		(6.33)		0.79
5. Punishes daughter for misbehaviour					
N: WB/HO	259/54	5	298/54	4	
Odds: WB ÷ HO	(4.80)		(5.52)		0.87
6. How much schooling for son					
N: WB/HO	257/56	6	261/91	6	
Odds: WB ÷ HO	(4.59)		(2.87)		1.60
7. How much schooling for daug					
N: WB/HO	254/59	7	254/98	7	
Odds: WB ÷ HO	(4.31)		(2.59)		1.66
8. What food to buy					
N: WB/HO	223/90	8	168/184	8	
Odds: WB ÷ HO	(2.48)		(0.91)		2.72**
9. Whether respondent should work outside?					
N: WB/HO	205/108	9	128/224	10	
Odds: WB ÷ HO	(1.90)		(0.57)		3.33***
10. Whether to purchase/ sell major goods					
N: WB/HO	174/139	10	130/222	9	
Odds: WB ÷ HO	(1.25)		(0.59)		2.12**

** Significant at the 0.005 level.
*** Significant at the 0.001 level.

Source: Field work by the authors.

Table 2.7.   Factors affecting women's autonomy, Nepal,
1993

	Benighat (hill)	Bagahi (plain)
Poverty (%)		
Landless	12.2	17.7
Poor	51.9	66.8
Non-poor	35.9	15.6
Position in household (%)		
Spouse	78.3	78.1
Daughter-in-law	21.7	26.9
Respondent's age (%)		
15–24	33.2	33.2
25–34	34.6	39.2
35–49	32.2	27.6
Respondent's education (%)		
0 years	75.6	97.7
1–5 years	17.6	3.6
6+ years	32.2	2.7
N	295	334

Source: Field work by the authors.

are landless compared to 13 per cent in the hills.[9] The measurement of other factors is straightforward and the justification for considering them was presented earlier.

We predicted that wage work would be a key intervening variable between measures of individual and contextual factors and autonomy. Access to wage labour is predicted to increase wives' power vis-à-vis husbands. Table 2.8 shows the effects of selected factors on the likelihood that women will work for wages. The first column of Table 2.8 shows the bi-variate association between each factor and the odds of wage work. Column 2 shows the additive effects of all factors, net of others. Column 3 shows effects from the 'preferred model', which captures the important features of the data.

Spouses (as opposed to daughters-in-law) and older (as opposed to younger) women are more likely to be employed. Both of these effects are moderately attenuated in the multi-variate model because they are corre-lated—older women are more likely to be a spouse of the head of household than a daughter-in-law.

The bi-variate effect of education is misleading. This effect, shown in col-umn 1, is due to the correlation of setting and education—women in the plains setting are more likely to report wage work and they have less education than women in the hill setting. Once we include a control on setting the educa-

Table 2.8. Effects of selected factors on whether wife works for a wage, Nepal, 1993

Selected factors	Wage work (yes/no): Odds ratios		
	Gross	Additive	Preferred
Poverty			
Landless (omitted category)	—	—	—
Poor[a]	0.22***	0.23***	0.52***
Non-poor[a]	0.05***	0.05***	0.27***
Position in household			
Daughter-in-law (omitted category)	—	—	—
Spouse	2.80***	1.96**	2.03**
Wife's age			
15–24 (omitted category)	—	—	—
25–34[a]	1.39***	1.29*	1.30*
35–49[a]	1.93***	1.66*	1.69*
Wife's education			
No schooling (omitted category)	—	—	—
1–5 years[a]	0.58**	0.97	1.08
6+ years[a]	0.34**	0.94	1.17
Setting			
Benighat (omitted category)	—	—	—
Bagahi	1.82***	1.52**	8.87***
Interactions			
Setting × poverty			
Bagahi × poor[a]			0.14***
Bagahi × non-poor[a]			0.02***
Model chi-square (df)		108.8	134.1
		(5)	(6)

* Significant at 0.10 level.
** Significant at 0.05 level.
*** Significant at 0.01 level.

[a] These pairs of coefficients are constrained such that the second one is obtained by squaring the first. For example, each odds ratio for the Non-poor row is obtained by squaring the corresponding ratio for the Poor row ($0.22^2 = 0.05$; $0.23^2 = 0.05$; etc.). These constraints result from a simple linear scoring of the three categories from 0 to 2. These linear scorings do not significantly worsen the fit of model to data.

Source: Field work by the authors.

tion effect becomes small, varies in direction across columns 2 and 3, and is statistically insignificant.

Column 1 shows that the poor are less likely to work for a wage than the landless (the odds of wage work are lowered by a factor of 0.22 if the woman is poor as opposed to landless). Non-poor wives are very unlikely to work for

Table 2.9. Expected odds of wage work (yes/no) and effects (odds ratios) of poverty status on these odds, Nepal, 1993

Poverty status	Benighat		Bagahi	
	Expected odds	Odds ratio	Expected odds	Odds ratio
Landless	0.56	1.0	4.36	1.0
Poor	0.29	0.52	0.31	0.07
Non-poor	0.15	0.27	0.02	0.005

Source: Calculated from Figures in Table 2.5.

a wage—their odds of wage work are only 0.05 (0.22×0.22) as great as the odds for the landless. This strong effect is not attenuated by controlling other factors shown in Table 2.8 (column 2). But the preferred model (column 3) contains a significant interaction between poverty status and setting. In a non-additive model, neither the main effect nor the interaction term can be interpreted independently (see Stolzenberg 1979); they must be considered jointly. We do this in Table 2.9, where we show the effects of poverty conditional on setting.

The expected odds of wage work (yes/no) decline with higher socio-economic status in both the hills and the plains. But note that the decline is much sharper in the plains. The odds of wage work in the plains are 4.36 for the landless but only 0.02 for the non-poor. The odds ratio, 0.005, equals the ratio of the former to the latter. In the hills, the ratio of these odds is 0.27— the non-poor are roughly one-fourth as likely to work as the landless.

In sum, then, the results in Table 2.9 show that landless and poorer women are more likely to work and that this relationship is especially strong in the plains setting. Landless women in the plains setting were especially likely to be engaged in wage work. Older women and women who are spouses of the household head are especially likely to be engaged in wage work.

Table 2.10 shows the effects of these same variables and wage work on autonomy—measured as freedom of movement and power in household decision-making. Earlier we analysed a set of items for each concept. Rather than analyse separate items, for our purposes here we have constructed simple additive indices of three items for each dimension of autonomy. We then dichotomize each index into the categories of high and low. The freedom of movement index is constructed from whether a woman can go alone to visit a health post, to fields outside the village, and to the next village. The questions we chose to represent greater decision-making power ask women who makes the decisions on: what food to buy, whether to purchase/sell major household goods, and whether the wife works. We have replicated the results presented here with separate items and conclude that these indices represent accurately the association between these items and factors shown in Table 2.8.

In Table 2.10 (as in Table 2.8) we show gross, additive, and preferred model effects. We focus our attention on estimates from the preferred model shown in the third column of both measures of autonomy. Regardless of the autonomy measure, there was little evidence of differential effects by setting. For instance, if one compares the landless, poor and non-poor categories the likelihood that wives report high freedom of movement or high decision-making power declines. In both settings, being a spouse of the household head (as opposed to a daughter-in-law) increases the odds on both freedom of movement and decision-making power. Education has strong effects on freedom of movement and wife's age has strong effects on decision-making power.

We conclude the following:

1. these two measures of autonomy are affected by different sets of factors, suggesting that the measures tap distinct aspects of the concept;
2. there is little evidence that co-variate effects vary by setting.

General arguments about these factors are consistent with effects observed in these two locales. The exception is wage work; we now turn to these complicated effects.

For both measures of autonomy, the preferred model contains an interaction between setting and wage work. We show these effects in Table 2.11. The pattern of results could not be more complex. Specifically, the estimated interactions are vicious—that is, the effects of work are opposite in the two settings. Moreover, the direction of the effects switches as we move from one autonomy measure to another. In the case of freedom of movement, the estimated effect of wage work lowers slightly (by a statistically insignificant factor of 0.84) the odds on high autonomy in the hills; in the plains setting wage work increases these odds dramatically (by a factor of 2.85). In contrast, for the decision-making power variable, wage work more than doubles (increases by a factor of 2.19) the odds on high autonomy in the hills; in contrast, wage work reduces substantially the odds on high decision-making power (by a factor of 0.35) in the plains setting. Our theory did not predict these complex interactions. We shall hazard a post hoc explanation. But the most important conclusion is a general one: the effects of wage work are specific to both place and dimension of autonomy.

As for a possible explanation: with respect to decision-making power the positive effects of work on autonomy are consistent with the theory outlined earlier. In the plains setting, the negative effects may be related to the very selective nature of work there—wage work is almost entirely the province of landless women. Work is available only in agricultural operations, where extensive patron–client relations favour men. In addition, the more restrictive macro-context in the plains setting may restrict women's ability to use any

Table 2.10.   Effects of selected factors on two measures of wife's autonomy, Nepal, 1993

Selected factors	Freedom of movement (high/low): odds ratio			Decision-making power (high/low): odds ratio		
	Gross	Additive	Preferred	Gross	Additive	Preferred
Works for wage						
No (omitted category)	—	—	—	—	—	—
Yes	1.2	1.41	0.84	0.96	0.68*	2.19*
Poverty						
Landless (omitted category)	—	—	—	—	—	—
Poor[a]	0.86	0.60**	0.62**	1.09	0.87	0.80*
Non-poor[a]	0.74	0.36**	0.38**	1.19	0.75	0.64*
Position in household						
Daughter-in-law (omitted category)	—	—	—	—	—	—
Spouse	1.65**	1.66*	1.54*	14.4***	10.6***	10.7***
Wife's age						
15–24 (omitted category)	—	—	—	—	—	—
25–34[a]	1.07	0.98	0.98	2.71***	1.91**	1.94***
35–49[a]	1.15	0.96	0.96	7.34***	3.65**	3.76***

Wife's education						
No schooling (omitted category)	—	—	—	—	—	—
1–5 years[a]	1.78***	1.54**	1.48*	0.89	1.25	1.20
6+ years[a]	3.17***	2.37**	2.19*	0.79	1.56	1.44
Setting						
Benighat (omitted category)	—	—	—	—	—	—
Bagahi	0.13***	0.11***	0.09***	0.33***	0.29***	0.43***
Interactions						
Setting × Works for wage (Bagahi × Yes)			3.4**			0.16***
Model chi-square (df)		145.7 (6)	152.6 (7)		213.3 (6)	227.5 (7)

* Significant at 0.10 level.
** Significant at 0.05 level.
*** Significant at 0.01 level.

[a] These pairs of coefficients are constrained such that the second one is obtained by squaring the first. For example, each odds ratio for the Non-poor row is obtained by squaring the corresponding ratio for the Poor row ($0.86^2 = 0.74$; $0.60^2 = 0.36$; etc.). These constraints result from a simple linear scoring of the three categories from 0 to 2. These linear scorings do not significantly worsen the fit of model to data.

Source: Field work by the authors.

Table 2.11. Effects of women's working for a wage on two
measures of autonomy, Nepal, 1993

Setting	Freedom of movement	Decision-making power
Benighat	0.84	2.19
Bagahi	2.85	0.35

Source: Field work by the authors.

greater leverage that might result from an independent source of income. As Jain (1970) discovered of Indian workers in Malaysia, men are so powerful in the plains village that even if women work for wages, they have little control over their earnings. For the freedom of movement measure there is virtually no effect in the hill setting. In the plains setting, wage work increases freedom of movement. This greater freedom of movement may be a logical necessity for the plains setting women who perform wage work.

Conclusion

Women living in the plains setting have very little autonomy. Their movement is severely restricted and most do not take a major part in many household decisions. By comparison, hill setting women have substantial autonomy—although with respect to other referents (e.g., men in these settings or women in Western industrialized countries) one would reach a different conclusion.

What accounts for these differences? Most of the difference can be traced to features of the social context. We have shown this by controlling several individual characteristics that do not attenuate the differences between settings. While both settings are patriarchal, the plains setting is intensely patriarchal. We have noted that the different intensities of patriarchy arose from historical and ecological peculiarities of the hill and tarai regions. For our purposes these differences are taken as given. We have shown that the gender division of labour in the plains is more extreme than in the hills. We have argued that this division of labour is the backbone of gender inequality. Furthermore, this division of labour is maintained by restrictions on women's autonomy—'the ability . . . to obtain information and use it as the basis for making decisions about one's private concerns and those of one's intimates' (Dyson and Moore 1983: 45). We have demonstrated dramatic differences in women's autonomy between settings using two sets of measures: one focusing on freedom of movement and the other focusing on the wife's role in household decisions. The gendered division of labour and the restrictions on women's autonomy together comprise a stratification system—the division of labour provides differential access to resources and limitations on autonomy perpetuate the gender division of labour. The more rigid gendered division of labour in the plains setting is consistent with the more rigid constraints on women's movement and decision-making.

This macro-explanation does not rule out individual variability within settings. Individual variability is expected because the forces of patriarchy are weakened under particular circumstances. For instance, we have argued that within settings older women, better-educated women, women who are spouses of the household head, and poorer women will have greater autonomy. Evidence we have presented is consistent with these expectations. Blumberg (1984) argues that the effects of more micro-structures would be attenuated by more intense forms of patriarchy. Thus one might expect greater effects of these factors in the plains setting than in the hill setting; we find no evidence to support these claims. Specifically, we could not reject the hypothesis of 'no difference across settings' in the effects of each factor on autonomy.

The biggest puzzle is the link between wage work and autonomy. There are strong associations between the likelihood that women will work for a wage and factors that we analyse (e.g., poverty, position in the household, age, and setting) but no *consistent* association between wage work and autonomy. We expected that wage work would increase women's power by providing them with direct access to resources. Clearly, such a general story is not consistent with these data and adds to the evidence that the effects of wage work are strongly context-specific. Positive effects of wage work on autonomy likely depend on the type of work available, the structure of work routines, and the degree of control women have over the wages they earn. As noted earlier, such conditions could account for the complex associations we have sketched.

Many lament the absence of strong theory in sociology. We take the opposite position here. We conclude by pointing out the relevance of core theoretical ideas about gender inequality (e.g., those taken as true; see Cole 1994) for this chapter—for explaining the dramatic variability in the gender division of labour and in women's autonomy across *and* within these two settings. For instance, consider this fundamental claim: the most powerful determinants of women's status are macro-level (setting or contextual) factors. As Cain (1993: 46) states:

One can think of many individual-level measures of women's economic dependence on men; however, the factors that condition an individual's experience . . . are located in a society's institutional structure. While there may exist substantial variation in the individual experience of women in a particular society, the distribution of such experiences will be constrained by institutionally determined bounds.

As a second example, Chafetz (1990: 105) states: 'the greater the division of labour, the greater men's resource power at both the macro and micro levels.' This idea is at the centre of explanations offered for the lower autonomy of women in the plains setting (compared to the hill setting). Finally, the set of more micro-effects we document can be accounted for by how women's access and control of resources are influenced by them. Our study focused on a specific dimension of gender inequality and our data were collected especially to measure this dimension. We suggest that the poor fit between theory and data in many prior studies may not have been because of inadequate theory. Instead, the problems may lie in the conceptualization of relevant dimensions of gender inequality and in appropriate measures of them. Our research agenda includes additional studies of this kind. These studies will allow additional assessments of whether these notions should comprise 'core' theoretical ideas.

Notes

We acknowledge the usefulness of draft survey instruments developed by Karen Mason, Herb Smith, and their colleagues for a study of many settings in five different Asian countries. We adopted sections of their survey instruments for use in our data collection. We acknowledge research support from the Mellon Foundation for data collection and analysis. Bhanu Niraula acknowledges post-doctoral fellowship support from the Rockefeller Foundation. We also thank Herb Smith, Tom Fricke, Susan Watkins, Etienne van de Walle, and Sonalde Desai for comments on previous drafts.

1. A narrow strip of lowland plains in Nepal's southern region is popularly known as the tarai.

2. The tarai is also an important area demographically and economically. As early as 1970 the tarai area contained over 30% of Nepal's population and produced over half of its gross domestic product.

3. The choice of two settings was not meant to allow generalizations to the national or even regional level. Instead and as stated above, the choice was intended to produce a sharp contrast in women's status allowing for a strong test of this contextual influence.

4. In Nepal, the lowest unit of government is the Village Development Committee (VDC). A VDC consists of 9 wards. In the hills, we limited our study to 2 contiguous wards, while in the plains we collected information from 5 wards.

5. The individual-wives questionnaire can be used to present similar data. But both Table 2.3 and the one that can be constructed from the wife's interview show that employment opportunities in the hills are much more diverse than in the plains (for further details, write to the authors).

6. The structure of the society is also important. In the hill villages we studied, more than 30% of the households are Brahmans. Brahmans traditionally do not plough the land. This creates round-the-year demand for manual labour in the hills. In contrast, only 4% of the tarai households are higher-caste.

7. Detailed description of caste-ethnicity in both the hills and the tarai is beyond the scope of this paper. But we would like to reiterate that the hills and the tarai are significantly different in their caste ritual. Note also that there is no 'untouchability' in Nepalese legal parlance. (For details on caste-ethnicity in Nepal, see Bista 1972; Gaige 1975; Levine 1987; Holmberg 1989; Bishop 1990).

8. Land is the single most important source of income, wealth, and status in both settings. However, the value of land may vary both in terms of its production and its proximity to roads and settlements. We used 3 measures of poverty: land per capita, production per capita, and land value per capita. All 3 show similar results with respect to women's status. We selected land value per capita as the best measure of level of economic condition.

9. Note that in Nepal, income inequality is higher when the household is used as the unit but is quite a bit lower when per capita income is considered (Nepal Rastra Bank 1989; World Bank 1991).

References

Acharya, M., and Bennett, L. (1981), *Status of Women in Nepal*, Kathmandu: Centre for Economic Development and Administration.

Axinn, W. G., Fricke, T., and Thornton, A. (1991), 'The Micro-demographic Community Study Approach: Improving Survey Data by Integrating the Ethnographic Method', *Sociological Methods and Research*, 20: 187–217.

Balk, Deborah (1994), 'Individual and Community Aspects of Women's Status and Fertility in Bangladesh', *Population Studies*, 48: 21–45.

Basu, Alaka M. (1992), *Culture, the Status of Women, and Demographic Behaviour*, Oxford: Clarendon Press.

Bishop, B. C. (1990), *Karnali under Stress: Livelihood Strategies and Seasonal Rhythms in Changing Nepal Himalaya*, Chicago: Chicago University Press.

Bista, D. B. (1972), *People of Nepal*, Kathmandu: Ratna Pustak Bhandar.

——(1982), 'The Process of Nepalization', in D. B. Bista *et al.* (eds.), *Anthropological and Linguistic Studies of the Gandaki Area in Nepal*, Tokyo: Institute for Linguistics and Culture Studies of Asia and Africa, 1–20.

Blumberg, Rae Lesser (1984), 'A General Theory of Gender Stratification', in Randall Collins (ed.), *Sociological Theory*, San Francisco: Jossey-Bass, 23–101.

Cain, M. T. (1993), 'Patriarchal Structure and Demographic Change', in N. Federici, K. O. Mason, and Solvi Sogner (eds.), *Women's Position and Demographic Change*, New York: Oxford University Press, 43–60.

Caldwell, J. C. (1982), *Theory of Fertility Decline*, London: Academic Press.

——and Hill, A. G. (1988), 'Introduction: Recent Developments Using Micro-approaches to Demographic Research', in J. C. Caldwell *et al.* (eds.), *Micro-approaches to Demographic Research*, London: Kegan Paul International, 1–9.

——Reddy, P. H., and Caldwell, P. (1988), *The Causes of Demographic Change: Experimental Research Design in South India*, Madison, Wisc.: University of Wisconsin Press.

Chafetz, Janet S. (1990), *Gender Equity: An Integrated Theory of Stability and Change*, London: Sage.

Cole, S. (1994), 'Why Sociology Doesn't Make Progress like the Natural Sciences', *Sociological Forum*, 9: 129–54.

Collins, Randall, and Coltrane, Scott (1991), *Sociology of Marriage and the Family*, Chicago: Nelson-Hall.

Dyson, T., and Moore, M. (1983), 'On Kinship Structure, Female Autonomy and Demographic Behaviour in India', *Population and Development Review*, 9: 35–60.

Fricke, T. E., Thornton, A., and Dahal, D. R. (1991), *Family Organization and the Wage Labor Transition in a Tamang Community of Nepal*, Ann Arbor: Institute for Social Research and Department of Anthropology, University of Michigan.

Gaige, F. H. (1975), *Regionalism and National Unity in Nepal*, Berkeley: University of California Press.

Gurung, Harka (1989), *Nature and Culture: Random Reflections*, Kathmandu: Jeewan Printing Support Press.

Holmberg, D. H. (1989), *Order in Paradox: Myth, Ritual, and Exchange among Nepal's Tamang*, Ithaca, NY: Cornell University Press.

Jain, Ravindra K. (1970), *South Indians on the Plantation Frontier in Malaysa*, New Haven: Yale University Press.

Levine, Nancy (1987), 'Caste, State, and the Ethnic Boundaries in Nepal', *Journal of Asian Studies*, 46: 71–88.

Mason, Karen O. (1984), *The Status of Women*, New York: Rockefeller Foundation.

——(1993), 'Women's Position as a Cause of Demographic Change', in N. Federici, K. O. Mason, and S. Sogner (eds.), *Women's Position and Demographic Change*, New York: Oxford University Press, 19–42.

Morgan, S. P., and Niraula, Bhanu B. (1994), 'Women's Status and Fertility in Two Nepali Villages', paper presented at the Annual Meetings of the American Sociological Association, Los Angeles.

Nepal Rastra Bank (1989), *Multipurpose Household Survey: A Study on Income Distribution, Employment and Consumption Patterns in Nepal*, Kathmandu: Nepal Rastra Bank.

Smith, H. L. (1989), 'Integrating Theory and Research on the Institutional Determinants of Fertility', *Demography*, 26: 171–84.

Spain, Daphne (1993), 'Gendered Spaces and Women's Status', *Sociological Theory*, 11: 137–51.

Stolzenberg, Ross M. (1979), 'The Measurement and Decomposition of Causal Effects in Nonlinear and Nonadditive models', in Karl F. Schuessler (ed.), *Sociological Methodology*, San Francisco: Jossey-Bass, 459–88.

Van de Walle, Francine, and van de Walle, Etienne (1993), 'Urban Women's Autonomy and Natural Fertility in the Sahel Region of Africa', in N. Federici, K. O. Mason, and S. Sogner (eds.), *Women's Position and Demographic Change*, Oxford: Clarendon Press, 61–79.

Webster's (1991), *Webster's New Collegiate Dictionary*, Springfield, Mass.: G. C. Merriam.

Whyte, Martin King (1978), *The Status of Women in Preindustrial Societies*, Princeton: Princeton University Press.

World Bank (1991), *Nepal: Poverty and Incomes. A World Bank Country Study*, Washington, DC: World Bank.

APPENDIX 2.1

Table 2.A1. Question wording and worksheet used to collect the data in Table 2.4

Now I would like to find out the tasks done by members of this household. Please tell me everyone in the house who (ask items a–q). Does anyone else to do this?

	Respondent	Husband	Son	Daughter	Another male family member	Another female family member	Paid help	No one
a. Works for income								
b. Cooks meals								
c. Cleans up after meals								
d. Buys food grains								
e. Handles the household money								
f. Cleans the house								
g. Buys clothing								
h. Washes the clothes								
i. Cares for the children								
j. Cleans outside the house								
k. Gets water								
l. Gets cooking fuel								
m. Tends animals								
n. Tends crops								
o. Processes crops								
p. Does other agricultural work								
q. Has time for daily leisure activities								

APPENDIX 2.2

Table 2.A2. Question wording and worksheet used to collect the data in Table 2.5

Now I would like to find out whether it is acceptable for you to go alone to certain places. Is it acceptable for you to go alone to . . .

Places	Yes	No	Depends	Don't know
a. The local market				
b. The local health centre				
c. Fields outside the village				
d. A community centre, park, or park in the village				
e. The home of relatives or friends in the village				
f. A nearby fair or shrine				
g. The next village				
h. A movie				

PART II

Nuptiality, Fertility, and Abortion Practices by Poverty Status

3 Quality of Life and Marital Experiences in Mexico

Orlandina de Oliveira

In this chapter I analyse the marital experiences of women with different social backgrounds. I am interested in examining the influence which the quality of life has on the first conjugal experience.[1] The concept of quality of life transcends strictly economic factors to include elements of a social character. In this article I avail myself of two factors to define quality of life: the availability of economic resources and the types of family experiences of women during childhood and adolescence.[2] I consider that these factors can affect individuals' life trajectories by opening or closing opportunities for study, work, and personal development. Differential access to structural opportunities and to normative and value frameworks depends on family and class backgrounds, although individuals can succeed in counteracting adverse circumstances through personal self-improvement projects.

The information utilized comes from 88 women's life history narratives. On the basis of these women's statements I analyse their perceptions of their conjugal experiences. I focus above all on the subjective features of those experiences: their reasons for marrying, perceptions of married life, and the meanings they attribute to marriage. It is important to note the continued scarcity of studies in Mexico which analyse marriage from the subjective perspective of the actors involved and which also consider the differences between social sectors. There is also a notorious absence of studies which take economic and social factors into account when defining individual quality of life and which evaluate their influence on the inception and later evolution of married life.[3]

In order to frame my findings within a broader context, in the first section of this study I review some of the earlier investigations conducted in Mexico on prevailing marriage patterns and women's perceptions of their marital unions. In the second section I analyse the relationships between social backgrounds and marital experiences. Initially I consider some of the qualitative information utilized. I then classify women into four types of situations according to two factors: (1) differential access to economic resources and (2) presence or absence of family conflicts and instability during childhood and adolescence. Later I compare their conjugal experiences. In the last section, I review the principal findings of the study.

Marriage Patterns and Experiences in Contemporary Mexico

In recent decades, Mexican society has experienced important economic and demographic changes. The process of family formation has not been unaffected by these transformations. Fertility has declined markedly and marriage patterns have changed. In this section I first refer to analyses which permit us to characterize marriage patterns in the country and their recent changes. I then refer to some works focusing on the study of values, beliefs, and customs with respect to conjugal unions and to the partners' rights and obligations.[4]

Recent marriage trends in Mexico

On the national level, early marriage is prevalent, adult celibacy is rare, and legal unions predominate although consensual unions are by no means negligible. Moreover, regional and rural–urban variations as well as variation among women with different demographic traits are considerable (Ojeda 1989; Quilodrán 1989, 1991, 1994).

In terms of the co-existence of legal and consensual unions, Mexico resembles the countries of Central America and the Caribbean and differs from other Latin American countries and other regions of the world, where marriage sanctioned by law predominates (Quilodrán 1992; Rossetti 1993). Consensual unions are a historical and cultural trait of Mexican society dating from the pre-Hispanic period; their relative importance has remained stable, with a slight downward tendency over the past years: 15 per cent in 1976 and 14 per cent in 1982.[5] Also, it is worth pointing out that consensual unions are less common in urban than in rural areas (Ojeda 1989; Quilodrán 1991, 1994).

The legalization of consensual unions over the course of a couple's life is another characteristic which Mexico shares with other countries (Pebley and Goldman 1986; Ariza, González de la Rocha, and Oliveira 1994; Quilodrán 1994). On the national level, in 1982 the figures for legalization of unions at some point after their formation reached almost 50 per cent, for first unions of at least five years' duration (Ojeda 1989). It is important to emphasize that the different types of unions are distinguished according to age at the time of formation, stability, propensity to second marriages, and fertility levels. Consensual unions occur at early ages, and are more unstable and less fertile than legal ones (Quilodrán and Potter 1981; Quilodrán 1982; Potter and Ojeda 1984).

With regard to the differences between social sectors, a central feature of my analysis, it has been found that consensual unions are more frequent among women of lower socio-economic levels. Also, legalization of unions during the couple's life is less frequent in the lower socio-economic strata (Ojeda 1989). Important differences have also been registered in terms of the age at couple formation: less-favoured social groups have a pattern of early female marriage, whereas marriage comes later for professionals, executives, and high public officials (Ojeda 1989).

Finally, I want to point out the most important changes in Mexican marriage patterns between 1960 and 1990. The proportion of individuals who never marry increased much more markedly among men than women. Additionally, the number of legal unions, civil marriages, and civil and religious marriages increased at the expense of the number of exclusively religious or consensual unions. The proportion of divorced and separated individuals rose notably among women; among men the increase was smaller because of their greater tendency to form new unions. Finally, the age at first union increased, especially for women: it rose from 20.7 to 22.0 years of age during the period analysed, whereas for men it remained around 24 (Quilodrán 1994).

Marital experiences: rituals, motives, and meanings

Case studies conducted in rural communities and in different geographical areas characterized by different marriage patterns have turned up results of great interest for understanding the values, customs, and practices linked to marriage in Mexico.

Until only a few decades ago, in some rural communities marriage was a decision of the family group; weddings were almost always arranged by the parents of the bride and groom. In this regard, González (1994) points out that social acceptance of courtships and engagements is an important change in the values and cultural patterns regulating marriage in recent years. Despite this, 'free' selection of spouses continues to be relative. Limits to freedom of choice are set by the social values and norms concerning whom one may marry. In general, it is preferable to marry a person who belongs to the same social stratum of the same community and to have the parents' approval, even though these norms may not always be explicit and may vary by region and generation. However, not complying with social norms can entail social sanctions such as the distancing of friends and relatives, loss of inheritance, and mistreatment of the bride by the husband's family. Similarly, during engagement, parents tend to control the prospective couple's meetings by withholding permission or demanding the presence of chaperones, although differences have been found according to the geographic area analysed (Aranda 1989; Quilodrán 1993a; González 1994).

Asking for the hand of the bride and the wedding feast are frequent practices among different social sectors in rural and urban Mexico. The parents of the groom request the hand of the bride even when the union is arranged consensually (Quilodrán 1993a). Aranda (1989) found that in a Oaxacan community one of the functions of the wedding feast is to initiate a relationship of mutual aid between families that will continue indefinitely. For her part, González Montes (1994) maintains that among the older population, a religious marriage and feast are what really legitimize a union, whereas for the younger people these rituals are principally symbols of social prestige. She points out that when there are no resources to cover the cost of the wedding, the union begins with the 'theft' of the bride, which can either take place without her consent or be arranged beforehand.

In terms of the expectations for marriage, over twenty years ago Elú de Leñero (1971) compared the motives for marrying with perceptions of marriage at the time of the interview among a group of urban women who used a family planning clinic. The results indicate that the women married first for love and affection, second to have children, and third for economic security. Only half the women whose expectations were to have love, affection, and economic security when they married found them in their lives as partners. Something very different happened with the children: to a great degree they did become the most important reason for satisfaction. On the basis of in-depth interviews with women from different regions and social groups, Quilodrán (1993*a*) also found that children represent the main reason for maintaining the marital union. García and Oliveira (1994), in analysing the meaning of motherhood among married women from different social sectors, stress that working-class women consider motherhood to be the central pillar of their lives and to give meaning to the marriage.

For their part, Benería and Roldán (1987) studied the normative expectations which regulate the interaction and legitimize exchanges between husband and wife. They point to various elements which allow us to understand the meaning of the marriage contract among working-class women in Mexico City. There is a constant re-negotiation of the rules of interaction throughout married life, and divergences from expectations cause family conflicts and violence. According to this study, women's expectations on getting married were that their husbands should contribute enough economic resources to maintain the family, respect their wives, not mistreat them physically or verbally, not humiliate them with scandalous infidelity, treat them gently, and recognize their contributions to the home. Newlywed women also expected love and affection. On the other hand, wives ought to carry out the domestic work and attend to the children, comply with the demand for conjugal sexual faithfulness, and respect their partners in the sense of 'obedience and deference'.

In the same vein, other studies mention that women, above all in the working class, agree to obey their husbands and to ask permission to leave the house, even when they have to work to 'help' maintain the household. Similarly, they consider it to be an obligation to their husbands to contribute economic resources for supporting the family (De Barbieri 1984; García and Oliveira 1994).

In addition to the duties of spouses, studies of perceptions about marriage show that *understanding* is seen as an essential element for the couple's survival. Likewise, the notion of *commitment* and the desire for *protection*, especially for the children, are very important (Quilodrán 1993*a*). García and Oliveira (1994) also mention that women from both the urban middle and working class who do not work in extra-domestic activities value marriage above all as a source of protection.

Quality of Life and Marital Experiences

In this section I analyse the quality of life of women with different social and family backgrounds, and I compare their conjugal experiences. I define quality of life in terms of economic resources and in terms of instability and conflict in the family of origin.

Methodological considerations

I base the relationship between social background and marital experiences on the analysis of in-depth interviews carried out in three urban centres in Mexico in 1990 by Brígida García and me.[6] We chose cities with very different traits in order to maximize the heterogeneity of the cases analysed and not with the idea of carrying out a comparative analysis of urban areas.[7] Of the many features included in the 1990 interview guide, in this study I refer to information from life histories on key events in childhood and adolescence, perceptions of the family of origin's economic conditions, age at the beginning of the conjugal union, divorces or separations, subsequent unions, reasons for getting married, perceptions of married life, and meaning attributed to the marriage.

Women were selected from two large cohorts: those 20–34 and 35–49 years of age who were married or living with a partner, had children, and worked in different extra-domestic activities. Most of the women interviewed (89.7 per cent) had only had one conjugal union, reflecting the general trend in the Mexican population. Regarding extra-domestic work, we chose an equal number of salaried and self-employed, full-time and part-time working women in both manual and non-manual occupations. Some women who were not working at the time of the interview were also considered. Due to the non-probabilistic sample employed and the small number of cases analysed, my results should not be seen as *empirical generalizations* valid beyond the women interviewed. Instead, they allow us to support, specify, or question already existing generalizations and to suggest hypotheses which can fruitfully direct future studies on the subject.

The information analysed in this investigation offers advantages over census data and available surveys for the study I propose because of its longitudinal and qualitative character. It is important to emphasize that in Mexico we do not have retrospective survey data which permit us to analyse the influence of women's social backgrounds on the formation of their conjugal unions. The available information is cross-sectional and refers to husbands' occupational traits at the time of the interview for women who have been in conjugal unions, or fathers' occupational traits for single women. For this reason, the existing analyses of variations in marriage patterns by social sector consider women's current demographic characteristics above all. Longitudinal data would permit a more accurate analysis of these variations.

Concerning the advantages of qualitative data, I want to point out two features. The first is that in our case it offers the possibility of considering the family of origin's internal dynamics as an indicator of the quality of life in addition to the economic dimension. In general, surveys do not capture information on family dynamics because of the topic's inherent difficulties and the high costs of applying open interviews to large samples. Second, a qualitative approach also allows us to capture the connections which the subjects themselves establish between events which have taken place during their lives. It permits us to analyse the meanings which women attribute to their marital experiences rather than inferring them from demographic traits.[8] However, it must be acknowledged that recalling experiences is an interpretation of the past which people being interviewed make on the basis of their current situations. Memory does not register a lineal succession of finished facts and events; it reconstructs the past (Cano and Radkau 1991).

Quality of life during the formative years

The childhood and adolescent experiences of the women interviewed varied greatly between individuals. Two dimensions are important for characterizing these differences between women in terms of quality of life. The first deals with economic needs and permits us to distinguish between poor and non-poor women. The second deals with family dynamics in terms of the presence or absence of conflict and family instability. Poverty and domestic violence are characteristics of Mexican reality. The proportion of poor households in the country has grown significantly during the economic crisis and adjustment of the 1980s and 1990s (Hernández Laos 1992). In turn, the physical and psychological violence at the heart of Mexican families for centuries has attained greater public visibility in recent years (Tuñón, Riquer, and Velázquez 1990). In another investigation I analyse economic hardship during childhood and adolescence as an element which limits women's possibilities for studying and getting better-paid jobs, and therefore for attaining the economic security which would allow them to terminate a violent conjugal union. Similarly, I pointed out that a conflict-ridden and violent environment during the formative years can generate greater acceptance of spousal violence as something natural (García and Oliveira 1994).

The distinction between poor and non-poor women rests on the basis of the perceptions of the very women interviewed; I do not use statistical measures of income or household resources. This qualitative approach allows us to incorporate the subjective dimension of 'relative deprivation' into the definition of poverty. *Poor women* are those who according to their perceptions confronted marked economic hardship in their childhood and adolescence. For them the economic situation was difficult and precarious: money was lacking, the father's income did not meet needs or he 'didn't bring money home'. In cases of extreme poverty, the women interviewed mentioned that they even went hungry:

There were times when my mother said, 'Oh, kids, well we have nothing to eat.' I was little, in first grade . . . My mother didn't have any money and she gave us dry tortillas with salt. (Cecilia, age 24, two children, Mexico City)

In other situations of economic precariousness, the needs may not have been so pressing but the women interviewed still considered that their parents earned very little and that their incomes were insufficient for maintaining many children. Often, as girls they had to work to help their families and in many cases they could not remain in school.

In contrast, *non-poor women* are those who consider that their families' economic resources were adequate for everyday survival. These women had very different experiences:

I had a very nice childhood. I had everything, and in adolescence too. . . . We used to travel a lot. (Esther, age 33, three children, Tijuana)

Likewise, because they did not confront serious economic difficulties, the great majority of these women were able to finish high school, many went to college, and some even went to graduate school. Moreover, in these cases a frequent pattern was to continue studying even after entering the labour market, although the predominant situation was one in which they first finished school and later began their working lives.

In terms of family dynamics, according to accounts of the women interviewed, we distinguish their families of origin according to the presence or absence of instability and conflict. On the one hand are *unstable and conflictive families*, those marked by at least one of the following features: the father's or mother's alcoholism or irresponsibility towards the home; physical violence between the spouses and towards the children; separations, divorces, and second unions; or family disintegration due to the parents' death or abandonment of the children. On the other hand are the *stable and less conflictive families*, those which have more harmonious relations between parents and children and in which at least one of the following features is present: love and respect; dialogue; family understanding and unity; responsibility; trust; or equality.

These different forms of family experiences can occur in families with different material conditions. However, the cases analysed suggest that family conflicts and instability can contribute to aggravating conditions of poverty and even cause economic difficulties for families with more resources. Thus, it is important to consider both dimensions and posit four types of situation:

1. women from poor, unstable, and conflictive families;
2. women from poor, stable, and less conflictive families;
3. women from unstable and conflictive families with resources; and
4. women from stable and less conflictive families with resources.

In general, the women from *poor, unstable, and conflictive families* (25 cases) say that during their childhood and adolescence they had dramatic experiences which have marked their lives: being daughters of single mothers, the death of the father or mother, abandonment by the mother, or separation of the parents. Thus, for example, Evangelina tells us that her birth was the result of her mother being raped by a relative:

[My mother] says that . . . when they left her alone, one of her cousins—that is, my father, who was older then her—came in and took advantage of her. She didn't know what was going on because she was 12 years old . . . Her father arrived and beat her and ran her out of the house . . . Later, when she had me . . . she went to work for a family. (Evangelina, age 37, three children, Mexico City)

For her part, Rocío relates that she did not live with her mother or siblings:

I was the daughter of a marriage which broke up. My mother left me with my paternal grandparents and then my father hooked up with another woman . . . and I didn't learn of my mother again until I was 15 . . . when I met a brother and a sister. The rest I don't know about: one died and the other—I don't know if she gave it away or it stayed. I don't know. (Rocío, age 44, five children, Tijuana)

The father's, stepfather's, or mother's alcoholism or physical violence directed at their partners or children repeatedly form part of the childhood and adolescent memories of the women interviewed from poor, unstable, and conflictive families. This made their already very precarious living conditions even more difficult.

There were seven kids . . . our life was—how should I put it? . . . very sad. My father often did not work. He spent his time just drinking. . . . Until my mother decided to separate . . . he got to where he hit her. (Cecilia, age 24, two children, Mexico City)

The women with scant economic resources who were interviewed also mention the 'unobliging' father's lack of responsibility in their childhood and adolescence; he did not regularly contribute to supporting the family:

at the same time he was a little irresponsible because he would get to drinking and didn't give my mother any money. (Gerarda, age 50, one child, Mérida)

Under these circumstances the mothers often worked to help support the family or took charge of looking after and supporting their children by themselves:

Look, I just lived with my mother. . . . my father was very . . . alcoholic. . . . the one who took care of us was my mother; she worked . . . to support us. (Antonia, age 44, eleven children, Mexico City)

On occasion, when faced with their spouses' irresponsibility, the mother left the home.

I come from . . . a broken marriage. . . . my parents separated when I was 10 years old. My mother left home because my father used to hit her a lot. My father was always a big womanizer and unobliging . . . he never helped with the expenses as he should have. (Gregoria, age 29, three children, Mexico City)

It is important to point out that poverty does not necessarily cause conflict and family instability. The women who grew up in *poor, stable, and less conflictive families* (20 cases) present a very different image of their childhood and adolescence. They perceive themselves as having been poor but not in extreme poverty. They value having had harmonious family relations; when they discuss their parents' relationship they speak of responsibility, unity, understanding, and emotional stability.

I had a very healthy, happy, and contented childhood. . . . sure, we had problems, but they were overcome. . . . I am a very emotionally stable person, and this is what my mother and father taught me. . . . there were [economic] deficiencies, but there was never a deficiency of love or understanding. (Juana, age 29, three children, Tijuana)

They turned their back on my father because my mother was from . . . a poor village neighbourhood. That's where our poverty began but I think that when you live comfortably and happily in poverty, when there is unity between the parents, I think that money isn't so important. (Imelda, age 39, two children, Mexico City)

These circumstances of poverty or conflict contrast markedly with those of the women born into *stable and less conflictive families with economic resources* (23 cases). In these cases, when the women interviewed refer to their families of origin, they consider that the economic situation was good or at least that they did not face serious difficulties. However, on occasion the mothers and siblings had to work to maintain their standard of living. Similarly, when they describe their parents' relationship, they speak of love, respect, dedication, dialogue, confidence, unity, and equality.

[My parents] were an extremely united couple . . . they went everywhere together. . . . They travelled together and were very happy. . . . They were known as a model couple. (Viviana, age 36, two children, Tijuana)

there was always a lot of respect between the two and among us. . . . I think there was equality. . . . I saw a peaceful, happy marriage. I didn't see fights or arguments. I didn't hear yelling or see blows, nothing like that. (Natalia, age 33, three children, Mérida)

Finally, the women interviewed who spent their childhood and adolescence in *unstable and conflictive families of origin with economic resources* (20 cases) had their lives marked by difficult situations: constant conflicts, separations, and alcoholism.

I lived in a family that was supposed to be very rich . . . [but] my parents got along very badly. I didn't like my childhood or my adolescence. . . . In my house everything was yelling, scenes, a mess. (Constanza, age 40, three children, Mérida)

As with the poor women, although at different levels, in certain situations family instability also contributed to worsening the living conditions of families with economic resources, and the mothers had to work to support their children.

My father was from a good family. . . . he made a lot of money but as fast as he made it, it went like water. He didn't know how to manage it. Then my mother had to work. . . . you see, my father dedicated himself to partying. . . . unfortunately drink overcame him and . . . my mother was the one who saw to trying to take care of us. (Martha, age 36, four children, Mérida)

Different Conjugal Experiences

I begin the analysis of conjugal experiences with the variations in age at marriage among women with different family backgrounds. I then consider the motives for marrying and their variations according to the earliness or lateness of the conjugal union. Finally, I analyse the perceptions of married life and the meaning of marriage. I base my argument on the hypothesis that both the availability of economic resources and the degree of stability in the family of origin can condition marital experiences.

Age of first union

In terms of the analysis of life cycles or individual trajectories, I conceive the first union as a fundamental transition in women's lives. Together with the birth of the first child, it marks the entry into adult life. In this qualitative analytic framework, the age at first union acquires special importance because it can condition other life-cycle transitions. Various studies indicate that marriage at an early age is associated with dropping out of school, early entry into the labour market, and high fertility. These features in turn can limit individuals' future opportunities (Elder 1978; Marini 1978; Carlson 1979; Michael and Tuma 1985; Cooney and Hogan 1991).

Previous studies show that age at first union varies according to social group (Ojeda 1989; Quilodrán 1990). My results show a similar pattern: women with poor backgrounds marry at earlier ages than those born into families with more economic resources. Moreover, analysis of the interviews suggests that if instability and conflict in the families of origin is added to scarce material conditions, the predisposition toward early marriage is accentuated even more.

In essence, the situation of women with *poor, unstable, and conflictive* family backgrounds contrasts markedly with that of women *with economic resources and a more harmonious family environment.* At one extreme, when the quality of life is very precarious both economically and in terms of the family environment, women are highly prone to marry at very young ages, sometimes even before they turn 15. Among this group of women, consensual unions are more common than in the other family situations analysed, although legal marriages predominate in all cases. This finding agrees with the national tendencies indicated. The majority of women interviewed who grew up in poor, conflictive households and married very young managed at most to complete primary school or a few years of secondary school, and they have had a high number of children (3.8 on average). Likewise, throughout their married lives, most have remained in the least-privileged social sectors. Only in exceptional cases have women with poor backgrounds managed to study beyond secondary school and rise to non-poor social sectors.

At the other extreme, women *with economic resources and a more harmonious family environment* during their formative years are more prone to late marriages; the majority marry after age 19. Moreover, many of them wait to form couples until after finishing their studies. Those studies are frequently university level or even higher, and these women have far lower levels of fertility (2.4 children on average). Almost all of them have maintained their original social position throughout their married lives. These are primarily women who have had broad social and family opportunities to move ahead. Some have managed to develop professional activities as part of a project of personal development. Others work to cover their personal expenses, and very few do so out of necessity to maintain their families' standard of living. There are very few cases in which women from stable and less conflictive families with economic resources become impoverished during their married lives.

In sum, these results confirm what has been found in other studies: early marriage can entail a serious obstacle to overcoming precarious living conditions confronted during childhood and adolescence. Indeed it can contribute to the impoverishment of women born into families with resources.

Motives for marriage

Unlike previous studies which indicate that love and affection hold a central place in the decision to marry (Elú de Leñero 1971), I find that only women with social backgrounds in more privileged, *stable, and less conflictive families with economic resources,* and who marry after age 20, do so because they are in love.

I got married because . . . I was very much in love. Probably him too. . . . I was 24 years old and we'd been engaged for five years. My family was not in favour because he's younger than me. I insisted a lot that he had . . . maturity, ability, intelligence. (Celia, age 37, two children, Mérida)

In contrast, marriage patterns in the less fortunate sectors (*poor women with unstable and conflictive families of origin*) are characterized by early unions motivated above all by the desire to flee from problems in the paternal or maternal home. In general, young women leave without much thought in order to get away from family conflicts because they fear their parents or want to try to change their lives. Under these circumstances, the couple almost always goes to live in the bride's in-laws' house in accordance with the patrilocal pattern of residence (González and Iracheta 1987).

I got married at 13, very much a girl. . . . I don't know why. . . . I didn't think of getting married. . . . [The engagement] only lasted a week. . . . then I went off with him. . . . My mother went to look for me but . . . out of fear that she would hit me . . . I didn't go back any more. (Antonia, age 44, eleven children, Mexico City)

He always had time for me and I talked to him about my problems. When my mother hit us for being such children and such a problem, I showed him where [she'd hit me] and how [the bruises] were and he cured them for me. He was a good person. He said to me, 'Will you go off with me?' and I went . . . I was 14 . . . I didn't think, really. (Oralia, age 24, five children, Mexico City)

It is important to emphasize that among women who have lived through less extreme situations, no clear pattern of motives for marriage manifests itself. Instead, there is a wide range of possibilities: some seek security or support, others do it for social convenience or because of pressure from the parents or boyfriends, and yet others want freedom—to flee from family problems or because they are in love or pregnant.

Perceptions of Married Life

Previous studies show that marital satisfaction varies according to the length of the partnership. Unlike women who have been married for over twenty years, those married for under five years are optimistic and in general consider that they have possibilities for personal development (Elú de Leñero 1971). My analysis refers almost exclusively to women who have been married for over ten years. Regardless of their social and family backgrounds, the women interviewed share the perception that marriage is a central change in life which is not always easy to *adapt or adjust to*. It is important to emphasize that there are significant differences in the problems confronted in married life when one compares women with different social backgrounds. In effect, regardless of the kinds of family experience in their families of origin, women with *poor* backgrounds say that they remain married because they have learned to endure and to overcome difficult situations and consider that it is better for the children. Very few stay together for love, affection, or the satisfactions that marriage brings; instead, they have confronted serious difficulties in their married lives: violence, alcoholism, lack of responsibility by the spouse, infidelity, jealousy, and prohibitions against leaving the house.[9] These results point in the same direction as various studies on relationships between couples in the urban working class in Mexico (De Barbieri 1984; Massolo and Díaz Ronner 1985; González de la Rocha 1986; Benería and Roldán 1987; García and Oliveira 1994).

These kinds of difficulties were also present in the married lives of women who grew up in households with greater resources, but much less often than for women raised in poor sectors. More exactly, women with *non-poor* backgrounds have confronted other conflicts more related to the search for greater autonomy, spousal demands with respect to child care, and problems with administering the family budget.[10] Likewise, non-poor women, including those whose homes were unstable and conflictive, state that over the years they have achieved more satisfactory partnerships than the women with poor backgrounds who were interviewed. The non-poor women assert more frequently that the relationship is progressing, not only because of the children, but also because of love and affection and because they have done well.

On occasion, there is even an explicit intention to break with the kinds of shared experience which prevailed in their families of origin.

[The marriage] is like an alliance that we have . . . between husband and wife with the children of one family. And to me it seems good for both of us and for the children. . . . Since we were both children of separated parents, it's that we don't want disunity between the two of us. (Lupita, age 39, married at 23, two children, Mérida)

The differences between social sectors in terms of conjugal satisfaction may be due to the characteristics of the sample utilized. We only interviewed married women; however, the women interviewed with more privileged backgrounds are more prone to separate and remarry. As a result, one possible explanatory hypothesis for the differences in marital satisfaction between social sectors would be that women with *poor backgrounds* tend to break off unsatisfactory marital relationships less frequently than non-poor women.[11] This assertion is based on the fact that because they have little schooling, receive low wages, and have more children, poor women confront greater economic difficulties in separating than those who come from more privileged sectors.[12] The latter women have higher levels of education, better-paid jobs, and lower levels of fertility. Another explanatory factor for the differences between social sectors may be associated with the fact that the conjugal relationships of the women interviewed who had poor backgrounds had lasted for a longer time than those of the non-poor women: 51.2 per cent of the poor women interviewed versus 40.5 per cent of the non-poor women had been married for fifteen years or longer.[13]

The Meaning of Marriage

Previous studies reviewed in the first section of this study show that women consider marriage to be a *commitment* in which *understanding* and *respect* between the spouses plays a central role. Similarly, they indicate that the *children* represent a fundamental element in the maintenance of the conjugal relationship. Moreover, they indicated that for many women, especially those who do not undertake extra-domestic activities, marriage means *protection*.

My results permit us to make additional conclusions about the influence of class backgrounds ·on the meaning attributed to marriage. We find that regardless of how the families of origin lived together, for women born into *poor households* marriage means *moral or economic support* above all: the possibility of *being mothers* and of having *companionship*. In contrast, for women from *families of origin with economic resources, understanding* occupies a central position, whereas moral and economic support are secondary. With respect to the children's role, it is important to emphasize that this emerges with greater clarity in poor women's discourse; they establish a more marked connection between marriage and maternity. Women from families with resources value the *home*, the *family, and the couple* in general and not so much the children in particular, as is the case among the poorer sectors.

Final Considerations

In this study I have analysed the marital experiences of women with different social and family backgrounds. I utilized in-depth interview data on various features relevant to the study of marriage: characteristics of the families of origin; age at first union; motives for marrying; perceptions of married life; and the meaning of marriage. The methodological strategy for establishing the connections between class background and marital experiences consisted first in constructing a typology based on two dimensions: the availability of economic resources and the presence of conflicts during childhood and adolescence. Later I compared the women's perceptions and lived experiences with different types of social situations and families of origin.

It is important to reiterate that due to the intentional character of the sample employed, my results are not generalizable beyond the cases analysed. Instead, in some cases the qualitative analysis I carried out allows us to support, specify, or question already existing generalizations. Similarly, the analysis of women's own perceptions has provided us with elements for deepening our understanding of the possible influences social background has on marital experiences. Moreover, the comparison between *extreme types* has made it possible to visualize more clearly the complex interrelations between the features analysed. My findings have suggested topics and hypotheses which need to be studied with both greater analytic depth and broader population coverage.

A central feature I want to point out is the nature of the interrelations between quality of life during the formative years and the different features analysed. With respect to *age at first union*, we found that this trait depends strongly on both the availability of economic resources and the internal dynamics of the family of origin. Similarly, we saw that the relationship manifested itself more clearly in the extreme cases. Women from *poor, unstable, and conflictive families* are more prone to early unions whereas women born into *non-poor, stable, and less conflictive families* marry later. In effect we can hypothesize that in statistical terms, an interaction between poverty and family instability and conflict would allow us to explain the greater probability of forming unions at early ages.

In relation to the influence of social and family background on *the motives for marrying*, my analysis suggests an even more complex structure of interrelations. Only in the extreme cases of women from poor, unstable, and conflictive families who marry young and those from non-poor, stable, and less conflictive families who marry later does a definite pattern of motives for marrying appear. The former do it to flee from family problems whereas the latter mostly assert that they marry for love. In other situations, the range of motives is much broader. Women marry both for love and under pressure from parents and boyfriends, for moral and economic support, and because of pregnancy, convenience, or custom. These results point to the need for deepening the study of the role of sentiments, social pressures, and the search for security in the formation of couples. Similarly, the results make clear the importance of analysing the influence of social and family background on the motives and age of marriage in terms of the two dimensions indicated: availability of resources and kinds of family experience.

In terms of *perceptions of married life*, the differences are much less marked and occur principally among women from different social sectors. The results suggest that regardless of the type of shared experiences in their families of origin, during their married years women from poor families confront problems of violence, alcoholism, lack of responsibility on the part of the spouse, jealousy, and prohibitions against leaving the house. In contrast, although they may confront problems of a different nature, the women interviewed who had non-poor social backgrounds state that over the years they have achieved satisfactory relationships and that they remain married not only for the children, as in the case of the working-class women, but also for love and affection.

With respect to the possible influence of social and family background on the women's perceptions of married life, it will be important to carry out studies with broader samples which include both married and separated or divorced women. This type of sample will allow us to counteract the possible selectivity effect which could be affecting the explanation of the differences between social sectors: that is, the women from poor sectors surely express greater dissatisfaction with conjugal life because they are less prone than women from non-poor families to break unions. It would also be important to analyse systematically to what degree age at marrying, the motives for doing so, and the length of the union are associated with different perceptions of married life.

As to the *meaning of marriage*, the most important differences also occur between women with different social backgrounds. As we saw, regardless of the kinds of shared experiences in the families of origin, for women who confronted difficult economic situations during their childhood and adolescence, marriage means above all *moral or economic support*, the possibility of *being mothers*, and having *companionship*. In contrast, for women from families with economic resources, moral or economic support recedes to a secondary level and *understanding* holds a central position.

In terms of the role of children, we also found differences between the *poor and non-poor sectors*. Women with poor backgrounds establish a clearer connection between marriage and motherhood. For these women, marrying allows them to be mothers and they frequently remain married for their children's sake. For women born into families with economic resources, it is more common to encounter the notion of having a home, a family, and a partner. Finally, it is important to point out that the more marked differences in terms of age at marriage, the motives for marrying, married life, and the meaning attributed to marriage occur between women born into poor families and those born into non-poor families.

Notes

I wish to acknowledge the valuable comments of Marina Ariza and Brígida García on the first version of this text, which was presented at the IUSSP Conference on Women, Poverty and Demographic Change. The English translation was done by Paul Liffman.

1. In general, conjugal unions means legal or consensual unions. Likewise, I use the terms 'marital', 'conjugal', and 'matrimonial experiences' interchangeably due to the high proportion of legal unions in the sample analysed.

2. For a discussion of the importance of taking family dynamics into account when studying the quality of life, see García (1995) and Basu (this volume).

3. As far as I know, only De Barbieri (1984) and García and Oliveira (1994) analyse differences in the meaning of work and motherhood between urban middle- and working-class women. Other studies do not posit differences by social group when they analyse the reasons for and meaning of marriage (Elú de Leñero 1971; Quilodrán 1993*a*). For their part, Benería and Roldán (1987) study conceptions about the marriage contract among working-class women exclusively. Finally, Aranda (1989) and González (1994) research the peasant sector. (As far as other countries are concerned,

see Bumpass *et al.* 1991; Trent and South 1992; Webster *et al.* 1995; and Tambashe *et al.* 1996, which are recent studies that deal with family background issues and their impact on different aspects of married life.)

4. For Mexico, various authors have analysed marriage patterns as well as the motivations for, conceptions of, and rituals of matrimony. See, among others, Aranda (1989); Ojeda (1989); Quilodrán (1993*a*, 1993*b*, 1994), Samuel *et al.* (1993); González (1994); Mummert (1994); and Samuel (1994). Elú de Leñero (1971) and Quilodrán (1993*a*) examine the motives for marrying and the meaning of marriage in women's lives. Finally, Vivas Mendoza (1993) analyses these same issues from the male perspective.

5. These percentages refer to the type of union at the time the survey was taken. If one considers the type of union at the time of its formation, consensual unions reached 25% in 1982.

6. The data analysed were collected as part of a research project on Fertility, Work and Women's Condition with financing from the Rockefeller Foundation. The principal findings of this research are presented in García and Oliveira (1994).

7. The interviews were carried out in Mexico City, the principal urban area of the country; Mérida, located in the South-east; and Tijuana, an important city on the US border.

8. For a discussion of the advantages and limitations of demographic surveys, see Oliveira and García (1986).

9. For an analysis of women with violent, alcoholic spouses who do not regularly contribute to supporting their families, see García and Oliveira (1994: ch. 6).

10. For an analysis of the same source of information from another point of view, see García and Oliveira (1994: ch. 8). The authors examine the relationships of couples in the urban middle and working class according to the women's degree of commitment to extra-domestic labour.

11. However, one must keep in mind that some authors have suggested that extreme poverty can also be a factor in the break-up of unions (see, among others, Bethencourt 1992; CEPAL 1994).

12. In a previous analysis we found that some working-class women maintain unsatisfactory relationships because they are afraid of their partners, fear their children's reproaches, are insecure about confronting life without a spouse, hope that the relationship will change, or consider matrimony to be a commitment which must be honoured (García and Oliveira 1994).

13. Recall that the poor women who were interviewed married earlier.

References

Aranda, Josefina (1989), 'Matrimonio, géneros y subordinación de las mujeres: el caso de Santo Tomás Jalieza, Oaxaca', Master's thesis in Social Anthropology, Escuela Nacional de Antropología e Historia, Mexico City.
Ariza, Marina, González de la Rocha, Mercedes, and Oliveira, Orlandina de (1994), 'Características, estrategias y dinámicas familiares en México, América Latina y el Caribe', paper presented to the Population and Quality of Life Independent Commission, Mexico, mimeo.

Basu, Kaushik (1994), *Agrarian Questions*, Delhi: Oxford University Press.

Benería, Lourdes, and Roldán, Marta (1987), *The Crossroads of Class and Gender: Industrial Homework, Subcontracting and Household Dynamics in Mexico City*, Chicago: The University of Chicago Press.

Bethencourt, Luisa (1992), 'Lo cotidiano de la sobrevivencia: organización doméstica y rol de la mujer', in Cariola Cecilia (coord.), *Sobrevivir en la pobreza: el fin de una ilusión*, Nueva Sociedad, Venezuela: CENDES, 81–102.

Bumpass, Larry, Castro Martin, Teresa, and Sweet, James (1991), 'The Impact of Family Background and Early Marital Factors on Marital Disruption', *Journal of Family Issues*, 12: 22–42.

Cano, Gabriela, and Radkau, Verena (1991), 'Lo privado y lo público o la mutación de los espacios (Historia de mujeres, 1920–1940)', in Vania Salles and Elsie McPhail (coords.), *Textos y pre-textos*, Mexico City: Programa Interdisciplinario de Estudios de la Mujer, El Colegio de México, 417–61.

Carlson, Elwood (1979), 'Family Background, School and Early Marriage', *Journal of Marriage and the Family*, 41: 341–53.

CEPAL [Comisión Económica para América Latina y el Caribe] (1994), *Situación y perspectivas de la familia en América Latina y El Caribe. Familia y Futuro: un programa regional en América Latina y el Caribe*, Santiago de Chile: CEPAL.

Cooney, Teresa M., and Hogan, Dennis P. (1991), 'Marriage in an Institutionalized Life Course: First Marriage among American Men in the Twentieth Century', *Journal of Marriage and the Family*, 53: 178–90.

De Barbieri, Teresita (1984), *Mujeres y vida cotidina*, Mexico City: Fondo de Cultura Económica and Instituto de Investigaciones Sociales, Universidad Nacional Autónoma de México.

Elder, Glen H., Jr. (1978), 'Family History and the Life Course', in Tamara Hareven (ed.), *Transitions: The Family and the Life Course in Historical Perspective*, New York: Academic Press, 17–64.

Elú de Leñero, Ma. Carmen (ed.) (1971), *Mujeres que hablan: implicaciones psico-sociales en el uso de métodos anticonceptivos*, Mexico City: Instituto Mexicano de Estudios Sociales del Instituto Nacional de Nutrición.

García, Brígida (1995), 'Dinámica familiar y calidad de vida', paper presented to the V Reunión Nacional de Investigación Demográfica en México, Sociedad Mexicana de Demografía, Mexico City, mimeo.

——and Oliveira, Orlandina de (1994), *Trabajo y vida familiar en México*, Mexico City: El Colegio de México.

González, Soledad, and Iracheta, P. (1987), 'La violencia en la vida de las mujeres campesinas: el distrito de Tenenago, 1880–1910', in Carmen Ramos *et al.*, *Presencia y transparencia: la mujer en la historia de México*, Mexico City: El Colegio de México, 111–41.

González de la Rocha, Mercedes (1986), *Los recursos de la pobreza: familias de bajos ingresos de Guadalajara*, Guadalajara: El Colegio de Jalisco-CIESAS-SPP.

González Montes, Soledad (1994), 'Cambios en los patrones en la nupcialidad rural en México', paper presented to the Workshop on Hogares, Familias: Desigualdad, Conflicto, Redes Solidarias y Parentales, Sociedad Mexicana de Demografía and Instituto Nacional de Estadística, Geografía e Informática, Aguascalientes, Mexico, mimeo.

Hernández Laos, Enrique (1992), *Crecimiento económico y pobreza en México: una agenda para la investigación*, Centro de Investigaciones Interdisciplinarias en Humanidades, Mexico City: Universidad Nacional Autónoma de México.

Juárez, Fatima (1990), 'La vinculación de eventos demográficos: un estudio sobre los patrones de nupcialidad', *Estudios Demográficos y Urbanos*, 5: 453–78.

Marini, Margaret Mooney (1978), 'The Transition to Adulthood: Sex Differences in Educational Attainment and Age at Marriage', *American Sociological Review*, 43: 483–507.

Massolo, Alejandra, and Díaz Ronner, Lucila (1985), 'Consumo y lucha urbana en la ciudad de México: mujeres protagonistas', Xochimilco, Mexico: Universidad Autónoma Metropolitana, mimeo.

Michael, Robert, and Tuma, Nancy Brandon (1985), 'Entry into Marriage and Parenthood by Young Men and Women: The Influence of Family Background', *Demography*, 22: 515–43.

Mummert, Gail (1994), 'Cambios en las estructuras y organizaciones familiares en un contexto de migración masculina y trabajo asalariado femenino: estudio de caso en un valle agrícola de Michoacán', paper presented to the Workshop on Hogares, Familias: Desigualdad, Conflicto, Redes Solidarias y Parentales, Sociedad Mexicana de Demografía and Instituto Nacional de Estadística, Geografía e Informática, Aguascalientes, Mexico, mimeo.

Ojeda, Norma (1989), *El curso de vida de las mujeres mexicanas: un análisis sociodemográfico*. Cuernavaca, México: Universidad Nacional Autónoma de México, Centro Regional de Investigaciones Multidisciplinarias.

Oliveira, Orlandina, and García, Brígida (1986), 'Encuestas, ¿Hasta dónde?', in *Problemas metodológicos en la investigación sociodemográfica*, Mexico City: Programa de Investigaciones Sociales en Población en América Latina and El Colegio de México, 65–80.

Pebley, Anne, and Goldman, Noreen (1986), 'Legalización de uniones consensuales en México', *Estudios Demográficos y Urbanos*, 1. 267–92.

Potter, Joseph, and Ojeda, Norma (1984), *El impacto sobre la fecundidad de la disolución de las primeras uniones*, Mexico City: Secretaría de Gobernación.

Quilodrán, Julieta (1982), 'Tipos de uniones maritales en México', in *Investigación Demográfica en México*, Mexico City: Consejo Nacional de Ciencia y Tecnología, 235–46.

——(1989), 'México: diferencias de nupcialidad por regiones y tamaños', *Estudios Demográficos y Urbanos*, 4: 595–613.

——(1990), 'Variaciones, niveles y tendencias de la nupcialiad', paper presented to the IV Reunión Nacional de Investigación Demográfica en México, Mexico City, mimeo.

——(1991), 'Entrance into Marital Union and into Motherhood by Social Sectors', in Mario Bronfman, Brígida García, Fátima Juárez, and Orlandina Oliveira (eds.), *Social Sectors and Reproduction in Mexico*, Demographic and Health Surveys, New York: The Population Council, 4–8.

——(1992), 'La vida conyugal en América Latina: contrastes y semejanzas', paper presented to the Workshop El Poblamiento de las Américas, International Union for the Scientific Study of Population, vol. 3, Veracruz, Mexico, pp. 245–64.

——(1993a), 'Historias conyugales: un análisis para México', paper presented to the General Congress of the International Union for the Scientific Study of Population, Montreal, mimeo.

——(1993b), 'La dinámica de la población y la formación de parejas', paper presented to the IV Conferencia Latinoamericana de Población, session on 'Mujer, familia y transición demográfica', Programa Latinoamericano de Actividades en Población, Mexico City, mimeo.

——(1994), 'El matrimonio y sus transformaciones', paper presented to the Workshop on Hogares, Familias: Desigualdad, Conflicto, Redes Solidarias y Parentales, Sociedad Mexicana de Demografía and Instituto Nacional de Estadística, Geografía e Informática, Aguascalientes, Mexico, mimeo.

——and Potter, Joseph (1981), 'Diferentes tipos de unión y fecundidad en México', paper presented to the Seminar on Tipos de Familia y Fecundidad en los Países en Desarrollo, São Paolo, mimeo.

Rossetti, Josefina (1993), 'Hacia un perfil de la familia actual en Latinoamérica y el Caribe', in Comisión Económica para América Latina (CEPAL), *Cambios en el perfil de las familias: la experiencia regional*, Santiago de Chile. CEPAL, 17–65.

Samuel, Olivia (1994), 'Cambios en la nupcialidad en México', paper presented to the Workshop on Hogares, Familias: Desigualdad, Conflicto, Redes Solidarias y Parentales, Sociedad Mexicana de Demografía and Instituto Nacional de Estadística, Geografía e Informática, Aguascalientes, Mexico, mimeo.

——Lerner, Susana, and Quesnel, André (1993), 'Hacia un enfoque demo-antropológico de la nupcialidad y su relación con nuevos esquemas de procreación', paper presented to the XII Congreso Internacional de Ciencias Antropológicas y Etnológicas, Mexico, mimeo.

Spainer, Graham B., Roos, P., and Shockey, J. (1985), 'Marital Trajectories of American Women: Variations in the Life Course', *Journal of Marriage and the Family*, 47: 993–1003.

Tambashe, B. Oleko, and Shapiro, David (1996), 'Family Background and Early Life Course Transitions in Kinshasa': *Journal of Marriage and the Family*, 58: 1029–37.

Trent, Katherine, and South, Scott (1992), 'Sociodemographic Status, Parental Background, Childhood Family Structure, and Attitudes toward Family Formation', *Journal of Marriage and the Family*, 54: 427–39.

Tuñón, Esperanza, Riquer, Florinda, and Velázquez, Margarita (1990), 'Perfil de la mujer en México', Consejo Nacional de Población, Mexico City, mimeo.

Vivas Mendoza, María Waleska (1993), 'Del lado de los hombres (algunas reflexiones en torno a la masculinidad)', Bachelor's thesis in Ethnology, Escuela de Antropología e Historia, Mexico City.

Webster, Pamela, Orbuch, Terri, and House, James (1995), 'Effects of Childhood Family Background on Adult Marital Quality and Perceived Stability', *American Journal of Sociology*, 101: 404–32.

4 Adolescent Women in Buenos Aires: The Influence of Social Class and Gender Images on Reproductive Behaviour

Edith A. Pantelides, Graciela Infesta Domínguez, and Rosa N. Geldstein

> I think that they should protect themselves. I always tell a girl . . . (if) she has been having sexual intercourse with her boyfriend for three years and she always goes to [the Virgin of] Luján every year to give thanks for not getting pregnant, that God will not always help her, because what does God care about her walking so many kilometres if afterwards she goes on doing the same thing? I don't know. I tell her she has to protect herself.
>
> (Carla, age 17, lower class)

Introduction

Interest in the determinants of adolescent reproductive behaviour in Argentina arose a few years ago from the observation that fertility rates for women below the age of 20 had risen, and were relatively high, for a country where fertility levels have been moderate and diminishing for more than seven decades. The fertility rate for the 15–19 age group reached its lowest level around 1960 (61 per thousand). By 1980 the rate had gone up to 81 per thousand. Although the rate diminished afterwards, it has not returned to its 1960s level, oscillating around 68–70 per thousand in the last few years (69.7 in 1991). Additionally, half of the provinces have adolescent fertility rates above 90 per thousand (Giusti and Pantelides 1991; Pantelides 1995).

This chapter presents partial results from a research agenda aimed at exploring the relationship between gender images and reproductive behaviour of male and female adolescents of the lower and upper middle class. On this occasion we focus our analysis on adolescent females, trying to exhibit differences in the behaviour of those belonging to different social classes.

We introduce social class into our study because we assume that social class determines differential access to the economic and cognitive resources required to manage one's own reproductive health (Balán and Ramos 1989).

The studies that explore the relationship between social class and reproductive behaviour in Argentina use education as a proxy for social class, and fertility is generally the dependent variable. Giusti and Pantelides (1991), Pantelides and Cerrutti (1992), Añaños (1993), and Infesta Domínguez (1993) found the usual negative relationship between educational levels and fertility among adolescents of different urban areas. In a study that measures fertility in relation to occupational status (also a proxy for social class), Infesta Domínguez (1993) found that 45 per cent of working adolescent mothers aged 18–19 residing in the Metropolitan Area of Buenos Aires were domestic servants as compared with 18 per cent of working adolescents without children. Conversely, almost 40 per cent of economically active adolescents without children worked as clerical employees, while only 13 per cent of those with children were in the same category.

Many of the studies to which we have had access are at the macro-level. Both independent and dependent variables have been measured at the aggregate level. In fact there appears to be little research on the concrete mechanisms (mediations) through which the status of women 'translates' into individual attitudes, motives, and behaviours that result in fertility as their outcome. We hypothesize that it is through the cultural images of gender roles, acting at the individual conscious level, that gender inequality 'produces' behaviour, in this case reproductive behaviour.

The concept of gender images is defined here as the set of different representations that both males and females have of (1) their own relative positions and roles of being male and female, (2) the opposite sex's positions and roles, and (3) the relative societal value of being male or female. Gender images are formed through the internalization of these societal values.

The concept of gender images may also help to consider simultaneously variables that have been individually related to adolescent fertility, such as self-esteem (Cvetkovich and Grote 1980; Plotnick 1992), achievement orientation (Devaney and Hubley, cited in Hayes 1987), perception of alternative opportunities, self-perception (Hayes 1987), and locus of control (McIntyre, Saudargas, and Howard 1991; Plotnick 1992). Such variables could be tapping aspects or dimensions of gender images.

We intend to show how gender images influence the adoption of reproductive behaviour that may enhance or diminish the probabilities of having an unintended pregnancy. We hypothesize that gender images are differentially processed by young women of different social classes.

Methodology

An exploratory approach was adopted for two reasons. First, there was no previous research that could guide us in the quantitative measurement of gender images. Second, a representative sample was difficult to obtain because the social climate did not allow a 'door to door' survey on issues related to sexual life and reproductive behaviour.

The universe of the study carried out in 1992 was composed of male and female adolescents of the lower and upper middle class between the ages of 15 and 18. The sampling area was the Greater Buenos Aires Metropolitan Area, an urban conglomerate of close to 11 million inhabitants, in which is concentrated one-third of Argentina's total population. The population of this area works exclusively in the secondary and tertiary sectors of the economy. The predominant religion is Roman Catholicism, although no recent questions on religion have been included in the censuses or in any other source of data. Around 95 per cent of the population is literate (INDEC 1993).

Regarding adolescents, 39 per cent of the population between the ages of 15 and 19 was not attending school at the time of the 1991 population census (INDEC 1993). In the same age group, 70 per cent did not work, although a small proportion were searching for a job (INDEC 1994).

Field work was done in two stages. In the first, a qualitative approach was adopted in order to explore issues deemed relevant according to the literature, and to reveal others that could be significant. This first stage required the use of two instruments: interviews with qualified informants and in-depth interviews with adolescents within the same age-brackets and social classes that would later be used in the second stage. Qualitative data were used both for the design of the survey's questionnaire and to illustrate and expand the interpretation of the survey's results, but there was no interpretative analysis of the material itself. In the second stage a survey was administered to an intentional (non-probabilistic) sample of 386 adolescents of which 211 were female. The distribution by age was predetermined so that each age comprised about 25 per cent of interviewees of each sex. This chapter will mainly be based on the survey's results, and the in-depth interviews will only be used to enrich and illustrate the analysis.

In both the in-depth interviews and the survey, around half of the sample of each sex was lower class, with the other half upper middle class. We wanted to work with two clearly differentiated social classes. Thus, we chose to leave aside the grey area of the lower middle and middle middle classes.

The determination of adolescents' social class is not straightforward. Many have no economic activity and the parents' characteristics are used to determine their class situation. In most studies, education is used as a proxy for social class. In this particular study social class was defined by father's occupation and mother's occupation (or by the step-parent's when the adolescent was not living with his/her biological parent). Lower-class occupations were those that needed little or no qualification (such as those found in the informal sector) plus those classified as 'operators and artisans of industry'. Upper middle-class occupations were those generally classified as 'professionals', 'managers', and owners of middle-sized commercial and industrial enterprises. When the father's and mother's occupations belonged to different social classes, we looked at their education. We placed parents with at least some college education in the upper middle class. When parents had very different educational levels, we gave priority to that of the parent with the highest level.

For the qualitative stage, upper middle-class adolescents were recruited through informal contacts and in a public school. Lower-class interviewees were recruited in a slum area, in the ward for adolescents of a public hospital, and in a neighbourhood association. For the survey we contacted students from public and private schools that cater to the upper middle and lower class. For the youngsters that had dropped out of school we resorted to the adolescent wards of two public hospitals, and to social workers and leaders from poor neighbourhoods. Finding of school drop-outs was difficult and the representation of this category is not proportional to its weight in the population mentioned above. Once adolescents were contacted, the response rate was almost 100 per cent and the adolescents did not pose any objections to talking about sensitive questions.

All individuals in the survey had some schooling. The majority of the respondents (84 per cent) had incomplete high school education, and 11 per cent had only incomplete or complete primary education, while 6 per cent had completed high school or started college. Thus, our sample is somewhat more educated than the general population of the same age.

More than three-quarters of the interviewees did not work, close to the 70 per cent found in the census (see above). Those who did performed administrative tasks or were domestic servants. Regarding marital status, 89 per cent were single, 3 per cent were legally married, and 8 per cent were living in *de facto* conjugal unions.[1]

Reproductive Behaviour and Social Class

Sexual initiation

In this chapter we propose to measure reproductive behaviour through two indicators: sexual initiation and contraceptive use.

Patterns of sexual initiation by age are not very different by class (Table 4.1). In both the lower and the upper middle class, most women start sexual relations at age 15 or 16 (this coincides with findings by Pantelides and Cerrutti 1992). There is some difference in the proportion of early initiations: there are no upper middle-class women in the category of having sexual intercourse at or below the age of 12. Also, fewer women belonging to the upper class first have sexual intercourse between the ages of 13 and 14. These differences are too small to allow for any attribution of significance to them.

Table 4.1. Age of sexually initiated female adolescents at first sexual intercourse by social class, Buenos Aires, 1992 (%)

Age at first sexual intercourse	Lower class	Upper middle class	Total
≤12	1.9	0.0	0.9
13–14	18.9	16.4	17.6
15–16	54.7	58.2	56.5
17–18	24.5	25.4	25.0
N	53	55	108

Source: Field work by the authors.

Although sexually initiated women of both classes start their sexual life almost 'in parallel', a smaller proportion of lower-class women first have sexual intercourse during adolescence. As a consequence, by age 18, 87 per cent of upper middle-class women have already initiated intercourse versus 74 per cent among the lower-class women.

We explored the existence of differences in the circumstances of sexual initiation between the classes. Although the majority of women in both social classes declare that they first had sexual intercourse with their formal boyfriend or husband, this is more so among those of the upper middle class, among whom 96 per cent give that answer (compared to 79 per cent in the lower class). On the other end of the spectrum, none of the upper middle-class women but 8 per cent of the lower class said that they first had sexual intercourse with somebody other than a formal boyfriend, a husband, a friend, or an acquaintance. This 'other' category must include relatives or completely unknown men.

It is interesting to observe the motives for first sexual intercourse (Table 4.2). Again, a majority in both social classes say that love was their motive, but the frequency is larger in the upper middle class.

Instead of having sexual relationships with somebody, I prefer knowing him beforehand. Because that's an instinct. Other people think with the instinct and I don't do it . . . Because one sexual relationship after another is like a doggy and I am not an animal . . . Besides being something intimate . . . I think two people must love each other because having a sexual relationship is a lot. (Amada, age 15, upper middle class)

I think that [one has sexual intercourse] with somebody one loves, because when one arrives there one reaches the most profound feelings. (María, age 17, lower class)

Moore and Rosenthal (1993: 96–7), citing Sue Lees (1986, 1989), argue that reputation is still 'a major issue for girls, so that sexual desire can only be expressed in the context of romantic love and commitment'. This may explain why desire is very seldom recognized as a motive.

Table 4.2. Motives for first sexual intercourse of sexually initiated female adolescents, by social class, Buenos Aires, 1992 (%)

Motives for first sexual intercourse	Lower class	Upper middle class	Total
Love	53.9	69.0	61.7
Desire	11.5	16.4	14.0
Curiosity	17.3	5.5	11.2
Pressure from partner	9.6	5.5	7.5
Threat, rape	7.7	0.0	3.7
Peer pressure	0.0	1.8	0.9
Was just the occasion	0.0	1.8	0.9
N	52	55	107

Source: Field work by the authors.

Initiation under physical pressure[2] is not mentioned by women of the upper middle class but has some importance among those in the lower classes. Moreover, initiation under psychological pressure is more frequent in the lower classes. These categories of response may be linked to the initiation with 'other' persons previously mentioned. We can also link all these responses to those regarding how they felt during first intercourse: while 33 per cent of women in the lower class said it was disagreeable, only 11 per cent of the upper middle class felt that way.

It seems that if there is any difference in risk of unplanned pregnancy between the lower- and the upper middle-class young women stemming from the experience of sexual initiation, it is more related to the circumstances of that initiation (with whom and how) than with their age at the moment.

Contraceptive knowledge and use

Practically all respondents know about the existence of contraceptive methods (100 per cent in the upper middle class and 92 per cent in the lower class). Adolescents from the first group can mention a larger number of methods: 70 per cent of them can mention four or more contraceptives, while in the lower class the proportion who can mention four methods declines to 35 per cent.

The condom was spontaneously named by almost all women of the higher class and 86 per cent of those of the lower class (Table 4.3). The latter mention the pill with higher frequency than the condom. These two methods are the most popular, and the differences in knowledge between classes are less noticeable. Regarding the other methods, the upper middle-class adolescents are able to mention other methods more frequently than girls in the lower class. Only one method is named more frequently in the lower

Table 4.3.   Percentage of female adolescents that spontaneously mention each contraceptive method, by social class, Buenos Aires, 1992 (%)

Method mentioned	Lower class	Upper middle class	Total
Pill	94.5	93.7	94.1
Condom	85.7	97.3	92.1
IUD	41.8	84.7	65.3
Diaphragm	20.9	57.7	41.1
Spermicides	12.1	35.1	24.8
Injection	35.2	8.1	20.3
Rhythm	8.8	23.4	16.8
Withdrawal	5.5	17.1	11.9
Sterilization	3.3	6.3	5.0
Abstinence	4.4	3.6	4.0
Other	2.2	1.8	2.0

Source: Field work by the authors.

strata: the injection (more than one-third of lower-class women as compared to 8 per cent of higher-class women). The more extensive knowledge of injection in the lower class can be explained in different ways. First, poor women of all ages tend to go to the pharmacist (and not to the physician) in search of a contraceptive method (Balán and Ramos 1989). Injection, which does not require instructions and is immediately administered, is preferred. Additionally, counselled by her friends and relatives and guided by her own experience, the woman of the lower strata looks for a method that does not require daily discipline. Another advantage of this method is that it is 'invisible' to her partner and (particularly important for adolescents) her parents. Finally, there exists a confusion between injection as a contraceptive and as an abortifacient. It is frequent, especially among the lower strata, to resort to the pharmacist when there is a delay in the menstrual period. When the pharmacist injects them with a menstrual regulator they consider it to be a contraceptive.

As is known by all researchers in the field, being able to mention a certain contraceptive does not necessarily mean that the adolescent knows its properties and how to use it correctly:

for example [I learned] about how to be careful, there are . . . I don't know . . . the condoms [*preservativos*] or 'preservatives' [*conservativos*], and with pills and all that.[3] (María, age 17, lower class, pregnant)

The only effective one [contraceptive method] that I know of . . . is the condom. But for AIDS the condom does not work because another form of AIDS was discovered, a smaller one, that goes through the condom . . . With AIDS I try not to get it when I

Table 4.4. Distribution of sexually initiated female adolescents according to who used contraception during first and last sexual intercourse, by social class, Buenos Aires, 1992 (%)

Who used the contraceptive in first sexual intercourse	Lower class	Upper middle class	Total
Male only	23.1	27.3	25.2
Female only	15.4	1.8	8.4
Both	11.5	50.9	31.8
Nobody	50.0	20.0	34.6
N[a]	52	55	107

Who used the contraceptive in last sexual intercourse	Lower class	Upper middle class	Total
Male only	13.3	13.2	13.3
Female only	26.7	24.5	25.5
Both	17.8	62.3	41.8
Nobody	42.2	0.0	19.4
N[b]	45	53	98

[a] Excludes 2 cases of no response in 'lower class'.
[b] Excludes 2 cases of no response and 18 cases that had only one sexual relationship.
Source: Field work by the authors.

go to the swimming pool. I sit on my own clothes, I don't sit on the place or on the towel they give me there, I don't sit down in places where sexual intercourse might have taken place. (Virginia, age 16, upper middle class)

Measurement of contraceptive use is a complex matter. Although the interviewee answers about her own experience, use of a method by one member of the couple protects both of them from the point of view of contraception (but not always from the point of view of sexually transmitted diseases—STDs). It is necessary to collect information regarding the couple's protection to determine if there was pregnancy risk in a situation of sexual intercourse. Adolescents themselves interpret the issue of protection in different ways.[4] Some refer only to what they themselves did (use or not use a contraceptive), while others refer to what the couple did, independently of who was using the contraceptive method. We analyse here contraceptive care, defined as the use of a contraceptive by either member of the couple.

Both in first and most recent sexual intercourse, women from the lower class were less likely to have protected intercourse (Table 4.4). Considering first sexual intercourse, half of the adolescents in the lower class were not protected on that occasion, while only one-fifth of the upper middle-class women had unprotected coitus. In most recent sexual intercourse, more than 40 per cent of women of the lower class still did not use contraception while no woman of the upper middle class had unprotected coitus.

Another difference between the women of the two strata is the issue of who uses the method: in first intercourse among higher-class women, both members of the couple use a contraceptive method in half of the cases (the preferred combination is the pill with a condom) as a double security measure and, probably, as a result of the AIDS epidemic; the proportion goes down to 12 per cent in the lower class. Similarly, only 2 per cent of higher-class women depended exclusively on a feminine method for their protection, while 15 per cent of lower-class women did so. In the in-depth interviews, moreover, it is more frequent among higher-class women to mention the use of two methods simultaneously. This is consistent with the opinion, held more frequently among upper-class women than among those in the lower class, that the use of contraception is a shared responsibility (see pp. 107–9 below).

Interesting changes occur between first and most recent sexual intercourse among those using contraceptive methods. On the one hand the proportion of those relying on two methods rises in both social classes. On the other hand, in both classes the responsibility for using contraception slips from men to women, especially in the upper middle class, given that in first intercourse lower-class women in charge of using contraception are already found more frequently than in the upper middle class. From other questions and the in-depth interviews we concluded that this reflects a more extended use of the pill (and, in the lower class, injection) to the detriment of the condom among couples who have a relationship they define as stable (which is more likely to be true in their most recent act of intercourse). The idea that relationships with a stable partner do not require protection against AIDS has been popularized in Argentina by the state, the Catholic Church, and the medical profession by means of public or personal communications.

The research included a question on which contraceptive method was used. In the *last protected act of intercourse*, the condom was the preferred method in both social classes, but especially in the upper class (70 per cent among the upper middle class and 61 per cent in the lower class), while the pill was a distant second (41 per cent in the upper class and 34 per cent in the lower class).[5]

A combination of answers to several questions allowed us to construct a variable that we called 'trajectory of contraceptive use'. This variable summarizes use at first intercourse, constancy in use, and use at most recent intercourse. The difference in protection against unwanted pregnancy among the two social classes, through the span of their lives beginning with sexual initiation, is shown very clearly in Table 4.5. Three-fourths of upper middle-class women used contraception continually starting at first sexual intercourse as compared to one-third of lower-class women. At the other extreme, one-fifth of lower-class women never had protected intercourse while none of the upper middle-class women were in the same situation.

Table 4.5. Contraceptive behaviour of sexually initiated female adolescents by social class, Buenos Aires, 1992 (%)

Type of contraceptive behaviour	Lower class	Upper middle class	Total
Always from first intercourse	33.3	74.5	55.2
Not in first intercourse, but always thereafter	17.8	13.7	15.6
Used in first intercourse, intermittently thereafter	13.3	7.8	10.4
Not in first intercourse, intermittently thereafter	15.6	3.9	9.4
Never used	20.0	0.0	9.4
N[a]	45	51	96

[a] Excludes those cases with only one sexual relationship.

Source: Field work by the authors.

The motives for using contraceptive methods during first intercourse are mostly linked to preventing unwanted pregnancy, although some adolescents (one-fourth in the upper middle class and 6 per cent in the lower class) mention pregnancy and STDs together. Motives for having unprotected first sexual intercourse in both classes are generally attributed to being inexperienced or unprepared (unplanned intercourse).

It is clear now that the differential risk of unplanned pregnancy between the women of the two classes lies in the use of contraception. Such a difference does not arise from the kind of method used but rather from the frequency of use.

Social Class and Gender Images

Regarding gender images, we are particularly interested in those that could be related to reproductive behaviour. We intend to show the existence of images of own and opposite gender that imply recognition of different degrees of autonomy and power. In the private domain, we indicate the presence of these images through the perceptions and valuations of gender roles in the family, in the couple, and in the practice of sexuality, whereas in the public sphere they are shown through perceptions and valuations about gender segmentation of occupations and the unequal opportunities in the labour market. We attempt to explore whether and how women perceive men qua men as the holders of power and authority, and perceive themselves qua women as powerless and devoid of authority. The responses of some interviewees to the in-depth interview are illustrative:

Table 4.6.   Percentage of female adolescents according to the definitions they give of gender roles, by social class, Buenos Aires, 1992

Definitions of gender roles	Lower class	Upper middle class
In the family the man should:		
work and support it	53.6	28.6
have the same responsibilities as the woman	10.1	36.6
In the family the woman should:		
be the mother and housekeeper	57.6	23.2
have the same responsibilities as the man	9.1	43.8
Men are more frequently found in executive positions because:		
they have more natural abilities than women	17.5	6.5
there is discrimination against women	18.6	50.0
A woman without children is an incomplete woman	47.4	20.5
Even when it is not mandatory, a woman should use her husband's surname	66.3	16.2
Men are more interested in sex than women are	71.7	46.8
Even though human beings try to escape their destiny, this is impossible	66.3	37.8

Source: Field work by the authors.

I have a question: can a woman be intelligent, knowledgeable and also marry, have children, be feminine? (Liliana, age 16, lower class)

Men are more intelligent, men get jobs more easily in this society. (Eva, age 18, lower class)

To measure images of gender we used a large set of questions. Some were open-ended, others were incomplete sentences that required the respondent to complete them, and some asked for agreement or disagreement with a statement. We have chosen some of those for which the answers indicated an unequivocal interpretation of the stimulus by the interviewees.

There were clear differences between social classes in their perception of appropriate gender roles within the family. We show here the two extremes of the range of opinions (Table 4.6, first two sets of answers). The majority of young women of the lower class repeat verbatim the 'traditional'[6] definitions of what are supposed to be the responsibilities of men and women.

I like to be a woman . . . I like men for company, as husbands, but women are more delicate and don't have to be worried so much about money. (Marcela, age 18, lower class)

Respondents from the upper middle class more readily state egalitarian definitions of roles. A still small but not insignificant proportion of them question the status quo (it is a 'machista' society).

it is more difficult [in society] for a woman than for a man to attain certain things, perhaps [because society] considers that certain things are [now] good for women that for men were considered [good] long ago, or [it] considers bad things for women but not for men . . . for example the issue of virginity. (Moira, age 16, upper middle class)

I think that some day I will do it [marry]. But at the beginning I would try without marrying, cohabiting. Because I wouldn't put up with him asking me to cook for him, to wash the dishes, [I wouldn't put up with] him working and wanting me to stay at home. (Carla, age 17, upper middle class)

The social mandates of motherhood and housekeeper are also more prevalent among women of the lower class, as the following quotations show.

Men and women should be equal but each one performs a different role; the man works more, and women take care of the children. (Candy, age 18, lower class)

I think that I want to be a housekeeper and stay at home all the time. Everybody tells me 'you are mad, cleaning all day long' . . . [I like] everything [having to do with housework], keep my house extra-clean. I love it, the only thing I don't know how to do is sewing, everything else I do. (Marcela, age 18, lower class)

Upper middle-class women are also more critical of society than their lower-class counterparts when it comes to the issue of executive working positions: half of the former think that men occupy those positions more frequently than women due to discrimination. The dependence of the woman on her husband for the definition of her identity is tapped by the sentence about the use of the husband's surname (which is not mandatory in Argentina). Two-thirds of lower-class interviewees agree with that statement, as compared with 16 per cent of those in the upper middle class. The agreement with the stereotype that men are more 'sexual' than women is high in both social strata. However, it is still higher in the lower class although some interviewees have doubts:

Sex fascinates me and I know that being a woman is like I have to check myself, isn't that so? (Eva, age 18, lower class)

That times are changing is reflected in the contradictions and ambiguities of the demands placed on the younger generations of women, and in the unsolved contradictions between the reproductive and the productive roles:

I want to marry and my father says that I have to study a lot. I know that sometimes women that study a lot do not marry but I don't like to do household work. I do it all the same. But my father insists all the time that my mother iron, cook, and that I help. But my mother did not study and I feel pressed from different sides. (Liliana, age 16, lower class)

In conclusion, images of gender that reflect a more 'traditional' outlook are always more prevalent among women in the lower strata than in the upper-middle strata.

Social Class, Images of Gender, and Risky Behaviour

Multi-variate analysis suffers from the limitation of our sample size. In spite of this we choose to present some results that we think are interesting and that show a consistent trend that could give us some confidence in their validity (Table 4.7).[7]

The expected relationship between gender images and risky behaviour holds only in the lower class. Among all selected indicators of gender images, those women with more traditional responses show higher frequencies of unprotected first intercourse. This is especially true for women who agree with the use of the husband's surname, and for those that have a fatalistic attitude. The number of cases in the upper middle class is too small to allow for any analysis and the proportions show erratic behaviour.[8]

Attribution of responsibility for the use of contraception was another issue we investigated. This variable was intended to measure the presence of attitudes regarding delegation of control, which may in turn result in a failure to use contraceptive protection (Table 4.8).

The relationship between gender images and attribution of responsibility for the use of contraception appears only in the lower class: women who hold traditional gender images tend to answer more frequently than women with modern attitudes that their partner is the one who should take care of contraception.[9]

Again, the number of cases of women in the upper middle class who decline to take responsibility (alone or together with their partner) is too small to analyse (see note 8 below). The information collected in the in-depth interviews, however, shows upper middle-class women to have more modern attitudes. An upper middle-class girl said:

women have to start to control the situation. For example with the condom. Many men do not like it when a woman carries a condom in her handbag. (Guillermina, age 18)

In-depth interviews allowed us to investigate the motives for attributing responsibility.

I think that using contraception is an issue for both partners. I don't like the condom ... I know it is better ... but I don't like to interrupt everything ... I would take pills but not because the woman is the one who has to use the contraceptive. If there were something equivalent [to the pill] for the man he would be able to use it. It's a matter of the two partners. He has to know if she is using contraceptives, what is she using, and everything. (Sofía, age 16, upper middle class)

Table 4.7. Percentage of adolescent females that had protected (P) or unprotected (U) first sexual intercourse, by images of gender and social class, Buenos Aires, 1992

Gender images	LOWER CLASS			UPPER MIDDLE CLASS		
	U	P	N	U	P	N
Men's family roles*[a]						
Traditional	54.5	45.5	33	27.3	72.7	11
Modern	0.0	100.0	5	26.1	73.9	23
Women's family roles**[a]						
Traditional	55.3	44.7	38	18.2	81.8	11
Modern	16.7	83.3	6	24.1	75.9	29
Childless women are incomplete**[b]						
Traditional	55.6	44.4	27	30.8	69.2	13
Modern	39.1	60.9	23	16.7	83.3	42
Women should use husband's surname****[b]						
Traditional	61.8	38.2	34	0.0	100.0	9
Modern	23.5	76.5	17	24.4	75.6	45
Men more interested in sex*[b]						
Traditional	63.3	36.7	30	20.8	79.2	24
Modern	33.3	66.7	21	20.0	80.0	30
We cannot escape destiny***[b]						
Traditional	63.9	36.1	36	13.0	87.0	23
Modern	13.3	86.7	15	25.8	74.2	31

Chi-square values:
    * Lower class: significant at the 0.05 level; upper middle class: no association.
    ** Lower class: significant at the 0.10 level; upper middle class: no association.
    *** Lower class: significant at the 0.01 level; upper middle class: no association.
**** Lower class: significant at the 0.01 level; upper middle class: significant at the 0.10 level.

[a] The category 'traditional' corresponds to the first answer in table 4.6, the category 'modern' to the second.
[b] The category 'traditional' corresponds to those who agree with the statement, the category 'modern' to those who disagree.
Source: Field work by the authors.

I think they [women] are as responsible as men but the truth is that the most effective method is the one that men, not women, use . . . Both have to look after contraception but if there existed a method equivalent to the condom that was for women's use, maybe things would be different. (Natalia, age 16, upper middle class)

Men [don't want to use the condom] . . . The woman is the one who has to use con-

Table 4.8. Percentage of adolescent females who considered that the responsibility for the use of contraception was the man's, by images of gender and social class, Buenos Aires, 1992

Gender images[a]	LOWER CLASS			UPPER MIDDLE CLASS		
	M	O	N	M	O	N
Men's family roles*						
Traditional	27.5	72.5	51	27.3	72.7	26
Modern	10.0	90.0	10	26.1	73.9	41
Women's family roles*						
Traditional	21.0	79.0	62	18.2	81.8	32
Modern	22.2	77.8	9	24.1	75.9	49
Childless women are incomplete**						
Traditional	32.6	67.4	43	30.8	69.2	23
Modern	13.0	87.0	46	16.7	83.3	88
Women should use husband's surname***						
Traditional	27.6	72.4	58	0.0	100.0	17
Modern	12.5	87.5	32	24.4	75.6	93
Men more interested in sex*						
Traditional	25.0	75.0	64	20.8	79.2	51
Modern	15.4	84.6	26	20.0	80.0	59
We cannot escape destiny****						
Traditional	30.5	69.5	59	13.0	87.0	41
Modern	6.3	93.7	32	25.8	74.2	69

M: Responsibility for contraception is with the man.
O: Responsibility for contraception is with the woman or with both.
Chi-square values:
* Lower and upper middle class: no association.
** Lower class: significant at the 0.05 level; upper middle class: no association.
*** Lower class: significant at the 0.10 level; upper middle class: no association.
**** Lower class: significant at the 0.01 level; upper middle class: no association.
[a] See notes *a* and *b* in Table 4.7.
Source: Field work by the authors.

traception if she doesn't want to become pregnant, if she doesn't want to ruin her life. (Ana, age 15, lower class)

I think it [using contraception] is a mutual thing. For example, if the man works, it would be great for him to be the one to use a method. But if he doesn't work, [the man and the woman] together have to buy pills and the woman should use them. I think that the woman has more chances of using contraceptives, the one that has more resources. (Eva, age 18, lower class)

Conclusions

Women of the lower class adopt reproductive behaviour that could lead to unplanned pregnancies more frequently than upper middle-class women. The difference lies not so much in the earlier sexual initiation of the former in comparison with the latter, but in their differential use of contraception. Upper-class women start to use contraception earlier in their sexual life, use contraception more frequently and more consistently throughout their sexual lives, and tend to use two methods simultaneously (as extra protection against pregnancy, but also as protection against AIDS).

Gender images that reflect a modern outlook are more prevalent in the upper than the lower class. Among women of the lower class, those that hold modern images of gender tend to adopt contraception more frequently than those who have traditional attitudes. Additionally, women with modern attitudes consider that the responsibility for the use of contraceptives lies more with women or with both men and women; they were more in control of their reproductive behaviour.

Notes

We are grateful for funding from the Rockefeller Foundation, under its programme on Women's Status and Fertility in Developing Countries, which made possible the research on which this chapter is based.
1. This research was designed with a focus on risky reproductive behaviour (regarding unexpected pregnancy and AIDS). Thus, the analysis was centred on the sexually initiated, independently of their being single, legally married, or in consensual unions. The proportion of these last two marital statuses is low among those 15–18 years old in the Greater Metropolitan Area of Buenos Aires.

In most cases the inclusion of the non-single does not alter the meaning of the analysis. However, in others, such as the motives for the use of contraception, the interpretation of the results may be different for the married and the non-married.
2. In other research (Pantelides and Cerrutti 1992), initiation under physical or psychological pressure in lower-class adolescents of the Greater Metropolitan Area of Buenos Aires was declared by 13% of interviewees.
3. In Spanish condoms are called *condones* or *preservativos*, while *conservativos* does not designate any contraceptive method: it means 'preservatives'.
4. The question used in our research was 'Did you do anything to protect yourself during your first/most recent sexual intercourse?' We deliberately left to the respondents the interpretation of 'protection' to explore whether the concept was linked to the risk of pregnancy and/or to the risk of infection from STDs.
5. The percentages add up to more than 100 because of combined use of methods, which, as we mention in the text, is very high.
6. Our definitions of 'traditional' and 'modern' gender roles are well expressed by Moore and Rosenthal (1993: 82–3): 'In Western society, traditionally, appropriate sex

roles for men have been as worker, primary breadwinner, head of the household, and holder of leadership roles in the community. These activities are assumed to be paralleled by typically male personality characteristics, such as assertiveness, confidence, bravery, and independence with associated interests in sports, active pursuits, and competition. The [traditional] female gender role has revolved around the bearing and nurturing of children as well as taking responsibility for household duties . . . Sexually speaking, the traditional sex role stereotype is for man to be the "hunter" and initiator of sexual activity, the one with the more powerful and demanding sex drive, the strong one, the powerful figure in a relationship. The traditional woman plays her role through being pleasant, cooperative, placating, flirtatious, and attending to her appearance and the pleasure of the male, while retaining a respectable and ladylike demeanour in public'.

7. Although the literature consistently advises against the use of significance tests on non-random samples, they have been used in such cases. We follow current usage.

8. Chi-square values indicate no association except in the case of the variable relating to the use of the husband's surname. For some cross-tabulations, the number of cases in our sample is not sufficient for the use of chi-square. 'The criteria usually used for deciding whether or not the number of cases is sufficient involve the expected frequencies in each cell. Whenever any of the expected frequencies is in the neighbourhood of 5 or smaller' the use of chi-square or similar tests is not recommended (Blalock 1979: 291). There are very few upper middle-class women who hold traditional points of view, and also very few that have unprotected sexual intercourse.

9. With the use of chi-square, however, some of the differences in percentages are shown to be non-significant. Those that remain significant are the ones related to childless women, the use of the husband's surname, and fatalistic attitudes.

References

Añaños, María Celina (1993), 'Composición social y comportamientos de unión en madres adolescentes: Rosario 1980–1991', in Centro de Estudios de Estado y Sociedad (CEDES) and Centro de Estudios de Poblacíon (CENEP), *Taller de Investigaciones Sociales en Salud Reproductiva y Sexualidad*, Buenos Aires: CEDES and CENEP, 50–79.

Balán, Jorge, and Ramos, Silvina Edith (1989), *La medicalización del comportamiento reproductivo*, Cuadernos del CEDES No. 29, Buenos Aires: Centro de Estudios de Estado y Sociedad.

Benson, Olivier (1974), *El laboratorio de ciencia política*, Buenos Aires: Amorrortu.

Blalock, Hubert (1979), *Social Statistics*, Washington, DC: McGraw-Hill.

Cortés, Fernando, and Rubalcava, Rosa María (1987), *Métodos estadísticos aplicados a la investigación en ciencias sociales: análisis de asociación*, Mexico City: El Colegio de México.

Cvetkovich, G., and Grote, B. (1980), 'Psychological development and the social problem of teenage illegitimacy', in C. Chilman (ed.), *Adolescent Pregnancy and Childbearing: Findings from Research*, Washington, DC: US Department of Health and Human Services, 15–41.

Devaney, B. L., and Hubley, K. S. (1981), *The Determinants of Adolescent Pregnancy and Childbearing: Final Report to the National Institute of Child Health and Human Development*. Washington, DC: Mathematical Policy Research.

Festinger, León, and Katz, Daniel (comps.) (1992), *Los métodos de investigación en las ciencias sociales*, Barcelona: Paidós.

Giusti, Alejandro, and Pantelides, Edith Alejandra (1991), *Fecundidad en la adolescencia: República Argentina 1980–1985*, Programa Nacional de Estadísticas de Salud, Series 8, No. 11, Buenos Aires: Dirección de Estadísticas de Salud.

Hayes, Cheryl D. (ed.) (1987), *Risking the Future: Adolescent Sexuality, Pregnancy and Childbearing*, Washington, DC: National Academy Press.

INDEC [Instituto Nacional de Estadísticas y Censos] (1993), *Censo Nacional de Población y Vivienda, 1991. Resultados Definitivos. Características Generales. Serie B, Capital Federal y 19 Partidos del Gran Buenos Aires*, Buenos Aires: INDEC.

—— (1994), *Censo Nacional de Población y Vivienda, 1991, Resultados Definitivos. Características Generales. Serie C, Capital Federal y 19 Partidos del Gran Buenos Aires*, Buenos Aires: INDEC.

Infesta Domínguez, Graciela (1993), 'Fecundidad adolescente: un análisis de los diferenciales socioeconómicos', paper presented to the II Jornadas Argentinas de Estudios de Poblacíon, Buenos Aires.

Lees, Sue (1986), *Losing Out: Sexuality and Adolescent Girls*, London: Hutchinson Education.

—— (1989), 'Learning to Love: Sexual Reputation, Morality and the Social Control of Girls', in M. Cain (ed.), *Growing Up Good: Policing the Behaviour of Girls in Europe*, London: Sage, 287–98.

McIntyre, A., Saudargas, R. A., and Howard, R. (1991), 'Attribution of Control and Teenage Pregnancy', *Journal of Applied Developmental Psychology*, 12: 55–61.

Moore, Susan, and Rosenthal, Doreen (1993), *Sexuality in Adolescence*, London: Routledge.

Pantelides, Edith Alejandra (1995), *La Maternidad precoz: la fecundidad adolescente en la Argentina*, Buenos Aires: UNICEF.

—— and Cerrutti, Marcela Sandra (1992), *Conducta reproductiva y embarazo en la adolescencia*, Cuadernos del CENEP No. 47, Buenos Aires: Centro de Estudios de Población.

Plotnick, R. D. (1992), *The Effect of Attitudes on Teenage Premarital Pregnancy and its Resolution*, University of Wisconsin-Madison, Institute of Research on Poverty, Discussion Paper No. 965–92, Madison, Wisc.: University of Wisconsin Institute of Research on Poverty.

5 Levels of Childbearing, Contraception, and Abortion in Brazil: Differentials by Poverty Status

Susheela Singh and Mario Monteiro

Introduction

The very large and rapid decline in fertility that occurred in Brazil, beginning in 1970 and continuing through the 1980s, has now been well documented (Carvalho and Wong 1990; Silva *et al.* 1990). The total fertility rate (TFR) declined from about 5.8 in 1970 to approximately 4.4 in 1980, and then to 3.5 in the mid-1980s. This decline in fertility is continuing, and the TFR has been estimated to be slightly under 3.0 by the early 1990s (United Nations 1994).

While the fertility decline has been universal, and has occurred among all socio-economic subgroups, some subgroups started out with higher TFRs, and still have substantially higher levels of childbearing. Differences in the level of the TFR by region, place of residence, and education were still substantial in 1986 (Arruda *et al.* 1987; Silva *et al.* 1990). Although there is less information on subgroups of women classified by income, the information available supports the conclusion that large differences existed before the decline in fertility, and that they still exist. In 1984, women in families with less than 1 minimum salary had an average of 5.9 children, compared to an average of 2.6 children per woman in families with an income of 5 or more minimum salaries (Instituto de la Mujer *et al.* 1993).

Broad structural changes such as rapid increases in urbanization (from 50 per cent to about 76 per cent over the past 25 years), in enrolment of the school-age population (from 16 per cent to about 45 per cent of females at the secondary level, in the last 25 years), and in the proletarianization of the rural labour force (Carvalho and Wong 1990), as well as wide swings in economic growth—including explosive growth from 1970–6, then slowdown and then crisis and economic decline in the 1980s (World Bank 1993)—are among the important factors accounting for overall fertility decline. But in addition, other factors have helped to account for the overall rapid pace and universality of the decline in fertility across all social classes. These include tremendous increases in exposure to the mass media and a consequent impact on family-size desires, and very large increases in knowledge of and access to modern contraception and induced abortion (Carvalho and Wong 1990).

Clearly, contraception is the primary proximate determinant of the large decline in fertility (Silva *et al.* 1990). The proportion married is an important factor explaining levels of fertility, but marriage patterns in Brazil have not changed greatly during the recent period, and cannot explain trends in fertility. Breastfeeding and post-partum abstinence also account for a small proportion of the variation in fertility, but these factors have also most likely not changed to any significant extent in the past two decades. Although the fourth main proximate determinant, induced abortion, is generally acknowledged to play an important role in the fertility transition in Brazil, information for quantifying trends in the level of abortion, and its current contribution in explaining the level of fertility, is very limited (Carvalho and Wong 1990; Singh and Wulf 1991, 1994). It is even more difficult to marshal data on induced abortion among subgroups of any kind, and certainly among income or poverty subgroups of women.

Poverty is one of the most difficult variables to measure, and levels of poverty are not usually collected in surveys or censuses in most developing countries (Ahlburg 1994). In Brazil, however, both the concept of poverty and a measure of it have been developed, and information on poverty has been collected in national government surveys and in censuses. However, even though poverty level—measured as the number of minimum salaries earned by a family—is collected in national censuses and surveys, this information was not obtained in the only national survey to focus explicitly on fertility behaviour—the 1986 Demographic and Health Survey (Arruda *et al.* 1987). Moreover, even within existing data sources, national-level information on both poverty and particular aspects of reproductive behaviour is available in only some surveys, and is often quite limited. One of the main aims of this chapter is to bring together the somewhat scattered information that is available on poverty levels among women of reproductive age, and that relates women's reproductive behaviour to poverty. The second aim is to analyse the limited information available on abortion and spontaneous foetal loss, as it relates to women's poverty level, using data on 'interrupted pregnancies' collected in a national survey on health and nutrition. Because of the nature of the data available, this chapter is largely exploratory.

In this chapter we first discuss the sources of data and their limitations, as well as some methodological points; we next describe differences in the distribution of women according to poverty within socio-economic subgroups, and overall trends in the proportion of women who are poor, from 1970 to 1989. We then summarize what is known about differences in fertility and contraceptive use according to the poverty status of women. National estimates of abortion are then discussed, the limited data on abortion and miscarriages from the 1989 Pesquisa Nacional de Saúde e Nutrição (PNSN) are presented, and estimates of the level of abortion among subgroups of women by poverty are then developed, based on varying assumptions concerning under-reporting.

Methodology

This chapter relies principally on secondary analyses of censuses and surveys that have been carried out by the Brazilian government (mainly by the Fundação Instituto Brasileiro de Geografía e Estatística, or IBGE) during the period 1970 to 1989. These include:

- the 1970 Census: the data used are from published sources only, based on a 1 per cent sample;
- the 1977 Pesquisa Nacional por Amostragem de Domicilios (PNAD) or National Household Sample Survey: the data used are from published sources only;
- the 1980 Census: the data used are from published tabulations only;
- the 1986 PNAD: the data used are from both published sources and special tabulations;
- the 1989 PNSN: the data presented are from special tabulations done for this chapter.

The 1986 Demographic and Health Survey (DHS) is cited in regard to the situation at the national level, but because the data from this survey lack a measure of poverty, they are not used extensively in this paper. Unfortunately, data from the 1991 Census, apart from simple population counts, are not yet available.

The PNAD and PNSN are based on nationally representative samples of households, and therefore of women of reproductive age. All of the above sources (other than the DIIS) obtained information to create the standard measure of poverty. In terms of information related to reproductive behaviour, the censuses generally provide the distribution of women by age and poverty, and the number of children ever born, as well as sometimes providing the number of stillbirths. The PNAD supplies the same measures, but can provide more information, depending on special supplements that may be added to the standard household questionnaire. The 1977 PNAD provides only the basic variables, while the 1986 PNAD added a special supplement on contraceptive use. The 1989 PNSN, whose principal aim was to measure maternal and child health, includes questions on the number of 'interrupted pregnancies' or foetal losses occurring at 27 weeks' gestation or less during the five years before the survey. However, the PNSN did not obtain information on contraceptive use, or on the total number of children ever born. Moreover, the PNSN did not obtain dates of interrupted pregnancies, or of events during the past five years; it simply obtained a count of births, stillbirths, and interrupted pregnancies. Nor did the PNSN obtain an event history that would document changes in the respondent's poverty, residence, or family status during the five years before the interview. Because of these data limitations, we present summary measures of events (births, pregnancies) during the past five years among various subgroups defined by their characteristics at the time of interview. For example, in the case of age, when pregnancies over the past five years are being considered, the appropriate age is not current age, but an age-range that is about 2.5 years younger: e.g., women aged 20–24 at the time of the interview ranged between 15 and 24 years of age over the five-year period preceding the survey, and at the midpoint of the period this group was about 17.5 to 22.5 years old.

Different measures of poverty are employed in Brazil. At least two are commonly employed: the mean number of minimum salaries per family and the mean number of minimum salaries per capita. The latter measure is the one mostly used here, because it takes into account variation in the number of persons in a family. Half a minimum salary per person is considered to be the level below which poverty exists. One-quarter of a minimum salary per capita or less is considered to be extreme poverty. The base minimum salary is corrected for inflation using the National Consumer Price Index (IBGE 1994) to allow for measurement of income at a constant value. This more or less allows comparison over time, but the adjustment has been criticized as being insufficient in periods of very rapid economic change (IBGE 1982; Silva 1985).

Poverty among Women of Reproductive Age

Poverty Distribution and Characteristics of Poor Women

Nationally, in 1989, about one-third of women aged 15–49 in Brazil were considered to be below the poverty line, that is, the per capita income in their families was less than half a minimum salary (Table 5.1). In 1989 this level represented an estimated 11.8 million women. Within this group, nearly half (about 15 per cent of all women) live in extreme poverty (with incomes of under one-quarter of a minimum salary per capita or no income at all), and the rest (17.5 per cent with one-quarter to one-half of a minimum salary per capita) are very poor.

The next highest poverty category—women in families with one-half to 1 minimum salary per capita—contains about one-quarter of women: this group is also considered to be quite poor. The other two income categories of women—those in families with 1–2 and with more than 2 minimum salaries per capita—each have about one-fifth of all women of reproductive age, and these may be considered as middle-income and higher-income women, respectively.

Some subgroups of women are poorer than the national average, while others are somewhat better off. The youngest women (15–19) are poorer than average (41 per cent are below the poverty line), and older women, those aged 35–49, are slightly worse off than average (close to 35 per cent below the poverty line). Women aged 25–29 are least poor (24 per cent are below the poverty line). Women who are heads of households are much poorer (43.5

Table 5.1. Distribution of women aged 15–49 by poverty level, according to age, position in family, region, place of residence, and education, Brazil, 1986 and 1989 (%)

Characteristic	Income per capita (in minimum salary units)							
	1986				1989			
	0–½	>½–1	>1–2	>2	0–½	>½–1	>1–2	>2
Age								
15–19	31.4	27.3	24.3	17.0	40.6	27.5	16.4	15.6
20–24	27.0	24.1	24.9	24.0	31.1	25.2	23.3	20.4
25–29	28.2	23.5	22.4	25.9	24.2	21.6	26.1	28.2
30–34	29.9	22.6	22.8	24.8	27.9	21.4	21.9	28.9
35–39	30.7	23.1	21.0	25.3	34.6	23.5	18.6	23.3
40–44	28.2	23.6	23.0	25.2	33.2	24.9	20.6	21.4
45–49	27.6	21.5	25.0	26.0	34.8	26.0	17.9	21.4
Position in family								
Head	30.9	23.9	19.6	25.5	43.5	20.7	17.7	18.2
Wife	29.1	24.3	23.2	23.4	29.5	24.3	22.3	23.9
Daughter	30.7	24.5	25.3	19.5	35.7	27.3	20.0	17.1
Other	21.9	21.4	20.5	36.2	21.7	18.4	17.0	42.9
Place of residence								
Urban	20.4	24.0	26.8	28.8	23.6	24.7	24.1	27.7
Rural	57.2	24.3	12.4	6.1	63.2	23.1	9.4	4.3
Region								
North (Urban)	25.9	24.7	24.3	25.1	22.7	25.2	24.2	27.9
North-East	54.7	23.3	11.7	10.3	60.3	18.8	10.7	10.2
South-East	17.4	23.1	28.8	30.8	20.2	26.2	25.7	27.9
South	23.6	27.4	26.9	22.1	24.7	26.8	23.3	25.2
Central-East	22.0	25.3	24.4	28.3	26.4	26.8	20.9	25.9
Education								
<4 Years	50.8	26.6	15.6	7.1	56.4	26.0	12.3	5.3
4–6 Years	27.7	29.6	27.4	15.4	31.6	29.6	24.1	14.7
7+ Years	9.2	16.6	27.6	46.7	13.5	18.6	25.2	42.8
Total Brazil	29.1	24.1	23.4	23.4	32.3	24.3	20.8	22.5

Source: Special tabulations of the 1986 National Househould Survey (PNAD) and the 1989 National Survey of Health and Nutrition (PNSN).

per cent live in families with less than half a minimum salary per capita) than women who are wives, living with a partner (29.5 per cent are below the poverty line).

The urban–rural differentials in poverty are extremely large: 23.6 per cent of urban women are poor, compared to 63.2 per cent of rural women. Women in the North-East region are also much more likely to be poor (60.3 per cent) than women in any other region (20–26 per cent of women in the other regions are poor). As may be expected, poverty is strongly correlated with women's level of education: 56.4 per cent of women with less than 4 years' education are poor, as compared with 31.6 per cent of those with 4–6 years of schooling—a sharp decline in poverty for such a small decline in schooling. The decline is even greater among women with 7 or more years of education— only about 13.5 per cent of this group lives in poverty.

Looking at all poor women as a group (leftmost column of Table 5.2) compared to the national average (rightmost column), we find that they are somewhat younger than average: 24.1 per cent are aged 15–19 compared to 19.2 per cent in the overall population, and only 58.6 per cent are aged 25 or more, compared to 62.9 per cent in Brazil as a whole. About 16 per cent of all poor women are heads of households, compared to 12 per cent nationally. Although rural women are much more likely to be poor than urban women, because of the high proportion of the total population that is urban (78 per cent in 1989) it is still the case that 57 per cent of poor women live in urban areas. More than half of all poor women have extremely rudimentary education—54 per cent have less than 4 years' schooling, compared to 31 per cent nationally. Nevertheless, about one-sixth of poor women are better educated, with 7 or more years' schooling.

Trends in the Distribution of Women of Reproductive Age by Poverty Level

Information is available on the distribution of women by poverty level for four points in time: 1970 (based on a 1 per cent sample of the census of that year); 1977 (based on the PNAD of that year); 1986 (also based on the PNAD of that year); and 1989 (based on the PNSN). The distribution of women 15–49 according to income per capita, for each five-year age group, is presented in Table 5.3 for these four time points.

There was clearly an extremely large decline in poverty in Brazil between 1970 and 1986: in 1970, 71.7 per cent of all women aged 15–49 lived in families with one-half or less of a minimum salary per capita, while, by 1986, only 29.1 per cent of women did so. The average annual rate of decline during the whole of the period (1970–86) in the proportion of women who were poor was 2.7 per cent per year. However, the rate of change was greater during the early part of this period, 1970–7, than it was during the later part: the average annual rate of change was about 3.7 per cent per year between 1970–7, while it was about 2 per cent per year during 1977–86.[1] All age groups of women show the same broad overall trends, and the change occurred at about the same as the average national rate for all age groups. While there is no doubt that the greater part of this large decline in poverty is probably real, given the industrial and urban transformation that Brazil experienced during

Table 5.2. Distribution of women aged 15–49 by age, position in family, region, place of residence, and education, according to poverty level, Brazil, 1989 (%)

Characteristic	Income per capita (in minimum salary units)				
	0–½	>½–1	>1–2	>2	Total
Age					
15–19	24.1	21.7	15.1	13.3	19.2
20–24	17.3	18.6	20.0	16.2	17.9
25–29	12.0	14.3	20.2	20.1	16.1
30–34	12.6	12.9	15.3	18.7	14.6
35–39	13.8	12.4	11.5	13.3	12.9
40–44	10.7	10.7	10.3	9.9	10.4
45–49	9.5	9.4	7.6	8.4	8.8
Position in family					
Head	15.9	10.1	10.1	9.6	11.9
Wife	51.2	56.0	60.0	59.3	56.0
Daughter	29.0	29.4	25.2	19.9	26.3
Other	3.9	4.5	4.8	11.2	5.9
Place of residence					
Urban	56.9	79.1	90.0	95.8	77.9
Rural	43.1	20.9	10.0	4.2	22.1
Region					
North (Urban)	2.3	3.4	3.8	4.0	3.2
North-East	50.5	21.0	13.9	12.3	27.1
South-East	28.7	49.5	56.7	57.0	45.9
South	12.4	17.9	18.2	18.2	16.3
Central East	6.1	8.3	7.5	8.6	7.5
Education					
<4 Years	54.3	33.3	18.4	7.3	31.1
4–6 Years	29.9	37.2	35.3	20.0	30.6
7+ Years	15.5	28.3	44.8	70.4	37.1
Not stated	0.4	1.1	1.4	2.3	1.2
Number of women	11,792,521	8,866,113	7,603,604	8,215,040	36,477,278

Source: Special tabulations of the 1989 PNSN.

this period, especially during the 1970s, it is possible that part of the apparent change is due to inadequate adjustment for the real value of income in the definition of the index of poverty (IBGE 1982).

It is interesting that economic stagnation at the national level during the late 1980s does show an effect on the extent of poverty among women: the proportion of all women 15–49 who were poor increased from 29.1 per cent in 1986 to 32.3 per cent in 1989, and in the case of this most recent trend, it was the youngest (15–24) and the oldest (35–49) age groups that saw the

Table 5.3. Distribution of women aged 15–49 according to poverty level, by age, Brazil, 1970–1989 (%)

Year	Age group	Income per capita (in minimum salary units)				
		0–½	>½–1	>1–2	>2	Total[a]
1970 Census						
	Total	71.7	14.6	8.3	5.4	100.0
	15–19	74.4	14.3	7.2	4.1	100.0
	20–24	69.3	16.1	8.9	5.7	100.0
	25–29	71.2	14.1	8.6	6.1	100.0
	30–34	73.2	13.4	8.1	5.4	100.0
	35–39	74.0	13.7	7.3	5.0	100.0
	40–44	69.8	14.9	9.3	6.0	100.0
	45–49	66.8	16.2	10.1	6.9	100.0
1977 PNAD						
	Total	46.1	24.5	16.4	13.0	100.0
	15–19	49.6	26.6	15.0	8.8	100.0
	20–24	41.6	26.8	18.6	13.1	100.0
	25–29	44.4	23.0	17.2	15.4	100.0
	30–34	48.5	21.9	15.1	14.5	100.0
	35–39	50.7	21.5	15.0	12.8	100.0
	40–44	45.1	23.9	16.7	14.4	100.0
	45–49	41.6	24.5	17.6	16.3	100.0
1986 PNAD						
	Total	29.1	24.1	23.4	23.4	100.0
	15–19	31.4	27.3	24.3	17.0	100.0
	20–24	27.0	24.1	24.9	24.0	100.0
	25–29	28.2	23.5	22.4	25.9	100.0
	30–34	29.9	22.6	22.8	24.8	100.1
	35–39	30.7	23.1	21.0	25.3	100.1
	40–44	28.2	23.6	23.0	25.2	100.0
	45–49	27.6	21.5	25.0	26.0	100.1
1989 PNSN						
	Total	32.3	24.3	20.8	22.5	100.0
	15–19	40.6	27.5	16.4	15.6	100.0
	20–24	31.1	25.2	23.3	20.4	100.0
	25–29	24.2	21.6	26.1	28.2	100.0
	30–34	27.9	21.4	21.9	28.9	100.0
	35–39	34.6	23.5	18.6	23.3	100.0
	40–44	33.2	24.9	20.6	21.4	100.0
	45–49	34.8	26.0	17.9	21.4	100.0

[a] Totals may not add to 100.0 because of rounding.

Sources: 1970 and 1977 data: IBGE (1982); 1986 and 1989 data: special tabulations of the 1986 PNAD and 1989 PNSN.

downturn in income. By comparison, women aged 25–29 and 30–34 saw slight improvements in their income distribution during this period.

Reproductive Behaviour and Poverty

Although, as mentioned earlier, only limited information is available on variations in reproductive behaviour according to the poverty status of women, it is nevertheless useful to review briefly what we do know about differences across poverty subgroups in the level of childbearing and in the main proximate determinant, contraception. Such information serves to place the question of the level of abortion, and differentials in abortion, within a broader context.

Marriage and Post-partum Infecundability

National-level information is not readily available on some proximate determinants of fertility by poverty level (e.g. marriage or union participation and post-partum infecundability). The DHS, which is the one national survey that focuses only on fertility and that measures these factors, does not provide a measure of poverty. However, the available information on these two proximate determinants suggest that they have not changed greatly in the last twenty years, and are not likely to play an important role in explaining trends in childbearing and pregnancy. Although marriage patterns have changed somewhat, with small increases in consensual union (Henriques 1989), and although it would be helpful to know how these changes differ across poverty subgroups, the small size of these changes, relative to the rise in contraceptive use, suggests that these two factors would not be highly significant in explaining differences in childbearing by poverty level.

Nationally, post-partum infecundability is not an important determinant of the national level of fertility: the mean duration of post-partum insusceptibility in 1986 was 5.6 months (Arruda *et al.* 1987: Table 2.7). Although the duration of breastfeeding is longer among the less educated, it is not longer in the poorest region, the North-East, but rather in the Central-East and North Central-West regions, suggesting that cultural differences, rather than poverty, may be related to duration of breastfeeding, and to the importance of post-partum insusceptibility. The difference between women living in urban and in rural areas is relatively small, and there are no important differences in post-partum abstinence across subgroups.

Data on differences in women's participation in marriage and consensual unions, according to education, urban/rural residence, and region, show that the better-educated, urban residents living in regions with larger proportions of urban residents have a somewhat later median age at first marriage (Arruda *et al.* 1987: Table 2.3). These results suggest that poor women, who are less educated and more likely to reside in rural areas, are likely to marry earlier, and more likely to be married or in a consensual union, than better-off women.

Contraceptive Use

Contraceptive use is the most important proximate determinant of the level of fertility in Brazil. By 1986, according to data from the two national surveys carried out in that year, the proportion of women currently in union who were using a method was quite high—66 per cent (of women aged 15–44), according to the DHS, and 60 per cent (of women aged 15–49), according to the PNAD.[2] However, the distribution according to method used is approximately the same. Considering that some unmarried women are sexually active, it is also relevant to consider contraceptive use among all women: these levels were 43.5 per cent according to the DHS, and 39.5 per cent according to the PNAD.

The PNAD, which also measured poverty, provides differentials in contraceptive use according to level of poverty (Table 5.4). According to the

Table 5.4.   Contraceptive method used among all women 15–49 and among women aged 15–29 and 30–49, by poverty level, Brazil, 1986 (%)

| Age-group and poverty level | Contraceptive Method | | | | | | | |
	No method	Sterilization	Pill	Rhythm	Coitus interruptus	Condom	IUD	Other
15–49								
All	60.5	16.1	17.3	2.7	1.2	0.8	0.5	0.9
<$^{1}/_{2}$	66.4	14.6	14.5	1.7	1.8	0.3	0.1	0.7
>$^{1}/_{2}$–1	58.8	17.1	19.4	2.0	1.0	0.6	0.4	0.8
>1–2	58.6	16.3	18.6	2.7	1.2	1.0	0.6	1.0
>2	56.8	16.7	17.3	4.5	0.7	1.6	1.1	1.1
15–29								
All	71.9	5.7	18.7	1.5	0.7	0.5	0.4	0.7
<$^{1}/_{2}$	74.4	6.9	15.6	1.2	1.0	0.3	0.2	0.5
>$^{1}/_{2}$–1	69.1	6.8	21.2	1.0	0.5	0.5	0.2	0.7
>1–2	72.4	4.6	19.6	1.5	0.5	0.3	0.5	0.7
>2	71.1	4.0	19.1	2.7	0.6	0.9	0.6	0.9
30–49								
All	46.8	28.6	15.6	4.0	1.9	1.3	0.7	1.1
<$^{1}/_{2}$	56.7	23.7	13.1	2.4	2.7	0.4	0.0	0.8
>$^{1}/_{2}$–1	45.1	30.9	16.9	3.3	1.6	0.8	0.6	0.9
>1–2	41.1	31.0	17.5	4.2	2.2	1.9	0.7	1.4
>2	41.8	30.2	15.5	6.4	0.8	2.3	1.6	1.4

Source: Special tabulations of the 1986 PNAD.

1986 PNAD, poor women were less likely to be using contraception: 32.5 per cent of all women aged 15–49 living in families with less than half a minimum salary per capita were using a method of contraception, compared to 43.3 per cent of women in the highest income category (Table 5.4). While this is a fairly large differential, it is not as large as might have been expected. Moreover almost half of the difference is due to the use of rhythm or other methods such as the condom, withdrawal, other modern female methods such as foam and jelly, diaphragm, and IUD, but all of these methods are rarely used. Thus, poor women are only somewhat less likely than wealthier women to use sterilization and the pill, the two most popular methods in Brazil: 29 per cent of all women in the poorest income group use one or the other of these two methods, compared to 34 per cent in the highest income group. These broad similarities may, however, conceal important differences in the timing of initial use—e.g., poor women may resort to sterilization only after having several children—and poor women may be less efficient and continual users of the pill, and may be more likely to experience contraceptive failures (Costa *et al.* 1990).

Differences in Childbearing by Poverty Level

The relationship between level of childbearing and poverty is strong, and in the expected negative direction: the average number of children ever born decreases as level of income rises (Table 5.5). This negative relationship is expected because women in families with higher income tend to have more alternatives or opportunities that compete with having a large family; they also tend to marry at a later age and to be better educated; in addition, better-off women are more knowledgeable and have more resources to seek contraceptive options and abortion, if this is necessary. The 1986 PNAD shows that women aged 40–44 who were below the poverty line had an average of 6.5 children, compared to 2.4 children among women in families with 2 or more minimum salaries per capita. This relative difference is even larger among younger women, because poor women have their first child at a younger age, and have a faster pace of childbearing: women aged 25–29 in families with less than half a minimum salary per capita had an average of 3.0 children, three times the number among the same age group at the highest income level, who had only 1.0 children on average.

Another aspect of fertility differences by poverty is seen in the proportion of women who have had at least one child. These proportions are shown in Table 5.6 for 1986, for each five-year age group, by poverty level. The earlier initiation of childbearing among poor women is evident: 12.8 per cent of poor 15–19-year-olds have already had a child, compared to 5.2 per cent among the teenagers in the highest income group. Equally striking is the finding that 63.3 per cent of poor 20–24-year-olds have already had a child, compared to 25.9 per cent of the 20–24 age group at the highest income level. Higher-income

Table 5.5. Mean number of children ever born, by age group and poverty level, Brazil, 1970–1986

Year	Age group	Income per capita (in minimum salary units)				
		0–½	>½–1	>1–2	>2	Total
1970 Census						
	Total	3.2	1.7	1.3	1.0	2.7
	15–19	0.1	0.1	0.0	0.0	0.1
	20–24	1.3	0.6	0.4	0.2	1.1
	25–29	3.1	1.5	1.1	0.8	2.6
	30–34	4.6	2.3	1.8	1.4	3.9
	35–39	5.8	2.9	2.3	1.8	5.0
	40–44	6.5	3.7	2.7	2.1	5.4
	45–49	6.7	4.3	3.1	2.2	5.6
1977 PNAD						
	Total	3.3	2.1	1.6	1.3	2.5
	15–19	0.2	0.1	0.1	0.0	0.1
	20–24	1.3	0.7	0.5	0.3	0.9
	25–29	3.0	1.7	1.2	0.9	2.1
	30–34	4.7	2.8	2.0	1.5	3.4
	35–39	6.0	3.9	2.8	2.1	4.6
	40–44	6.9	5.0	3.5	2.5	5.2
	45–49	7.3	5.7	4.1	2.8	5.6
1986 PNAD						
	Total	3.3	2.2	1.7	1.3	2.2
	15–19	0.2	0.2	0.1	0.1	0.1
	20–24	1.4	1.0	0.5	0.4	0.8
	25–29	3.0	2.0	1.3	1.0	1.9
	30–34	4.2	2.8	2.1	1.5	2.7
	35–39	5.4	3.6	2.8	2.1	3.6
	40–44	6.5	4.7	3.7	2.4	4.4
	45–49	6.7	5.3	4.6	2.8	4.9

Sources: 1970 and 1977 data: IBGE (1982); 1986 data: special tabulations of the 1986 PNAD.

women are also somewhat more likely not to have children at all: between 14–18 per cent of the highest-income women aged 40–49 had had no children, compared to about 6–8 per cent of the lowest income group.

Trends in Fertility Differentials, by Poverty Level

The strong negative relationship between level of childbearing and economic level that existed during the 1970s continues to exist even as overall fertility

Table 5.6. Distribution of women aged 15–49 who have had a child, by age group and poverty level, Brazil, 1986 PNAD (%)

Age group	Income per capita (in minimum salary units)				
	0–½	>½–1	>1–2	>2	Total
15–19	12.8	12.7	8.7	5.2	10.6
20–24	63.3	54.8	36.7	25.9	45.6
25–29	88.8	82.6	67.7	55.0	73.8
30–34	94.0	90.9	81.2	72.2	85.0
35–39	93.6	92.1	87.6	83.0	89.3
40–44	93.5	93.1	90.9	82.2	90.0
45–49	91.7	88.2	90.9	85.7	89.2
15–49	70.1	65.2	58.0	55.8	62.7

Source: IBGE (1991).

has declined at all poverty levels. These patterns of differences by poverty are shown in Table 5.5 for three years: 1970 (Census), 1977 (PNAD), and 1986 (PNAD). However, it is not possible to analyse the declines by specific poverty-level groups over time, because the classification by poverty has changed in such a way as to shift the whole distribution upward. Since the level of fertility within each poverty subgroup has hardly changed over time, and has even risen in a few instances, it is clearly the changing composition of the population according to the poverty levels that accounts for the decline in fertility.

However, as discussed above, while some of this 'improvement' in average income may be real, it is likely that the adjustment of the definition of poverty was insufficient, and that a given poverty level (e.g. women in families with less than half a minimum salary per person) contained relatively poorer women in the more recent years than it did in 1970, for example. This may explain the apparent absence of fertility declines within poverty categories. As a result, it is unfortunately not possible, with the data available, to quantify the proportion of fertility decline that is due to real improvements in income distribution, i.e., to the shift in composition according to poverty, and the amount that occurred regardless of income (i.e., at all income levels).

Pregnancy, Abortion, and Poverty

When presenting results from the 1989 PNSN on pregnancy loss, and while utilizing these data to produce estimates of the level of induced abortion by poverty status of women, we recognize that under-reporting of pregnancy loss is likely to be very high, and that this fact greatly weakens the value of these results and estimates. We nevertheless opted to use these data for three reasons: (1) the total absence of any other national information in Brazil on pregnancy loss according to women's poverty status; (2) the recognized high levels of induced abortion in Brazil; and (3) we consider it important even to have approximate estimates of differences in the practice of abortion across poverty subgroups. Our estimates of abortion according to poverty are based mainly on the information on interrupted pregnancies collected in the 1989 PNSN. This survey also measured poverty, which makes it possible to obtain information on interrupted pregnancies according to women's poverty status. However, an important element in using these data to make estimates of induced abortion is the availability of earlier independent estimates of the overall national level of induced abortion, based on a different data source— hospitalization statistics (Singh and Wulf 1994).

We first discuss existing national estimates of the level of abortion; we then present information from the 1989 PNSN on reported differences in the level of interrupted pregnancy according to poverty level. Next, we discuss a range of possible patterns of under-reporting across poverty subgroups, and use these assumptions to correct for under-reporting and to make a series of estimates of levels of abortion by poverty-level subgroups in Brazil.

National Estimates of the Level of Abortion

Estimates show that the national level of abortion in Brazil is quite high, implying that abortion is most likely an important determinant of the level of fertility in the country as a whole (Carvalho and Wong 1990; Singh and Wulf 1994). National-level estimates of the extent of induced abortion have been made on the basis of existing statistics showing the number of women hospitalized due to abortion complications, and by applying a range of assumptions as to the likely number of total abortions performed for each woman that is hospitalized. This ratio, or multiplier, has been assumed to range between 3 and 7 across countries in Latin America. In the case of Brazil during the recent time period, the applicable ratio was conservatively assumed to be at the midpoint of this range, that is, a ratio of 5 induced abortions for every woman hospitalized. Estimates for 1991, based on moderate or conservative assumptions, produced a count of 1.443 million abortions in Brazil annually, or an abortion rate of 3.81 per 100 women per year. Abortions are estimated to be equivalent to 30.7 per cent of all pregnancies, and 44.4 per cent of live births. The level of abortion was found to be moderately high even in the early 1980s, when, on the basis of hospitalization statistics and assuming a moderate ratio of 5 abortions for each hospitalized case, the total number of abortions was estimated to be almost one million, equivalent to 26 per cent of all births (Singh and Wulf 1991). This finding suggests that abortion was at a high level throughout the 1980s, and that abortion has probably played an important role

in fertility decline in Brazil. Another estimate, which was based on information concerning hospitalization due to abortion collected in the 1986 DHS survey, was also analysed. This estimate yielded a national total of 1.4 million
induced abortions in 1985, or an estimated 34.9 per cent of all births (Singh
and Wulf 1991). However, data are not available to establish when the rise in
abortion began. Applying a ratio of 5:1 produced an estimated total of 1.443
million induced abortions in a recent year (1991) for Brazil. Information from
the national system of health statistics, DATASUS, suggests that in the late
1980s the number of hospitalized abortion cases has been relatively stable; in
addition, it is generally recognized, although there is little published work
on this subject, that the conditions under which abortion is being provided
continue to produce a high number of hospitalizations (Costa *et al.* 1990;
LaGuardia *et al.* 1990; Costa 1994).[3] As a result, for purposes of developing
estimates of abortion among poverty subgroups for the period 1984–9 (the
five-year period for which the 1989 PNSN has obtained information on
interrupted pregnancies and on poverty), we assumed that the annual number
of induced abortions during the late 1980s was approximately the same as the
number for 1991, that is, about 1.44 million.

Findings from the 1989 PNSN concerning Interrupted Pregnancies

In the 1989 PNSN, women were asked whether they had lost any pregnancies
of 27 weeks' gestation or less during the past five years, and if so, how many
such pregnancies they had lost. Spontaneous pregnancy loss or miscarriage
was not distinguished from induced abortion. Before attempting to estimate
what proportion of reported interrupted pregnancies are likely to be due to
induced abortion rather than spontaneous pregnancy loss, we present some
results on the level of interrupted pregnancies and on differentials among
subgroups of women, based on all reported interrupted pregnancies.

Table 5.7 shows the number of interrupted pregnancies per 100 live births,
based on events in the five years before the survey. Overall, there are 13.3
reported interrupted pregnancies for every 100 live births. Large differences
are found among subgroups: the two highest income groups show a greater
probability of an interrupted pregnancy, given that a pregnancy has occurred,
than the poorest subgroup (16–18 per cent for women with 1–2 and 2+
minimum salaries per capita, compared to about 9 per cent for women with
one-half or less of a minimum salary), while the remaining income group falls
somewhere within this range. The oldest women—those 40–49 years old—
report ratios of interrupted pregnancies to live births that are at least twice
as high as those of younger women, at every poverty level. Women who are
classified as daughters within their households have the highest ratio of
interrupted pregnancies (38 per cent of live births), and this is true more or
less across all poverty groups. (An unusual result is found for the poverty
level of 1–2 minimum incomes per capita, and this needs to be examined more

128   *Susheela Singh and Mario Monteiro*

Table 5.7. Mean number of interrupted pregnancies per 100 live births among women aged 15–49 during the five years before the survey, by level of poverty and by by age, position in family, region, place of residence, and education, Brazil, 1989

Characteristic	Income per capita (in minimum salary units)				
	0–½	>½–1	>1–2	>2	Total
Age					
15–19	9.6	8.3	10.8	17.7	10.2
20–29	6.8	13.3	15.9	13.7	11.6
30–39	10.2	15.4	10.9	18.3	13.1
40–49	17.8	28.4	71.0	67.5	29.0
Position in family					
Head	8.9	23.4	11.6	32.9	13.7
Wife	9.0	13.2	16.7	16.0	12.8
Daughter	29.8	43.1	17.6	85.2	37.6
Other	23.5	17.8	10.6	20.3	18.8
Residence					
Urban	11.3	17.5	16.9	18.0	15.6
Rural	7.5	8.3	12.4	10.1	8.2
Region					
North (Urban)	6.8	9.0	7.3	16.9	9.5
North-East	9.5	11.6	19.2	23.6	11.7
South-East	10.5	20.2	16.8	16.9	15.9
South	8.0	10.0	15.8	19.4	12.8
Central-East	7.9	12.2	11.5	10.9	10.6
Education					
<4 Years	9.8	13.7	14.7	22.7	11.5
4–6 Years	7.8	13.0	20.3	17.0	13.1
7+ Years	12.0	21.3	13.3	17.5	16.2
Total Brazil	9.4	14.7	16.2	17.6	13.3

Source: Special tabulations of the 1989 PNSN.

closely.) Urban women have much higher ratios than rural women (15.6 per cent compared to 8.2 per cent). The South-East region also has a somewhat higher than average ratio (16 per cent) compared to substantially below-average levels in the North (Urban) and Central-East regions. Better-educated women report higher ratios of interrupted pregnancies (about 16 per cent among those with 7 or more years of education) than the less educated (11.5 per cent among women with less than 4 years of education).

Some of these differences are in the direction of what might be expected in terms of better reporting—better-educated, urban women may be expected to report more of their interrupted pregnancies, whether miscarriages or induced abortions. However, some of the differences are also consistent with expectations about which subgroups are likely to have higher levels of induced abortion (assuming that spontaneous abortion does not differ substantially among subgroups): we would expect older women to have reached their desired family size, and to be more highly motivated to avoid a birth, and to obtain an induced abortion; similarly, we would expect daughters (unmarried young women) and 'Other' members of the household (mainly domestic workers, who are typically unmarried) also to be more highly motivated to avoid an unplanned birth; finally, the major differentials (higher ratios of interrupted pregnancies to live births among better-off, urban, educated women) are consistent with expectations concerning the higher opportunity cost of an additional unplanned birth, and greater motivation to avoid such a birth, as well as ability to pay for an abortion.

Looking at the number of reported interrupted pregnancies in a different manner, we calculated that in the five-year period, about 7 such pregnancies occurred per 100 women (Table 5.8). This quasi-abortion rate is almost uniform across poverty levels, and apart from a few noticeable differentials, the uniformity of this measure is remarkable. This measure is somewhat related to the rate of childbearing itself—those subgroups that are in the peak periods of exposure to pregnancy and childbearing are the groups that have the highest rates. These include women aged 20–39, women who are in union, and those living in the North-East region, the region which has the highest level of fertility. Young women (15–19) and unmarried women (daughters, 'Other' household members), both of whom would be expected to have lower levels of sexual activity than older women, or than wives and women who are heads of households, have the lowest interrupted pregnancy rates, in all poverty groups. The differences according to other characteristics are smaller, and the rate is indeed fairly uniform across other subgroups. The higher degree of uniformity across subgroups for this measure (Table 5.8), in combination with what appear to be plausible variations in the ratio of interrupted pregnancies to live births (Table 5.7), supports the interpretation that under-reporting is fairly even across subgroups, and across poverty levels, but that actual levels of induced abortion (the variable element in the interrupted pregnancy measure) vary by subgroups.

Estimates of the Number of Reported Induced Abortions, based on the 1989 PNSN

Since the total number of interrupted pregnancies includes miscarriages, as well as induced abortions, in order to proceed to calculate estimates of induced abortion we need to estimate the proportion of pregnancy terminations that

Table 5.8. Mean number of interrupted pregnancies per 100 women aged 15–49 during the five years before the survey, by level of poverty and by age, position in family, region, place of residence, and education, Brazil, 1989

Characteristic	Income per capita (in minimum salary units)				
	0–½	>½–1	>1–2	>2	Total
Age					
15–19	2.3	1.3	2.2	2.0	2.0
20–29	6.9	11.1	11.4	7.8	9.2
30–39	9.5	9.6	5.2	9.7	8.7
40–49	6.3	5.1	6.6	5.0	5.8
Position in family					
Head	6.8	10.8	4.8	7.8	7.5
Wife	9.4	10.5	11.5	10.0	10.3
Daughter	1.1	1.3	0.4	1.4	1.1
Other	3.5	1.3	1.4	1.5	1.9
Place of residence					
Urban	6.8	7.7	7.4	7.2	7.3
Rural	5.8	6.0	8.9	5.2	6.1
Region					
North (Urban)	5.3	6.0	4.5	7.2	5.8
North-East	7.1	8.1	12.6	9.5	8.1
South-East	6.4	8.2	6.7	6.7	7.1
South	4.3	4.8	7.4	7.8	6.0
Central-East	4.5	6.6	6.0	5.3	5.6
Education					
<4 Years	7.7	9.0	7.7	7.2	8.0
4–6 Years	4.7	6.8	9.9	5.9	6.8
7+ Years	4.9	6.4	5.7	7.7	6.6
Total Brazil	6.4	7.4	7.5	7.2	7.0

Source: Special tabulations of the 1989 PNSN.

are accounted for by miscarriages. We assumed that only miscarriages that occur at a relatively advanced stage of gestation (e.g., from 13 weeks to 27 weeks) are likely to have been events significant enough (in terms of the severity of bleeding and discharge of tissue) to be both remembered and reported by women.[4] In fact a small number of earlier miscarriages would doubtless have been reported, and some later ones not reported. A convenient method of applying this assumption to estimate the number of miscarriages reported in the survey, and one that has the advantage of being independent of the survey, is to apply a biological 'constant' (the proportion of live births to late miscarriages) to the number of live births, nationally and for subgroups. This proportion may be calculated from life tables of foetal deaths. Spontaneous pregnancy loss at gestations of 13 to 27 weeks' duration has been estimated to account for 4.13 per cent of live births (Goldhaber and Fireman 1991).[5] Applying this percentage to the number of live births produces estimates of the number of miscarriages for Brazil as a whole, and for age and poverty subgroups (Table 5.9). These miscarriages, which are included among the reported number of interrupted pregnancies, are then subtracted from total reported interrupted pregnancies to obtain an estimate of the number of induced abortions reported in the PNSN.[6]

At the national level, we estimate that there were 796,188 miscarriages and 1,768,688 induced abortions (a total of 2,564,876 interrupted pregnancies were reported during the five-year period before the survey). Reported induced abortions as a percentage of live births are shown in the last panel, as an indicator of the size of differentials according to age and poverty.

The Level of Under-reporting and Correction Factors

Once we have estimated the total number of induced abortions that were reported in the 1989 PNSN for the five-year period, we can compare this number to another national estimate of the total number of induced abortions in Brazil that was derived independently, based on other data sources. The total number of PNSN 'induced abortions' is divided by 5 to obtain an approximate annual number, 353,700: this number represents only 25 per cent of the estimated national total of induced abortions (1.44 million). Under-reporting at the national level is therefore estimated to be approximately 75 per cent, and the overall correction factor would be 4.0 (this factor multiplied by the number reported in the survey would yield the 'correct' total number of abortions). This is a very high level of under-reporting. Although such a high level might be expected, given that abortion is illegal and women are not likely to feel free to report these events in a general household survey, it is nevertheless an impressive fact that even though abortion in the United States is legal, the estimated level of under-reporting in Brazil is similar to that found among non-whites in the United States (a correction factor of 3.64) and only somewhat worse than that for all women in the United States in 1984–7 (a correction factor of 2.86, based on an evaluation of data from the 1988 National Survey of Family Growth (Jones and Forrest 1992)).

Given the inadequacies of the available data, but needing nevertheless to determine what little these data can tell us about differences by poverty level, we took a quasi-simulation approach to making estimates of the level of abortion for income subgroups. Although the most rational assumptions have been made and they do provide a range that most likely includes the true abortion levels (described below), these estimates necessarily suffer from the

Table 5.9.   Total pregnancies, interrupted pregnancies, estimated miscarriages, estimated number of induced abortions, and reported induced abortions as a percent age of live births, according to poverty level and age, Brazil, 1984–1989

Measure	Income per capita (in minimum salary units)				
	0–½	>½–1	>1–2	>2	Total
Total pregnancies					
15–19	762,058	330,945	255,161	146,682	1,494,846
20–29	3,735,174	2,752,144	2,545,973	1,944,371	10,977,662
30–39	3,198,226	1,611,425	1,089,032	1,654,153	7,552,836
40–49	999,672	412,180	217,568	188,281	1,817,701
Total	8,695,130	5,106,694	4,107,734	3,933,487	21,843,045
Interrupted pregnancies					
15–19	66,436	25,323	24,946	22,080	138,785
20–29	237,555	322,968	349,466	234,049	1,144,038
30–39	295,366	215,624	106,958	255,575	873,523
40–49	151,231	91,098	90,304	75,897	408,530
Total	750,588	655,013	571,674	587,601	2,564,876
Live births					
15–19	695,622	305,622	230,215	124,602	1,356,061
20–29	3,497,619	2,429,176	2,196,507	1,710,322	9,833,624
30–39	2,902,860	1,395,801	982,074	1,398,578	6,679,313
40–49	848,441	321,082	127,264	112,384	1,409,171
Total	7,944,542	4,451,681	3,536,060	3,345,886	19,278,169
Estimated miscarriages (4.13% of live births)					
15–19	28,729	12,622	9,508	5,146	56,005
20–29	144,452	100,325	90,716	70,636	406,129
30–39	119,888	57,647	40,560	57,761	275,856
40–49	35,041	13,261	5,256	4,641	58,199
Total	328,110	183,854	146,039	138,185	796,188
Estimated number of induced abortions reported in PNSN					
15–19	37,707	12,701	15,438	16,934	82,780
20–29	93,103	222,643	258,750	163,413	737,909
30–39	175,478	157,977	66,398	197,814	597,667
40–49	116,190	77,837	85,048	71,256	350,331
Total	422,478	471,159	425,635	449,416	1,768,688
Reported induced abortions as a percentage of live births					
15–19	5.42	4.16	6.71	13.59	6.10
20–29	2.66	9.17	11.78	9.55	7.50
30–39	6.04	11.32	6.76	14.14	8.95
40–49	13.69	24.24	66.83	63.40	24.86
Total	5.32	10.58	12.04	13.43	9.17

Source: Special tabulations of the 1989 PNSN.

limitations of the assumptions on which they are based, and at best will give only a rough picture of the actual situation.

We developed two assumptions concerning the level of under-reporting across poverty-status subgroups, building upon two theories:

A. that under-reporting will be greater in lower social-status subgroups—supported by the very large difference found between the poorest subgroup and the three higher-income subgroups in the reported mean number of interrupted pregnancies per 100 live births (Table 5.7);[7]
B. that under-reporting might be similar across poverty-status subgroups—supported by the very similar levels of reported interrupted pregnancies per 100 women across poverty-status subgroups.

Based on the average national level of reporting of induced abortions—24.56 per cent—Assumption A was developed by taking this average level and creating a range around it: we assume a quite wide range across poverty-status subgroups, from 16 per cent reported induced abortions among women in families with under one-half minimum salary per capita to 38 per cent among women in families with 2 or more minimum salaries per capita (see Table 5.10). Assumption B is that all four poverty-status subgroups have the same level, i.e., the average national level of under-reporting. Although results are presented for age groups, we did not develop any hypothesis concerning differences in under-reporting according to age. Instead, all age groups within a given poverty group were assumed to have the average level of under-reporting of that poverty group. In addition, uniformity was assumed across the five-year period.

These two assumptions are viewed as the two extremes of a range that spans the likely situation. We consider these to be the two ends of the likely range because it is very improbable that low socio-economic status groups would have better reporting, both in general and concerning abortion, when compared to higher-status groups. In addition, the assumed range in under-reporting across poverty-status subgroups—between 16 per cent and 38 per cent—is quite large, with the highest status group having more than twice the reported proportion of the lowest (wider than the range observed across subgroups in the United States, for example), and it seems unlikely that the range would be larger than this.

Estimates of the Level of Abortion among Poverty Subgroups

Estimates of the abortion rate per 100 women per year, of abortions as a proportion of live births, and of abortions per 100 pregnancies are presented, for both assumptions, in Table 5.10. As might be expected, the national-level results are very similar to those published earlier in Singh and Wulf (1994), given that reported numbers from the PNSN were weighted up to the national total for 1991 estimated in Singh and Wulf's study. On the besis of PNSN

Table 5.10. Estimates of the total number of induced abortions, the abortion rate per 100 women, abortion as a percentage of live births, and abortions per 100 pregnancies, Brazil, 1984–1989, based on 1989 PNSN data and on two assumptions about the level of under-reporting in the 1989 PNSN

Measure	Income per capita (in minimum salary units)				
	0–½	>½–1	>1–2	>2	Total
ASSUMPTION A: WIDEST RANGE OF CORRECTION FACTORS					
Assumed per cent reported	16	24	30	38	24.57
Correction factor	6.25	4.17	3.33	2.63	4.07
I. Estimated number of induced abortions					
15–19	235,668	52,920	51,460	44,563	384,611
20–29	581,896	927,679	862,501	430,033	2,802,109
30–39	1,096,737	658,239	221,328	520,562	2,496,866
40–49	726,190	324,322	283,493	187,515	1,521,520
Total	2,640,490	1,963,161	1,418,782	1,182,673	7,205,107
II. Number of women (1989 PNSN)					
15–19	2,844,498	1,923,916	1,146,397	1,090,550	7,005,361
20–29	3,454,999	2,915,990	3,055,393	2,986,195	12,412,577
30–39	3,109,341	2,243,395	2,042,086	2,634,547	10,029,369
40–49	2,383,683	1,782,812	1,359,728	1,503,748	7,029,971
Total	11,792,521	8,866,113	7,603,604	8,215,040	36,477,278
III. Number of pregnancies (live births from PNSN+estimated induced abortions)					
15–19	931,290	358,542	281,675	169,165	1,740,672
20–29	4,079,515	3,356,855	3,059,008	2,140,355	12,635,733
30–39	3,999,597	2,054,040	1,203,402	1,919,140	9,176,179
40–49	1,574,631	645,404	410,757	299,899	2,930,691
Total	10,585,032	6,414,842	4,954,842	4,528,559	26,483,276
IV. Estimated abortion rates (number of abortions per 100 women per year)					
15–19	1.66	0.55	0.90	0.82	1.10
20–29	3.37	6.36	5.65	2.88	4.51
30–39	7.05	5.87	2.17	3.95	4.98
40–49	6.09	3.64	4.17	2.49	4.33
Total	4.48	4.43	3.73	2.88	3.95
V. Estimate of abortions as a percentage of live births					
15–19	33.9	17.3	22.4	35.8	28.4
20–29	16.6	38.2	39.3	25.1	28.5
30–39	37.8	47.2	22.5	37.2	37.4
40–49	85.6	101.0	222.8	166.9	108.0

Table 5.10. (cont.)

Measure	Income per capita (in minimum salary units)				
	0–½	>½–1	>1–2	>2	Total
Total	33.2	44.1	40.1	35.3	37.4

VI. Estimate of abortion ratio (abortions per 100 pregnancies)

15–19	25.3	14.8	18.3	26.3	22.7
20–29	14.3	27.6	28.2	20.1	21.8
30–39	27.4	32.0	18.4	27.1	27.4
40–49	46.1	50.3	69.0	62.5	53.7
Total	24.9	30.6	28.6	26.1	27.2

ASSUMPTION B: ALL POVERTY LEVELS HAVE THE SAME CORRECTION FACTOR

Assumed per cent reported	24.57	24.57	24.57	24.57	24.57
Correction factor	4.07	4.07	4.07	4.07	4.07

I. Estimated number of induced abortions

15–19	153,498	51,703	62,846	68,935	336,982
20–29	379,008	906,342	1,053,329	665,226	3,003,905
30–39	714,341	643,100	270,297	805,267	2,433,004
40–49	472,992	316,863	346,216	290,069	1,426,140
Total	1,719,839	1,918,008	1,732,688	1,829,497	7,200,031

II. Number of women (1989 PNSN)

15–19	2,844,498	1,923,916	1,146,397	1,090,550	7,005,361
20–29	3,454,999	2,915,990	3,055,393	2,986,195	12,412,577
30–39	3,109,341	2,243,395	2,042,086	2,634,547	10,029,369
40–49	2,383,683	1,782,812	1,359,728	1,503,748	7,029,971
Total	11,792,521	8,866,113	7,603,604	8,215,040	36,477,278

III. Number of pregnancies (live births from PNSN+estimated induced abortions)

15–19	931,290	358,542	281,675	169,165	1,693,043
20–29	4,079,515	3,356,855	3,059,008	2,140,355	12,837,529
30–39	3,999,597	2,054,040	1,203,402	1,919,140	9,112,317
40–49	1,574,631	645,404	410,757	299,899	2,835,311
Total	10,585,032	6,414,842	4,954,842	4,528,559	26,478,200

IV. Estimated abortion rates (number of abortions per 100 women per year)

15–19	1.08	0.54	1.10	1.26	0.96
20–29	2.19	6.22	6.89	4.46	4.84
30–39	4.59	5.73	2.65	6.11	4.85
40–49	3.97	3.55	5.09	3.86	4.06
Total	2.92	4.33	4.56	4.45	3.95

Table 5.10.   (cont.)

Measure	Income per capita (in minimum salary units)				
	0–½	>½–1	>1–2	>2	Total
V. Estimate of abortions as a percentage of live births					
15–19	22.1	16.9	27.3	55.3	24.9
20–29	10.8	37.3	48.0	38.9	30.5
30–39	24.6	46.1	27.5	57.6	36.4
40–49	55.7	98.7	272.0	258.1	101.2
Total	21.6	43.1	49.0	54.7	37.3
VI. Estimate of abortion ratio (abortions per 100 pregnancies)					
15–19	18.1	14.5	21.4	35.6	19.9
20–29	9.8	27.2	32.4	28.0	23.4
30–39	19.7	31.5	21.6	36.5	26.7
40–49	35.8	49.7	73.1	72.1	50.3
Total	17.8	30.1	32.9	35.3	27.2

Source: Estimates by the authors.

data for the period 1985–9, the abortion rate is estimated to be 3.95 per 100 women per year, while the number of abortions per 100 births is 37.4, and the number of abortions per 100 pregnancies is 27.2.[8]

Both assumptions show that teenagers are much less likely to have induced abortions than are older women—these assumptions yield an overall abortion rate of close to 1 per 100 teenagers per year, compared to about 4–5 per 100 women aged 20–49, with relatively little difference by age among women over 20. Other studies and other related information support the conclusion that teenagers have lower abortion rates than older women—e.g., their number of hospital complications are proportional to their live births. Unmarried women (mostly teenagers) do not have a higher likelihood of complications than married women (Singh and Wulf 1993), and a much higher proportion of teenagers than of older women are not married, and therefore are not sexually active.

A second finding from these data is that the age group 40–49 is estimated to have an abortion rate almost as high as those of women aged 20–39: assuming equal under-reporting across subgroups, the rate for 40–49-year-olds is 4.06, compared to about 4.85 for women aged 20–39; and assuming greater under-reporting among poor women, the rate for 40–49-year-olds is 4.33, compared to 4.51–4.98 for 20–39-year-olds. These very high abortion rates for 40–49-year-olds are implausible, given the high proportion sterilized and the decline in fecundity at these ages. When the much higher level of *reported* interrupted pregnancies among older women is taken into consideration

(Table 5.7), it seems likely that this age group has better than average reporting of abortions on the PNSN, and that the correction factor for this age group should be lower than the average correction factor. It is nevertheless noteworthy, and plausible, that this oldest age group should have a higher probability than younger women of resolving a pregnancy by abortion (the abortion ratio). This result is found in estimates based on both assumptions concerning under-reporting and in results from the unadjusted PNSN data— the abortion ratio, either per 100 live births or per 100 pregnancies, is much higher among women aged 40–49. Moreover, this pattern is found at all poverty levels. In addition, results from both assumptions show that *higher-income* women aged 40–49 are more likely than *lower-income* women aged 40–49 to resolve a pregnancy by abortion.

However, the two extremes of the range of assumptions produce different conclusions concerning the overall pattern of the level of abortion across poverty-status subgroups. This is to be expected, given the direction of the assumptions that have been made according to poverty status, and given the actual variations by poverty in the level of reporting of abortion. Reported levels of interrupted pregnancy and of induced abortion appear to be higher among better-off women. The findings that are based on the assumption that all poverty-status groups have the same level of under-reporting reflect poverty-status differentials in reported levels of abortion, and show, at the overall level, that the lowest income group of women have an abortion rate of 2.92 per 100 women per year, while the three higher-income groups are very similar, ranging from rates of 4.33 to 4.56 (Table 5.10, Assumption B, panel IV). On the other hand, the alternative set of estimates, based on the assumption that under-reporting is lower among higher-income women and greater among lower-income women, not only smooths out the observed differences, but in fact reverses them, showing higher levels of abortion among lower-income women than among higher-income women. According to this set of estimates, the two lowest income groups have similar abortion rates of 4.43–4.48 per 100 women, and the rate steadily decreases as income rises, to 3.73 among women in families with 1–2 minimum salaries per capita, and further declines to 2.88 at the highest income level.

Estimates of the number of abortions per 100 live births, and per 100 pregnancies (Table 5.10, panels V and VI respectively, for each of Assumptions A and B), show more consistency in the pattern by poverty level than did the abortion rate: for both assumptions, the lowest income level has lower proportions resolving a pregnancy by abortion. The difference is smaller under the assumption that lower-income women have higher under-reporting (Assumption A): for example, there are an estimated 33.2 abortions per 100 live births among women in families with less than half a minimum salary per capita, compared to 40.3 among women with incomes above this level. This difference is much larger when under-reporting is assumed to be even (Assumption B): there are an estimated 21.6 abortions per 100 live births among the lowest income group of women, compared to 48.4 among women with incomes above this level.

It would have been desirable to be able to draw from these estimates at least a general conclusion as to whether lower-income women have higher or lower abortion levels than higher-income women. Some of these results point in the direction of poor women being somewhat less likely than better-off women to seek an abortion once a pregnancy has occurred, overall, and certainly this appears to be so among the oldest group, women aged 40–49. It is possible that poor women also have a lower abortion rate (the number of abortions per 100 women per year), if we accept the hypothesis that women are equally likely to under-report abortions in a survey situation, regardless of their socio-economic status. The limited data available on differences in contraceptive use and fertility according to income status also suggest that better-off women probably have a higher rate of abortion. On the other hand, under the assumption that low-income women are more likely than higher-income women to under-report abortions, we would conclude that the two lower-income subgroups (less than one-half and one-half to 1 minimum salary per capita) have a somewhat higher abortion rate than the two higher-income subgroups.

The data currently available to us do not allow us to resolve the issue of whether under-reporting is likely to be about the same across income subgroups, or whether it is negatively related to income. Moreover, these results are not inconsistent with the possibility that lower-income women nevertheless have a higher abortion rate (abortions per 100 women). If women in the low-income group have higher proportions who are sexually active, somewhat lower contraceptive use, higher failure rates and resulting higher pregnancy rates, but a small desired family size, their abortion rate per 100 women could be higher than that of higher-income women, even though their probability of resolving a pregnancy by abortion (once the pregnancy has occurred) is somewhat lower.

However, although it is possible that lower-income women have a higher abortion rate than that of higher-income women, the weight of the data discussed here—the relatively similar levels of contraceptive use across income groups (lower-income women are only somewhat less likely to use a method, and only at ages 30–49) and the very large fertility differentials by income (higher-income women have much smaller numbers of children)—suggests that higher-income groups probably have higher abortion rates. These estimates also allow us to draw an even more general conclusion, that abortion is quite high at all income levels, and that it is very high among some income and age subgroups. Even the lowest estimated level for either set of assumptions, about 2.9 abortions per 100 women per year, is at the level reported in the United States, which is recognized to be moderately high. To put these estimates into perspective, it is useful to mention rates in a few other countries: in the mid- to late 1980s, the abortion rate in the Netherlands was

0.53 per 100 women per year; in Canada it was 1.2; in Cuba it was 5.8; while in the former USSR, where abortion was remarkably high, the rate was 18.1 (Henshaw 1990).

Summary and Conclusions

In Brazil, poverty levels among women of reproductive age and in the population as a whole declined sharply during the 1970s, and continued to do so at a slower pace during the early 1980s. However, during the late 1980s the proportion of poor women rose again, probably as a result of the severe economic crisis that affected the country during those years. By 1989, about one-third of women aged 15–49 were considered to be below the poverty line, and about half of those lived in extreme poverty.

Average family size has historically been much larger among poor women, and it continues to be much higher among poor women, even though at the national level fertility has declined from almost 6 children per woman in 1970 to about 3 children per woman in the early 1990s. Data for 1986 show that the mean number of children ever born among women aged 40–44 who lived in families with less than half a minimum salary per capita was 6.5; by comparison, this mean was 4.7, 3.7, and 2.4 among the three successively higher-income subgroups. This pattern is very similar to that found in 1970 and in 1977, implying that much of the national decline in fertility was achieved by the upward shift in income distribution, rather than by declines in childbearing within income groups.

Since the 1970s, fertility decline has largely been achieved by increased contraceptive use and sterilization, as well as by the practice of induced abortion. For both poor and non-poor women, it is chiefly effective methods (sterilization and the pill) that are used. Data for 1986, the most recent year for which information on contraceptive use among poverty subgroups is available, show that differences in use across poverty groups are very small among younger women (15–29), but that among women aged 30–49, use is higher among those of higher income.

The estimates developed in this chapter of the level of induced abortion for income subgroups suggest that the lowest income subgroup of women is less likely than better-off women to resolve a pregnancy by abortion (based on two measures, the number of abortions per 100 live births and the number per 100 pregnancies). However, these estimates do not provide a definitive answer to the question whether the abortion rate (the number of abortions per 100 women per year) differs according to poverty status. Depending on the pattern of under-reporting, poor women may have a higher abortion rate than better-off women (assuming that under-reporting of abortions in the PNSN is greater among lower-income women) or a lower abortion rate than better-off women (if under-reporting is the same across all poverty subgroups).

Nevertheless, circumstantial evidence from income-status differences in contraceptive use (relatively small) and in fertility (relatively large) suggests that higher-income women probably have a higher abortion rate. Regardless of under-reporting, however, it is clear that the level of induced abortion in Brazil is at least moderately high at all income levels.

Notes

1. Data from the 1980 Census, on poverty by family income levels, rather than by per capita income, suggest that the rate of change was higher between 1977–80, and then slowed down to a level that was under 2% per year, between 1980 and 1986.

2. This difference is partly due to the difference in base populations and possibly to differences in questioning or probing.

3. The use of Cytotec or Misoprostol to induce abortion increased quite rapidly in the late 1980s, and reached what has probably been its highest level in 1991, before government restrictions began to reduce use of the drug for purposes of abortion. However, use of this method has by no means disappeared (*Veja* 1994). Although the use of this new method caused a temporary rise in the number of hospitalizations, women soon learned what the side-effects of the method were and what treatment was appropriate, and the pattern of hospitalization soon stabilized.

4. It is accepted that reporting of very early spontaneous abortions, e.g. those under 8 weeks' gestation, is very low. The likelihood of reporting spontaneous abortions in general, and even those of gestations later than 8 weeks, is probably dependent on many factors. Whether the pregnancy was wanted, level of education, and access to and use of modern medical care are probably important factors; knowledge of the reproductive system as well as beliefs and customs surrounding pregnancy and menstruation are also important determinants of when a foetus is recognized and therefore of when a miscarriage is considered to have occurred (Weisner 1982). A later miscarriage, which entails more severe bleeding and more obvious discharge of foetal tissue, is probably more likely to be reported, especially if complications arise.

5. Goldhaber and Fireman's paper is a new study, improving on estimates previously made by Harlap *et al.* (1980). However, their findings on levels of pregnancy loss at later gestations, which are used in our analysis, do not differ much from those of Harlap *et al.* In addition, data collected in the World Fertility Surveys support the assumption made here concerning the level of spontaneous abortion reported in fertility surveys: for several Sub-Saharan African countries in the 1970s, where induced abortion was quite low, and almost all reported pregnancy loss would be spontaneous, results show that pregnancy losses were equivalent to about 4% of all pregnancies (Casterline 1989). This proportion is very similar to the one that we assume in our analysis.

The fact that the level of spontaneous abortion is influenced by the level of induced abortion has been recognized and treated elsewhere (Figa-Talamanca and Repetto 1988; Hammerslough 1992). Induced abortions lower the level of spontaneous abortion because some pregnancies that would have been lost as a result of natural causes at a later gestation have already been terminated. For the purposes of this analysis, the impact of induced abortion will be to lower the number of spontaneous abortions, resulting in a small conservative bias to our estimate of induced abortions, which is obtained by subtracting the estimated number of late miscarriages from the total number of reported interrupted pregnancies.

6. Stillbirths, which are of 28 weeks' or longer gestation, are not included in the reported number of interrupted pregnancies, and do not enter into these estimates.

7. This assumption is supported by results from other countries, such as those from the study on the under-reporting of abortion in surveys in the United States, where lower-status subgroups were found to have higher under-reporting (Jones and Forrest 1992).

8. The number of women is slightly less for 1989 compared to 1991, and the average annual number of births during 1985–9 is slightly greater than that for 1991, as the fertility decline continues. Therefore the two sets of estimates are not exactly the same.

References

Ahlburg, D. A. (1994), 'Population Growth and Poverty', in R. Cassen (ed.), *Population and Development: Old Debates, New Conclusions*, New Brunswick, NJ: Transaction Publishers, 127–47.

Arruda, J. M., Rutenberg, N., Morris, L., and Ferraz, E. A. (1987), *Pesquisa Nacional Sobre Saúde Materno-Infantil e Planejamento Familiar, Brasil, 1986*, Rio de Janeiro: BEMFAM and IRD.

Carvalho, J. A. de, and Wong, L. R. (1990), 'La transición de la fecundidad en el Brasil: causas y consecuencias', paper presented at the IUSSP Seminar on Fertility Transition in Latin America, Buenos Aires.

Casterline, J. (1989), 'Collecting Data on Pregnancy Loss: A Review of Evidence from the World Fertility Survey', *Studies in Family Planning*, 20: 81–95.

Costa, S. H. (1994), personal communication and unpublished tabulations from 1993 survey of women hospitalized due to abortion complications in Rio de Janeiro, mimeo.

——and Vessey, M. (1994), 'Misoprostol and Illegal Abortion in Rio de Janeiro, Brazil', *Lancet*, 341(1), 1258–61.

——Martin, I. R., Silva Freitas, S. R., and Pinto, C. S. (1990), 'Family Planning among Low-Income Women in Rio de Janeiro: 1984–1985', *International Family Planning Perspectives*, 16: 16–22.

Figa-Talamanca, I., and Repetto, F. (1988), 'Correcting Spontaneous Abortion for the Presence of Induced Abortion', *American Journal of Public Health*, 78: 40–2.

Goldhaber, M. K., and Fireman, B. H. (1991), 'The Fetal Life Table Revisited: Spontaneous Abortion Rates in Three Kaiser Permanent Cohorts', *Epidemiology*, 2: 33–9.

Hammerslough, C. (1992), 'Estimating the Probability of Spontaneous Abortion in the Presence of Induced Abortion and Vice Versa', *Public Health Reports*, 107: 269–77.

Harlap, S., Shiono, P. H., and Ramcharan, S. (1980), 'A Life Table of Spontaneous Abortions and the Effects of Age, Parity and other Variables', in E. B. Hook and I. Porter (eds.), *Human Embryonic and Fetal Death*, New York: Academic Press, 120–40.

Henriques, M. H. F. T. (1989), 'Brazil: Changes in Nuptiality and their Fertility

Implications', in International Population Conference, *Proceedings, Volume 3*, New Delhi: IUSSP, 163–74.

Henshaw, S. K. (1990), 'Induced Abortion: A World Review', *Family Planning Perspectives*, 22: 76–89.

IBGE [Fundação Instituto Brasileiro de Geografía e Estatística] (1982), *Perfil estatístico de criancas e maes no Brasil: características sócio-demográficas 1970–1977*, Rio de Janeiro: IBGE.

——(1986), *Pesquisa Nacional por Amostragem de Domicilios (PNAD)*, Rio de Janeiro: IBGE.

——(1989), *Pesquisa Nacional de Saude e Nutriçao (PNSN)*, Rio de Janeiro: IBGE.

——(1991), *Anticoncepção—1986, Volume 1*, Rio de Janeiro: IBGE.

——(1994), *Criancas e adolescentes: indicadores socias, Volume 4, 1992*, Rio de Janeiro: IBGE.

Institute for Resource Development (1986), *Demographic and Health Survey (DHS)*, Rio de Janeiro: Institute for Resource Development/Macro Systems.

Instituto de la Mujer, Ministerio de Asuntos Sociales de España, and Facultad Latinoamericana de Ciencias Sociales (1993), *Mulheres Latinoamericanas em Dados: Brasil*, Madrid: Instituto de la Mujer.

Jones, E. F., and Forrest, J. D. (1992), 'Underreporting of Abortion in Surveys of US Women: 1976–1988', *Demography*, 29: 113–26.

LaGuardia, K., Rotholz, M. V., and Belfort, P. (1990), 'A 10-Year Review of Maternal Mortality in a Municipal Hospital in Rio de Janeiro: A Cause for Concern', *Obstetrics and Gynecology*, 75: 27–32.

Martins, I. R., Costa, S. H., Freitas, S. R. da S., and Pinto, C. S. (1991), 'Aborto induzido em mulheres de baixa renda: dimensão de um problema', *Cadernos de Saúde Pública, RJ*, 7: 251–66.

Miller, Lilian Maria (1994), 'A Distribuição da renda pessoal', in Fundação Instituto Brasileiro de Geografía e Estatística (IBGE), *Indicadores sociais: uma análise da década de 1980*, Rio de Janeiro: IBGE.

Silva, N. do V. (1985), 'Os deserdados do milagre: O estado social da nacao em 1985', unpub. paper.

——Henriques, M. H. F. T., and de Souza, A. (1990), *An Analysis of Reproductive Behaviour in Brazil*, Columbia, Md.: Demographic and Health Surveys.

Singh, S., and Wulf, D. (1991), 'Estimating Abortion Levels in Brazil, Colombia and Peru, Using Hospital Admissions and Fertility Survey Data', *International Family Planning Perspectives*, 17: 8–14.

——(1993), 'The Likelihood of Induced Abortion among Women Hospitalized for Abortion Complications in Four Latin American Countries', *International Family Planning Perspectives*, 19: 134–41.

——(1994), 'Estimated Levels of Induced Abortion in Six Latin American Countries', *International Family Planning Perspectives*, 20: 4–13.

United Nations (1994), *The Sex and Age Distribution of the World Populations, 1994 Revision: Preliminary Release Version*, New York: United Nations.

Veja (1994), 'O comprimido do náo', *Veja: News Magazine*, 13 July.

Weisner, M. H. (1982), *Aborto Inducido: Estudio antropológico en mujeres urbanas de bajo nivel socioeconómico*, Santiago: Universidad de Chile.

World Bank (1993), *Social Indicators of Development, 1993*, Washington, DC: Johns Hopkins University Press.

PART III

Strategies to Alleviate Poverty: Women's Extra-domestic Work and Migration

6 Daughters and Wives: Marital Status, Poverty, and Young Women's Employment in Sri Lanka

Anju Malhotra and Deborah S. DeGraff

Introduction

Women's labour force activity is regarded as one of the most important factors defining women's lives: it influences not only their economic role, but also their power in the household, their fertility levels, and the nutrition and welfare of their families (Acharya and Bennett 1983; Bruce and Dwyer 1988; Desai and Jain 1994). Research on developing societies in the last two decades has highlighted the complexity in the patterns and determinants of female labour force participation (Blumberg 1991; King and Evenson 1983; Leslie and Paolisso 1989; Popkin 1983; Youssef 1976). A much-emphasized theme emerging from these works is that differences in socio-economic class, familial responsibilities, and labour force settings must be taken into account in examining which women work for pay and why.

An important yet largely unexplored question arising in this context is whether differences in women's roles as unmarried daughters versus wives are relevant in shaping women's labour force activity. Given the importance of marriage in most Asian societies, it is likely that freedoms and restrictions, familial obligations and expectations, and contributions to survival or mobility strategies would all be perceived differently for daughters as compared to wives (or daughters-in-law). The employment status of women, therefore, may be a reflection not only of economic need, individual ability, and individual preferences, but also of the culturally appropriate definitions of women's roles according to marital status.

In spite of increasing attention in recent years to women's employment issues in developing countries, little consideration has been given to the importance of marital status in determining women's labour force behaviour. The literature on women's employment in developing countries has focused largely on married women, since much of the theoretical debate surrounding women's labour force participation has centred either on fertility or on issues of role conflict and opportunity costs associated with domestic versus paid work. A few studies examine the economic role of single women and show that it too can be critical to household strategies of survival as well as upward mobility (Greenhalgh 1988; Salaff 1981; Wolf 1991). None the less, how the economic roles of unmarried adult daughters and married women may differ remains largely uninvestigated.

In this chapter, we examine ways in which the employment status of young women in Sri Lanka may be conditioned by both the economic status of their families and their position within the family as daughters or wives. Our argument is twofold. First, given the centrality of marriage in Sri Lanka, the dynamics of women's employment and economic contributions to the family cannot be fully understood without considering the role of marital status. Whether a young woman is married or single may affect the aspirations of individual women, the expectations, roles, and constraints imposed at the household level, and the employment conditions and opportunities available in the labour market.[1] Secondly, we argue that within a context of high rates of unemployment and labour market imperfections, the relationship between socio-economic status and employment is shaped not only by motivations based on economic need, and on individual preferences and human capital, but also by the ability to obtain a job through access to appropriate contacts and resources. Marital status may also influence this dimension of young women's employment, as it defines, in part, the contacts and resources available.

In our analysis we focus on Sri Lanka, a society with low levels of economic development and high rates of female unemployment, but with high levels of social welfare and education, late but universal marriage, low fertility, and a historical tradition of greater gender equality than is common throughout much of South Asia. The question that concerns us here is that in this unusual socio-economic context, which young women work for pay and why? To what extent is a woman's household economic status, especially poverty status, an important determinant of employment, and to what degree is this relationship shaped by a woman's position as a daughter or a wife? To answer these questions we estimate a multi-variate model of young women's employment, conditional on marital status. Our interpretation of the empirical results is enhanced by the availability of unusually rich descriptive information on the process of job-seeking and the disposition of wages of young women. Whether or not young women share their earnings, and the means through which they acquired their current jobs, are important factors that can shed light on our two central concerns of familial responsibilities and resource availability. We focus on young women because of the importance of women's labour force entrance in shaping the subsequent labour market involvement and economic roles of women in Sri Lanka.

Theoretical Context

In this section we provide an overview of the theoretical arguments surrounding women's employment in developing countries in general, and in

Sri Lanka in particular. First, we discuss the importance of socio-economic status in shaping women's economic activity. Next, we consider the ways in which marital status might influence the process through which the economic roles of young women are determined. Finally, we describe specific features of the Sri Lankan context which may have a bearing on women's employment.

Socio-economic Status

The relationship between socio-economic status and women's employment is complex. The standard argument based on modernization and development theories has been that an increase in human capital, through education and exposure to modern-sector opportunities, should lead to higher rates of female labour force participation (Choi and Brinton 1993). In developing societies, upper-class women are generally the forerunners in obtaining higher levels of education; thus women's employment should be positively related to socio-economic class.

This argument has, however, been challenged by evidence to the contrary in many developing-country contexts: in societies as disparate as Indonesia and Peru, it is poor women who are more likely to work for pay (Buvinic and Lycette 1988). The two reasons most often cited to explain this pattern are economic need and gender inequality. Poor women, it is argued, are more likely to be in the labour force due to sheer necessity and the demands for survival. Studies find that the earnings of adult women are proportionately more important in poor families than among the better off (Buvinic and Lycette 1988). Secondly, research in several Asian societies suggests that gender inequality often creates greater barriers to the employment of women from the middle and upper classes than among the poor. Upper-class status may be associated with stronger norms regarding sexual purity, familial control, and the observation of purdah or seclusion in cultures such as Pakistan or parts of North India (Sathar and Desai 1994; Sharma 1980). In other cultures, such as Indonesia and Taiwan, implicit norms may lead middle- and upper-class women to aspire to a life in which they do not work outside the home, symbolizing their class status (Greenhalgh 1991; Hull 1979).

At the same time, the evidence for a negative relationship between socio-economic class and female employment is not unequivocal. In many societies, job access may be denied to poor women despite their greater need to work because they lack the training and skills needed to obtain jobs (Sathar and Desai 1994). Poor women also may be less able effectively to utilize systematic channels for obtaining jobs in the public and private sectors. Furthermore, in addition to child care, the domestic burdens of providing daily food, water, fuel, and other necessities are often extensive and time-consuming for women in developing societies (DaVanzo and Lee 1983; Desai and Jain 1994). Wealthier women are more likely to have access to labour-saving devices and/or domestic help, and are therefore in a better position, ceteris paribus, to enter the labour market.

The complexity and the sometimes paradoxical nature of the relationship between economic status and women's employment has led some to posit a curvilinear association. That is, women at both ends of the class spectrum are more likely to work, but for different reasons: poor women work because they have to, while wealthier women work because they want to and are well positioned to do so. In Indonesia, for example, historical tradition has supported norms of women as economic participants, but largely among the lower classes. Modernization and associated changes, especially a modest amount of literacy, do not appear to be promoting increased labour force participation among middle-class women. Rather, these changes are making most middle-class women more successful at fulfilling 'Western' traditions of domestic roles.[2] Among the elite, however, it is considered acceptable for women to aspire to personal fulfilment and economic freedom, and they possess the human capital and resources that provide access to modern-sector jobs. Employment patterns, therefore, show a U-shaped relationship with class levels (Hull 1979; Malhotra 1991).

Thus, theoretical arguments can provide good reasons for expecting either a positive or a negative as well as a curvilinear relationship between economic status and women's economic activity. The actual situation in a given society is likely to be based on its social and economic organization, the degree to which economic need motivates market work, and the differing ability of women of different classes to acquire a job.

Marital Status

In most of the literature on Third World women, marital status is missing in the discussion of the links between poverty, women's position, and their economic roles. The incorporation of marriage as a factor is generally limited to noting that marriage affects *levels* of labour force participation. Married women are thought to be less likely to undertake employment because their lives are more committed to domestic functions, childbearing, and child rearing. In sociological terms, this is usually stated as greater role conflict between the spheres of domesticity and employment, and in economic terms as greater opportunity costs among married women of working outside the home (Blau and Robins 1989; Connelly 1992; Connelly *et al.* 1995; Doan and Popkin 1989; Floge 1989; Leibowitz *et al.* 1992; Mason and Kuhlthau 1992; Michalopoulous *et al.* 1992; Oppong 1983; Presser and Baldwin 1980; Richter *et al.* 1992, 1994; Wong and Levine 1992).

Other than noting differences in the levels of women's economic activity by marital status, the possible effect of marital status on the *determinants* of female employment is rarely considered. However, given the centrality of marriage for women in the social and economic organization of most Asian societies, it is likely that many of the factors related to employment function differently for married and single women. In the interrelationships discussed above, in particular, it is possible that the effect of socio-economic class on women's employment is likely to differ according to marital status. We argue that such interactions operate at the macro-, household, and individual levels.

Macro-level factors generally define the demand for labour in a society. The nature of the labour market as well as societal norms often have important implications for the employment opportunities of women (Desai and Jain 1994; Sathar and Desai 1994). For example, due to high levels of occupational segregation in most developing countries, the jobs open to women may not be compatible with child care, which results in higher employment rates among single women. These jobs may also require levels of training available primarily to wealthier women. In certain countries, the nature of economic development and explicit government policy may open the doors of modern-sector employment to women of a certain class as well as marital status, e.g., middle-class single women in Taiwan and Malaysia (Chia 1987; Greenhalgh 1988). The labour market may also be discriminatory due to real or perceived differences in productivity, turnover rates, or costs (in terms of wages, benefits, leave) associated with married as opposed to single women (Ahooja-Patel 1986). Moreover, social norms regarding the acceptance or desirability of a woman's being employed may differ by economic status and by marital status, thereby shaping the demand for labour.

At the household and individual levels, familial obligations and roles, freedom of movement, individual aspirations, and the domestic division of labour are all factors that may differ for single versus married women, and consequently may result in differences in the determination of the supply of labour to paid employment (Greenhalgh 1991; King and Evenson 1983; Oppong 1983; Rexroat 1990). For example, an extended as opposed to nuclear family structure may be more relevant in determining the employment of married women than of single women, possibly because of ready access to child care, but also because of the availability of alternative family members for employment. The presence of other potential income earners may affect married women more strongly precisely because of their child care responsibilities. Similarly, in some South Asian contexts, responsibility for domestic tasks and rules of seclusion tend to be enforced more strictly for married women than for single women. In other parts of the region, however, concerns about the sexual purity of unmarried women is so strong that rules of seclusion apply very strictly to daughters, but only modestly to wives and daughters-in-law (Sharma 1980).

In most Asian cultures, this distinction in the roles and obligations of a daughter as opposed to a wife/daughter-in-law is so strong that it has major repercussions for almost every aspect of a woman's life. For example, in certain cultures, altruism, self-sacrifice, and obligation to the family may be much stronger motivating forces for employment among married women than among single women, especially if the welfare of children is involved. A similar contribution might not be expected of daughters, and consequently, they may be freer to act on their preferences regarding employment. Support for such an argument is provided by Wolf's (1991) work in the relatively gender-egalitarian setting of Central Java. Her findings show that even when daughters work in factories, they rarely turn over their earnings to parents for general household consumption. Work in this case is seen by both parents and daughters as a means of personal fulfilment and some degree of independence for the woman, rather than as a means of enriching the family.

On the other hand, a contrasting situation exists in Taiwan, where it has been shown that employment as a form of family obligation can apply with *greater* force to daughters. In the strongly patriarchal setting of Chinese culture, families have adapted to modernization and industrialization by expecting daughters to contribute to the household strategy of educational investment in sons by working before they are married. In this case, single women turn over large portions of their earnings to parents and assist parental aspirations for social mobility. Moreover, the obligation does not hold once women are married, since they are no longer considered members of the parental household (Greenhalgh 1988).

Finally, given labour demand and supply conditions, marital status may also influence women's employment through the process of job seeking and acquisition itself. For example, if there is imperfect information in the labour market, an employed male relative may serve as an important source of information regarding employment opportunities for young women. If men perceive their own welfare to be more strongly affected by the employment of their wives than by the employment of their sisters or daughters, this effect will be stronger for married women than for single women. Similar arguments hold for the role of male relatives in facilitating job acquisition if jobs for women are scarce.

In sum, this discussion suggests that while in many situations labour market forces, social norms, and family obligations favour the employment of single women, this is not always the case. In certain contexts the reverse is true and these factors can favour the employment of married women. Therefore, in analysing the determinants of women's labour force participation in developing countries, it is important to allow for differences by marital status. This is particularly so for young women, a substantial percentage of whom may not yet be married, and whose economic roles are in the process of being defined.

Sri Lanka

The setting for our analysis is Sri Lanka, an island nation of about 17 million people located near the south-eastern coast of India. In terms of the social and cultural context, we expect Sri Lanka more closely to resemble Indonesia, and other South-east Asian countries, than Northern India, Pakistan, or

Bangladesh (Dyson and Moore 1983). Historically, the position of women in Sri Lanka has been relatively favourable, especially by South Asian standards. This is partially due to the practice of matrilineal and bilineal descent systems which allow for some degree of inheritance rights among women and provide considerable natal family support for daughters before and after marriage (Nayar 1977; Metthananda 1990). Equally important have been women's access to education and relatively late entry into marriage. Even in the 1945–55 decade, close to half of all women were literate, and the singulate mean age at marriage for women was 20.7 years. Currently, women are almost at parity with men regarding education—83 per cent literate in 1990 compared to 88 per cent for men—and have comparable enrolment rates in secondary school (Central Bank of Sri Lanka 1990; De Silva 1990; World Bank 1994). Moreover, while marriage continues to be almost universal, the average age at which women marry is around 25, a late marriage pattern relative to both developed and developing societies (Department of Census and Statistics 1988; De Silva 1990).

Sri Lanka is also noted for a remarkably high level of social development among South Asian countries. The total fertility rate declined from 5.3 in 1953 to 2.5 in 1992, and the infant mortality rate of 18 in 1992 is comparable or superior to other demographically advanced Asian countries like Thailand (26) or South Korea (14) (Department of Census and Statistics 1988; World Bank 1994).

Although Sri Lanka ranks high on indicators of social welfare, it has not experienced high levels of economic progress. The 1960s and 1970s witnessed several economic crises which some have attributed to adverse trade conditions, price inflation, foreign exchange shortages, and a burgeoning, over-educated labour force. Although somewhat alleviated in the 1980s by economic liberalization, increased remittances from the Middle East, and emphasis on export industries such as textiles, economic uncertainty has continued, in part due to the violence unleashed by a northern-based secessionist movement (Central Bank of Sri Lanka 1990; United Nations 1986). Thus, although per capita income rose (in absolute dollars) from US$390 in 1985 to US$540 in 1992, Sri Lanka continues to Figure in the World Bank's listing of the world's poorest nations (United Nations 1986; World Bank 1994).

Economic conditions have been particularly detrimental to opportunities for female employment in Sri Lanka. Despite positive indicators on gender equality such as matrilineal descent kinship, late marriage, and relatively high female education, indicators on women's economic role show a less favourable picture. Even with strong interest in labour force activity among women, rates of female employment have been low, around 20 per cent throughout the 1960s, 1970s, and 1980s (Malhotra *et al.* 1992). As a result, unemployment rates for women have been high during much of this period: around 23 per cent in the 1980s, double the unemployment rate for men (Central Bank of Sri Lanka 1990; United Nations 1986, 1991).

Gender discrimination in the labour market is also a factor contributing to low levels of economic participation among women. Occupational sex segregation is severe, with only a handful of occupations, such as teaching and unskilled and semi-skilled production work (often in textiles or tourism) open to women. Despite similarity in educational levels to men, women's share of clerical work is less than 20 per cent (Ahooja-Patel 1986). Biases in employment often originate with the educational system, in which women are typically limited to a generalized liberal arts education and are seriously under-represented in vocational and professional training. This results in qualifications and aspirations among women which are suitable for a narrow range of jobs for which competition is severe (Ahooja-Patel 1986; Kiribamune and Samarasinghe 1990).

The Marga Survey, a study of female economic activity conducted in the early 1980s, also indicates strong labour market discrimination by marital status. Not only do employers 'prefer' male workers, a large degree of their bias is directed against married women due to the perceived need for extra facilities and higher costs in the form of absenteeism and maternity leave. While Sri Lankan law does require special concessions and benefits for married women, the study shows that these are rarely enforced in actuality; however, the laws are an important basis for the perception of greater difficulties involved in employing married women (Ahooja-Patel 1986).

Analytical Approach

The discussion above indicates that Sri Lanka presents an unusual context for investigating the intersection of marital status, poverty, and women's economic roles. On the one hand, normative traditions of relative freedom and access to education for women, as well as the value of daughters in the parental household, indicate that women, particularly those who are single, should have strong social support for a productive role outside the home. On the other hand, poor economic opportunities and a discriminatory labour market structure suggest substantial barriers to the labour force participation of women, especially married women.

In such a context, what factors are important in determining young women's economic roles, and is the process conditioned by marital status? Is young women's labour force participation largely a response to poverty? This analysis takes a two-pronged approach towards investigating these questions. First, using a standard reduced-form model, we estimate women's employment in the paid labour force as a function of socio-economic class and of selected individual and household factors. In addition to socio-economic status measures, these variables include:

1. a woman's personal characteristics, including age, education, and work experience;

2. household structure, in terms of its composition by gender and generation;
3. cultural ideology of the family, in terms of religion/ethnicity; and
4. an indicator of labour market conditions, in terms of urban residence.[3]

Since differential effects by marital status are a prime concern, we estimate models for single and married women separately as well as jointly.[4] This allows us to determine whether there are differences across marital status in the process that results in young women's employment, rather than just examining differences in the outcome, or level of employment.

The multi-variate models are estimated using a logit specification because of the dichotomous (0,1) dependent variables.[5] The logistic function underlying the logit specification is as follows:

$$P_i = \exp\left(\sum \beta_k X_{ik}\right) / \left(1 + \exp\left(\sum \beta_k X_{ik}\right)\right),$$

where P_i is the probability that the observed dependent variable, Y_i, takes on a value of 1 for observation i, the X_{ik} are the values of the k explanatory variables, and the β_k are the coefficients to be estimated. Parameter estimates are derived using the maximum-likelihood technique. The sign and magnitude of a logit coefficient are similar in interpretation to regression coefficients in that a larger value indicates a larger effect, a positive (negative) value indicates a positive (negative) effect, and significance tests for coefficients are conducted in the same manner. However, the coefficients do not represent linear effects of the explanatory variables on the observed dependent variable, as they do in OLS regression. Rather, they represent linear effects on the log-odds ratio of observing a value of 1 for the dependent variable:

$$\log(P_i/(1 - P_i)) = \sum \beta_k X_{ik}.$$

The appropriate interpretation of a significant positive (negative) coefficient in the present context is that it increases (decreases) the relative probability of being employed versus not being employed.

To facilitate the interpretation of the multi-variate results, we also take a more detailed descriptive look at how women acquire jobs and the disposition of their earnings once employed. Information on job acquisition can provide a fuller understanding of the importance of appropriate resources and the ability to utilize the system in obtaining jobs in a context of high unemployment and an imperfect labour market. Similarly, knowledge of patterns of the pooling of women's earnings with family income offers insights into the motivations for paid work and the relevance of women's work to the satisfaction of personal versus familial goals (Acharya and Bennett 1983; Blumberg 1991; Mencher 1988; Miller 1981). Given the theoretical discussion, we expect differences by socio-economic class and marital status in these aspects of women's employment.

Data and Variables

The data for this analysis are from the second wave of a two-wave panel study of young women in the Kalutara district of Sri Lanka. The study sample consists of 1,460 women aged 18–33 at the time of data collection in 1992. The first wave of the study was conducted in 1989. At that time, a probability sample of 1,527 young women aged 15–30, regardless of marital status, was selected with the assistance of the Government Department of Census and Statistics, using an updated sampling frame based on 1981 Census results. Of these women, 1,460 (92 per cent) were successfully re-interviewed in 1992. Our analysis is conducted on the 577 currently married women and 812 never-married women.[6] These data are especially valuable because in addition to employment information and standard socio-economic and demographic data, they contain substantial information regarding the process of job seeking and the disposition of wages, as well as complete work histories beginning at age 15.[7] The survey also asked detailed questions about household composition. The data set is limited, however, in that it does not provide specifics regarding occupation, hours of work, and wage levels.

The Dependent Variable

For the multi-variate analysis, we use a dichotomous measure of a woman's work status as the dependent variable: whether or not she is currently engaged in paid employment.[8] Given the considerable documentation in recent literature showing that women's economic role in developing countries can be substantial even when they are not working for pay, we were concerned about non-paid economic activity as well (Anker *et al.* 1982; Goldschmidt-Clermont 1987). However, non-paid work was found to be negligible among the women in our sample.[9]

Independent Variables

Socio-economic Status

Our measure for socio-economic status is based on the ownership of consumer durables. To most Sri Lankans, the possession of consumer goods is a very clear indicator of family wealth as well as social standing. We chose the consumer durables measure over one based on income for several reasons. Our young female respondents were frequently unable to provide information on income, creating a large number of missing cases. Information on consumer durables, on the other hand, was well reported. Income was also seen as an incomplete measure of the economic position of farm families. Furthermore, in modelling employment, family income is more likely to be an endogenous than an exogenous factor, and detailed data on individuals' wages that would allow young women's contribution to be isolated is not available. Finally, it is often argued that indicators of consumption are better than indicators of income as measures of socio-economic status because consumption measures smooth out periodic or seasonal variations that can be deceiving in income measures.[10]

The relative standing of the consumer durables was determined by their cost and social prestige in Sri Lanka. Households with none of a set of specified possessions were considered to be the poorest. Those owning only a radio were considered somewhat better off, while the ownership of a bicycle was considered mid-range and that of a television somewhat higher, with the ownership of a refrigerator serving to classify the family in the highest socio-economic class. A household in any given class could at the same time own any or all of the items that define a lower-class status.[11]

Respondent's Characteristics

The three variables measuring individual traits of the woman herself are age, education, and work experience. Age is measured in continuous years, and we would expect a positive relationship between employment and age.[12] Work experience is measured as the number of years a woman has worked for pay or in a voluntary position since age 15.[13] We posit a curvilinear effect of work experience on employment status: additional experience is helpful in getting or maintaining a job only up to a point. Thus this variable is included in the model in quadratic form.[14]

As education in Sri Lanka is widespread, and a considerable proportion of women have secondary schooling (89 per cent in our sample), we do not find much variation at lower levels of schooling. Therefore, we use a dichotomous measure of education: less than ten years, or ten or more years, of schooling.[15] Since higher education increases human capital and may be critical to modern-sector jobs, we would generally expect a positive relationship between education and employment, especially in the absence of data on wages. However, given that Sri Lanka has an abundant, well-educated labour force, this relationship may not be very strong. Furthermore, education effects are often related to class effects; to the extent that schooling captures attitudes, norms, or ability to tap modern-sector opportunities, it may reflect class differences not measured through the indicator based on consumer durables.[16]

Household Composition

Since we have detailed information on the membership of each household, instead of a single measure of household structure (such as nuclear or extended), we incorporate substantially more information by using measures of the presence or number of relevant household members by gender and generation.[17] When the specifics of household composition are considered, there are reasons to expect not only different, but in some cases opposite, effects on the employment of single versus married women. The household composition variables are as follows:

1. Number of same-generation women (mostly sisters and sisters-in-law). Women of the same generation may serve as substitute labour-market workers as part of the household strategy on the division of labour, thus having a negative effect on the employment of women. However, for married women, they may free mothers for employment by providing easily accessible child care.

2. Number of same-generation men (mostly brothers, brothers-in-law, and, for married women, husbands). Since men of this generation are likely to be working, especially if married, we would expect a negative effect of their presence on women's employment.

3. Presence of mother or mother-in-law. This variable is likely to be most important for married women since grandmothers are often the prime candidates for substitute child care.[18] In fact, considerable literature documents the fact that in many developing-country contexts, elder women may actually be the primary, rather than substitute, caretakers of children (Desai and Jain 1994; Oppong 1983).

4. Presence of father or father-in-law. As with the presence of younger men, we expect this variable to have a negative effect on women's employment, perhaps more so for single women, whose fathers are likely to be the major earners in the household.

5. Number of other older relatives. Due to the different life-cycle stages of single versus married women, we expect older relations to be a source of additional economic support for single women, but an additional economic burden in the households of married women. Thus, we would expect opposite signs in the effect of this variable on women's employment, particularly since older relatives may also facilitate the employment of married women by taking on child care.

6. Presence of children (for married women only). Since one of the aspects most emphasized in the literature is the conflict between the maternal role and non-domestic work, we would expect a negative relationship between presence of children and employment.[19]

Other Family and Societal Characteristics

Variables included in this grouping are urban residence, religion/ethnicity, and, for married women only, the husband's occupational status. Urban residence is measured dichotomously and is a very rough indicator of labour market conditions. Due to the greater concentration of modern-sector and industrial jobs in urban areas, we would expect greater employment opportunities for an educated labour force in urban areas. At the same time, employment differentials by urban residence may not be very strong in Sri Lanka, since terrain, small geographic size, and widespread access to welfare and educational facilities have meant that there are often few physical, cultural, and economic distinctions between rural and urban areas.

The two major ethnic groups in Kalutara are the Sinhalese and the Moors.[20] Ethnicity also overlaps with religion in that the Sinhalese are always either Buddhist or Christian while the Moors are all Muslims. In terms of family obligations and women's roles, ethnic traditions of support and freedom for daughters tend to be more prevalent among the Sinhalese, whether Buddhist or Christian, than among the Moors.[21] Moors have been influenced by Islamic traditions and are generally seen as more 'conservative' in their treatment of daughters in terms of early marriages, less education, and considerably less freedom of movement. We use a two-category measure of ethnicity (and religion) by differentiating between the Sinhalese and the Moors, with the expectation of lower employment levels among Moor women.

For married women only, we include a dichotomous measure of their husbands' employment status: whether or not he is in a skilled or professional occupation. This variable is likely to be related to socio-economic class, particularly since young married couples who live independently may not yet have accumulated many consumer durables, even if they are from the upper class. For example, if Sri Lanka demonstrates patterns similar to Taiwan, the wives of men who hold a relatively high-status job may choose not to work as a sign of this status. On the other hand, if Sri Lankan norms do not encourage a domestic-oriented life-style for prosperous wives, then husbands' professional employment status may have a positive effect on their wives' employment. Such an effect may be attitudinal in that husbands in high-status occupations are more supportive of wives working. It could also be resource-related in that well-placed husbands are better connected to official channels through which their wives can obtain jobs, and are better able to afford labour-saving devices and domestic help.[22]

Empirical Results

Descriptive statistics for the independent variables and current employment status are presented for all sample women and separately for single and married women in Table 6.1. The table shows that, as is the case in most societies, single women have a considerably higher rate of employment as compared to married women: 28 per cent as opposed to 11 per cent. However, the overall rate for the women in our sample is low: only 21 per cent of the women in this young cohort are gainfully employed. The relatively high education level in Sri Lanka is evident in that almost 40 per cent of the women in our sample have schooling beyond the tenth grade. However, possibly because they are younger, a considerably higher proportion of single women have ten or more years of schooling (48 per cent) than do married women (26 per cent). Also, some women may choose to delay marriage in order to further their education. This issue is discussed more fully below.

Table 6.1. Means of independent and dependent variables used in modelling female employment in Sri Lanka, total and by marital status, 1992

Variable	All women		Single women		Married women	
Currently employed	0.21		0.28		0.11	
Respondent's Characteristics						
Married	0.42		—		—	
Age	24.53	(4.20)	22.81	(3.68)	26.95	(3.68)
10+ years of education	0.39		0.48		0.26	
Years of work experience	1.53	(2.55)	1.48	(2.31)	1.59	(2.86)
Experience squared	8.83	(25.26)	7.50	(20.32)	10.69	(30.82)
Family and Societal Characteristics						
Urban residence	0.34		0.31		0.38	
Ethnicity						
Sinhalese	0.78		0.83		0.71	
Moor	0.22		0.17		0.29	
Husband skilled/professional	—		—		0.44	
Household Composition						
Number of same-generation women	0.82	(1.01)	1.09	(1.03)	0.44	(0.85)
Number of same-generation men	1.31	(1.01)	1.23	(1.08)	1.42	(0.89)
Mother or mother-in-law	0.70		0.86		0.48	
Father or father-in-law	0.58		0.76		0.33	
Number of other older relatives	0.10	(0.40)	0.15	(0.50)	0.03	(0.19)
Any children	—		—		0.81	
Class Status						
Lowest	0.06		0.05		0.07	
Low	0.27		0.27		0.27	
Middle	0.19		0.19		0.20	
High	0.29		0.30		0.28	
Highest	0.19		0.18		0.19	
N	1389		812		577	

Note: Standard deviations for non-dichotomous variables are presented in parentheses.
Source: Survey of young women in the Kalutara district of Sri Lanka.

Ethnic differentials in marriage are reflected in the fact that a much higher proportion of married as compared to single women are from a Moor background. Almost half of the married women have a parent, in-law, or other relative from the older generation residing with them, and a vast majority (81 per cent) are mothers. Single women, in contrast, are much more likely to live with relatives of each gender and generation, except for same-generation men.

Table 6.2. Distribution of employment of Sri Lankan women by class and marital status, 1992 (%)

Marital status	Class status					
	Total	Lowest	Low	Middle	High	Highest
Percentage employed						
Single	27.8	46.3	24.6	28.0	28.7	26.0
Married	11.4	14.0	14.9	3.5	9.4	16.8

Source: Survey of young women in the Kalutara district of Sri Lanka.

Socio-economic class shows relatively lower concentration at the extremes as opposed to the middle three categories; only a small percentage (6 per cent) of the women in our sample reside in extremely poor households. The distributions for this variable are very similar by marital status.

Table 6.2 shows differences in employment status by socio-economic class and marital status. Among single women, the poor are most likely to be employed (46 per cent as opposed to 24 to 29 per cent for the other classes). However, among married women, we see a U-shaped pattern, so that not only poor women, but also the best-off, show the highest levels of employment, suggesting that the ability to acquire a job through greater access to resources, and/or stronger motivations to work outside the home, may also be factors for this group of women. At the bi-variate level, therefore, Kalutara women show either a negative or a curvilinear relationship between socio-economic status and women's employment, depending on marital status. Poverty status is associated with a greater propensity to work regardless of marital status, whereas higher rates of employment among women who are better off is evident only among the married. This is evidence for possible differences in access to, and motivations for, paid work among married and single women.

The degree to which these relationships hold once controls are introduced can be determined through multi-variate analysis. Since our dependent variable is dichotomous, we use logistic regression to model the log-odds of the likelihood of being employed as a function of the four sets of factors discussed previously: socio-economic class, personal characteristics, household composition, and other family/societal characteristics. As differences by marital status are of major interest, we estimate three models with all the factors common to both married and single women: one for the combined sample but with a dummy variable for marital status, and two separately for each group of women. We also estimate a fourth model for married women only, in which we include the two variables unique to them: husband's profession and presence of children.

Table 6.3 presents the results for all four logit models.[23] In examining

160 *Anju Malhotra and Deborah S. DeGraff*

Table 6.3. Logit coefficients for the effect of personal, household, and economic characteristics on the current employment status of Sri Lankan women, total and by marital status, 1992

	All women (1)	Single women (2)	Married, model 1 (3)	Married, model 2 (4)
Respondent's Characteristics				
Married	-0.656***	—	—	—
Age	-0.034	-0.031	0.008	0.029
10+ years of education	0.221	0.041	0.888**	0.766**
Years of work experience	0.794***	0.797***	0.905***	0.883***
Experience squared	-0.038***	-0.044***	-0.043***	-0.043***
Family and Societal Characteristics				
Urban residence	-0.414**	-0.330	-0.836*	-0.799*
Ethnicity				
Sinhalese	—	—	—	—
Moor	-0.513	-0.728*	0.274	0.579
Husband skilled/professional	—	—	—	0.784**
Household Composition				
Number of same-generation women	0.108	0.093	0.074	0.093

Number of same-generation men	−0.213**	−0.180*	−0.482*	−0.566**
Mother or mother-in-law	−0.387*	−0.964***	0.513	0.656
Father or father-in-law	−0.406**	−0.590***	0.283	0.072
Number of other older relatives	−0.264	−0.433**	0.462	0.152
Any children	—	—	—	−0.865**
Class Status				
Lowest	0.868**	0.872**	1.917**	2.081**
Low	0.282	−0.055	1.869***	1.897***
Middle	—	—	—	—
High	0.069	0.006	0.952	0.734
Highest	0.527*	0.358	1.605**	1.613**
Model chi-square	416.4 (16df)***	233.7 (15df)***	164.3 (15df)***	174.1 (17df)***
N	1,389	812	577	577

* $p < 0.10$.
** $p < 0.05$.
*** $p < 0.001$.

Source: Survey of young women in the Kalutara district of Sri Lanka.

columns 2 and 3 of this table, it is apparent that there are important differences by marital status in the effects on women's employment among each of the four groups of variables considered. As a result, the joint model in column 1 shows more muted effects and will not be discussed in detail, other than to note the strong negative effect of the marital status variable.

Despite controls, the socio-economic class effects show the same pattern as was evident in the bi-variate table. For married women, a clear curvilinear relationship exists where both the poor and the wealthier are more likely to be employed than are the middle class. In contrast, while poverty also increases the likelihood of paid work among single women, there is little evidence of a curvilinear relationship. These results suggest that among poor families, both daughters and wives/daughters-in-law contribute towards household strategies for survival by getting jobs. However, differentiation among the economic roles of married and single women seems to occur among wealthier families. Here, unmarried daughters do not seem to be part of the strategy for social and economic mobility, and/or are less inclined to work for personal fulfilment, among families that are well off; however, the opposite holds for married women from upper-class families.

In order to investigate further the motivations for employment of single as opposed to married women, we examine the manner in which women dispose of their earnings if employed. Shared income, rather than independent use of women's wages, is an important indicator of familial rather than personal motivations behind work. Therefore, if employment among women of a particular class and/or marital status is a vital part of the family strategy for survival or mobility, we would expect working women to contribute a substantial part of their earnings to the household.

In examining the disposition of wages by employed women in our sample we find that there are *no cases* where a working woman turns her entire earnings over to the family. On this dimension, therefore, Kalutaran women are fairly autonomous. However, there is variation in the degree of that autonomy. Fig. 6.1 shows the extent to which employed women share their wages with the family. As a survival and needs-based argument would suggest, poorer single and married women are the most likely to contribute their wages towards family needs. However, the relationship with socio-economic class differs markedly by marital status. In fact, the differences for married and single women in the disposition of wages are parallel to those we have seen in employment patterns: a negative relationship for single women and a curvilinear one for married women. This parallelism provides additional support for the argument that household strategies of survival as well as mobility are a major basis for women's employment. Moreover, while familial obligations function in the same way for poor women regardless of marital status, this is not the case for wealthier women. Unmarried daughters in families that are better off keep their money to themselves when they work, and this decreases family motivation to have them work.[24] On the other hand, wives and

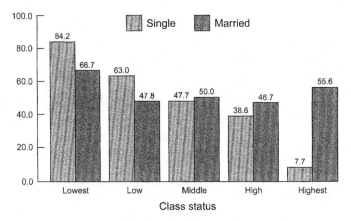

Fig. 6.1. Percentage of Employed Women who Share Wages with the Family, by Class and Marital Status, Sri Lanka, 1992.

daughters-in-law, even in wealthier households, contribute to the family and, as such, there is greater family motivation to have them work. This is consistent with married women playing more of a caretaker role in which they are expected to contribute significantly to the maintenance of the family, either through market work, home production, or both, and in which their own aspirations are closely tied to that of the family. In contrast, single women, unless they are poor, enjoy a more care-receiver role, in which these expectations are lacking, and their aspirations are largely independent of the family.

A second reason why wealthier married women may be more likely to work is their greater access to effective means of securing employment. We are fortunate in having substantial detail regarding the process of job acquisition, and can therefore examine the extent to which the data support such reasoning. Fig. 6.2 shows, separately for employed married and single women, the main source of enquiry for obtaining one's current job by socio-economic class. The possible sources are categorized as friends or relatives, self-initiated search (direct contact with employer, newspaper or other advertisement), and government schemes. The latter typically involve government-sponsored apprenticeships in selected industries. There are distinct differences by socio-economic class, but the pattern is more exaggerated for married women. The main source of job enquiry for poor women is friends/relatives. In contrast, women of higher economic classes find their jobs either through self-initiated enquiry or through government schemes. This last aspect is extremely surprising, since it would be expected that government schemes are intended to benefit the poor. However, these distributions show quite clearly that poor women are, in fact, barred from access to these schemes. It is likely, therefore, that personal connections and an understanding of official systems is required

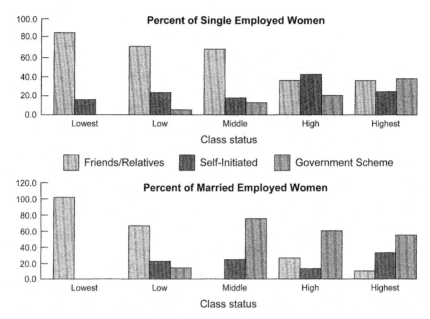

Fig. 6.2. Main Source of Enquiry for Employed Women's Current Job by Class and Marital Status, Sri Lanka, 1992 (%)

to obtain these jobs.[25] Moreover, among wealthier women, there is a substantially higher concentration of jobs acquired through government schemes for women who are married. This supports the argument that well-placed husbands facilitate job acquisition, thus contributing to the higher rates of employment for this group of women.

The relevance of resources, including human capital, as a basis for the employment of married women is also evident in the differential effect of higher education. Table 6.3 shows that highly educated married women are more likely to work, while this variable is irrelevant to the employment of single women.[26] If the labour market is particularly discriminatory against married women then it is possible that they have to be especially well qualified in order to obtain a job. Furthermore, greater opportunity costs of market work for married women (because of greater domestic responsibilities) implies a higher reservation wage for labour market entry than for single women. Thus, higher education is more likely to be a significant factor for these women. Highly educated single women, although perhaps more attractive to employers, may be more inclined to postpone employment until a professional job can be obtained, if they are not expected to contribute to the family. Similar desires on the part of highly educated married women to hold out for a professional job may be outweighed by familial financial obligations.

Turning to the effects of household composition, the presence of men or women of the same generation has similar effects regardless of marital status. The presence of young women makes no difference in either case, but the presence of young men is an important determinant of employment for all women. Clearly this is an effect related to gender roles in the family: young women are much less likely to work in the labour market if there are also young men in the household. Given that for married women this category consists mostly of employed husbands, the effect is stronger for them.

At the same time, however, the coefficients for the presence of members of the older generation demonstrate the difference in the family's expectations about a young woman's role based on whether or not she is married. There is no significant effect from this group of variables for married women, although all the coefficients are positive. Thus, in Sri Lanka, having an extended family in which elders reside with the couple does not on the whole facilitate or prevent married women's participation in paid employment. The only exception to this is, perhaps, the presence of a mother or mother-in-law: this presence may be facilitative, possibly in terms of child care, but also (as the coefficient remains positive in model 2, where presence of children is accounted for) in terms of other domestic work.[27]

For single women, in contrast, the presence of a mother shows a very strong *negative* effect: having a mother in the household makes it less likely that an unmarried daughter works for pay. Similarly, the presence of a father or other elders also shows a strong negative effect for single women. Again, this suggests that in Sri Lankan families, unmarried daughters are more likely to be perceived as care-receivers rather than as care-givers. That is, as long as there are any older adults present in the household, unmarried women are not expected to work in the labour force.

Model 2 for married women shows that the inclusion of the two variables unique to these womenh—the presence of children and husband's profession—does not alter the above comparison in any significant manner. As expected, mothers are less likely to be employed than non-mothers. We also observe a positive effect of the husband's professional/skilled occupational status on the wife's employment. As hypothesized above, this could be indicative of more positive attitudes towards the employment of wives among professional men. Also, in keeping with Fig. 6.2, it suggests that wives of well-placed husbands are more likely to benefit from the advantages, contacts, and resources attached to their husbands' jobs, which may facilitate their own employment.

Finally, the other family and societal factors also show differences by marittal status. Although urban residence has a negative estimated coefficient for both married and single women, the effect on employment is substantial and significant only for married women. This may be due to greater discrimination against married women in the more formalized and modern-sector labour market of urban areas. The nature of work, tighter labour market conditions, and a more strongly perceived government presence in urban areas could all contribute to this result. In contrast, the effect of coming from a Moor ethnic background is negative only for single women. Thus, the conservatism of Moor families applies more strictly to unmarried daughters than to wives and daughters-in-law, possibly due to greater concerns regarding the sexual purity of unmarried daughters.

Discussion and Conclusions

The results of this analysis point towards important differences by marital status as well as by socio-economic class in the relevance of survival and mobility strategies, familial obligations and roles, and ability to secure employment in defining the employment patterns of young Sri Lankan women. In answering the question of which young women work and why, we find not only that economic factors are relevant, in terms of household needs and aspirations and the ability to utilize resources effectively, but also that cultural factors are of great importance, in terms of women's position in the family as unmarried daughters as opposed to wives or daughters-in-law.

Our analysis provides strong confirmation for the importance of marital status when considering young women's employment in Sri Lanka. In particular, the effects of socio-economic status on women's economic roles are significantly shaped by whether or not a woman is married. Furthermore, each of the four major categories of explanatory variables included in our model of young women's employment provides evidence of differential effects by marital status. Thus, not only does this study confirm the often-observed phenomenon of greater labour force participation among single women; more importantly, it highlights the usually neglected issue of the extent to which the determinants of women's work status vary by marital status. Within the Sri Lankan context of late entry into marriage, this issue is especially important to our understanding of the workings of the labour market, the position of women in society, and the implications of poverty for women's roles.

Our findings show that, as in many countries, poverty promotes women's market work in Sri Lanka, regardless of marital status. Women's employment is part of a household survival strategy among the poor, as evidenced by the greater propensity of poor working women, both single and married, to contribute their earnings to the household. Thus economic need overrides differences across marital status in expectations, opportunities, and aspirations among poor women.

However, this is not the case among wealthier women. Here we see clear differences by marital status in the effect of economic class on young women's employment. Upper-class status leads to a greater likelihood of employment among young married women, but not among young single women. Married women who are better off seem to aspire to and/or be expected to contribute to maintaining or improving the socio-economic position of the household.

Thus, employment is not solely poverty-driven among young married women. In contrast, these same dynamics do not operate for single women from wealthier families; they are not more likely to work than are their middle-class counterparts and their labour force participation appears to be more oriented towards personal fulfilment rather than part of a household strategy of upward mobility. These findings suggest a distinction in role definition for young women by marital status among upper-class families. Unmarried daughters are more often viewed as receiving care, and as such, their role is not strongly prescribed by family obligations and responsibilities. This family context, along with an unfavourable employment climate, reduces the incentives for these young women to work. On the other hand, familial responsibilities are more important in prescribing the economic role of young married women. They are more often in the position of providing care by contributing to the financial position of the family.

Furthermore, the interplay of poverty and marital status as determinants of women's employment is not only important on the supply side of the labour market, it may also condition women's ability to obtain employment in an imperfect and saturated labour market. Working women of higher economic status are much more likely to have acquired employment through a government scheme than are poor women, who rely primarily on family contacts. Moreover, this difference in mode of job acquisition between poor and non-poor women is more pronounced among married women than among single women. Thus wealthier married women are especially well placed to take advantage of formal systems of job seeking, perhaps benefiting from the knowledge of (and/or influence over) government employment on the part of their well-positioned husbands. These findings underscore the importance of expanding the analysis of young women's employment beyond a consideration of labour supply issues to encompass the dimensions of labour demand and the process of job acquisition.

Notes

1. In Sri Lanka, young unmarried women almost always reside in the home of their parents or possibly with other relatives. It is very unusual for a single woman to establish her own household.

2. It has been argued by some that the traditional Western division of labour, where women are limited to domestic work, has not necessarily applied to many non-Western contexts, at least historically. However, modernization often brings with it an idealization of post-war Western norms in these societies, even when those norms have already become outdated in the Western countries from which they originated (Hull 1979).

3. Although the larger macro-context is represented by the cultural and socio-economic conditions in Sri Lanka, our full conceptualization of a model of women's

employment includes macro-indicators of variations in labour market structure and social norms *within* Sri Lanka. Due to data limitations, however, we are confined to using urban residence as the only indicator of the macro-context.

4. In many countries it may be the case that women's employment and marital status are jointly determined behaviours and, in such cases, marital status should be treated as an endogenous variable in a model of young women's employment. In the context of Sri Lanka, however, this is less likely to be relevant. Marriage is almost universal; thus whether to marry is not a choice. While the timing of marriage is more likely to be subject to choice, it has been argued before that it is generally not conditioned on the employment behaviour of young women (Malhotra *et al.* 1992).

5. Estimation of models with a dichotomous dependent variable usually calls for either a logit or a probit specification. The choice between a logit and a probit specification is usually arbitrary because the underlying distributions differ only at extreme values. The logit results presented here have all been re-estimated using a probit specification and the two sets of results are substantively identical.

6. Since one of our prime interests relates to differentials between unmarried daughters and married wives or daughters-in-law, we do not include the 17 currently widowed or divorced women in our analysis.

7. Given the unfavourable employment conditions for women in Sri Lanka, a growing number of young women are seeking and obtaining employment in the Middle East. We were somewhat concerned that overseas migration for employment might be more common among single women than married women, potentially producing a sample selection bias in the data. However, the information on sample loss between the two waves of data collection does not support this. The propensity to migrate out of the sample was of comparable magnitude for married and single women.

8. For definitional purposes, it is important to distinguish our dichotomous measure of employment status from a variable that measures participation in the labour force. The labour force is defined as consisting of those who are employed as well as those who are actively looking for work. While this latter category is usually not very large, due to the poor employment opportunities for women in Sri Lanka, unemployed women seeking work are a significantly large group in our sample (34% among single women and 30% among married women). For a detailed discussion of unemployment among young women in Sri Lanka see Malhotra and DeGraff (1995).

9. Non-wage economic activity is usually in the form of unpaid family or farm labour. The survey questionnaire from which our data are derived was very sensitive to this concern, and asked specific questions regarding non-paid work. However, although we changed the wording in the second wave in order to probe further, the number of women doing farm or family work was consistently less than 1%. Thus, it seems that young women in Kalutara are simply not engaged in this type of labour activity. To some extent, our findings are supported by cross-national data which show extremely low rates of female participation in family enterprises in Sri Lanka (Greenhalgh 1991). This may be partially due to the fact that Sri Lankan agriculture is heavily estate- rather than family-oriented; agricultural work is often on tea or rubber plantations and therefore is largely wage labour.

10. In addition to information on consumer durables, we also had a measure of monthly household expenditures. We experimented with a measure of the natural logarithm of household expenses per capita, but, although the results were similar, we decided against it due to the same concerns about endogeneity as for household income.

It is quite common in studies of demographic or labour force behaviour to use measures of productive assets (e.g., land or livestock), dwelling conditions (e.g., piped water or housing material), and/or consumer durables in lieu of a measure of income. Examples of studies which make use of a measure of consumer durables include Desai (1992), Horton (1988), Kelley and Schmidt (1988), Knodel *et al.* (1990), and Muhuri and Preston (1991).

11. Questions about the ownership of consumer durables were patterned after the Demographic and Health Surveys and, as such, provide information on a wider array of consumer durables than the 4 used here. Given the detailed data, we experimented with various combinations of consumer durable possessions of similar status and the measures were found to be very robust across alternative definitions.

12. Age is often included in quadratic form in employment models. However, since our sample consists of a relatively young cohort, we expect these women to be on the linear part of the curve, and therefore do not include a squared term. Exploratory analysis showed no indications of a curvilinear relationship.

13. The measure for work experience has a considerably larger share of paid work experience than voluntary work experience. About 15% of the women had ever done voluntary work while 31% had ever worked for pay. The multi-variate results for the effect of this variable were found to be the same with or without the inclusion of voluntary work in the definition.

We tested for collinearity between age and experience, but found that although positively related, they are not highly correlated.

14. Although it is standard practice to include previous work experience in models of current employment status, we were somewhat concerned that this variable might also be a determinant of the acquisition of consumer durables, our measure of socio-economic class. However, cross-tabulations of the two variables provide no evidence of a systematic relationship, and the parameter estimates for the consumer durables variables are robust to the exclusion of the work experience variables.

15. The tenth year of schooling was chosen as the cutoff because students in Sri Lanka are awarded the O-level graduation at this stage; this is equivalent to high-school graduation.

16. In some developing-country settings the class effect has been so evident through education that there is a distinct *negative* relationship between employment and schooling. This is often the case in societies where upper-class status is associated with a negative attitude towards women working for pay and/or seclusion of women (Sathar and Desai 1994).

17. The exact ages of other household members are not available.

18. In Sri Lanka, in addition to living independently, married couples show equal tendencies of living with the wife's or the husband's parents. Given that a woman is likely to have more rights and fewer obligations in her parents' household as compared to her in-laws' household, we had thought that this distinction would be relevant for their employment status. However, in our experimental analysis with a three-category residence variable (independent, parents, in-laws), we found no significant effects of residence status.

19. The presence of any children was chosen over more standard measures of children, such as number of children in each of several age categories, because the relatively low fertility in Sri Lanka, combined with the narrow age range of respondents, resulted in little variance in such measures.

20. Sri Lanka has three major ethnic groups: Sinhalese, Tamils, and Moors. Sinhalese constitute the largest ethnic group, or about $^3/_4$ of the population. The Tamil population is not evenly distributed throughout the island, but tends to be heavily concentrated in the northern areas around the Jaffna peninsula. Kalutara is a district in which the Tamil presence is negligible.

21. Sinhalese traditions reflect the indigenous bilineal and matrilineal culture of the island. Buddhist and Christian patterns are undifferentiated mainly because most Christians are converts from Buddhism; in most aspects of family life, they continue the Sinhalese traditions.

22. The effect of husband's occupation may also be need-based, as in the case where the husband is unemployed, for example. In our sample, however, only 2 husbands were currently unemployed.

23. The chi-squared statistic included for each model is the standard measure of explanatory power for a logit model. It is a measure of the difference in the value of the log-likelihood function between the estimated model and the null model in which all coefficients are restricted to 0. In each case, the model chi-squared statistic is significant at the 0.001 level, indicating the relatively good explanatory power of our model. The R^2 statistic that is typically used to measure goodness of fit in the context of OLS regression models is not appropriate here as it assumes a linear estimation procedure. None the less, several 'pseudo-R^2' statistics have been proposed for logit models, although there is disagreement as to which, if any, of these measures should be used. One such measure is calculated as $(1 - L(\Omega) / L(\omega))$, where $L(\Omega)$ is the value of the estimated log-likelihood function and $L(\omega)$ is the value of the log-likelihood function under the null hypothesis (Kmenta 1986). For our 4 models this measure produces pseudo-R^2 values of 29.15, 24.31, 40.03, and 42.43 respectively.

24. This is not to argue that parents derive no satisfaction from their unmarried daughter's employment, independent of contributions to family income. However, the absence of such a contribution would reduce the benefit to the family.

25. Our data also show an interesting pattern: blue-collar employment is much more prominent among wealthier than poor women; it is also more prominent among married women. Such a pattern is contrary to what is commonly found in most countries: that upper-class women are more heavily represented in white-collar jobs. In the Sri Lankan case, however, access to government schemes is the key to the puzzle: jobs in government schemes are almost entirely skilled, blue-collar work (textiles, cottage industry, etc.), and it is wealthier and married women who have the best access to such employment.

26. While all but 2 married women have finished their schooling, 11% of the single women are still in school. We were concerned about the endogeneity of being in school for this group of women (women are in school because they cannot find a job or women are not married yet because they want more schooling). In lieu of modelling schooling jointly with employment (which is beyond the scope of this chapter), we checked for the sensitivity of our results by re-estimating the model for single women excluding those still in school. On the whole, the results are highly robust for the other coefficients. The education coefficient itself is sensitive to the exclusion of women in school, but not enough to alter the substantive interpretation: it increases from 0.04 to 0.26, but is not significant ($p = 0.19$). This is because women still in school are the best educated and also the least employed; thus, their exclusion leads to a positive, but very weak, effect of schooling for the remaining women. While this does not constitute a

formal test, the overall consistency of results makes us confident that there is little endogeneity bias in our model.

27. The *P*-values for the coefficient of the presence of mother or mother-in-law in the models for married women are 0.21 and 0.13, respectively. In alternative specifications of the model this coefficient is sometimes significant at the 10% level. Thus there is very weak support for a positive effect. One possible explanation for this effect's being weaker than expected is that it is not uncommon for the mother, mother-in-law, or other relatives who might perform child care or other domestic work to live near, but not with, the young married couple. This mitigates the importance of co-residence. Unfortunately, as is typically the case, we do not have information on the location of non-resident relatives.

References

Acharya, Meena, and Bennett, Lynn (1983), *Women and the Subsistence Sector: Economic Participation and Household Decision Making in Nepal*, Washington, DC: World Bank.

Ahooja-Patel, Krishna (1986), 'Employment of Women in Sri Lanka: The Situation in Colombo', in R. Anker and C. Hein (eds.), *Sex Inequalities in Urban Employment in the Third World*, Geneva: International Labour Office, 213–33.

Anker, Richard, Buvinic, M., and Youssef, N. (1982), *Women's Roles and Population Trends in the Third World*, London: Croom Helm.

Blau, David M., and Robins, Philip K. (1989), 'Fertility, Employment and Child Care Costs', *Demography*, 26: 287–300.

Blumberg, Rae Lesser (1991), 'Introduction: The "Triple Overlap" of Gender Stratification, Economy and the Family', in R. L. Blumberg (ed.), *Gender, Family and Economy: The Triple Overlap*, Newbury Park, Calif.: Sage Publications, 7–34.

Bruce, Judith, and Dwyer, Daisy (1988), 'Introduction', in D. Dwyer and J. Bruce (eds.), *A Home Divided: Women and Income in the Third World*, Stanford: Stanford University Press, 1–19.

Buvinic, Mayra, and Lycette, Margaret A. (1988), 'Women, Poverty, and Development in the Third World', in John P. Lewis (ed.), *Strengthening the Poor: What Have We Learned?*, New Brunswick, NJ: Transaction Books, 149–62.

Central Bank of Sri Lanka (1990), *Socio-economic Achievements of Sri Lanka*, Colombo: Central Bank of Sri Lanka, Statistics Department.

Chia, Sio Yoe (1987), 'Women's Economic Participation in Malaysia', in *Women's Economic Participation in Asia and the Pacific*, Bangkok: United Nations, ESCAP, 163–90.

Choi, Moonkyung, and Brinton, Mary C. (1993), 'Industrialization and Women's Work in the Formal and Informal Sectors: The Case of South Korea', paper presented at the Annual Meetings of the Population Association of America, Cincinnati, Ohio.

Connelly, Rachel (1992), 'Self-employment and Providing Child Care: Employment Strategies for Mothers with Young Children', *Demography*, 29: 17–31.

——DeGraff, Deborah S., and Levison, Deborah (1996), 'Women's Employment and Child Care in Brazil', *Economic Development and Cultural Change*, 44: 619–56.

DaVanzo, Julie, and Lee, Donald Lye Poh (1983), 'The Compatibility of Child Care and Nonmarket Activities: Preliminary Evidence from Malaysia', in Mayra Buvinic, Margaret A. Lycette, and William Paul McGreevey (eds.), *Women and Poverty in the Third World*, Baltimore: Johns Hopkins University Press, 62–91.

Department of Census and Statistics (1988), *Sri Lanka Demographic and Health Survey, 1987*, Colombo: Government of Sri Lanka, Ministry of Plan Implementation.

Desai, Sonalde (1992), 'Children at Risk: The Role of Family Structure in Latin America and West Africa', *Population and Development Review*, 19: 689–717.

—— and Jain, Devaki (1994), 'Maternal Employment and Changes in Family Dynamics: The Social Context of Women's Work in Rural South India', *Population and Development Review*, 20: 115–36.

De Silva, W. Indralal (1990), 'Age at Marriage in Sri Lanka: Stabilizing or Declining?', *Journal of Biosocial Science*, 22: 395–404.

Doan, Rebecca Miles, and Popkin, Barry M. (1989), 'Women's Work and Child Care Arrangements in the Philippines', paper presented at the Annual Meetings of the Population Association of America, Baltimore, Md.

Dyson, Tim, and Moore, Mick (1983), 'On Kinship Structure, Female Autonomy and Demographic Behavior in India', *Population and Development Review*, 9: 35–60.

Floge, Liliane (1989), 'Changing Household Structure, Child-Care Availability, and Employment among Mothers of Preschool Children', *Journal of Marriage and the Family*, 51: 51–63.

Goldschmidt-Clermont, Luisella (1987), *Economic Evaluations of Women's Unpaid Household Work*, Geneva: International Labour Office.

Greenhalgh, Susan (1988), 'Intergenerational Contracts: Familial Roots of Sexual Stratification in Taiwan', in D. Dwyer and J. Bruce (eds.), *A Home Divided: Women and Income in the Third World*, Stanford: Stanford University Press, 39–70.

—— (1991), *Women in the Informal Enterprise: Empowerment or Exploitation?*, New York: Research Division, The Population Council.

Horton, Susan (1988), 'Birth Order and Child Nutritional Status: Evidence from the Philippines', *Economic Development and Cultural Change*, 36: 341–54.

Hull, Valerie J. (1979), *A Women's Place: Social Class Variations in Women's Work Patterns in a Javanese Village*, Djakarta: Population Studies Centre, Gadjah Mada University.

Kelley, Allen C., and Schmidt, Robert M. (1988), 'The Demographic Transition and Population Policy in Egypt', in T. Paul Schultz (ed.), *Research in Population Economics, Vol. 6*, Greenwich, Connecticut: JAI Press, 69–110.

King, Elizabeth, and Evenson, Robert (1983), 'Time Allocation and Home Production in Philippine Rural Households', in Mayra Buvinic, Margaret A. Lycette, and William Paul McGreevey (eds.), *Women and Poverty in the Third World*, Baltimore: Johns Hopkins University Press, 35–61.

Kiribamune, Sirima, and Samarasinghe, Vidyamali (1990), 'Introduction', in S. Kiribamune and V. Samarasinghe (eds.), *Women at the Crossroads: A Sri Lankan Perspective*, New Delhi: Vikas Publishing House PVT, pp. xi–xxi.

Kmenta, Jan (1986), *Elements of Econometrics*, New York: Macmillan Publishing Company.

Knodel, John, Havanon, Napaporn, and Sittirai, Werasit (1990), 'Family Size and the Education of Children in the Context of Rapid Fertility Decline', *Population and Development Review*, 16: 31–62.

Leibowitz, Arleen, Klerman, Jacob Alex, and Waite, Linda J. (1992), 'Employment of New Mothers and Child Care Choices', *Journal of Human Resources*, 27: 112–33.

Leslie, J., and Paolisso, M. (1989), *Women, Work and Child Welfare in the Third World*, Boulder, Colo.: Westview Press.

Malhotra, Anju (1991), 'Gender and the Dynamics of Marriage Timing: Rural–Urban Differences in Java', paper presented at the Annual Meetings of the American Sociological Association, Los Angeles.

——Tsui, A., and DeSilva, V. (1992), 'Personal Preferences and the Family Context of Marriage Timing in Sri Lanka', paper presented at the Annual Meetings of the Population Association of America, Denver.

——and DeGraff, Deborah S. (1995), 'Entry and Success in the Labor Force: Young Women's Employment in Sri Lanka', paper presented at the Annual Meetings of the Population Association of America, San Francisco.

Mason, Karen O., and Kuhlthau, Karen (1992), 'The Perceived Impact of Child Care Costs on Women's Labor Supply and Fertility', *Demography*, 29: 523–44.

Mencher, Joan (1988), 'Women's Work and Poverty: Women's Contribution to Household Maintenance in South India', in D. Dwyer and J. Bruce (eds.), *A Home Divided: Women and Income in the Third World*, Stanford: Stanford University Press, 99–119.

Metthananda, Tilaka (1990), 'Women in Sri Lanka: Tradition and Change', in S. Kiribamune and V. Samarasinghe (eds.), *Women at the Crossroads: A Sri Lankan Perspective*, New Delhi: Vikas Publishing House PVT, 41–71.

Michalopoulos, Charles, Robins, Philip K., and Garfinkel, Irwin (1992), 'A Structural Model of Labor Supply and Child Care Demand', *Journal of Human Resources*, 27: 166–203.

Miller, Barbara P. (1981), *The Endangered Sex: Neglect of Female Children in Rural India*, Ithaca, NY: Cornell University Press.

Muhuri, Pradip, and Preston, Samuel H. (1991), 'Effects of Family Composition on Mortality Differentials by Sex among Children in Matlab, Bangladesh', *Population and Development Review*, 17: 415–34.

Nayar, Usha (1977), 'Women in Sri Lanka', *Social Change*, 7: 3–45.

Oppong, Christine (1983), 'Women's Roles, Opportunity Costs, and Fertility', in Rodolfo A. Bulatao and Ronald D. Lee (eds.), *Determinants of Fertility in Developing Countries, Vol. 1*, New York: Academic Press, 547–89.

Popkin, Barry M. (1983), 'Rural Women, Work and Child Welfare in the Philippines', in Mayra Buvinic, Margaret A. Lycette, and William Paul McGreevey (eds.), *Women and Poverty in the Third World*, Baltimore: Johns Hopkins University Press, 157–76.

Presser, Harriet, and Baldwin, Wendy (1980), 'Child Care as a Constraint on Employment: Prevalence, Correlates, and Bearing on the Work and Fertility Nexus', *American Journal of Sociology*, 85: 1202–13.

Rexroat, Cynthia (1990), 'Race and Marital Status Differences in the Labor Force Behavior of Female Family Heads: The Effect of Household Structure', *Journal of Marriage and the Family*, 52: 591–601.

Richter, Kerry, Podhisita, Chai, Soonthorndhada, Kusol, and Chamratrithirong, Apichat (1992), *Child Care in Urban Thailand: Choice and Constraint in a Changing Society*, Bangkok, Thailand: Mahidol University.

——————(1994), 'The Impact of Child Care on Fertility in Urban Thailand', *Demography*, 31: 651–62.

Salaff, Janet (1981), *Working Daughters of Hong Kong: Filial Piety or Power in the Family?*, Cambridge: Cambridge University Press.

Sathar, Zeba, and Desai, Sonalde (1994), 'Work Patterns in Rural Pakistan: Intersections between Gender, Family and Class', paper presented at the Annual Meetings of the Population Association of America, Miami.

Sharma, Ursula (1980), *Women, Work and Property in North-West India*, New York: Tavistock Publications.

United Nations (1986), *Socioeconomic Development and Fertility Decline in Sri Lanka*, New York: United Nations.

——(1991), *The World's Women, Trends and Statistics: 1970–1990*, New York: United Nations.

Wolf, Diane L. (1991), 'Female Autonomy, the Family, and Industrialization in Java', in R. L. Blumberg (ed.), *Gender, Family and Economy: The Triple Overlap*, Newbury Park, Calif.: Sage Publications, 128–48.

Wong, Rebeca, and Levine, Ruth (1992), 'The Effect of Household Structure on Women's Economic Activity and Fertility: Evidence from Recent Mothers in Urban Mexico', *Economic Development and Cultural Change*, 41: 89–102.

World Bank (1993), *World Development Report 1993: Investing in Health*, Oxford: Oxford University Press.

——(1994), *World Development Report 1994: Infrastructure for Development*, Oxford: Oxford University Press.

Youssef, N. G. (1976), *Women and Work in Developing Societies*, Westport, Conn.: Greenwood Press.

7 Class and Gender in Rural Pakistan: Differentials in Economic Activity

Zeba Sathar and Sonalde Desai

Introduction

Despite substantial gains in per capita income in the last few decades, Pakistan continues to experience sharp inequalities in income. Regional inequalities in income are pronounced and, as Table 7.1 shows, pockets of poverty are concentrated in rural areas (Gazdar, Howes, and Zaidi 1994). While regional inequalities are the subject of continuous concern (Hasan and Pasha 1986; Malik 1991) gender-based inequalities in wealth, control over resources, opportunities for economic activity, and earnings by gender have rarely been addressed.

Consequently, research, public policies, and public perceptions all continue to view the household as a basic unit of analysis when discussing poverty and assume that the burden of poverty is equally shared by different members of a household. Thus, when discussing issues related to poverty, public discourse has focused mainly on inequalities based on social class. In contrast, discussions of gender inequality have focused mainly on discrimination against girls and women in health, nutrition, and education or on cultural practices constraining women's physical autonomy. In this chapter, we merge these two perspectives by addressing the question, 'Is women's experience of poverty qualitatively different from men's experience of poverty?'

In examining the male and female experience of poverty, we focus primarily on the difference in men's and women's patterns of economic activity. In this context, it is important to note the sensitive nature of female employment in South Asia, where the separation between the male and female sphere of activities is strong, where reported rates of economic activity are extremely low, and where patriarchal families usually preclude most females from making independent decisions regarding work outside the home. Against this backdrop, gender differences in economic activities represent a delicate balance between social and economic pressures. Social pressures favour women's isolation from the labour force in order to ensure their segregation from unrelated males and restrict their physical mobility. Economic pressures favour women's participation in the labour force in order to generate and supplement

Table 7.1. Estimates of poverty for Pakistan by region over time[a]

	Urban	Rural
1984–5	38.8	45.6
1991	31.4	34.5

[a] These figures represent the head count of persons below the poverty line of Rs.288 (for a family of 2 adults and 4 children) per capita per month at 1991–2 rural prices.

Source: Gazdar, Howes, and Zaidi (1994).

household income and to meet household labour requirements, particularly requirements for agricultural labour. Since the balance between social and economic pressures is likely to differ across economic classes, the purpose here is to focus on poor women and their choices, or lack thereof, in terms of income generation.

In a departure from usual procedures, we not only address the issue of gender differences in employment within households but also look at the likelihood of interdependence between employment of males and females in the same household. We ask whether women are independent actors making their own labour force participation decisions or merely part of the 'surplus' labour force assigned to do whatever men cannot or do not want to do. Additionally, we ask whether this interdependence is greater and the choices narrower for women from less privileged classes.

This focus on poverty highlights the dilemma women face in balancing social considerations against economic ones. In the case of Bangladesh, increasing landlessness and poverty have led to almost a revolution in terms of the proportions of women who are now involved in waged employment in road works, garment industries, and income-generation schemes. Even within Pakistan the rapidly increasing participation of women in the urban informal sector is a result of increasing economic pressures for women to supplement family income or to support themselves when they are widowed or divorced (Kazi and Raza 1991). Similar pressures are likely to change the balance of social-economic trade-offs in rural Pakistan as well. The results from this chapter will provide insights on where and among which groups we can expect the change to begin.

Data and Methods

The results presented in this chapter are drawn from the Pakistan Integrated Household Survey (PIHS) conducted in 1991. Based on the World Bank Liv-

ing Standards Measurement Surveys format, this survey was designed ex-
pressly to assess levels of living and poverty in Pakistan. The survey comprises
a national sample of 4,711 households in both urban and rural areas. Since this
chapter is restricted to rural Pakistan, we utilize data from 2,397 households
representing the rural sector. In particular we focus on the work patterns of
6,394 men and 5,825 women aged 10 and above who live in these households.

Apart from detailed modules on consumption and expenditure, the PIHS
utilized special modules on time use and labour on family farms and other
enterprises owned by households in order to ensure that family-based employment was not missed out. In addition, the PIHS, unlike the usual Labour Force
Surveys in Pakistan, involved specially trained female enumerators who
directly questioned women. In the past, men usually answered questions relating to female family members. This departure from convention is expected to
yield much more accurate information on female employment. The additional questions designed to capture economic activities and the addition of
female enumerators makes this an ideal data-set for investigating the work
patterns of women. The PIHS also collected data on women's domestic activities, such as time spent on cooking, fetching water, and caring for children. At
the household level, information was also collected on the educational and
employment patterns of all individuals. We are also able to assess, at the household level, the composition and structure, land ownership, land-tenure status,
and aggregate levels of household expenditure.

Although we provide some descriptive statistics for household expenditure,
we have based our definition of social class mainly on ownership of means of
production, for two reasons:

1. we define social class in a classical sense, and consequently focus mainly
   on the ownership of means of production—land, cattle, and business
   enterprise or petty shop;
2. given our interest in studying the determinants of economic activity, using
   income or expenditure as one of the indicators of social class would not
   be appropriate, since economic activity determines income rather than
   the other way around.

Most of rural Pakistan's economy is comprised of agriculture. However, the
non-agricultural sector has been expanding considerably since the last decade,
when there were only a handful of commercial non-agricultural enterprises
apart from mills and factories involved in processing or marketing agricultural produce located in rural areas. In spite of land reform legislation in 1959
and 1972, land distribution is highly skewed. Even after these reforms, it has
been shown that nearly 30 per cent of agricultural land is owned by large farmers, who constitute only 0.5 per cent of the total number of landowners in the
country (Hussain 1989). Smaller-sized landholdings are more common. Land
ownership patterns are particularly skewed in rural Sindh and in Southern
Punjab.

Generally, rural households can be stratified in terms of social class by size of land owned, in combination with other land-tenurial arrangements: households owning land which they cultivate; households that are sharecroppers (usually turning over half the output to the landlord) but do not own land; or households that neither own nor cultivate land. Some of those households who have no access to land either through ownership or tenancy own and live off livestock or a family business; a substantial proportion have no assets at all. There can be some overlap between the categorization of households and consequently household members from any class can be engaged in different types of employment (e.g. both waged labour and farm labour).

In this chapter, our categorization of social class is based on a combination of land-tenure and other asset ownership statuses. In order to obtain this classification, we combined various pieces of economic information about these rural households. The combined category consists of landowners, tenant farmers (sharecroppers) who do not own any land, families for whom land ownership information is missing, landless families who own livestock, landless families who own a business or petty shop, and landless families who own neither livestock nor a business.

Table 7.2 shows some of the characteristics associated with this classification, such as real income[1] (calculated by the World Bank by using a combination of expenditure and consumption items for each household, adjusting for regional price variations). As column 1 in Table 2 indicates, sharecroppers and

Table 7.2. Real expenditure levels by economic categories and by region for rural Pakistan, 1991

	Real monthly expenditure (Rs.) (1)	Monthly per capita expenditure (Rs.) (2)	Number of persons in household (3)
Economic Categories			
Landless	2,940	547	6.2
Sharecropper	3,021	433	8.0
Livestock	3,719	572	6.9
Business	3,253	475	7.4
Landowners	4,055	509	8.4
Missing information	4,373	591	8.7
Region			
Sindh	3,251	535	7.1
NWFP	4,470	473	9.1
Baluchistan	3,977	528	8.6
Punjab	3,251	511	7.1

Source: Pakistan Integrated Household Survey (PIHS), 1991.

landless households are the poorest, while landowners and families with missing data on landholding pattern are the richest, with business- and livestock-owning families falling in between. High incomes of families with missing land data suggests that families with large farms may be more reluctant to reveal the size of their holdings, possibly due to land ceiling legislation.[2]

But absolute household expenditure differences do not always translate into per capita expenditure differences, since household size differs across these different social classes. When looking at per capita expenditure, landless families do not appear to be quite so poor. The existence of small families among landless households is intriguing since it may be due to lower fertility, higher migration, or higher family fragmentation. This pattern will be further investigated in future research. In general, the proportion of young children (under 15) to adults is very similar across all classes. The substantially higher household size in landowning households, those with missing information on land size, and sharecropper households versus landless households is likely to reflect a tendency of the landless not to live in extended households. The former three categories consist of a substantially greater number of both adults and children.

The regional classification of households shows Punjab to be the poorest and NWFP (North-West Frontier Province) seems to be by far the richest in absolute household expenditure. In terms of per capita expenditure, however, Sindh seems to be the richest. In results not reported here, we observed that South Punjab was considerably poorer than North Punjab. North Punjab has the highest per capita expenditure in the country.

The dependent variables used in this analysis consist of several dimensions of economic activity: overall labour force participation; participation in the 'inside' domain of economic work, consisting of work on the family farm or in the family business; and 'outside' work for wages, whether in agricultural labour or in the non-agricultural workforce. Additionally, we also present descriptive statistics for the intensity of participation by reporting the hours spent on each type of economic activity in the week prior to the survey. This information is reported purely for descriptive purposes for those individuals who participated in the labour force and is not analysed in multi-variate analyses.

Tables 7.3 through 7.5 report descriptive statistics on level of economic activity by independent variables of interest. Tables 7.6 through 7.9 report results from logistic regressions, with participation in each type of economic activity as well as overall participation as the dependent variables.

Findings

Women's work across class in rural Pakistan

The under-enumeration of women's work in the context of rural Pakistan is a recognized deficiency which reflects deeply ingrained values of women themselves, their household members, and enumerators (Afzal and Nasir 1987). According to the most recently conducted census, taken in 1981, only 2 per cent of women were economically active. The recording of women's economic activity is particularly problematic in areas such as the informal sector and in the agricultural sector, where many tasks undertaken by women are classified as productive activities when undertaken by men but are classified and reported as household work when done by women. Examples of such activities range from cutting wheat to fetching firewood to milking cows and selling eggs.

It is widely known and acknowledged that low reported levels of economic activity are due to a combination of two factors:

1. restrictive definitions of economic activities exclude many of the activities done by women;
2. male interviewers are unable to question women directly and so rely on proxy reports by male members of the family, who frequently under-report female activities because of the cultural mores discouraging women's economic participation.

The PIHS data allow us to tackle both these problems: the detailed employment questions separately asked for unpaid family workers on the family farm or business, and the detailed time-use module specially administered to women by female interviewers, allow a broader definition of women's work and account for a variety of economically productive activities. Though a range of activities are included as economically oriented, we differentiate between work on family farms or in a family enterprise from waged work outside the home. This distinction is particularly important from the viewpoint of receiving remuneration for work performed and also from the viewpoint of leaving the confines of the home or family-owned fields, which of course is connected with women's mobility and extra-familial dealings and exposure.

The most important finding from the PIHS is that over 40 per cent of females over the age of 10 are engaged in some type of economically productive activity in rural areas. This level of participation is much higher than that recorded in other national-sample labour force surveys but is close to the figure yielded by the Agricultural Census of 1980. The next two most pressing questions are how pervasive female employment is and whether economic activity among women is restricted to any particular economic class. Table 7.3 shows that there is significant variation in the level of female economic activity across the major agricultural status classifications—however, the pattern is not necessarily the one that would have been expected a priori.

Essentially, women belonging to sharecropping households have the highest overall level of economic activity, followed by those whose families own land and next by those whose families own livestock. Though this level is substantially lower for women whose households have a family business, even these women have a 34 per cent economic activity rate. The economic

Table 7.3. Levels of economic activity by type of work, gender, and economic class, rural Pakistan, 1991 (%)

Economic class	Work on own farm in agriculture		Work in own business		Non-agricultural wage work		Agricultural wage work		All work	
	Male	Female	Male	Female	Male	Female	Male	Female	Male	Female
Landless	2	6	1	3	52	5	4	3	57	16
Sharecroppers	63	53	5	4	11	1	3	10	75	56
Livestock	30	41	0	4	35	3	7	10	61	48
Business	18	22	45	10	14	2	3	7	65	34
Landowners	53	46	6	4	15	0	1	4	67	50
Information missing on land	45	45	3	5	16	4	2	13	60	52
All	37	36	11	5	23	2	3	7	65	43

Source: Pakistan Integrated Household Survey (PIHS) 1991.

activity rate is lowest for those rural households that own neither land, live-stock, nor business. Since this group is composed of many households that are essentially assetless and therefore quite poor, it is interesting to note that many women do not work even though they certainly must feel strong economic pressures to do so. Lack of access to means of production precludes women in this group from being involved in economic activity.

While sharecroppers do belong to the poorest of households and are extremely vulnerable in the feudal structure (living off rented land or the land-lord's land for just a share of the produce) they still have access to some land and therefore to a source of livelihood. Landowners, no matter how small their holdings, are better off in terms of land tenure status. There is even a similar-ity between sharecropping and landowning households: in both, women engage substantially in farm work. Assetless households are the ones where women make very little contribution to economic activity.

The Interaction of Class and Gender: Differential employment patterns of males and females across class

The next question is whether the impact of social class on opportunities to earn income is the same for men and women. Here the results are again unex-pected. Both men and women are most likely to work in agriculture on their own farms (Table 7.3). However, in the other three categories of work, gen-der differences are pronounced. Men are more likely to work in a family busi-ness than women, whereas women are more likely to work as agricultural wage labourers than men. However, the gender differences in these two activities are minor compared to the gender differences in non-agricultural work. While a substantial 23 per cent of males do non-agricultural wage work, only a minus-cule 2 per cent of women are found in the corresponding category. This dif-ference encompasses the full range of reasons leading to the asymmetry behind women's and men's work: wage work involves leaving home and often migrating to urban areas and is therefore not 'desirable' from the point of view of female seclusion and sex segregation; employers may generally prefer men, who are readily available for these jobs; non-agricultural wage work pays sub-stantially more than agricultural wage work and hence women are shut out of these occupations; and family demands reduce women's willingness to work in jobs requiring a substantial amount of travel time. In contrast, agricultural labour is usually seasonal in nature and low-paying—for both these reasons it is more readily accepted by the same potential pool of women, who may ide-ally prefer better-paid non-agricultural wage work.

Given the divergence in work patterns of males and females in rural Pak-istan, it is likely that class and gender interact to produce differing class employment patterns for men. For a start, the majority of males, regardless of class, engage in economic activity. Of course this is not in the least bit sur-prising, since men are regarded as the primary breadwinners. Men from sharecropping households work the most, followed by landowners and those who own businesses. Men from those households without assets such as land, livestock, and business work the least but are still many times more likely to be involved in economic activity compared to females in those households (Table 7.3). This is because this group of men are most likely to be involved in wage work, which as we have already pointed out is a domain mostly closed to women in rural areas.

It is interesting to add that regional differences in work patterns are almost as stark for men as for women. Men and women in NWFP and Baluchistan are much less likely to work than those in Punjab and Sindh. Regional differences in women's economic activities presented in Table 7.4 also show some contrasting patterns. The poorest regions, rural Sindh and Punjab, contain the largest proportions of women agricultural wage workers. Economic activity among women is lowest in NWFP and Baluchistan, where cultural reasons may be strong in preventing women from being involved in economic activities, particularly outside the home. It must be remembered that to a large extent the high rate of wage work in Sindh and Punjab reflects the greater availability of cotton-picking, which has recently been taking up a greater share of agricultural production.

Next, we consider the intensity of activity in terms of hours worked (Table 7.5). The average hours worked by women are longest for those who have no land, business, or livestock. In fact it is worth noting that these hours are 50 per cent longer than those worked by women whose families own land. It is likely that women from 'assetless' families who do work are most likely to belong to the poorest households while those women whose husbands are in relatively better-paid farm jobs may be most likely not to work at all. Women belonging to sharecropping households also work longer hours, as do those

Table 7.4. Levels of economic activity by type of work, gender, and region, rural Pakistan, 1991 (%)

Region	Work on own farm		Work in own business		Non-agricultural wage work		Agricultural wage work	
	Male	Female	Male	Female	Male	Female	Male	Female
Sindh	45	44	6	5	24	3	4	8
NWFP	26	38	12	4	24	0	1	2
Baluchistan	21	27	6	5	25	1	2	1
North Punjab	40	36	15	5	23	2	4	5
South Punjab	39	26	50	8	18	1	2	16
All	37	36	11	5	23	2	3	7

Source: Pakistan Integrated Household Survey (PIHS), 1991.

Table 7.5. Work patterns of men and women by selected characteristics, rural Pakistan, 1991

	Participation in all economic work (%)		Hours of work per week		Hours of household work per week
	Males	Females	Males	Females	Females
Provinces					
Punjab	68	42	44	21	31
Sindh	71	51	47	23	38
NWFP	55	39	45	16	30
Baluchistan	53	31	47	20	27
Agro-climatic Region					
Rain-fed	68	43	45	22	33
Irrigated	61	44	46	18	31
Family type					
Complex	67	42	47	21	34
Nuclear	67	48	46	21	37
Extended	66	42	44	21	30
Laterally extended	62	40	44	17	26
Economic class					
Missing information	60	52	48	28	37
No land/business/livestock	57	16	48	26	34
No land or business, but livestock	61	48	52	19	33
No land, but business	65	34	43	24	31
Sharecropper	75	56	43	24	32
Landowner	67	50	41	17	31
Total	65	43	45	20	32

Source: Pakistan Integrated Household Survey (PIHS), 1991.

women whose households have a family business. Women in livestock-owning households work relatively fewer hours, as do women from land-owning households.

In contrast to females, there is lesser variation in the average number of hours worked by males in different economic categories: nevertheless land-owning men work the shortest hours and surprisingly those that own livestock work the longest hours. The difference in the hours worked by sharecroppers and landowners is not substantial for males. It is interesting to note that males from 'assetless' households work approximately the overall average number of hours, while women in this category work the longest hours. This confirms that while men in this group, regardless of poverty, do work and their average hours worked therefore even out, in the case of women only those really on the fringes of survival take up work which is long and tedious.

In a multi-variate analysis for hours of work (not reported here) we found different employment outcomes for males and females by economic category in rural areas. 'Assetless' women are certainly more circumscribed in their opportunities for work and when they do find work, they have to put in long hours. Almost all members of sharecropping households work long hours but women in these households seem to work especially longer hours.

At this point it is also necessary to point out that although women seemingly spend shorter hours engaged in economic activity, almost all women spend a considerable number of hours in household work, which extends from fetching water to repairing the house to cooking, cleaning, and caring for children. Women on average do about 32 hours of domestic work in a week: furthermore, this average does not vary much at all across households belonging to different economic categories.

A strong manifestation of patriarchal society is that women's economic activity within groups may be highly dependent on men's economic activity. This can be seen most clearly in the differences in employment patterns between rain-fed and irrigated areas. In the former areas, participation in waged work by men is much higher because of the decidedly subsistence nature of farming, and the search for jobs leads to frequent out-migration of males. Women are then left with the responsibility of assuming most farm duties. A large proportion of them participate in farm work and they work longer hours on average than women in the irrigated areas. In the irrigated areas, where farming is more intensive, there is less of a trade-off between men's and women's work in the agricultural sector.

Multi-variate analysis of female labour force participation (Table 7.6) more or less reinforces earlier findings: women from households involved in livestock and in business are more likely to participate in economic work (including family work) than women in land-owning families. Women from households with no assets or those who own livestock or are sharecroppers are the ones most likely to participate in wage work. Differences in household work are not striking or particularly significant. Regional variations in women's participation in economic work are also maintained.

The corresponding analysis for males presented in Table 7.7 reaffirms that social class has quite a different impact on their labour force participation. Men from business-owning families are most likely to work but men from poor households are more heavily engaged in wage work. All other groups fall in between, in terms of intensities of wage work and own farm/business work.

Other intervening factors which influence female employment

If education is to be regarded as an additional variable ranking persons by class, assuming that those with some education in rural Pakistan are unlikely

Table 7.6. Logit analysis of female labour force participation, rural Pakistan, 1991

	All work participation	Wage work participation	Family work participation	Household work participation
Constant	-1.61**	-3.19**	-2.02**	1.31**
Rain-fed (Irrigated area omitted)	0.22**	-0.60**	0.34**	0.12
Province (Punjab omitted)				
Sindh	0.31**	-0.33**	0.50**	-0.27*
NWFP	-0.36**	-1.58**	-0.09	0.19
Baluchistan	-0.89**	-1.63**	-0.68**	-0.14
Economic Class (Landowner omitted)				
Missing information	-0.19	1.39**	-0.23	-0.36
No land/business/livestock	-1.82**	0.65**	-2.48**	-0.04
No land or business, but livestock	1.72**	0.47**	2.24**	0.13
No land, but business (may have livestock)	1.18**	0.05	1.69**	-0.10
Sharecropper	0.10	0.85**	0.07	-0.09
Operational land size in acres	0.00	0.00	0.00	0.00
Age				
Age	0.12**	0.06**	0.14**	0.13**
Age squared	0.00**	0.00**	0.00**	0.00**
Education (No education omitted)				
Primary education	-0.90**	-0.97**	-0.76**	-1.05**
Post-primary education	-1.15**	-1.13**	-1.12**	-0.60**
Chi-square (14df)	1,003	310	1,137	712

* $p \leq 0.05$.
** $p \leq 0.01$.

Source: Estimates by the authors.

Table 7.7.   Logit analysis of male labour force participation, rural Pakistan, 1991

	All work participation	Wage work participation	Family work participation
Constant	−2.66**	−5.09**	−1.96**
	−0.08	0.22**	−0.33*
Rain-fed (Irrigated area omitted)			
Province (Punjab omitted)			
Sindh	0.10	−0.11	0.18*
NWFP	−0.70**	−0.12	−0.64**
Baluchistan	−0.96**	−0.19	−1.05**
Economic Class (Landowner omitted)			
Missing information	−0.67**	−0.02	−0.64**
No land/business/livestock	−0.79**	1.98**	−4.52**
No land or business, but livestock	0.39**	−0.58**	3.23**
No land, but business			
(may have livestock)	0.61**	−2.07	4.31**
Sharecropper	0.17	−0.18	0.16*
Operational land size in acres	0.00	−0.01**	0.00**
Age			
Age	0.26**	0.23**	0.16**
Age squared	0.00**	0.00**	0.00**
Education (No education omitted)			
Primary education	−0.37**	−0.24*	−0.20*
Post primary education	−0.47**	0.03	−0.52**
Chi-square (14df)	1,718	1,441	2,110

*$p \leq 0.05$.
**$p \leq 0.01$.
Source: Estimates by the authors.

to belong to poor families, then the results from Tables 7.6 and 7.7 show that education reduces both wage and family work for males and particularly for females. If education is to be viewed at all as a class variable, then it would imply that receiving an education in the rural setting reduces the pressure for work and certainly its intensity in terms of hours worked. While for women it can be argued that education may simply be viewed as a source of social status, certainly for males it is viewed as a vehicle for enhancing employment prospects and income.

The provincial results confirm the predominance of female waged work in Punjab and the much greater prevalence of farm work in the other three

Table 7.8. Logit analysis of female labour force participation, rural Pakistan, 1991

	All work participation	Outside work participation	Inside work participation	Domestic work participation
Number of males aged 10–15	–0.05	–0.21**	–0.01	0.00
Number of females aged 10–15	–0.03	0.14*	–0.06	–0.20**
Number of adult males	–0.12**	–0.20**	–0.10**	–0.03
Number of adult females	–0.07*	0.00	–0.07*	–0.09*
Chi-square (18df)	1,088	362	1,198	742

$*p < 0.05.$
$**p < 0.01.$

Source: Estimates by the authors.

poorer provinces, excepting Baluchistan. Unfortunately the data do not permit disaggregation of economic categories at the provincial level but it is quite well known that women in Baluchistan and in some parts of North-West Frontier Province do face far more constraints on entering employment.

As pointed out already, men are regarded as the prime breadwinners, while the economic activities of women are usually regarded as subsidiary earners. In the best-off households, women pride themselves on not having the 'need' to work, while in the poorest households—where the need for generating income is strongest—women's access to economic activity is severely restricted. The effect of employment patterns of males on the levels of women's economic activity can be seen in Table 7.8, where the number of males (both those aged 10–15 and those aged 15 and older) have a significant negative impact on the 'outside work' of females in that family. The presence of additional females does not have a significant negative impact on the 'outside work' of women but on domestic work. The number of adult males also has a strong negative impact on the own farm/business work of women.

While it is usually assumed that men in a patriarchal society are the primary providers it seems that women do share this responsibility to a considerable extent. Larger families, particularly those with greater numbers of adult men and women, reduce the burden of work for male members (Table 7.9). Family size is related to family structure. Typically, nuclear households tend to be smaller and hence the burden of work—both outside and domestic work—is greater for women living in nuclear families. Living in extended families can be beneficial to men as well, since the presence of other men to take over the household farm chores seems to encourage other men in the family to seek

Table 7.9. Logit analysis of male labour force participation, rural Pakistan, 1991

	All work participation	Outside work participation	Inside work participation
Number of males aged 10–15	–0.18**	–0.21**	–0.02
Number of females aged 10–15	–0.08**	–0.05	–0.02
Number of adult males	–0.10**	0.06*	–0.19**
Number of adult females	0.00	0.07*	–0.03
Chi-square (18df)	1,804	1,483	2,235

$*p < 0.05.$
$**p < 0.01.$

Source: Estimates by the authors.

off-farm employment. The presence of other men—brothers, sons, or father—may also allow related males to migrate in search of better-paying opportunities, particularly if this means migration to a nearby town. Interestingly, the presence of young boys reduces overall work but also the chances of doing off-farm work among related males.

Discussion

The PIHS data have enabled us to document empirical evidence in support of the widespread involvement of rural women in economic activity. Though women across all the major economic groups do work, and size of landholding surprisingly does not make much of a difference in whether landed women do or do not work, the type of work undertaken and the length of hours spent on it are significantly different across classes. This observed pattern is not similarly reflected in patterns of male economic activity.

Though segregation by sex is regarded as highly desirable, it seems that inside work (i.e. work on one's own business or farm) is hardly regarded as economic activity. In a patriarchal set-up where the head of household totally controls earnings, these women are essentially unpaid family helpers who do not receive any remuneration for their work. No conflict arises to threaten the supremacy of the patriarchal family. The possibility of change in the status quo occurs primarily when men seeking wage employment have to migrate and leave farming or businesses in the hands of women. Then the evidence does show that power changes hands and women begin to play an active role (Friedman and Wei 1988). Otherwise, 'inside' work can hardly be expected to empower women; it certainly does not necessarily give them direct access to earnings.

But let us consider what may fast become the more crucial role of 'outside' work. At present, with only slight changes in the rural areas (with the exception of the considerable out-migration of men, which is concentrated in non-irrigated areas), opportunities for outside work are concentrated in agricultural wage work. This is menial work, low-paid and seasonal. However, women—particularly those living in cotton-picking areas—may end up receiving considerable cash in hand for their labour. Here there is a possibility that with increasing labour shortages in rural Pakistan, women's labour may become increasingly crucial and valuable. At the moment this type of work is being performed by the poorest women with the fewest options. Their families are left with little or no choice but to allow them to accept this lowest rung of work. Here is an instance where segregation from strange men stops being an issue because of dire poverty.

The most striking result from this chapter is the supporting evidence that barely any women in rural Pakistan are involved in non-agricultural wage work. Not only are opportunities for such employment rare, they also involve travelling long distances and/or living away from home, which are options not normally available to women. Also, non-agricultural wage work usually requires some minimal level of education, and we know that educational rates, especially for adult women in rural areas, are exceedingly low.

However, this is an area where change can be expected because, while until recently the demand for girls' schooling was very weak, it is now on the rise. While one strong positive reason for educating boys was that it would enable them to find jobs, this reason was usually not given for schooling girls. The evidence is clear that given economic pressures on a family most households would certainly give preference to spending on their sons' schooling over their daughters' (Sathar and Lloyd 1993). But as already pointed out this trend may be changing. In addition, there may be an expansion in job opportunities specifically for females in the non-farm wage sector as a result of recently launched schemes to recruit village family planning and health workers and female teachers. All of these new positions will need to be filled by women with at least a minimum of primary-level education. At present, education is hardly linked to expansion of job opportunities. Hence, parents mainly seek to educate girls so that they will make better mothers and housewives. This is not a significant motivation, particularly when sons also have to be educated.

At the moment, family structures, low educational attainment, and lack of remunerative employment possibilities restrict women to working in the home or on the family farm, and thus contribute to the low status of Pakistani girls and women vis-à-vis that of men. Any changes would require substantial expansion of wage opportunities. Agricultural wage work opportunities are limited and tend to be seasonal, for both men and women. Moreover, wages in this sector are also low. Hence, even in the rural areas, the only possibilities of expansion are in the non-agricultural sector. This would provide a niche for educated girls in rural areas and provide them with opportunities of generating a substantial income for their families without having to migrate to urban areas. Until now, unlike urban women, the handful of educated women living in rural areas have been unlikely to have any power within their households or any additional status in society apart from that acquired through husbands and fathers.

Conclusions

In conclusion, several points emerge from this analysis. Women in rural areas do participate widely in economic activities; their work is certainly much more integral to households and the economy than the contribution of urban women. Women from almost all classes do work, but the burden of long hours of work is greatest amongst the poorest groups, i.e. the sharecroppers and those households that do not own land, livestock, or any business.

Women from the poorest households have very few choices; they are the most likely to have to take up agricultural wage work, since more remunerative non-agricultural wage work is practically non-existent for females. Most importantly, since poor women's families do not own many assets (particularly land, where they could undertake 'inside' work), they are the ones who are most likely to undertake 'outside' work or who are left with little or no access to economic activity.

Education does not lead to greater chances of economic activity for males or females. While in the case of males it can be argued that they have to work fewer hours but are able to make up for this in terms of remuneration, in the case of females there are hardly any opportunities for highly remunerated work based on educational skills. The only positive change which can be expected to overthrow the status quo in rural Pakistan, where feudal structures and social and economic hierarchies predominate, is for the demand for female education to rise due to the increase in job opportunities in the waged sector in rural areas. This would re-arrange the existing unequal job structure, in which long hours of low-paid work is the only option for poor women in rural areas. The results presented in this chapter suggest that the burden of poverty and lack of rural development is disproportionately borne by women. Access to productive resources, particularly land, provides women with their only means of generating income for themselves and their families. Although a similar process operates for men, a large proportion of men manage to find work in the non-agricultural sector. Hence, belonging to a 'land-poor' household (one of the key indicators of poverty) does not have the same negative consequences for men as it does for women. Similarly, lack of non-agricultural employment opportunities in rural areas has substantial negative consequences for women, both in terms of their ability to find work and in terms of parental motivation to educate women.

These results point to a need to locate gender inequality in the context of such institutional and developmental issues as distribution of land and control over productive resources, rural development and opportunities for non-agricultural work, and agricultural productivity. Thus, although both men and women are deeply affected by macro-processes influencing the nature of the rural economy as a whole, gender inequality in the family and society and cultural norms circumscribing women's physical movement limit women's ability to cope with the negative consequences associated with these macro-processes.

Notes

1. Given the seasonal variability in income and the difficulties in computing farm income, expenditure has increasingly been used as a proxy for income. Underlying this approach is the rationale that expenditure patterns are based on long-term permanent income and are free from seasonal variation.
2. However, the number of families with missing data on landholding is very small, approximately 4% of our sample, and in the rest of this chapter we rarely discuss the results for this category.

References

Afzal, Muhammad, and Nasir, M. (1987), 'Is Female Labour Force Participation Really Low and Declining in Pakistan? A Look at Alternative Data Sources', *Pakistan Development Review*, 26.

Gazdar, H., Howes, S., and Zaidi, S. (1994), 'Poverty in Pakistan: Measurement, Trends and Patterns', paper prepared for the World Bank, mimeo.

Hasan, T., and Pasha, H. (1986), 'Development Rankings of Districts in Pakistan', in I. Nabi (ed.), *The Quality of Life in Pakistan: Studies in Social Sector Economics*, Lahore: Vanguard.

Hussain, Akmal (1989), 'Pakistan: Land Reforms Reconsidered', in Hazma Alvi and John Harriss (eds.), *Sociology of 'Developing Societies': South Asia*, Houndsmills, England: Macmillan, 59–69.

Kazi, S., and Raza, B. (1991), 'Duality of Female Employment in Pakistan', *Pakistan Development Review*, 30: 733–40.

Malik, S. J. (1991), 'Poverty in Pakistan 1984–85 and 1987–88', in M. Lipton and J. van der Gaag (eds.), *Including the Poor*, Oxford: Oxford University Press, 487–519.

Pakistan, National Institute of Population Studies (1992), *Pakistan Demographic and Health Survey, 1990/1991*, Islamabad: National Institute of Population Studies.

Sathar, Z., and Lloyd, C. (1993), *Who Gets Primary Schooling in Pakistan? Inequalities among and within Families*, New York: Population Council.

8 Female Migration in Relation to Female Labour Force Participation: Implications for the Alleviation of Poverty

Hania Zlotnik

According to the World Bank, more than a billion people live in poverty, struggling to survive on very low incomes, and the weight of poverty falls more heavily on certain groups, particularly on women who, as members of poor households, are generally faced with heavier workloads than men, are less educated, and have less access to remunerative activities (World Bank 1990). Although progress has been made in raising average incomes, the problem of ensuring that major sectors of society do not fall behind in terms of having access to an adequate income has been less tractable. Given that migration has generally been viewed as a process through which people can improve their likelihood of earning better wages (Todaro 1976), it is pertinent to enquire to what extent it has been or can be a means of combating poverty.

Undoubtedly, the final decades of the twentieth century have witnessed a sharp increase in population mobility. As is increasingly recognized, the process of development itself puts in motion forces that give rise to migration and, since a growing number of countries have embarked on such a process, large-scale movements of people have ensued. Both men and women have moved either within their countries or internationally in search of better economic opportunities. Migration statistics, despite their many deficiencies, indicate that the number of migrant women at the world level is comparable to that of men (United Nations 1993). Yet, it is only recently that the participation of women in migration has begun to be considered from an economic perspective. Not only has the general tendency to disregard women's work as 'non-productive' militated against considering female migration in relation to economic activity but, in addition, the observation that most women migrate for non-economic reasons has provided a strong rationale for ignoring their economic roles. Indeed, so ingrained is the view that women's migration matters little that even the women themselves tend to downplay their role in it and most of the sparse information available on reasons for migration tend to validate the view that women generally migrate to accompany or join family members or to get married (United Nations 1993). However, the fact that high proportions of men also do so has not prevented researchers from assuming that men can act as independent decision-makers intent on maximizing the economic gains that migration may bring.

In fact, both men and women are subject to a variety of constraints that impinge upon the decision to migrate, not least the extent to which they have assets at their disposal or the necessary skills to make the best of a new environment. In that respect, women are disadvantaged, since they generally lack control over resources, have limited access to income of their own, and tend to be poorer in human capital because they lack educational opportunities. In conditions of poverty, those disadvantages become accentuated and are likely to curtail the possibility of migration. Indeed, despite the common claim that poverty is a major cause of migration, the evidence suggests that as the degree of deprivation rises the likelihood of migration declines (Rodgers 1984). Yet, when the majority of a country's population can be classified as poor, it is not surprising to find that the poor also predominate among migrants and the issue is to determine if migration is a means of reducing their level of deprivation.

Unfortunately, the ideal data needed to assess the role of migration in alleviating or reducing poverty are not generally available. One of the difficulties lies in the fact that migration is a punctual event, while poverty may be long-lasting if not structural in nature. Thus, although migration may bring about a positive change in the economic status of a migrant or a household, that change may not be sufficient to get the person or persons involved out of poverty and keep them thus in the long run. In addition, the methods used to ascertain poverty status are difficult to reconcile with the approaches used to study migration and therefore preclude a direct assessment of the relations between both. Because this point has particular relevance for the study of female migration in relation to poverty, it will be addressed in some detail below.

The Measurement of Poverty

Traditionally, poverty status has been determined in terms of income. Since in most societies a large proportion of the population receives no income on an individual basis, income is measured at the household level. Household income is generally estimated by aggregating the income received by each and every household member over a specified period. Since households with the same income may have very different standards of living, depending on the number of household members involved, household income is then adjusted for household composition. Adjustments may also be made for price differentials across space and over time, and for the use of assets (by imputing rents, for instance, to owner-occupied property). To determine which households are poor, a standard level of income is established by determining the cost of goods and services that are deemed essential for the well-being of a household. Households whose income falls below the standard, which is usually denominated the 'poverty line', are then considered poor (Bilsborrow, De Graff, and Anker 1992).

Although this approach to determine who is poor accords well with a general concept of poverty, it is less than ideal for application in developing countries where significant proportions of the goods consumed and the services used do not derive from market activities. Thus, subsistence farming for family consumption, the free gathering of food or fuel, and the production of food and goods at home for family use would not be reflected in household income and would bias results, the more so since the importance of productive activities in the home tends to increase as the income of the household declines (Bilsborrow, De Graff, and Anker 1992). Since women are generally in charge of performing the activities that are not reflected in household income, it is their work that goes unrecorded and that produces misleading assessments of the degree of poverty. However, one may argue that women only engage in those activities because they are poor and are therefore deprived of alternatives. Poverty thus appears to be a multi-faceted condition that is not easily summarized by a single indicator such as household income.

It is in order to reflect the various aspects of poverty that the basic needs approach to its measurement was developed. Although the identification of what constitutes a 'basic need' has been a matter of some debate and the list of basic needs considered has varied from one context to another, the aim is to set minimum standards regarding food consumption, type of housing, and access to public services (Bilsborrow, De Graff, and Anker 1992). Thus, in an application of the basic needs approach carried out in Colombia, four criteria were used to identify poor households. Households that fulfilled at least one of the specifications were considered poor. The criteria were:

1. inadequate housing, meaning housing with dirt floors in urban areas or housing built with precarious materials and having dirt floors in rural areas;
2. lack of water or sanitation;
3. overcrowding, meaning more than three persons per room;
4. lack of schooling, meaning that there was at least one child aged 7 to 11 who was a relative of the head of household and did not attend school (Fresnada 1991).

A survey showed that, according to the unsatisfied basic needs criteria just outlined, 37 per cent of the Colombian population was poor in 1988, a figure that is to be compared with the nearly 51 per cent that appeared as poor according to an income criterion. Persons belonging to households that were classified as poor with respect to both income and unsatisfied basic needs made up nearly 26 per cent of the population.

A common problem with the approaches outlined above is that their unit of analysis is the household. Consequently, they provide little information about women since, at most, they focus on the characteristics of the head of the household, who is generally a man. Although households headed by women are often more likely to be poor than those headed by men, the incidence of poverty depends also on other factors. For instance, in Colombia in 1988, female-headed households were less likely to be poor than male-headed households in rural areas, particularly if the women who were heads of households had children under age 5 with them. However, the reverse was true in urban areas, where female heads of household with young children were 28 per cent more likely to be poor than their male counterparts (see Table 8.1). This reversal of the differentials may be associated with migration, since it is likely that women living alone with young children in rural areas have husbands elsewhere earning a living and helping them to maintain a slightly better status than that of average male-headed households in rural areas. Unfortunately the survey report gives no indication of whether and to what extent migration is in play. The level of remittances, for instance, is not reported. However, the data do indicate that, for all types of households, the incidence of poverty is lower in urban areas. Rural–urban migration may thus be an effective strategy to improve one's economic standing.

Clearly, in contexts where migration is being used as a household survival strategy whereby selected members of the household migrate in order to secure the income needed to support those left behind, the tools used to measure poverty need to be more sensitive to the processes taking place. Although there is a sense that the role of migrant women in providing support to the family members left behind has been increasing, the data available on that issue are still too sparse to lead to solid conclusions. In particular, given that migrant women tend to be concentrated in low-income occupations and that their wages are generally lower than those of their male counterparts, it is not clear whether they are able to contribute as much as migrant men to the well-being of their non-migrant families in the place of origin. Some researchers argue that, despite their lower wages, migrant women have lower

Table 8.1.   Proportion of the population living in poverty, by sex of the head of the household, presence of children under 5, and place of residence, Colombia, 1998 (%)

Type of household	Total	Urban	Rural
All households	56.0	39.4	71.1
Man, without children	48.5	30.2	65.5
Woman, without children	47.1	33.6	64.0
Man, with children	71.1	56.8	81.5
Woman, with children	74.8	72.5	76.9

Source: Fresnada (1991: table 22).

expenditures at the place of destination and are able to save more for their families. It is also suggested that filial piety is stronger among daughters than among sons and, consequently, that the former are more reliable sources of income once they leave the place of origin (Hugo 1993, 1994; Lim 1994). Be that as it may, the fact is that a growing number of women are migrating on their own for the purpose of taking up employment and that migrant women in general tend to have higher labour force participation rates than non-migrants. It is therefore important to establish how migrant women fare in the labour market and whether migration is beneficial in terms of improving their employment opportunities.

This type of enquiry can usefully be tied to the consideration of a migrant woman's poverty status by noting that the characteristics of a person's employment are a fundamental determinant of the person's economic situation. Since poor persons have few assets other than their labour, the employment that they secure can be used as an indicator of their vulnerability in economic terms (Bilsborrow, De Graff, and Anker 1992). In particular, low-status occupations that are associated with low earnings and poor working conditions have proved to be closely associated with poverty. Though the association is not perfect, it will nevertheless be used in the rest of this chapter to assess the status of female migrants in terms of work and poverty.

Migrant Women and Work

Any attempt to carry out an international study of the labour force participation of women is hampered by the lack of comparability of the statistics available. Not only do the concepts and methods used to ascertain who is economically active vary from country to country but, in addition, there is a tendency to disregard the work performed by women on the grounds that it is not productive (Waring 1990). In developing countries and, particularly, in rural areas, women often work as 'unpaid family members', growing food or raising livestock for household consumption. Although their work is essential for family survival, they do not receive a salary and consequently tend to be excluded from labour force statistics.

Although considerable effort has been devoted to devising data collection techniques that can capture the true extent of the labour force participation of women (e.g. Dixon-Mueller 1985; Anker *et al.* 1988), their application has not yet been wide enough to generate a useful basis for international comparisons. Consequently, the data on the labour force participation of women are still generally weak and tend to indicate that the proportion of economically active women is still fairly low in most developing countries. Indeed, since 1970, the share of women in the labour force has changed little or shown a tendency to decline in most low-income countries. Increases have been more common among middle-income and upper middle-income countries, but in general women still account for relative low proportions of the labour force in formal employment. Even in high-income countries, women account for, on average, only 38 per cent of the labour force (World Bank 1994). It is therefore not surprising to find that migrant women also tend to account for low proportions of the migrant labour force and to display low rates of economic activity, although the latter are often higher than those of non-migrant women.

Since the 1970s, the number of women migrating specifically for employment reasons has been growing and that change has been attributed to the rise in manufacturing activities in certain countries. Because women have traditionally been under-represented among production workers, their share of the labour force in manufacturing remains low. However, it has been growing at very high rates in a number of developing countries, including Hong Kong, Peninsular Malaysia, the Philippines, Singapore, the Republic of Korea, and Thailand in South-East Asia; India, Nepal, Pakistan, and Sri Lanka in South Asia; Brazil, Costa Rica, the Dominican Republic, El Salvador, Honduras, Mexico, and Panama in Latin America; and Egypt in Africa (Zlotnik 1993). Several of those countries have been implementing a strategy aimed at fostering export-led growth which has involved, among other things, the establishment of export processing zones, that is, industrial sites operating under special legislation that allows the duty-free import of raw materials for the assembly and manufacture of goods which are primarily destined for export.

In 1986, 176 export processing zones were operating in 47 developing countries and they employed 1.9 million persons. About half of those employees were women directly engaged in the production process (Kreye, Heinrichs, and Frobel 1987). Although export processing zones have undoubtedly had an important effect on the incorporation of women, and particularly migrant women, into the industrial labour force, their impact on women's economic position has been mixed. On the one hand, export processing zones have provided jobs for unskilled women whose labour market prospects are generally dim. On the other, the conditions of employment typical of export processing zones have not been conducive to economic mobility or the improvement of skills. Thus, the majority of women working in export processing zones are young, single, and working in remunerated employment for the first time. They are preferred over other types of workers because their very characteristics provide good rationalizations for paying them low wages. Their lack of experience and the fact that they have no dependants and are therefore not 'primary wage earners' justifies their low salaries. Lack of promotion opportunities and the practice of dismissing workers if they get married or pregnant implies that the average length of women's employment in export processing zones is only a few years. Despite these drawbacks, export processing zones provide a better employment opportunity than the other two common areas of work for unskilled women: domestic service and informal activities.

Indeed, domestic service remains one of the major occupations of working women in developing countries. Historically, the economic and social changes brought about by industrialization increased the demand for female labour, not only in factories but, mainly, in the area of domestic work, which was considered a natural extension of the normal activities of women. Thus, in 1870, 50 per cent of all employed women in the United States were domestic workers and the equivalent proportion in England in 1901 was 40 per cent (Weinert 1991). In the course of time, the strong economic growth experienced by developed countries after the Second World War led to improved working conditions and the expansion of job opportunities for women in other sectors of the economy, so that the supply of workers willing to undertake domestic service virtually dried up. Today, most developed countries and some developing countries import foreign female workers to carry out such tasks. It is perhaps the sharp rise in the number of women migrating to become domestic workers abroad that has most attracted the attention of those studying the relations between female migration and economic activity.

Yet women have been migrating for centuries to become domestic workers. Most migration, however, has taken and still takes place within countries, and it is an indication of the lower status of migrants that they are generally more concentrated in domestic services than non-migrants. Given that, whenever women have a choice, they tend to avoid working in someone else's home as servants, the fact that women migrate in order to undertake such tasks suggests that they are driven more by necessity than by choice. That is indeed the finding of a survey carried out among foreign domestic workers in Caracas, Venezuela (Torrealba 1992). Among the female workers interviewed, 48 per cent declared that they were domestic workers because they needed to work, that is, to earn some income. A further 35 per cent indicated that domestic service was the only activity for which they had the necessary skills. The characteristics of the women concerned justified this view: 63 per cent had not completed primary education and a further 25 per cent had completed at most that level of education. Most had never worked in any other activity and the few who had done had generally been employed in the service sector as waitresses or sales personnel. In a number of cases, the women concerned had dropped out of school in order to start working, thereby jeopardizing their future employment prospects.

In general, the salaries reported by the women interviewed were low. Nearly four out of every five earned between US$6.00 and US$7.50 a day. Those who lived in received food and board free of charge but were also likely to work longer hours than those who lived out. Most of the women in the sample (83 per cent) had at least one child. Only 17 per cent of those who lived in their place of work had their children with them and even among those who lived elsewhere, 53 per cent did not live with their children. Most helped support their children by sending money or goods to the relatives that were taking care of them.

Although this survey refers only to Venezuela, the situation of domestic workers is similar the world over. Because domestic work is poorly regulated, the women performing it have few rights and almost no protection against abuses. In addition, the conditions of work prevent many women from having a normal family life and, because the low salaries paid are not conducive to improving the situation of the women's dependants, domestic work is at most a means of survival. However, domestic work may represent a better source of income than doing piecework at home or performing odd jobs in the informal sector. It may also be more profitable if performed in rich countries by migrants from less well-off places. That is undoubtedly one of the reasons propelling the rise of the participation of women in international labour migration during the past twenty years.

Domestic Service in the International Context

At the international level, domestic service provides women with one of the few opportunities to migrate legally as workers to rich countries. Indeed, countries that generally discourage the admission of unskilled migrant workers nevertheless admit domestic workers, often stipulating that they must be women. Legal admission both provides some guarantee of fair treatment for the prospective worker (minimum wages and access to health care are thus mandated) and binds that worker to a particular type of employment if not to a particular employer. Government regulations regarding the treatment of foreign domestic workers are therefore responsible for maintaining those workers in a dependent and low-status position.

Examples of countries that have special provisions to admit foreign domestic workers include the oil-producing countries of Western Asia, Hong Kong, Singapore, Canada, the United Kingdom, and the United States. In addition, the growing demand for domestic workers in countries that lack the necessary provisions to admit them or that apply those provisions restrictively has led to considerable undocumented migration of women willing to undertake domestic work. Thus, foreign domestic workers in countries such as Argentina, Italy, Spain, and Venezuela generally work illegally after having entered the country with a tourist visa. Regularization drives in those countries have allowed the legalization of the status of foreign domestic workers, but many remain undocumented. For that reason, it is difficult to know the true extent of the participation of international female migrants in domestic work.

According to the 1980 Census of Argentina, 39,400 foreign-born persons worked in domestic service, representing 5.3 per cent of the economically active international migrants in the country at the time. The distribution by sex of those workers is not given, but they are likely to be mostly women. According to data classified by country of origin, persons born in Paraguay accounted for the largest proportion of all foreign-born domestic workers (45 per cent), and those born in the remaining neighbouring countries (Bolivia,

Brazil, Chile, and Uruguay) accounted for a further 43 per cent. Assuming that all domestic workers were women, they comprised 42 per cent of all the female migrant workers originating in the five countries neighbouring Argentina (CELADE 1989).

Among the 61,400 foreign-born domestic workers enumerated in Venezuela in 1981, 82 per cent or slightly over 50,000 originated in Colombia. The Dominican Republic and Ecuador accounted for smaller contingents. Assuming once more that all domestic workers were women, they accounted for 47 per cent of the economically active female migrants originating in those three countries (CELADE 1989). In contrast, all foreign-born domestic workers in Venezuela accounted for only 10 per cent of the foreign-born workforce in the country. That is, in Venezuela as in Argentina, female international migrants originating in neighbouring countries tended to be highly concentrated in domestic services.

In Italy, the migration of domestic workers and others willing to take unskilled jobs occurred largely at the margin of the law until the late 1980s, when regularization drives were carried out and steps towards the eventual adoption of a new immigration law were taken. During the first of those regularizations, which took place in 1987–8 and applied only to employed foreigners, 105,000 persons legalized their status, 28 per cent of whom were women. Among the latter, 57 per cent worked in domestic service (OECD 1990). Although the data available are not classified by the citizenship of those regularizing their status, it is known that the majority of legalized domestic workers were Filipino women.

Indeed, the Philippines is known as a major source of female migrant labour. According to official statistics, in 1987 alone, 81,000 Filipino women were employed abroad as domestic workers out of a total of 139,000 female migrant workers granted permits to leave that year. The destinations of those domestic workers included Hong Kong (30,000), Singapore (17,000), Saudi Arabia (9,000), the United Arab Emirates (8,000), other oil-producing countries in Western Asia (7,000), Greece (1,600), and Italy (1,500). Out of the 81,000 workers employed, 49,000 or 61 per cent were being hired for the first time, the rest being rehired by foreign employers (United Nations 1994).

The results of the 1991 Census of Hong Kong largely corroborate the importance of Filipino migration in relation to domestic service. As Table 8.2 shows, the Census enumerated 56,800 female Filipino workers. This group was highly concentrated in the so-called 'elementary occupations', which include domestic service. Among Filipino women such a category accounted for a full 95 per cent of all workers. Among other migrants, only those originating in Thailand displayed a markedly high proportion of economically active women in the elementary occupations (66 per cent) and those originating in India and Pakistan displayed a proportion in those occupations similar to that exhibited by the Hong Kong Chinese (about a third). However, in terms of absolute numbers, the Hong Kong Chinese dominated, accounting for 46 per cent of all

Table 8.2. Distribution of the economically active female population by citizenship and occupation, Hong Kong, 1991 (%)

	British	Hong Kong British	Hong Kong Chinese	Other Chinese	Philippines	India and Pakistan	Thailand	Japan	United States	Canada	Portugal	Other countries	Total
Economically active women ('000)	631.9	12.7	289.2	9.1	56.8	1.7	6.2	1.0	2.5	2.0	5.2	10.5	1,028.7
Professional	3.6	14.8	0.9	1.8	0.4	12.1	0.2	9.5	31.0	25.6	4.5	11.5	3.0
Associate professionals	14.9	23.4	4.9	5.8	0.8	7.9	0.6	23.9	20.9	19.6	16.7	13.3	11.3
Administrative and managerial	4.9	11.9	4.4	7.6	0.5	13.8	2.4	21.0	29.3	33.2	9.8	15.8	4.9
Clerical	39.2	26.8	13.4	13.6	1.0	15.0	3.1	13.0	9.2	13.5	36.6	14.2	28.8
Sales and services	13.6	11.1	12.3	12.7	1.8	11.9	13.2	23.2	4.1	5.2	12.3	12.6	12.5
Crafts	3.7	2.0	7.2	7.9	0.1	1.7	2.7	0.7	0.3	0.8	3.8	2.2	4.4
Machine operators	10.5	3.4	20.5	27.7	0.2	4.4	10.3	0.0	1.2	0.4	10.2	6.7	12.7
Elementary occupations	9.1	4.4	35.2	22.2	95.3	33.0	65.7	8.8	3.8	1.8	5.7	22.8	21.7
Other	0.5	2.2	1.2	0.7	0.0	0.2	1.7	0.0	0.3	0.0	0.4	0.9	0.7

Source: Hong Kong, Census Planning Section (1992: main tables, table C20).

women engaged in elementary occupations in Hong Kong, and migrants from the Philippines came second, accounting for 24 per cent of those workers. Clearly, not only are Filipino women strongly concentrated in a single occupation but their presence is crucial in satisfying local demand for domestic workers.[1]

The case of Filipino women in domestic service is interesting because the partial information available indicates that the women concerned do not necessarily fit the typical profile of the domestic worker. One characteristic is especially telling: Filipino women in domestic service tend to be better educated than other women in that occupation. Furthermore, it is common for Filipino migrant women engaged in domestic service to report that they had a white-collar occupation before migration. Thus, unlike other women, they are potentially qualified for better jobs than the ones open to them overseas. Yet, they opt for migration under restrictive conditions because domestic service abroad pays considerably higher salaries than those they can obtain at home performing higher-status occupations. Filipino women do not appear, therefore, to be migrating internationally because of absolute necessity but are prompted instead by the desire to improve their lot and that of their families.

The experience of women from other major sources of international domestic workers is different. Thus, migrant women from Indonesia or Sri Lanka, most of whom work in the oil-producing countries of Western Asia, are more likely to fit the mould of the typical domestic worker. The numbers involved are large. Indonesia alone granted work permits to 204,000 female migrant workers during 1983–8, 96 per cent of whom were intending to work in domestic service (Hugo 1991). Though the information available on the characteristics of migrants is scanty, a few studies on Sri Lankan female migrants indicate that a high proportion originates in rural areas and that many are married women who leave their families behind in order to earn an income abroad that ensures their survival. Their remittances are crucial for the well-being of the family and they are mostly used for consumption. Thus, returning female migrants often find that very little has been saved during their absence. The cost of securing a job abroad is often responsible for reducing potential savings and may force the woman's family to go into debt. Clearly, therefore, very poor families are unlikely to be able to afford the costs involved in international migration.

Although a great deal of diversity characterizes both the sources and the destinations of female international migrants engaged in domestic service, it seems safe to say that most are only moderately poor in their countries of origin and are therefore willing to face the risks involved in international migration and domestic work abroad in order to improve the economic status of their families. Generally, women find that the conditions of domestic work abroad are similar to those in the home country and, despite the potentially greater risks of abuse, higher salaries are enticing. Women, therefore, act rationally in choosing to engage in migration for work purposes, and therefore prove that, just like men, they are capable of sound economic accounting. It is regrettable that their choices are still so limited.

The Occupational Distribution of Female Internal Migrants

Despite the increase in the number of jobs in domestic service abroad, the major demand for domestic workers is still in the home country and, very often, recourse to internal migrants is needed to meet that demand. There is, however, considerable variation among countries regarding the extent of women's employment in domestic service and the relative participation of migrant women in that occupation. In this section, the data available for a number of countries will be used to illustrate the diversity of situations. Since most of the data presented have been obtained from censuses, it is important to bear in mind their possible deficiencies, especially in terms of their coverage of women's economic activity. Given that domestic work involves the provision of services in private homes and that it is generally not validated by an official contract, the potential for misreporting is high. It is also possible that women engaged in such activities may be reluctant to report them because of their low status. Lastly, most censuses fail to make a sufficiently detailed tabulation by occupation and migrant status. Hence, sometimes it is not possible to distinguish women engaged in domestic services from those in other types of services. In such cases, the total number of women in the service sector will be assumed to represent domestic workers. Although such interpretation is not strictly correct, the preponderance of such workers in the service category justifies it. With those caveats in mind, let us consider the cases of a number of developing countries having the required data.

For Northern Africa, data are available for Egypt and the Libyan Arab Jamahiriya. In Egypt in 1976, the proportion of economically active women working in the service sector was low, amounting to only 6.6 per cent among non-migrant women and 15.2 per cent among migrants (see Table 8.3). Although the latter proportion was more than twice the former, services was by no means the occupational category containing the greatest number of migrant women. In fact, migrant women were more likely to be in the professional and technical category than in services. Clerical occupations were also an important source of employment for migrant women. It would therefore appear that migrant women in Egypt were positively selected in terms of occupational status and, although they were more likely to work in services than the non-migrant female population, they were also less likely to be in agriculture than their non-migrant counterparts. Consequently, for the few migrant women who were reported as economically active (amounting to only 9 per cent of all migrant women), migration was associated with an average improvement of occupational status.

In contrast with Egypt, where non-migrant women in the labour force dis-

Table 8.3. Distribution of the economically active female population by migration status and occupation, selected countries (%)

	Migrant women	Non-migrant women
Egypt 1976[a]		
Economically active women (000)	199.8	498.4
Professional and technical	34.1	22.5
Administrative and managerial	2.5	1.4
Clerical	21.0	18.7
Sales	4.0	5.0
Services	15.2	6.6
Agricultural	3.3	14.9
Production and labourers	5.8	9.3
Not stated	14.2	21.5
Libyan Arab Jamahiriya 1973[b]		
Economically active women (000)	10.5	17.2
Professional and technical	27.9	17.3
Administrative and managerial	0.0	0.0
Clerical	2.0	1.3
Sales	0.5	0.2
Services	34.6	13.9
Agriculture	30.3	59.6
Production and transport	3.7	7.4
Not stated	0.9	0.4
Sierra Leone 1974[c]		
Professional and administrative	4.3	2.1
Clerical	4.3	1.6
Sales	35.9	16.0
Specialized services	2.9	1.5
Agriculture	50.0	77.3
Production	2.5	1.5
Lesotho 1978–9[d]		
Employed women (000)	183.8	78.6
Professional and administrative	1.7	0.8
Clerical, sales, and services	5.8	5.6
Agriculture	86.4	87.2
Production, transport, and construction	5.3	5.1
Not classifiable	0.9	1.3
Nepal 1981[e]		
Economically active women (000)	226.6	2,144.4
Professional and technical	0.7	0.4
Clerical	0.3	0.1
Sales	1.4	0.4
Services	0.2	0.1

Table 8.3.   (cont.)

	Migrant women	Non-migrant women
Agriculture	92.7	96.4
Production	3.2	1.6
Other	1.6	0.9
Peninsular Malaysia 1982[f]		
Professional	14.4	7.9
Administrative	0.7	0.5
Clerical	21.0	12.8
Sales	6.1	9.2
Services	20.9	12.9
Agriculture	16.6	34.9
Production	20.3	21.8
Peninsular Malaysia 1986[f]		
Professional	15.5	9.7
Administrative	1.5	0.8
Clerical	19.2	14.6
Sales	7.6	11.3
Services	23.5	14.4
Agriculture	14.1	28.1
Production	18.4	21.1
Philippines (urban) 1973[g]		
Professional and administrative	10.3	19.3
Clerical and sales	25.2	37.5
Transport and communications	0.7	1.0
Crafts and labourers	7.2	10.7
Domestic services	50.2	26.1
Other services	3.9	3.2
Agriculture and mining	2.4	2.3
Thailand (rural) 1980[h]		
Economically active women (000)	529.8	9,141.2
Professional and technical	6.7	1.6
Administrative and managerial	0.5	0.1
Clerical	1.7	0.3
Sales	8.8	5.1
Agriculture	67.7	86.5
Mining	0.4	0.1
Transport	0.1	0.0
Crafts and production	10.9	5.3
Services	3.2	1.1
Not stated	0.1	0.0
Thailand (urban) 1980[h]		
Economically active women (000)	243.6	1,146.6
Professional and technical	11.2	13.2

Table 8.3. (cont.)

	Migrant women	Non-migrant women
Administrative and managerial	1.9	2.7
Clerical	7.3	9.3
Sales	20.0	30.5
Agriculture	4.1	8.6
Mining	0.1	0.0
Transport	0.4	0.2
Crafts and production	23.6	21.5
Services	31.1	13.7
Not stated	0.4	0.3
Mexico 1990[i]		
Economically active women (000)	387.9	5,104.2
Professional and managerial	12.1	12.3
Crafts, machinists, and transport	15.6	16.0
Clerical	16.8	21.6
Sales	10.5	13.6
Education, public sector, and security	15.7	17.5
Peddlers	2.0	2.4
Domestic services	21.4	10.5
Agriculture	3.6	3.3
Not stated	2.2	2.8

[a] For Egypt, the population considered is aged 15 and over.
[b] For the Libyan Arab Jamahiriya, the data refer to the economically active female population aged 10 and over; migrants are persons who changed place of residence within the country at some time prior to enumeration.
[c] For Sierra Leone, migrants are persons born outside of their place of enumeration (lifetime migrants) and the figures for non-migrant women refer to the total economically active female population.
[d] For Lesotho, the data refer to women aged 14 and over who were employed at the time of interview.
[e] For Nepal, migrants are persons born outside of their place of enumeration.
[f] For Peninsular Malaysia, the data refer to economically active women aged 15–64.
[g] For the Philippines, the data refer only to economically active women aged 15 and over in urban areas; migrants are persons who moved during the 5 years preceding the survey. The figures for non-migrant women refer to the total economically active female population in urban areas.
[h] For Thailand, the data refer to economically active women aged 11 and over; migrants are persons who moved between 1975 and 1980.
[i] For Mexico, the data refer to economically active women aged 12 and over; migrants are persons who had moved since 1985 and international migrants are excluded.

Sources: Egypt, Central Agency for Public Mobilisation and Statistics (1980: vol. 2, tables 15A and 20); Okoye (1981: table 15); Sierra Leone, Central Statistical Office (n.d.: table 11.9); Swee-Heng (1989: tables 6.4 and 6.6); Nepal, Central Bureau of Statistics (1988: table 7.23); Libyan Arab Jamahiriya, (n.d.: table 116); Lesotho, Department of Statistics (n.d.); Eviota and Smith (1984: table 9.8); Thailand, National Statistical Office (1984: table 13.B); INEGI (1993: table 7).

played a variety of occupations, in the Libyan Arab Jamahiriya the small number of women who were identified as economically active in 1973 were largely concentrated in agricultural activities (60 per cent were in that category among non-migrants). Migrant women, however, were more likely to be working in the service sector than in agriculture (see Table 8.3). Migrant women were also more likely to work in professional and technical occupations than their non-migrant counterparts. Data indicating whether migration had taken place within a state or between states (not shown) suggest that women migrating between states and thus moving, on average, over longer distances than intra-state migrants were less likely to work in agriculture than other migrants. Among all migrant women, the declining share of agricultural occupations was largely absorbed by an increase in the share of service occupations, where domestic work probably predominated. Thus, whereas 35 per cent of all migrant women worked in services, only 14 per cent of non-migrant women did so. It would appear, therefore, that migration allowed economically active women in the Libyan Arab Jamahiriya to diversify their occupations somewhat and, if educated, to find employment in professional or technical occupations or, if not, to join the service sector.

For Western Africa, the case of Sierra Leone in 1974 illustrates the typical occupational pattern of women in that region (Table 8.3). Among non-migrant women, the large majority (77 per cent) were concentrated in agriculture, with sales occupations attracting a further 16 per cent. Among lifetime migrant women, those two occupational categories accounted for 50 and 36 per cent, respectively. The category of 'sales' should probably be interpreted widely to encompass petty trade. West African women have traditionally engaged in such trade which, among other things, is associated with a higher degree of spatial mobility. Consequently, it is not surprising to find that migrant women are more highly concentrated in sales than non-migrant women. Most of the trading activities carried out by women occur within the informal sector and probably compare favourably with agricultural activities in terms of profit-making. It thus appears that, again in this case, the occupational structure of migrant women is more favourable than that of non-migrants, especially in terms of the income-earning opportunities that migration may open up for them.

In Southern Africa, Lesotho illustrates yet another case of an agricultural society, where, in 1978–9, 87 per cent of all economically active women worked in agriculture (Table 8.3). In contrast with other countries where agricultural activities predominate, there was very little difference in Lesotho between migrant and non-migrant women in terms of their concentration in agricultural activities, though migrant women moving over longer distances (between districts) had a lower propensity to work in agriculture (80 per cent did so) than those moving over shorter distances (among those moving within districts, 89 per cent worked in agriculture). Migration therefore seemed to be associated with only a small degree of improvement of occupational status.

Poverty and the lack of other income-earning opportunities are likely to have kept most migrant women in the agricultural sector.

A similar situation prevailed in Nepal, where 96.4 per cent of the non-migrant female labour force was engaged in agricultural activities in 1981. Among migrant women, the proportion in agriculture was lower (92.7 per cent) but not by much. In societies that are still largely agricultural, the lack of non-farm employment is probably responsible for keeping women on the land. In those cases, generalized poverty prevents households from hiring domestic workers and, consequently, the participation of women in the service sector is very low (Table 8.3).

In South-Eastern Asia, the case of Peninsular Malaysia illustrates a society in transition, where agricultural activities are still important (34 per cent of the non-migrant female labour force in 1982 worked in agriculture) but where participation in service activities is growing, particularly among female migrants (Table 8.3). By 1982, non-migrant women in Peninsular Malaysia already displayed a fairly diversified distribution by occupation where, next to agriculture, production was an important employment category. Migrant women were also well represented in production but the biggest differences between them and non-migrant women was in relation to service, clerical, and professional occupations. Information classified by both education and migration status (not shown) indicates that female migrants with at least some secondary education were more likely to be in the professional, clerical, and service occupations than non-migrants with similar educational attainment. Among those with only primary education, in contrast, migrants surpassed non-migrants only in service occupations (in 1982, 30 per cent of female migrants with primary education were in those occupations, compared to 15 per cent among their non-migrant counterparts). For the less educated female migrants, the gains made by the service sector were largely accounted for by declines in their participation in agriculture. This trade-off suggests that their migration, though caused by poverty, nevertheless provided a means of securing non-farm employment (in the form of domestic work) for those who could no longer be profitably employed in the agricultural sector.

For the Philippines and Thailand, two countries where agriculture was still a major occupation during the 1970s and early 1980s, the data available permit us to focus on migrants in urban areas. The 1973 data for the Philippines clearly indicate the tendency of recent migrant women (meaning those who had migrated between 1968 and 1973) to find employment in domestic service (Table 8.3). Thus, whereas only 26 per cent of the economically active women in urban areas were domestic workers, half of all recent female migrants in the labour force exercised that occupation and, among those aged 15–24 and single, 71 per cent did. In 1973, the cities of the Philippines had almost no other employment opportunities for unskilled women, since production activities (i.e. crafts and labourers) absorbed only 11 per cent of all economically active women in urban areas. Given that the other important source of employment for women, clerical and sales occupations, required higher levels of skills, unskilled migrant women could not but be relegated to lower-status jobs in the service sector.

In Thailand in 1980, the crafts and production occupations together with sales provided employment to over half of all economically active non-migrant women in urban areas, though services were also an important source of employment. Women who had migrated between 1975 and 1980 differed from their non-migrant counterparts in being more concentrated in services (31 versus 14 per cent) and less in sales (20 versus 31 per cent). Data distinguishing urban–urban from rural–urban migrants (not shown) further indicate that the latter tended to be even more concentrated in services than all recent migrants (40 per cent of all recent rural–urban female migrants who worked were employed in service occupations). In contrast, for those remaining in or moving to rural areas, the possibility of working in services was rare (see Table 8.3). Domestic service therefore appeared to be concentrated mostly in urban areas and to provide, as expected, an employment outlet for unskilled women, especially for those originating in rural areas.

In Latin America, the data for Mexico yielded by the 1990 Census show that the distribution by occupation of economically active female migrants was very similar to that of non-migrant women, with the largest difference between the two being in domestic service (21 per cent of migrant women were domestic workers whereas only 11 per cent of non-migrant women were in that occupation). The higher concentration of migrant women in domestic service occurred at the expense of a reduction in their participation in higher-status occupations, including clerical work, sales, and civil service jobs (see Table 8.3). Data by age (not shown) indicate that the major difference between female migrants and non-migrants regarding domestic service was found in age group 12–19, where 45 per cent of the migrant women but only 20 per cent of the non-migrants were concentrated in that occupation. At no other age were similar concentrations noticeable. As already noted in the case of the Philippines, women who were young, single, lacking in marketable skills, and in need of earning an income had little choice but to resort to domestic service. It is worth noting that, despite Mexico's drive to promote export-led growth and increase employment in production, the proportion of women in those occupations remained generally low, especially among migrants. Consequently, poor and unskilled women who migrated were still more likely to find employment as domestic workers than in factories or assembly plants.

In the case of Colombia, data for two points in time indicate how the structure of the labour force changed and how such changes have affected the insertion of female migrant workers into the labour market. In 1964, domestic services clearly dominated as the main source of employment for female migrants, whether they moved to Bogota, other urban areas, or rural areas (see Table 8.4). By 1977, the number of jobs in production had increased in urban areas and migrant women were being channelled to them. Such a change not

Table 8.4. Distribution of economically active women by migration status, destination, and occupation, Colombia, 1964 and 1977 (%)

	Bogotá		Other urban areas[a]		Rural areas	
	Migrants	Non-migrants[b]	Migrants	Non-migrants[b]	Migrants	Non-migrants[b]
Economically active women 1964						
Professional and technical	7.2	10.1	11.3	9.7	16.2	5.1
Employers (non-professional)	0.4	1.9	0.9	2.3	3.4	7.4
White-collar workers	11.5	24.8	8.3	16.3	3.5	3.4
Blue-collar workers	6.5	12.5	5.5	10.1	1.2	3.3
Own-account workers	3.4	9.5	7.9	20.3	9.3	33.1
Domestic services	61.4	28.6	53.4	29.4	48.8	21.3
Other services	5.8	6.3	8.0	4.9	4.6	2.8
Family workers	3.7	6.3	4.8	7.0	13.0	23.6
Employed women 1977						
Professional and technical	10.0	13.2	9.1	11.9	—	—
Administrative and managerial	2.9	1.2	2.5	0.9	—	—
Clerical	13.4	28.9	11.4	25.8	—	—
Sales	17.2	16.4	17.3	15.0	—	—
Services	23.9	24.0	24.4	25.3	—	—
Agriculture	1.6	0.2	2.2	0.2	—	—
Production	31.1	16.2	33.1	20.9	—	—

Note: A dash (—) indicates that the data are not available.

[a] For 1977, the data refer to only 7 cities: Bogotá, Barranquilla, Bucamaranga, Cali, Manizales, Medellín, and Pasto.

[b] In 1964 the data for non-migrants refers to residents of the respective places; in 1977 the equivalent data refer to natives.

Sources: Youssef, Buvinic, and Kudat (1979: table 9); García Castro (1980: table 18).

Table 8.5. Distribution before and after migration of female migrants aged 14 or over, by occupation, Ecuador, 1977 (%)

Occupation	Urban survey		Rural survey	
	Prior to migration	Time of interview	Prior to migration	Time of interview
Number of women (000)	131.0	188.0	136.0	297.0
Per cent not working	64.8	52.7	70.6	34.8
Professional	3.8	1.6	2.2	3.0
Clerical	0.8	1.1	0.7	2.0
Commerce	10.7	13.8	1.5	7.1
Services	21.4	69.7	14.7	72.4
Agriculture	37.4	1.1	51.5	1.3
Production	26.0	12.8	29.4	14.1

Source: Yang and Bilsborrow (n.d.: table 4).

only provided women with alternative employment opportunities but was also symptomatic of a development process that was gaining momentum. Thus, despite the fact that a high proportion of the population in Colombia can still be considered poor according to standard measures (see Table 8.1), migration appears to have led to a modest improvement in the occupational status of women.

In Ecuador, a survey of rural–urban migrants carried out in 1977 gathered information about migration both in the areas of origin of migrants and at their destination. One of its findings was that migrant women moving from rural areas to cities tended to find employment mostly in the service sector even though a considerably smaller proportion had worked in that sector before migration (Table 8.5). Although the reports obtained in urban areas from the migrants themselves did not fully coincide with those obtained in rural areas from close relatives, they both suggested that, for women, migration implied in many cases a change of occupation from agriculture or petty trade to domestic service. Migration in those circumstances did not bring about a major improvement in the status of the migrant women involved, but it probably produced economic benefits by the mere fact of giving women access to remunerated employment.

Conclusion

Although the number of cases considered and the differences in the data available are not conducive to a solid assessment of the effects of migration on women's occupational status and its potential for reducing or alleviating poverty, a pattern nevertheless seems to emerge from the cases presented. At low levels of development, when the occupational structure of a country is still highly dominated by agricultural work, women who migrate and remain economically active have little choice but to engage in agricultural activities. Although more detailed information about the qualitative changes in the type of agricultural work performed before and after migration would be necessary to reach definitive conclusions about the relation between migration and the alleviation of poverty, it is likely that in this case the potential effect of migration on poverty is small. This hypothesis is based on the fact that most women working in agriculture do so as unpaid family members and are usually engaged in subsistence farming. At best, migration may allow them to gain access to better land. At worst, landlessness may prompt migration and cause women to move as agricultural wage labourers, thus joining the ranks of one of society's lowest-status groups.

As development proceeds, employment opportunities in urban manufacturing rise and fuel migration to urban centres. Although at first most of the industrial jobs are reserved for men, both men and women move to urban areas in considerable numbers. The concentration of resources in cities improves the status of a growing part of the population, who thus become able to hire domestic workers. Consequently, unskilled women who need to work have one possible source of paid employment. Because rural–urban migration predominates, many migrant women who remain economically active exchange agricultural work for domestic service. Although the conditions of work in the latter are far from ideal, it nevertheless provides women with the opportunity of earning an income and gaining some degree of independence within the family. Domestic service also provides some alleviation of poverty by at least ensuring that the women involved have room and board. However, in so doing, it deprives them of a normal family life and is likely to demand very long hours of work. To the extent that migration is necessary to permit women to obtain jobs in domestic service, it is likely to contribute to the alleviation of poverty, although it certainly does not ensure that the women concerned improve their economic status in the long run.

In yet more advanced countries, the employment opportunities open to women in the formal sector of the economy grow. According to the experience of the few countries at that stage of development, employment for women tends to rise in the production sector. Although that sector generally offers only low-wage, low-status jobs, it nevertheless provides unskilled women with a viable alternative to domestic service. In a number of countries, migration has been instrumental in taking women to the manufacturing jobs available. However, domestic service tends to compete strongly with the production sector as a source of employment, particularly for young and poorly educated female migrants. To the extent that production jobs provide an alternative employment outlet for unskilled women and migration is involved in securing those jobs, migration probably contributes to the alleviation of poverty in the short term. Yet, just as in the case of domestic service, the lack of promotion prospects for unskilled women within the production sector is not conducive to the long-term improvement of their economic status.

In selected cases, economic growth and development have been successful in increasing the demand for domestic workers while at the same time curtailing the growth of the pool of women willing or needing to undertake such work. Under those conditions, foreign female workers have filled the gap. Although the situation varies considerably from one country to another, the foreign women involved often originate in nearby countries and are characterized by their low levels of education and skills. The evidence available indicates that moderate poverty is at the root of their decision to migrate internationally to become domestic workers. Because the wages that they earn abroad are usually considerably higher than those that similar employment would provide in their country of origin, their migration has a positive impact in combating poverty. However, the restrictions to which international female migrant workers are subject while abroad prevent any sustained improvement of their status and their economic gains, though real, may be short-lived.

By necessity, these conclusions are highly tentative. The lack of data linking migration and poverty directly, and especially the migration of women with some measure of their relative deprivation, both as members of households or family groups and as individuals, precludes firmer results. However, the partial and indirect information considered in this chapter suggests that there is much to be learned about the interactions between poverty status and migration. The widespread view that poverty leads to migration and to the perpetuation of poverty elsewhere, or that the alleviation of poverty can be the solution to the 'migration problem', suggests that both migration and poverty are equally negative. Recognizing that one is an answer to the other and that, even if poor, migrants are not irrational is a major step in the right direction. It is also crucial to stress that women are more than mere pawns of their families and that they generally make the best use of the opportunities open to them. Although migration may not be the solution to poverty, the availability of better employment opportunities certainly is and spatial mobility may be required to gain access to them. As always, women are ready to migrate if they have reason to expect gains from such a course of action.

Notes

The views and opinions expressed in this chapter are those of the author and do not necessarily represent those of the United Nations.

The author thanks Lucie Laurian for her assistance in preparing and analysing the data presented in this chapter.

1. This situation could change now that Hong Kong has been handed over to China.

References

Anker, R., Khan, M. E., and Gupta, R. B. (1988), *Women's Participation in the Labour Force: A Method Test in India for Improving its Measurement*, Geneva: International Labour Office.

Bilsborrow, Richard E., DeGraff, Deborah S., and Anker, Richard (1992), 'Poverty Monitoring and Rapid Assessment Surveys', Geneva: International Labour Office, mimeo.

CELADE [Centro Latinoamericano de Demografía] (1989), 'Investigación de la migración internacional en Latinoamérica (IMILA)', *Boletín Demográfico*, 22(43), special issue.

Dixon-Mueller, R. (1985), *Women's Work in Third World Agriculture*, Geneva: International Labour Office.

Egypt, Central Agency for Public Mobilisation and Statistics (1980), *1976 Population and Housing Census: Fertility and Internal Migration and Movement of Workers and Students*. Cairo: Central Agency for Public Mobilisation and Statistics.

Eviota, Elizabeth U., and Smith, Peter C. (1984), 'The Migration of Women in the Philippines', in James T. Fawcett, Siew-Ean Khoo, and Peter C. Smith, *Women in the Cities of Asia*, Boulder, Colo.: Westview Press, 165–90.

Fresnada Bautista, Oscar (1991), 'Dimensión y características de la pobreza en Colombia', *Boletín de Estadística*, 464: 159–230.

García Castro, Mary (1980), *Migración laboral femenina en Colombia*, Bogotá: Programa de las Naciones Unidas, Oficina Internacional del Trabajo sobre Migraciones Laborales.

Hong Kong, Census Planning Section (1992), *Hong Kong 1991 Population Census*, Hong Kong: Census Planning Section.

Hugo, Graeme (1991), 'Women on the Move: Changing Patterns of Population Movements of Women in Indonesia', mimeo.

——(1993), 'Migrant Women in Developing Countries', in United Nations, *Internal Migration of Women in Developing Countries*, New York: United Nations, 37–73.

——(1994), 'Migration as a Survival Strategy: The Family Dimension of Migration', paper presented at the Expert Meeting on Population Distribution and Migration, Santa Cruz, Bolivia.

INEGI [Instituto Nacional de Estadística Geografía e Informática] (1993), *Migración: Tabulados Temáticos. XI Censo de Población y Vivienda 1990*, Aguascalientas, Mexico: (INEGI).

Kreye, O., Heinrichs, J., and Frobel, F. (1987), *Export Processing Zones in Developing Countries: Results from a New Survey*, Geneva: International Labour Office.

Lesotho, Department of Statistics (n.d.), *1978/79 National Sample Survey*, Maseru: Department of Statistics.

Libyan Arab Jamahiriya (n.d.), *1973 Population Census: Final All-Country Results*, Tripoli: National Statistical Office.

Lim, Lin Lean (1994), 'The Status of Women and International Migration', in United Nations, *International Migration Policies and the Status of Female Migrants*, New York: United Nations, 29–55.

Maguid, Alicia (1990), *Argentina: Migración y pobreza durante la década del 80*, Paris: Centre de Recherche et de Documentation sur l'Amérique Latine (CREDAL).

Nepal, Central Bureau of Statistics (1988), *Population Monograph of Nepal*, Kathmandu: Central Bureau of Statistics.

OECD [Organisation for Economic Co-operation and Development] (1990), *SOPEMI 1989*, Paris: OECD.

Okoye, C. S. (1981), *Population Distribution, Urbanization and Migration in Sierra Leone: Census Analysis, Vol. 4*, Freetown: Central Statistical Office.

Rodgers, Gerry (1984), *Poverty and Population,* Geneva: International Labour Office.

Sierra Leone, Central Statistical Office (n.d.), *Sierra Leone 1974 Population Census: National Data*, Freetown: Central Statistical Office.

Swee-Heng, Tan (1989), 'Female Migration Trends and Patterns in Peninsular Malaysia, 1981–1986', paper presented at the Population Studies Unit Colloquium on Women and Development: Implications for Planning and Population Dynamics, University of Malaysia, Kuala Lumpur.

Thailand, National Statistical Office (1984), *1980 Population and Housing Census. Subject Report No. 2: Migration*, Bangkok: National Statistical Office.

Todaro, Michael (1976), *Internal Migration in Developing Countries,* Geneva: International Labour Office.

Torrealba, Ricardo (1992), *Trabajadoras migrantes en el servicio doméstico en Venezuela*, Geneva: International Labour Office.

United Nations (1993), *Internal Migration of Women in Developing Countries*, New York: United Nations.

—— (1994), 'Measuring the Extent of Female International Migration', in *International Migration Policies and the Status of Female Migrants*, New York: United Nations, 56–79.

Waring, Marilyn (1990), *If Women Counted: A New Feminist Economics*, San Francisco: HarperCollins.

Weinert, Patricia (1991), *Foreign Female Domestic Workers: Help Wanted!*, Geneva: International Labour Office.

World Bank (1990), *World Development Report 1990: Poverty*, Oxford: Oxford University Press.

—— (1994), *Infrastructure for Development: World Development Report 1994*, Oxford: Oxford University Press.

Yang, Xiushi, and Bilsborrow, Richard E. (n.d.), 'Survey Locals and Biases in Migration Analysis', mimeo.

Youssef, Nadia, Buvinic, Mayra, and Kudat, Ayse (1979), *Women in Migration: A Third World Focus. Report of the International Center for Advancement of Women*, Washington, DC: United States Agency for International Development.

Zlotnik, Hania (1993), 'Women as Migrants and Workers in Developing Countries', *International Journal of Contemporary Sociology*, 30(1), special issue: 39–62.

9 Women's Status and Demographic Change: The Case of Mexico–US Migration

Katharine M. Donato and Shawn Malia Kanaiaupuni

A persistent finding in contemporary international migration research is that people move in search of economic opportunity. At the macro-level, much of the literature has attempted to explain migration by examining the sources of economic inequality in sending and receiving nations (see Massey 1988; Piore 1979). At the micro-level, studies have shown that the decision to migrate is strongly related to the economic status of families and households. Because of demographic and economic pressures at home, poor families seek to maximize their income by sending at least one member abroad to search for work.

This is the way we typically think about the relationship between economic status and international migration. However, if we add gender, the relationship becomes complex. Recently, Lim (1993) argued that women's economic and social position relative to men's is a crucial determinant of female migration. Women's relative status taps a dimension of stratification, and at the same time it incorporates the idea that gender ideology is an essential component of women's migration.

Our main objective in this chapter is to extend Lim's ideas to the study of international migration from Mexico to the United States. We begin by developing a model of female migration and identifying the ways in which economic status influences women's movement across the Mexico–US border. In a subsequent section, we assess the prevailing patterns of female Mexico–US migration and examine the effect of women's relative status net of the socioeconomic status of migrants, households, and communities. Although some have criticized this practice,[1] we treat women as a separate analytical category because we believe that the effect of status on women's decision to migrate from Mexico is inextricably tied to the ideology that governs women's behaviour in origin communities.

A Model of Female Migration

For a long time, the theoretical logic explaining women's mobility in Mexico predicted their migration on the basis of men's. This is primarily because migration from central and western Mexico was male-led and considered a rite of passage for men (Massey *et al.* 1987). Only after men accumulated experience by making repeated trips to the United States did daughters, wives, and other relatives become involved in the process (Massey *et al.* 1994; Mines and Massey 1985; Reichert and Massey 1980).

Recent studies have made substantial inroads by exploring the role that women play in Mexican migration (see Goldring 1995; Kanaiaupuni and Neuman 1994; Donato 1993, 1994; Kanaiaupuni 1993; Hondagneu-Sotelo 1992; Stier and Tienda 1992; Lindstrom 1991; Mummert 1988; Arias and Mummert 1987; Mines and Massey 1985; Oliviera 1984; Ranney and Kossoudji 1984; Simon and DeLey 1984; Fernandez-Kelly 1983; Reichert and Massey 1979, 1980). Studies have shown that women from Mexico usually migrate with family members instead of migrating alone (Donato 1994; Kanaiaupuni 1994; Lindstrom 1991; Cárdenas and Flores 1986). They are also more likely to work at destinations in the United States than in Mexico (Donato and Kanaiaupuni 1993), in part because paid labour opportunities in Mexico are more limited in terms of availability, wages, social mores, and sexual discrimination than in the United States (Gonzalez de la Rocha 1988; Benería and Roldán 1987).

Furthermore, other studies have shown that when Mexican women accompany their families to the United States, long-term migration is common (Massey 1987; Cárdenas and Flores 1986). Women migrants typically join their husbands at some point after the men have established US connections (Chavez 1988). Sometimes they leave their children behind; three-quarters of one sample of *Latina* women in the United States did so (Brice-Laporte and Couch 1976). But on the whole, migrant women play crucial roles integrating their families and children into US destinations. They develop links to communities outside of work because of their activities associated with the educational and health services of their children (Hondagneu-Sotelo 1994).

These efforts have documented a variety of micro- and macro-level factors that influence the migratory behaviour of women (see Guest 1993; Brown 1991; Baydar *et al.* 1990; Guest and Praditwong 1989; Bilsborrow *et al.* 1987; Brown and Goetz 1987; Findley 1987). For example, because decisions are made by individuals, personal attributes, such as age and education, are salient determinants of female migration. Education may increase the exposure and options available to women, whereas women's age may create certain limits to women's mobility. For example, Mexican women are under-represented among undocumented Mexican migrants by their late twenties because their marital responsibilities usually involve maintaining homes in Mexico (Massey *et al.* 1987; Fernandez-Kelly 1983).

To a large extent, a woman's decision to migrate is also shaped by powerful social norms, which play an important role in maintaining the pattern of male-dominated migration. In Mexico, norms emphasize patriarchy and machismo, and result in strong conjugal families that influence individual action (Rouse 1989). For women, as primary caretakers of households and families, this means subordination to men (Lund Skar 1993; Tanori-Villa 1989; González de la Rocha 1988; Loyden Sosa 1986; Casillas 1985; Solórzano de Rivera 1980; Lomnitz 1977; Elú de Leñero 1969; Lewis 1959, 1960). Abiding by these rules, men are obligated to provide for the economic needs of their families and to protect their wives (Lindstrom 1991; Benería and Roldán 1987). Norms also guide Mexican women's behaviour in the migration process; they are often afraid to migrate and lack the economic and social resources to do so, and if they migrate, they are usually accompanied by male family members (Donato 1993; Kanaiaupuni 1993; Lindstrom 1991).

As a consequence, women's migration is intimately linked to their households, which are the units where decisions occur about who migrates (see Grasmuck and Pessar 1991; Massey *et al.* 1987; Harbison 1981; Hugo 1981). In Mexico, households adopt a strategy of sending at least one member, usually the male household head or son, to work in the United States. Gender is central in these decisions (see Pedraza 1991) because they are shaped to a large extent by cultural beliefs and traditional values about the roles of women and men in families (Kanaiaupuni 1995; Hondagneu-Sotelo 1992, 1994).

The economic status of families is relevant because the decision to migrate is dependent on an efficient division of labour in households (Selby *et al.* 1990; Weist 1983). Often migration is a response to the socio-economic status of families and threats to that status (Grindle 1988; Massey *et al.* 1987; Dinerman 1982). For example, Findley and Diallo (1993) found that female migration is one way families respond to difficult economic conditions. Women from poorer families are more likely to migrate than those from households with more income; subsequently, as expectations rise, increasing income in a community encourages further migration. In addition, there is some evidence that Mexican families responded to the economic crises of 1982 and 1987 by keeping potential migrants home because it was difficult to accumulate the money necessary to cross the border (Donato *et al.* 1992).[2]

The broader economic and ideological context within which individuals and families reside therefore influences female migration in a variety of ways (Goldring 1995; Massey *et al.* 1994; Boyd 1989; Bilsborrow 1984; Arizpe 1982; Dinerman 1982). Mexican-origin communities with long-standing traditions of US migration, for example, may provide women with access to the educational and employment skills necessary for their territorial displacement. They may also offer women access to migrant networks, which often provide the necessary resources to protect women during the migration process. Additionally, the availability of these opportunities to men may trigger the migration of women who move for reasons related to family reunification (Donato 1993).

A closely related factor is women's relative status in origin communities. Women's status relative to men's is inextricably tied to the normative context that governs the behaviour of women, and directly affects the motives behind migration and the composition of migrant flows (Lim 1993). For example, women's decision-making autonomy (relative to men's), or women's relative ability to place their own welfare above that of their families, may influence whether women migrate. In addition, women may also migrate if they experience worse employment prospects than men in their origin communities (Kanaiaupuni *et al.* 1995), or if they have more access than men to the resources available from migrant networks.

Finally, global conditions that reflect the politics of migration in the United States and Mexico may both push and pull women to migrate to the United States. For example, immigration policies have long shaped Mexico–US migration (Donato 1994). Some policies specifically recruited men as agricultural workers (see Rodriguez 1985; Galarza 1964), and the result was that migration was passed down from fathers to sons, and brothers who were US migrants maintained strong ties with each other (Massey and Liang 1989; Massey *et al.* 1987; Reichert and Massey 1979).

Other policies, such as amendments to the Immigration and Nationality Act passed in 1965 and 1976, influenced women's migration. For example, after the 1965 amendments created a single visa queue for Mexican migrants by exempting Western Hemisphere immigrants from country-specific eligibility requirements and numerical limits (Roney 1992), many women migrated with US visas to reunite with their families. Beginning in 1977, however, all migrants were subject to the same numerical limits and preferences. Although legal immigration from Mexico was subsequently halved and illegal migration subsequently surged, women's migration dropped dramatically, in part because mothers of minor US children were no longer eligible for legal entry.

Recent legislation may also have affected female migration from Mexico. The Immigration Reform and Control Act (IRCA) was designed to restrict illegal migration by increasing border enforcement, implementing employer sanctions, and offering amnesty to illegals already resident in the United States. Despite its extensive provisions, however, IRCA-related effects were only observed for women (see Donato 1993; Donato *et al.* 1992). Their chance of migrating on an illegal first journey to the United States declined in the two years immediately following IRCA's implementation. However, by 1990, women's chance of migrating with and without documents rose to high levels and was no doubt related to the millions of migrants who were eligible for IRCA's amnesty.[3]

Finally, the Immigration Act (IMMACT) of 1990 may have influenced women's migration from Mexico because it allocated 55,000 visas to family members of IRCA's newly legalized migrants each year between 1992 and 1994. Moreover, recent evidence suggests that the demand for these visas exceeded their supply. To the extent that women's entry reflects a process of family reunification, IMMACT is therefore likely to raise the chances that Mexican women will migrate to the United States.

Despite the multiplicity of factors that have been hypothesized to affect women's migration, we argue that no study has conceptualized status as inextricably linked to gender ideology and the roles of women migrants. Therefore, it is unclear whether and how women's relative status affects their chances of migrating once other indicators of economic position are considered. We specify below a multi-level model which emphasizes individual, familial, and community determinants of women's migration, and includes measures of women's position relative to men's. It provides us with insights about the structural factors and processes that shape the spread of female migration.

Our main objective is to develop, operationalize, and evaluate different measures of women's status relative to men's, and examine how they affect the process of female migration from Mexico to the United States. To do this, we use data from 24 Mexican communities which differ considerably in size and economic development. These data are longitudinal, provide a large sample size, include samples of settled US migrants, and yield reliable information on Mexican immigration up through 1992.

Data

The following analyses are based on data from the Mexican Migration Project (MMP), which surveyed Mexican communities during the winters of 1987–8 through 1991–2 (MMP 1995). The communities are located in six Mexican states which have traditionally sent many migrants to the United States (Jones 1988; North and Houstoun 1976; Dagodag 1975). Within each, a simple random sample of 150 to 200 households was drawn up, and households were interviewed during December and January in successive years between 1987 and 1992. Because these months are the best times to locate US migrants in Mexico, the sample is representative of housing units occupied in these communities during the winter months of 1987–92.

This sample was supplemented with a non-random survey of out-migrants located in US destination areas during the summer after each period of Mexican fieldwork. Using data from Mexican communities, fieldworkers uncovered where in the United States migrants went and then travelled to those locations to interview householders that had established themselves permanently. Because snowball sampling methods were used to compile samples of 20 out-migrant households per community, the US sample data were weighted by the inverse of the sample fraction employed for each survey site (Massey and Parrado 1994).[4] To the extent that these data represent out-migrants from sample communities, they provide some control for biases due to selective emigration.

Respondents were interviewed using ethnosurvey methods (Massey 1987; Massey *et al.* 1987). Information was collected on the social, economic, and demographic characteristics of persons in sample households. The ethnosurvey asked whether household members, including the head, spouse, and resident children, had ever been to the United States. If so, the survey also obtained information about the first and most recent journey to the United States, including the date of initial entry, duration, occupation, wage, place of destination, and legal status. Although retrospective histories obviously contain some recall error, checks for internal consistency revealed that migrants were able to remember with considerable accuracy the years when they left for the United States (see Massey 1985).

Although not strictly representative of all migrant-sending areas, the communities were chosen to include a range of economic and cultural characteristics in the principal sending states of Mexico. Table 9.1 documents the extent to which communities vary in their composition and urbanization, resulting in different levels of preparation for work in the United States. The approximately 200 households sampled in each community produced Mexican sampling fractions that ranged from 0.029 to 0.699, depending on the number of households in the sampling frame. Overall refusal rates ranged from a high of 15.2 per cent to a low of 1.0 per cent. Although the variation may suggest problems with the study, field reports discovered that high rates reflected distrust resulting from local political conditions.

One limitation of this sample for our purposes is that the communities were chosen from areas having a long history of US migration. Because women are less likely to have migrated in the past, our sample may under-estimate women's current involvement in international migration. We therefore interpret our findings with caution (and request our readers to do so), but are comforted by the fact that sample communities varied considerably with respect to characteristics important for this study: sex composition among migrants, prevalence of migration, and year of earliest migration.

Methods

For this analysis, we used the woman's birthdate and date of the first journey to the US to construct a year-by-year life history up to the date of the first journey to the US. This information was compiled for all female household heads and married women at the time of the survey, and included all years of life between the ages of 12 and 70. The procedure built a discrete-time person-year file that follows each subject from birth to the date of the survey or the initial journey, whichever came first.

The person-year file provided the basis for estimating an age–period model of the probability of making a first journey to the United States. We then specified a multinomial model that distinguishes legal from illegal migration as two types of migration by allowing for a complete set of binary contrasts (Maddala 1983). The category of no migration served as the reference category for contrasts with migration types. The model therefore recognizes distinct boundaries between legal and illegal migration, yet does not impose a rank ordering on them.

The outcome measure was whether the woman migrated without legal documents, migrated with legal documents, or did not migrate during the person-year in question. If a woman did not migrate in a given year, the migration variable was coded 3; if she migrated without legal documents, it was coded 1; and if she migrated with legal documents, it was coded 2. For migrants, all later years of life were then excluded from the file.

For each year in which a migration took place, we also created time-varying variables to record personal, household, and community characteristics when the journey was taken. For example, we recorded the legal status of migrants when respondents made their journey. Legal migrants had valid US documents that entitled them to work in the United States, whereas illegal migrants did not. We also coded whether or not respondents were married,[5] and their years of education.

Household attributes included the physical and social assets important to the migration decision. For example, the number of young children may constrain the amount of time available to women. Children also create greater consumption needs, often motivating men to migrate and prompting women to join the labour force. We therefore measured the number of children under 18 in the household in each year, and expect that they will restrict the migration of women. In addition, given the well-established relationship between previous experience and subsequent migration (Massey *et al.* 1987), we hypothesize that the migration of other family members will raise the odds of a woman's migration because it offers more ties to the United States.

Community conditions are related to migration outcomes because they shape the experiences of households in which individuals make decisions. For example, a thriving economy in an industrial community with many factories enables households to allocate their labour locally. In times of economic need, households survive by sending more members into the labour force (Selby *et al.* 1990). In agricultural villages, where land is often distributed unequally and mechanized forms of agricultural production displace workers, comparable opportunities may not be available. The consequence is that, to survive, rural *campesinos* are likely to find work in the United States (Massey 1987; Arizpe 1982). We therefore measured some of these conditions by including in our models the availability of education and labour force opportunities in the manual sector. We expect that living in areas with greater access to education and employment opportunities creates an environment where residents have more information about the world and greater tolerance for women's mobility outside the home.

The historical precedence of migration in an origin community also influences the likelihood of women's migration. Because Mexican migration to the United States has historically been quite common, we included a continuous measure of migration to tap the maturity and intensity of the process in each community (see Massey *et al.* 1994). Over time, migration becomes institutionalized as a way of household survival in many communities and leads to

Table 9.1. Characteristics of the 24 Mexican communities sampled for study of Mexico–US migration, 1987–1992

Type of community and name	State	1990 population	Survey year	Sample size	Smpling fraction	Refusal rate (%)	US sample	Year of earliest migration	Percentage of population living in US	Percentage female
Metropolitan Areas										
León	Guan.	867,920[a]	1987	200	0.232	11.9	0	1920	2.3	16.9
Morelia	Mich.	492,901[a]	1991	200	0.056	8.3	20	1928	5.7	30.0
Irapuato	Guan.	362,915[a]	1991	200	0.100	5.7	20	1909	0.3	35.0
Uruapan	Mich.	217,068[a]	1992	200	0.184	8.3	13	1941	18.4	25.9
Smaller Urban Areas										
Ciudad Guzmán	Jal.	74,068	1992	201	0.119	7.4	20	1934	19.7	36.3
San Fco. del Rincón	Guan.	52,291	1987	200	0.256	3.4	20	1920	21.2	24.5
Salvatierra	Guan.	33,123	1992	200	0.072	9.5	15	1920	23.4	34.1
Los Reyes	Mich.	32,474	1989	200	0.029	3.7	20	1925	32.4	30.3
Ameca	Jal.	30,882	1991	200	0.113	4.4	20	1942	29.9	18.6
Yuriria	Guan.	23,726	1992	200	0.113	12.7	15	1915	3.9	23.6
San Felipe del Torres	Guan.	20,614	1990	200	0.053	4.7	20	1920	11.2	21.6

Ixtlán del Río	Nay.	19,645	1990	200	0.045	2.9	20	1915	36.9	38.5
Romita	Guan.	16,535	1988	200	0.073	5.7	20	1929	0.9	34.4
Las Varas	Nay.	11,541	1990	200	0.074	1.0	20	1943	53.8	35.7
Towns										
Nahautzen	Mich.	7,025	1990	200	0.139	5.7	20	1940	5.6	15.2
Ario de Rayón	Mich.	6,429	1989	200	0.143	5.0	20	1935	40.6	32.4
Unión de San Antonio	Jal.	4,760	1988	200	0.250	11.5	20	1906	3.9	13.4
San Diego de Alejandría	Jal.	3,516	1988	200	0.392	3.8	20	1916	30.8	18.5
Juchipila	Zac.	7,750	1991	364	0.212	12.7	20	1921	n.a.	12.0
Ranchos										
Santa María del Valle	Jal.	2,321	1988	200	0.375	1.0	20	1923	10.8	22.3
La Yerbabuena	Mich.	2,240	1989	150	0.335	15.2	20	1923	0.6	38.7
Mineral de Pozos	Guan.	1,737	1988	150	0.605	8.5	10	1941	1.1	21.3
La Soledad	Guan.	1,080	1991	100	0.699	2.9	20	1924	3.0	22.9
Contitlán	Zac.	5,785	1991	116	0.498	2.5	0	1919	n.a.	15.0

n.a. = not available at present.

[a] Population of metropolitan area.

Source: M M P (1995).

changes in social attitudes and behaviours, facilitating women's migration (Massey *et al.* 1994; Fletcher and Taylor 1992; Stark 1984).

Our two indicators of women's status relative to men's are built on sex-specific migration prevalence and labour force activity rates. Presumably, having more migrants in an origin community suggests support for women's mobility, and access for women to migration networks. However, it is likely that Mexican women do not have direct access to these networks. Created and perpetuated by men (see Hondagneu-Sotelo 1994), migrant social networks may hinder women's access.

If women's relative status plays an important role in the migration decision-making process for women, then the sex ratio among persons who have ever migrated from a community will significantly affect women's initial migration. Although it is unclear a priori whether and how women's status in US migration will differentially influence the two migration contrasts, we expect that as the ratio of men to women migrants rises, the probability of women's migration will decrease. In this case, male migrants will predominate among the out-migrant population and attitudinal changes about female migration from the community are not likely. Thus, the chances of women's migration will be low.

The second measure of women's status in the community was a proxy for their status in the labour market. As women's representation among workers in the manual sector increases, we argue that migration is less necessary for female than male migrants, especially a risky migration involving a border crossing without documents. Furthermore, with greater job security in their home communities, women are likely to adhere to traditional gender roles which restrict their migratory behaviour. Therefore, with the opportunity of earning income in origin communities, we expect the likelihood of illegal versus no migration to drop as the proportion of female to male labour force participation rates rises. In contrast, we expect that women's relative employment status in origin communities will have little, if any, effect on their chances of legal versus no migration because it is often linked to women's family connections in the United States rather than economic conditions at home.

Finally, we specified period dummies for single years from 1980 to 1992 because they provide a basis for assessing the magnitude of female migration and trends in the initial migration event that women undertake: making a first journey. They also permit us to evaluate whether and how changes in US policy and Mexican economic conditions influence women's migration net of personal and household characteristics.

If IRCA had an effect, then we expect declines in illegal migration probabilities after 1986 compared to a baseline period from 1980 to 1985. If IMMACT led to the reunification of families, then we expect increases in legal migration probabilities after 1990 compared to the prior five-year period. On the other hand, the economic crises of 1982 and 1987 in Mexico should have reduced women's migration in the years immediately after the crises because families were unable to meet the costs of migration for their members, even for those with US experience. We expect that this effect was short-lived, however, and that by the end of the 1980s, the economic distress experienced by Mexican families encouraged women's migration because making ends meet had become more difficult (Arizpe 1989).

Our strategy is as follows. We begin by describing the measures of household and community economic status we use. These are presented in Table 9.2 and Figs. 9.1–9.4. Subsequently, we present multi-variate models in Table 9.3, and discuss their implications in the final section.

Economic Status of Households

As mentioned earlier, we argue that economic need in households and communities affects the chances that women migrate on a first journey to the US. This section describes the measures we use to assess economic status. We begin with our measure of the socio-economic status of households. In developing nations, the link between poverty and households depends on their access to resources, such as land, cattle, labour, credit, tools, and technology, and the means of income generation through labour market opportunities (Youssef 1983).

Therefore, to derive a summary measure of household status, we gave each respondent one point for each of the following household assets: tile floors, at least five rooms, at least five hectares of land, and having owned a business. We then summed these scores, and the result was a measure of socio-economic status that ranges from 0 (low) to 4 (high).

Table 9.2 describes how each of the individual measures and the average socio-economic score vary by migrant status. The evidence clearly suggests that legal migrants were the wealthiest, followed by non-migrants, and then

Table 9.2. Socio-economic status of Mexican households in the 24 Mexican communities, 1987–1992 (%)

Asset	Undocumented migrant	Legal migrant	Non-migrant
Land	4.7	8.5	6.5
Rooms	8.3	17.8	15.1
Tile floors	10.4	22.9	14.2
Owns business	8.6	14.0	10.4
Socio-economic status score	0.320	0.632	0.461

Source: M M P (1995).

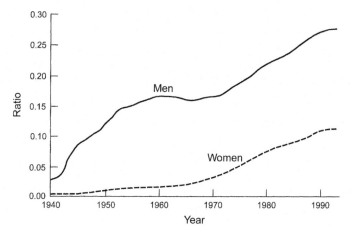

Fig. 9.1.   Male and female migration prevalence ratios by year, 24 Mexican communities, 1940–1993

Source: Mexican Migration Project (1995).

undocumented migrants. Approximately 23 per cent of legal migrants had households with tile floors, compared to 14 per cent of non-migrants and just 10 per cent of illegal migrants. Socio-economic status scores also reveal differences by migrant status, with average scores for legals being roughly twice that for illegals.

Women's Relative Status in Origin Communities

The status of women in their origin communities provides the context that influences their chances of migrating. Figs. 9.1–9.4 provide a closer look at our measures of women's status relative to men's in Mexican communities. Our first indicator, women's relative status in US migration, is derived from the data in Fig. 9.1, which describes how the proportion of women and men who have ever migrated has changed since 1940.

Among men, we see a gradual increase in their migration prevalence; by 1992, approximately 27 per cent of the community's living population were men who had ever migrated (compared to less than 5 per cent in 1940). The timing and magnitude of women's migration, however, varied quite dramatically from men's. The increase in the proportion of women who had ever migrated was observed in the late 1960s, and despite continuous increases, by 1992 the proportion of women who had ever migrated averaged slightly more than 10 per cent.

These trends suggest that the sex ratio of women's to men's migration has increased over time.[6] Fig. 9.2 reveals this pattern. After 1960, the sex ratio of

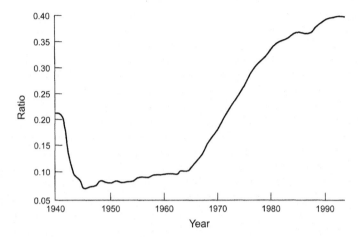

Fig. 9.2. Ratio of female to male migration prevalence by year, 24 Mexican communities, 1940–1993

Source: Mexican Migration Project (1995).

migrants in the living population of origin communities began to rise; by 1970, it was roughly 15 per cent and, after 1980, 35 per cent. The high sex ratios document women's growing presence in migration since 1960, and they contrast sharply with the low ratios (approximately 10 per cent) found in the 1945–60 period, when many Mexican men were recruited for temporary agricultural employment in the United States (Massey and Liang 1989). We hypothesize that the shifts in women's relative position to men's in US migration are related to women's migratory behaviour.

We derived the second indicator of women's position relative to men's from labour force activity rates. Fig. 9.3 illustrates how women's and men's labour force participation have changed in Mexican origin communities since 1932. In all years, men's activity has been much higher than women's. Among men, labour force activity grew during the 1940s, levelled off in the 1950s, and rose again to peak in the 1990s. Women's participation rose gradually after 1965, peaked around 1980, and dropped off thereafter.

Women's relative status in the manual sector is revealed in Fig. 9.4, which presents the female-to-male ratio of the sex-specific activity rates. Here we see that women's representation relative to men's in this sector grew briefly in the mid-1940s but then levelled off in the 1950s and early 1960s. Thereafter, women's labour force activity grew in proportion to men's, as the demand for female workers rose and peaked around 1980. In the 1980s, however, women's status relative to men's began to decline as the disparity between men's and women's activity widened. These trends were due in part to Mexico's economic crisis in the late 1970s and early 1980s (Szasz 1992;

Fig. 9.3. Labour force paticipation rates by sex and year, 24 Mexican communities, 1932–1993

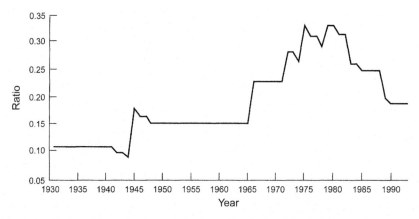

Fig. 9.4. Ratio of female to male labour force participation rates by year, 24 Mexican communities, 1930–1993

Gonzalez de la Rocha 1988; Chant 1985). At the outset of the crisis, women entered the labour market to help their families survive. Later in the 1980s, when the exigencies of the recession diminished, women's labour market activity dropped.

To sum up, these figures illustrate substantial shifts in women's relative status in US migration and the Mexican labour force. They therefore represent two ways in which the social and economic landscapes of Mexican origin communities have changed in the twentieth century. As a result, we expect them to be related to changes in women's migration behaviour; we examine these expectations in detail below.

Migrating on a First Journey to the US

We now examine how economic status influences the odds of not migrating compared to the two forms of migrating: with and without documents. Table 9.3 contains two models. The first predicts the probability of illegal, and then legal, migration (versus not migrating), using personal and household characteristics. Our emphasis here is on how the socio-economic status of households influences women's migration. The second model predicts the same set of contrasts using the same variables as well as community-level attributes, including measures of women's relative status. We focus our attention on (1) whether and how the effect of household socio-economic status changes, and (2) how women's relative status affects their chance of migration net of relevant controls.

The left-hand columns in Table 9.3 contain the estimates and standard errors from the basic model, which controls for age, marital status (equal to 1 if the person is in union at the beginning of the person-year and 0 otherwise), education (in years), and characteristics of households (the number of children less than 12 years of age, the number of male migrants, the number of female migrants, and socio-economic status). The right-hand columns present estimates and standard errors obtained from a second model, which includes personal and household attributes as well as period dummies and characteristics of origin communities. The latter includes human capital stock (the proportion of the population with at least six years of education), labour force activity in the manual sector (labour force participation rates), prevalence of migration (the proportion of the living population who have ever migrated), and women's relative status in US migration and the Mexican manual labour force (the sex ratio of male to female migrants and the ratio of female to male labour force participation rates).

Results from the basic model show that household status was an important indicator of women's illegal migration. The chance of women migrating illegally versus not migrating dropped as the socio-economic status of households rose. With respect to legal migration, however, household status had no effect.

Moreover, having young children also exhibited different effects on the chances of migrating versus not migrating. Surprisingly, minor children did not lower the odds of women migrating without legal documents (although the coefficient is negative), but they facilitated women's legal migration. To a large extent, we believe these findings underscore the status differences reported earlier for the two types of migrant women (see Table 9.2). Women who migrated with legal documents had more resources and were of higher status than women who crossed without documents. As a result, the presence of minor children did not inhibit the legal migration of women.

With respect to our other controls, coefficients in Table 9.3 suggest

Table 9.3. Multinomial logistic regression estimates for women from the 24 Mexican communities, 1987–1992[a]

Independent variables	Basic model				Full model			
	Undocumented/No migration		Legal/No migration		Undocumented/No migration		Legal/No migration	
	Estimate	Standard error	Estimate	Standard error	Estimate	Standard error	Estimate	Standard error
Personal attributes								
Age (ref = <15 years)								
15–19	1.266*	0.229	-0.592*	0.238	1.173*	0.230	-0.572*	0.238
20–24	1.633*	0.228	-0.168	0.221	1.509*	0.230	-0.111	0.223
25–29	1.466*	0.239	0.225	0.223	1.320*	0.242	0.304	0.226
30–34	0.138	0.304	-1.072*	0.313	-0.055	0.308	-1.017*	0.317
35–39	0.970*	0.289	-0.545	0.309	0.692*	0.294	-0.484	0.314
40–44	0.337	0.351	-0.696*	0.348	-0.035	0.355	-0.645	0.354
45–49	1.410*	0.291	-0.325	0.340	0.889*	0.297	-0.279	0.346
50–54	0.525	0.396	0.565	0.293	-0.107	0.402	0.617*	0.301
55+	-0.552	0.508	-0.071	0.320	-1.372*	0.514	-0.064	0.334
Married (ref = not married)	1.093*	0.119	0.693*	0.237	1.027*	0.121	0.688*	0.239
Education (years)	0.074*	0.010	0.141*	0.013	0.011	0.011	0.139*	0.014

Household characteristics

Number of minor children	-0.012	0.025	0.064*	0.031	-0.056*	0.026	0.047	0.031
Number of male migrants	0.428*	0.022	0.371*	0.034	0.321*	0.025	0.359*	0.037
Number of female migrants	0.389*	0.041	0.219*	0.068	0.350*	0.043	0.229*	0.070
Socio-economic status	-0.296*	0.069	0.066	0.069	-0.292*	0.069	0.075	0.070

Community characteristics

Prevalence of migration	—	—	—	—	5.305*	1.438	8.244*	1.888
LFP rate in manufacturing sector	—	—	—	—	2.548	1.330	-1.388	1.737
Percentage with 6+ years education	—	—	—	—	0.763*	0.396	0.641	0.627
Relative status of men and women: proportion of								
male to female migrants	—	—	—	—	-0.001	0.002	-0.006*	0.003
female to male LFP rates	—	—	—	—	-1.687*	0.361	-0.376	0.434

Period of journey (ref = before 1965)

1965–9	—	—	—	—	1.346*	0.330	1.309*	0.239
1970–4	—	—	—	—	2.978*	0.282	1.090*	0.268
1975–9	—	—	—	—	2.710*	0.295	0.372	0.318
1980	—	—	—	—	3.057*	0.332	-0.302	0.499
1981	—	—	—	—	2.536*	0.354	-0.964	0.614
1982	—	—	—	—	2.495*	0.357	0.254	0.448

Table 9.3.   (cont.)

Independent variables	Basic model				Full model			
	Undocumented/ No migration		Legal/ No migration		Undocumented/ No migration		Legal/ No migration	
	Estimate	Standard error	Estimate	Standard error	Estimate	Standard error	Estimate	Standard error
1983	—	—	—	—	1.189*	0.450	-1.640	0.759
1984	—	—	—	—	2.035*	0.383	-0.486	0.524
1985	—	—	—	—	2.422*	0.371	-1.008	0.613
1986	—	—	—	—	2.115*	0.388	0.110	0.477
1987	—	—	—	—	1.551*	0.427	-0.087	0.502
1988	—	—	—	—	1.823*	0.416	-0.065	0.509
1989	—	—	—	—	2.813*	0.382	-1.061	0.644
1990	—	—	—	—	1.907*	0.455	0.498	0.514
1991	—	—	—	—	2.116*	0.508	0.050	0.623
1992	—	—	—	—	2.853*	0.516	0.132	0.749
Intercept	-7.210*	0.220	-7.038*	0.188	-10.198*	0.704	-7.468*	0.827
Chi-square	901.2				1,901.2			
Person-years	129,189				129,189			

[a] Weighted by relative probability of being included in the sample: 1/sampling fraction.

* $p < 0.05$.

Source: M M P (1995).

different age–migration profiles for the two contrasts of interest. The odds of illegal migration versus no migration were lowest in childhood, but they grew in adolescence and peaked among women in their twenties. Thereafter, they declined except for women aged 35–39 and those aged 45–49, just past child-bearing years. In contrast, the odds of migrating legally on a first journey versus not migrating were low for women of all ages. Particularly noteworthy in this respect were the odds for teenagers, women aged 30–34, and those aged 40–44. For these women, the odds of legal migration were lower than for girls in the reference category (those less than 15 years of age).

Being married and educated increased a woman's chance of making a first illegal and legal journey to the United States. The marriage effect was consistent with prior research; most Mexican women migrate on a first journey after they marry (Kanaiaupuni 1994). Furthermore, as the number of male and female migrant relatives increased, the odds of migration (both undocumented and legal) versus no migration grew.

After we controlled for period and community attributes, including women's relative status, only a few of the above-mentioned effects changed. The positive effect for education disappeared when we predicted the odds of illegal versus no migration, whereas that for minor children became significant and negative. Furthermore, women aged 50–54 were now more likely to migrate legally versus not migrating.

Especially noteworthy, we argue, is that the significant effect for household socio-economic status remained after we controlled for community-level attributes. Consistent with the basic model, as household status increased the chance of women migrating illegally dropped. Also consistent with this model was that household status had no effect on the odds of women migrating legally. These findings are in line with the argument that women who migrate illegally are often prompted by precarious economic circumstances experienced in their community of origin. Women with legal documents, on the other hand, migrate to join relatives across the border rather than in search of employment opportunities per se.

Our proxies for local community conditions suggest that the prevalence of migration and level of human capital raised the chances of women migrating without documents versus not migrating. The migration prevalence of a community also raised the odds of legal versus no migration, although the overall skill level in communities had no effect on the chance of women making a legal journey to the US.

Indicators of women's relative position significantly affected women's migration but in different ways. That is, as the ratio of male to female migrants increased, the chance of women migrating with legal documents (versus not migrating) on a first journey dropped significantly. Although the effect is small, it suggests that men's growing representation among migrants in origin communities lowered the odds that women would migrate on a first journey to the US. More men also lowered the migration chances of women without documents, although not significantly. Thus, as men outnumbered women in the out-migrant population, women were less likely to make a first legal journey to the US. In contrast, women's growing labour force participation relative to men's reduced the likelihood that women would migrate on an illegal journey to the United States. Therefore, as women's prospects for employment in Mexico strengthened relative to men's, the likelihood that women would migrate on a first journey without documents declined.

The period effects stand proxy for global political and economic conditions. Interestingly, these conditions played a large role in determining the odds of illegal migration. Compared to the referent period, the odds of illegal versus no migration were higher in the late 1960s, the 1970s, the 1980s, and the early 1990s. During the late 1970s and early 1980s, a time of economic growth and development in Mexico, coefficients were quite high for illegal US female migration. This was also a period when most US settlers in our data-set were likely to have left for the United States. By 1983, however, the situation had reversed itself. Because of a severe financial crisis in Mexico and the rising costs of migration, the odds of illegal versus no migration dropped considerably. But this effect was not sustained, and the odds of illegal versus no migration peaked again in 1989 and in 1992.

This ebb and flow provides some evidence that US policy influenced the flow of illegal female migrants, but not always in the expected direction. Although rising coefficients in the late 1980s may suggest that economic need pushed Mexican families to turn to women as US migrants, it is also possible that efforts to reform immigration flows have resulted in *more* women migrants who are making their first journey to the US without documents. Because women's migration was probably linked to IRCA's amnesty provisions, the provision of amnesty to millions of previously illegal migrants reduced the risks of migrating for many family members who had not migrated before. It therefore provided an impetus for many Mexican women to migrate on an initial journey to the US—even without documents.

In contrast, period coefficients exhibited few notable effects on the odds of crossing legally versus not migrating. Compared to the reference period (prior to 1965), only coefficients for the late 1960s and early 1970s raised the odds of legal migration. No significant effects appeared for the 1980s and early 1990s, suggesting that the chances of legal versus no migration were independent of the dramatic shifts that occurred in the Mexican economy and US immigration policy during that period.

Conclusion

Our interest in how women's relative status affected Mexico–US migration was motivated by the failure of prior studies to include it. The neglect was especially puzzling in light of the work by Lim, who argued that it is a crucial determinant of women's migration. Thus, we argued that whether captured in US migration flows or in Mexican labour force activity rates, women's status relative to men's affects the migration decisions of women.

We investigated how women's relative status affects their initial migration decisions net of the socio-economic status of households, other household and community attributes, and personal characteristics. We concluded that socio-economic status, in households and communities, is an essential component of the migration process. Unlike the prior studies, however, we concluded that status may also be conceptualized in the relative positions of men and women in origin communities.

Overall, the analysis yields several important conclusions. First, there appears to be a greater tolerance of women's undocumented migration than legal migration, in part because of the lower socio-economic status of their households. The economic situation of undocumented migrant women is critical to the overall patterns manifested in our data. The chance of migrating is less elastic for undocumented women than for legals, driven more by the need to survive than by non-economic factors.

Second, the significant negative effects of women's relative status suggest that Mexican women have not been able to place their own welfare above that of men and their families. Despite women's growing representation in the US migration flows, for example, the predominance of men relative to women lowers the chances of women migrating. Moreover, growing employment opportunities for women in their origin community relative to those for men depress women's mobility.

Finally, period effects suggest that the chance of illegal migration is strongly shaped by the global political and economic conditions migrants face—whether in the form of US policy or economic recessions in Mexico. However, the chance of women migrating with documents to the United States is largely unaffected by these conditions. Taken together, these insights raise questions about the exact nature of the complex interrelationships that influence a woman's decision to migrate, and they provide the basis for future work on women's migration from Mexico to the United States.

Notes

This research was presented at the IUSSP Conference on Women, Poverty and Demographic Change. It was made possible by grants from the National Institute of Child Health and Human Development (HD-24041), the Sloan Foundation, and the American Sociological Association, whose support is gratefully acknowledged.

1. Some writers have argued that introducing sex into analytical frameworks is inappropriate (see Morokvasic 1983; Leeds 1976; Amin 1974). Harbison (1981), for example, has argued that sex differences do not require different models, just different weights on the motivations to migrate.

2. In the 1980s, rising inflation, exchange-rate uncertainty, and foreign debt set the context for migration decisions. Wages in Mexico were quite competitive with those in the United States until February 1982, when the peso was dramatically devalued. Inflation and further devaluation occurred again that year, so that by December the minimum wage had lost three-quarters of its dollar value while the peso value of US wages had soared. This situation repeated itself in 1987, when Mexican wages dropped after another year of record inflation rates.

3. There were two ways that illegal migrants could be eligible for amnesty under IRCA. The first applied to undocumented migrants living in the United States since 1982 (known as Legally Authorized Workers or LAWS), and the second offered amnesty to illegal agricultural workers employed in the United States for at least 90 days between 1984 and 1986 (known as Special Agricultural Workers or SAWS).

4. In Mexico, sampling fractions were calculated by dividing the number of sample households by the number of eligible households in the sampling frame. In the United States, sampling fractions were computed as the number of sample households divided by the estimated number of households in the out-migrant community. The size of the out-migrant population was measured for each community using data on the current location of offspring of the household head (see Massey and Parrado 1994 for further description of the random sampling methods employed in Mexican communities and the derivation of out-migration population size).

5. We are unable to differentiate among the types of unions, and therefore note that unions may be of a civil, religious, or cohabiting nature.

6. The sex ratio of men to women migrants is a cumulative one and calculated over the life of the community (see Massey *et al.* 1994 for further details).

References

Amin, S. A. (ed.) (1974), *Modern Migrations in Western Africa*, London: Oxford University Press.

Arias, P., and Mummert, G. (1987), 'Familia, mercados de trabajo y migración en el Centro-Occidente de México', *Nueva Antropología*, 4: 105–27.

Arizpe, L. (1982), 'The Rural Exodus in Mexico and Mexican Migration to the United States', *International Migration Review*, 15: 626–49.

——(1989), 'On Cultural and Social Sustainability', *Development*, 1: 5–10.

Baydar, N., White, M. J., Simkins, C., and Babakol, O. (1990), 'Effects of Agricultural Development Policies on Migration in Peninsular Malaysia', *Demography*, 27: 97–109.

Benería, L., and Roldán, M. (1987), *The Crossroads of Class and Gender: Industrial Homework, Subcontracting, and Household Dynamics in Mexico City*, Chicago: University of Chicago Press.

Bilsborrow, R. E. (1984), 'The Need for and Design of Community-Level Questionnaires', in R. E. Bilsborrow, A. S. Oberai, and G. Standing (eds.), *Migration Surveys in Low Income Countries: Guidelines for Survey and Questionnaire Design*, London: Croom-Helm, 407–86.

—— McDevitt, T. M., Kossoudji, S., and Fuller, R. (1987), 'The Impact of Origin Community Characteristics on Rural–Urban Out-migration in a Developing Country', *Demography*, 24: 191–210.

Boyd, M. (1989), 'Family and Personal Networks in International Migration: Recent Developments and New Agendas', *International Migration Review*, 23: 638–70.

Brice-Laporte, Roys, and Couch, R. Stephen (1976), *Exploratory Fieldwork on Latino Migrants and Indochinese Refugees*, Washington, DC: Research Institute on Migration and Ethnic Studies, Smithsonian Institution.

Brown, L. A. (1991), *Place, Migration and Development in the Third World: An Alternative View*, London: Routledge.

——and Goetz, A. (1987), 'Development-Related Contextual Effects and Individual Attributes in Third World Migration Processes: a Venezuelan Example', *Demography*, 24: 497–516.

Cárdenas, G., and Flores, E. T. (1986), *The Migration and Settlement of Undocumented Women*, Austin, Tex.: CMAS Publications.

Casillas Moreno, A. (1985), *La mujer en dos comunidades de emigrantes (Chihuahua)*, Mexico city: Consejo Nacional de Fomento Educativo.

Chant, S. (1985), 'Family Formation and Female Roles in Queretaro, Mexico', *Bulletin of Latin American Research*, 4: 17–32.

Chavez, L. (1988), 'Settlers and Sojourners: The Case of Mexicans in the United States', *Human Organization*, 47: 95–108.

Dagodag, W. T. (1975), 'Source Regions and Composition of Illegal Mexican Immigration to California', *International Migration Review*, 9: 499–511.

Dinerman, I. R. (1982), *Migrants and Stay-at-Homes: A Comparative Study of Rural Migration from Michoacán, Mexico*, San Diego: Center for US–Mexican Studies, University of California, San Diego.

Donato, K. M. (1993), 'Current Trends and Patterns of Female Migration: Evidence from Mexico', *International Migration Review*, 27: 748–71.

——(1994), 'US Policy and Mexican Migration to the United States, 1942–92', *Social Science Quarterly*, 75: 705–29.

——Durand, J., and Massey, D. S. (1992), 'Stemming the Tide? Assessing the Deterrent Effects of the Immigration Reform and Control Act', *Demography*, 29: 139–57.

——and Kanaiaupuni, S. (1993), 'The Labour Force Activity of Mexican Migrant Women', paper presented at the Southern Demographic Association meetings, New Orleans.

Durand, J., and Massey, D. S. (1992), 'Mexico–U.S. Migration: A Critical Review', *Latin American Research Review*, 27: 3–42.

Elú de Leñero, M. (1969), *¿Hacia donde va la mujer mexicana?*, Mexico City: Instituto Mexicano de Estudios Sociales.

Fernandez-Kelly, M. P. (1983), 'Mexican Border Industrialization, Female Labour Force Participation and Migration', in J. Nash and M. P. Fernandez Kelly (eds.), *Women, Men and the International Division of Labor*, New York: SUNY Press, 205–23.

Findley, S. E. (1987), 'An Interactive Contextual Model of Migration in Ilocos Norte, the Philippines', *Demography*, 24: 163–90.

——and Diallo, A. (1993), 'Social Appearances and Economic Realities of Female Migration in Rural Mali', in United Nations, *Internal Migration of Women in Developing Countries*, New York: United Nations, 195–206.

Fletcher, P., and Taylor, E. (1992), 'Migration and the Transformation of a Mexican Village House Economy', paper presented at the Binational Conference on Mexico–US Migration, Chicago.

Galarza, Ernest (1964), *Merchants of Labour: The Mexican Bracero Story*, Santa Barbara, Calif.: McNally and Loftin.

Goldring, Luin (1995), 'Gendered Memory: Reconstruction of Rurality among Mexican Transnational Migrants', in Lu M. DuPuis and P. Vandergeest (eds.), *Nature, Rurality and Culture: The Social Construction of Rural Development and Environmental Conservation*, Philadelphia: Temple University Press.

González de la Rocha, M. (1988), 'Economic Crisis, Domestic Reorganization and Women's Work in Guadalajara, México', *Bulletin of Latin American Research*, 2: 207–23.

Grasmuck, S., and Pessar, R. P. (1991), *Between Two Islands: Dominican International Migration*, Berkeley: University of California Press.

Grindle, M. (1988), *Searching for Rural Development*, Ithaca, NY: Cornell Press.

Guest, P. (1993), 'The Determinants of Female Migration from a Multilevel Perspective', in United Nations, *Internal Migration of Women in Developing Countries*, New York: United Nations, 223–42.

——and Praditwong, T. (1989), 'A Contextual Model of Thai Migration', paper presented at the Annual Meetings of the Population Association of America, Baltimore.

Harbison, S. F. (1981), 'Family Structure and Family Strategy in Migration Decision Making', in G. F. De Jong and R. W. Gardner (eds.), *Migration Decision Making: Multidisciplinary Approaches to Microlevel Studies in Developed Countries*, New York: Pergamon Press, 225–51.

Hondagneu-Sotelo, P. (1992), 'Overcoming Patriarchal Constraints: The Reconstruction of Gender Relations among Mexican Immigrant Women and Men', *Gender and Society*, 6: 393–415.

——(1994), *Gendered Transitions: Mexican Experiences of Immigration*, Berkeley: University of California Press.

Hugo, G. J. (1981), 'Village-Community Ties, Village Norms and Ethnic and Social Networks: A Review of Evidence from the Third World', in G. F. de Jong and R. W. Gardner (eds.), *Migration Decision Making: Multidisciplinary Approaches in Microlevel Studies in Developed and Developing Countries*, New York: Pergamon Press, 186–224.

Jones, R. C. (1988), 'Micro Source Regions of Mexican Undocumented Migration', *National Geographic Research*, 4: 11–22.

Kanaiaupuni, S. M. (1993), 'Household Organization Strategies: The Migration and Work Activities of Women and Men in Mexican Families', paper presented at the Annual Meetings of the Population Association of America, Cincinnati, Ohio.

——(1994), 'The Role of Women in the Social Process of Migration: Household Organizational Strategies among Mexican Migrant Families', Ph.D. dissertation, University of Chicago.

——(1995), '*Mujeres y Hombres*: A Gender Analysis of the Determinants of Migration from Mexico', paper presented at the Annual Meetings of the American Sociological Association, Washington, DC.

——and Neuman, K. (1994), 'The Diversity of Experience: Women and Migration from Mexico', paper presented at the Annual Meetings of the Latin American Studies Association, Atlanta.

——Kandel, W. A., and Donato, K. M. (1995), 'Women and Opportunity: Returns to Human Capital for Internal and International Migrants from Mexico', paper presented at the Annual Meetings of the Population Association of America, San Francisco.

Leeds, A. (1976), 'Women in the Migratory Process: A Reductionist Outlook', *Anthropological Quarterly*, 49: 66–9.

Lewis, O. (1959), *Five Families*, New York: John Wiley and Sons.

——(1960), *Tepoztlan, Village in Mexico*, Calif.: Holt, Rinehart and Winston.

Lim, L. L. (1993), 'Effects of Women's Position on their Migration', in N. Federici, K. Oppenheim Mason, and S. Sogner (eds.), *Women's Position and Demographic Change*, Oxford: Clarendon Press, 225–42.

Lindstrom, D. P. (1991), 'The Differential Role of Family Networks in Individual Migration Decisions', paper presented at the Annual Meetings of the Population Association of America, Washington, DC.

Lomnitz, L. (1977), *Networks and Marginality: Life in a Mexican Shantytown*, New York: Academic Press.

Loyden Sosa, H. (1986), *Mujeres Campesinas: Estudios sobre la Mujer*, Mexico City: El Colegio de México.

Lund Skar, S. (1993), 'The Gendered Dynamics of Quechua Colonisation: Relations of Centre and Periphery in Peru', in G. Buijs (ed.), *Migrant Women: Crossing Boundaries and Changing Identities*, Providence, RI: Berg, 21–34.

Maddala, G. S. (1983), *Limited Dependent and Qualitative Variables in Econometrics*, New York: Cambridge University Press.

Massey, D. S. (1985), 'The Settlement Process among Mexican Migrants to the United States: New Methods and Findings', in *Immigration Statistics: A Story of Neglect*, Washington, DC: National Academy Press, 255–92.

——(1987), 'Understanding Mexican Migration to the United States', *American Journal of Sociology*, 92: 1372–1403.

——(1988), 'Economic Development and International Migration in Comparative Perspective', *Population and Development Review*, 14: 383–413.

——Alarcón, R., Durand, J., and González, H. (1987), *Return to Aztlan: The Social Process of International Migration from Western Mexico*, Berkeley: University of California Press.

——Goldring, L., and Durand, J. (1994), 'Continuities in Transnational Migration: An Analysis of 19 Mexican Communities', *American Journal of Sociology*, 99: 1492–1533.

——and Liang, Z. (1989), 'The Long Term Consequences of a Temporary Worker Program: The US Bracero Experience', *Population Research and Policy Review*, 8: 199–226.

——and Parrado, E. (1994), 'Migradollars: The Remittances and Savings of Mexican Migrants to the U.S.A.', *Population Research and Policy Review*, 13: 3–30.

Mines, R., and Massey, D. S. (1985), 'Patterns of Migration to the United States from Two Mexican Communities', *Latin American Research Review*, 20: 104–24.

MMP [Mexican Migration Project] (1995), *Documentation of Data Files*, Philadelphia: Population Studies Center, University of Pennsylvania.

Morokvasic, M. (1983), 'Why do Women Migrate? Towards an Understanding of the Sex-Selectivity in the Migratory Movements of Labour', *Studi Emigrazione/Estudes Migrations*, 20: 132–41.

Mummert, G. (1988), 'Mujeres de migrantes y mujeres migrantes de Michoacan:

Nuevos papeles para las que se quedan y para las que se van', in T. Calvo and G. López (eds.), *Movimientos de Población en el Occidente de México*, Mexico City: El Colegio de Michoacan, CEMCA, 281–98.

North, D. S., and Houstoun, M. F. (1976), *The Characteristics and Role of Illegal Aliens in the U.S. Labour Market: An Exploratory Study*, Washington, DC: Litton.

Oliveira, O. de (1984), 'Migración femenina, organización familiar y mercados laborales en México', *Comercio Exterior*, 34: 676–87.

Pedraza, S. (1991), 'Women and Migration: The Social Consequences of Gender', *Annual Review of Sociology*, 17: 303–25.

Piore, J. M. (1979), *Birds of Passage: Migrant Labor in Industrial Societies*, New York: Cambridge University Press.

Ranney, S., and Kossoudji, S. A. (1984), 'The Labour Market Experience of Female Migrants: The case of Temporary Mexican Migration to the U.S.', *International Migration Review*, 18: 1120–43.

Reichert, J., and Massey, D. S. (1979), 'Patterns of U.S. Migration from a Mexican Sending Community: A Comparison of Legal and Illegal Migrants', *International Migration Review*, 13: 599–623.

——— (1980), 'History and Trends in U.S.-bound Migration from a Mexican Town', *International Migration Review*, 14: 475–91.

Rodríguez, J. (1985), 'Immigration by Single Mexican Women to the United States', M. A. thesis, University of Texas at Austin.

Roney, Lisa S. (1992), 'Immigration Policy over the Past Quarter Century—Who Immigrated and Why?', paper presented at the Annual Meetings of the Population Association of America, Denver.

Rouse, R. (1989), 'Mexican Migration to the United States: Family Relations in Development of a Transnational Migrant Circuit', Ph.D. dissertation, Stanford University.

Selby, H., Murphy, A., and Lorenzen, S. A. (1990), *The Mexican Urban Household: Organizing for Self-Defense*, Austin, Tex.: University of Texas Press.

Simon, R. J., and DeLey, M. (1984), 'The Work Experience of Undocumented Mexican Women Migrants in Los Angeles', *International Migration Review*, 18: 1212–29.

Stark, O. (1984), 'Rural to Urban Migration in LDCs: A Relative Deprivation Approach', *Economic Development and Cultural Change*, 32: 475–86.

Stier, H., and Tienda, M. (1992), 'Family, Work and Women: The Labor Supply of Hispanic Immigrant Women', *International Migration Review*, 26: 1291–1313.

Szasz, I. (1992), 'La migración femenina en México: Tendencias emergentes', paper presented at the Workshop on Territorial Mobility in Latin America, York University, Toronto.

Tanory-Villa, C. A. (1989), *La mujer migrante y el empleo: El caso de la industria maquiladora en la frontera norte*, Mexico City: Instituto Nacional de Antropología e Historia.

Weist, R. (1983), 'La dependencia externa y la perpetuación de la migración temporal a los Estados Unidos', *Relaciones*, 15: 12–25.

Youssef, P. (1983), 'Establishing the Economic Condition of Woman-Headed Households in the Third World: A New Approach', in M. Buvinic, M. A. Lycette, and W. P. MacGreevey (eds.), *Women and Poverty in the Third World*, Baltimore: Johns Hopkins University Press, 216–43.

10 Household Social Dynamics and the Retention of Rural Population: A Malian Case Study of the Link between Patriarchy and the Sustained Ruralization of Sub-Saharan Africa

Michael Tawanda

Introduction

Compared to a projected world urbanization level of approximately 50 per cent by the year 2000, the corresponding figure for Africa is only about 41 per cent (United Nations 1991). Given this disparity, it is important to deal with the question of why African rural areas continue to retain the larger share of the national population. In this paper, I propose and test what I shall refer to as a patriarchal household model of Africa's retention of rural population. The central dynamic in the model is provided by social-system continuity, and my main hypothesis is that men and women who are highly subordinate to the patriarch are less likely to engage in rural out-migration than individuals whose level of subordination is low. A secondary working hypothesis is that the migration effects of household social dynamics are stronger than the migration effects of household economic characteristics. To evaluate these propositions, we employ the STATA M-logit procedure on data from the Kayes region of Mali, West Africa, to estimate a multinomial logistic regression model of rural out-migration.

The Social Lacuna in the Migration Literature: Bringing the Patriarch Back In

There are currently four perspectives relevant to Africa's population distribution. These include the macro-structural approach of political economy (Meillasoux 1972; Abu-Lughod 1976; Amin 1977; Portes and Walton 1981), the purely demographic model, the individualistic paradigm of classical economics (Todaro 1969; Harris and Todaro 1970; Barnum and Sabot 1977) and the household survival models of migration (DaVanzo 1981; Harbison 1981; Findley 1987). However, despite the fact that a patriarchal household social order[1] constitutes the typical pre-migration context for the rural African out-migrant, in none of these approaches are social dynamics at origin fully integrated. The tendency instead is to emphasize the migration, or non-migration, effect of economic factors.

The foregoing notwithstanding, the household survival model is one approach which theoretically incorporates the migration effects of social context at origin. Nevertheless, to the extent that patriarchal household processes are incorporated into the model, they are misconceptualized. Following Becker's (1976, 1981) new household economics approach, however, this perspective conventionally vests the migration decision in *altruistically* motivated household heads, who are perceived as concerned primarily with the *economic* survival needs of the household. These needs include immediate food and other maintenance requirements (see Adams 1977; Minvielle 1985) as well as capital investment in items such as tractors, or commercial enterprise (see Coulibaly *et al.* 1980; Minvielle 1985).

African fertility analysts have already pointed out that the household economics perspective is based on two false premises, namely, intra-household consensualism and a joint household utility function (Caldwell 1982; Oppong 1983; Ryder 1984; Cain 1989). On the contrary, and courtesy of traditional religion, patriarchs are ideologized as custodians of corporate group resources, and as mediators between the living on the one hand and the ancestors and the Supreme Being on the other (Andah 1990). With this perceived 'hot line' to the supernatural, patriarchs are therefore under no obligation either to consult with, or heed the suggestions of, siblings.

Similarly, social differentiation on the basis of age and gender suggests that patriarchs' solicitation of input from women and children into the migration decision may be construed as a sign of weakness. Conversely, unsolicited input from persons of a lesser status may be regarded as an affront. In fact, the economic anthropologist A. F. Robertson (1991: 41) has argued that 'the [patriarchal] household can look less like a democratic republic than a little despotic state'.

In view of the foregoing, I suggest that a more realistic household model of migration is one which, without negating on the role of economic motives, places greater emphasis on the role of power and of status. More specifically, I suggest that the continuity of the social order upon which the patriarch's status is based also constitutes a prime objective in his migration decision-making process.

The Model

From the perspective of the patriarch concerned with both system continuity and household economic survival, different migration destinations imply varying risks of household fission on the one hand and potential material gains on the other. Compared to both rural–urban and international migration, rural–

rural migration implies fewer risks of household fission: the first two types of migration expose migrants to alternative value systems, as well as to alternatives to economic dependence on the patriarch. On the other hand, rural–urban and international migration imply entry into more lucrative labour markets. Therefore, a major dilemma confronting the patriarch is how to benefit from the expected higher material gains associated with rural–urban and international migration, while minimizing the attendant risk of household fission.

One way in which the patriarch's dilemma can be resolved is by confining highly subordinate household members to rural–rural migration, while using human capital characteristics as criteria for rural out-migration. For highly subordinate males and females, restriction to rural–rural migration denies them exposure to urban value systems which may undermine patriarchal authority. Furthermore, control of female spatial mobility through female rural–rural marriage migration ensures continuity of lineage in the offspring which wives provide (Meillasoux 1981) as well as perpetuation of attitudes of male domination on the one hand and female subordination on the other.

One African study, which nevertheless excludes females, provides some evidence that social-system survival can be an important consideration in the migration decision-making process. Mazur (1984), in his study of male migration in Mali, found that sons of the incumbent were more likely to remain in the rural household than his brothers, uncles, and nephews. The researcher concluded that sons' lower migration propensities anticipated their future assumption of household headship. By including females in our investigation, we can test for gender specificity in the migration effects of subordination to the patriarch, and thereby provide a more complete understanding of the social dynamics underlying the retention of rural population.

Data and Methods

Sources of Data

The study utilizes multi-level, longitudinal data obtained by the Centre d'Études et de Recherche sur la Population pour le Développement (CERPOD) of the Sahel Institute in Bamako, Mali. This survey of the Kayes Region of Mali, conducted from 1983 to 1989,[2] provides detailed inter-survey data, and various household- and village-level information. The data, therefore, allow us to evaluate the independent effects of household- and village-level economic characteristics, as well as the relative migration impact of personal factors and household social dynamics.

The Study Area

Mali has a number of characteristics which make it ideal for present purposes. The country is the least urbanized (United Nations 1991) and one of the poorest on the African continent (World Bank 1986). This conjunction of underdevelopment with low urbanization lends credence to the theory that development is associated with urbanization, and also highlights the need for research on the antecedents of population distribution.

The Kayes study area itself is situated in the Malian portion of the Upper Senegal River Valley, which is one of the least economically developed areas in the Western Sahel (Findley and Ouedraogo 1992). The region is also inhabited by a number of patriarchal ethnic groups, including the Soninke, the Khassonke, and a number of smaller ethnic groups including the Toucouler, Bambara, Maure, and Malinke.

Sampling

Sampling began with a 1982 survey of 14 per cent (1,219) of the registered Senegalese, Malian, and Mauritanian immigrant working population in the Paris and Seine-Maritime areas, the two main immigrant catchment areas in France. In this survey respondents named their villages of origin, which were then arranged into two strata: villages with 20 or more emigrants and villages with 1–19 emigrants currently in France. Thirty-three villages from each of these strata were selected, to represent areas of high and medium out-migration. Thirty-three villages with no emigrants were then added to this list of 66, to represent areas with little or no emigration to France. Of the total of 99 villages, 39 were Malian, 12 Mauritanian, and 48 Senegalese (Findley and Ouedraogo 1992). Different sampling fractions were then employed in each strata to obtain a Probability Proportionate to Size (PPS) sample of about 100 individuals per village. In 1982 the total sample equalled 1,032 households with 12,558 individuals, including migrants as well as non-migrants; the Malian sub-sample comprised 324 households with 4,910 individuals.

The 1989 follow-up survey identified all 324 of the 1982 households, even though either household headship or composition may have changed in the interim. In addition, 3 new households which had hived off from some of the original households were also interviewed, bringing the total number of house-holds to 327. The reason for this stability of households is the existence of both horizontal extension—approximately 21 per cent of the sample households had at least one co-resident brother of the household head—and vertical extension—about 17 per cent had at least one married or formerly married co-resident son of the household head. In addition, 37.5 per cent of married men in the Kayes region in 1987 had more than one wife (République du Mali 1991), a practice which increases the likelihood of vertical extension. By 1989, the number of individuals had also increased to 7,263.

Our sample comprised 317 of the 327 households interviewed in 1989, located in 39 villages: the 3 new households identified in 1989 were omitted, since some of their membership are included in the 1982 count of 324 house-holds; 5 were discarded at source (CERPOD 1982) due to excessive missing values; 2 female-headed households were discarded because they do not fit our model of the patriarchal household. At the individual level the sample comprised 2,863 persons of at least 7 years of age. We selected age 7 as the lower age cut-off point, as this is the age when the rural dweller is expected to begin to make productive contributions to the household economy.

Analytical Framework

In our patriarchal household model, individuals whose socio-demographic characteristics influence the likelihood of migration are conceived as situated in, and also influenced by, household-level social and economic dynamics. We do not include education in the model due to the low levels of education among subjects in our sample. Households are themselves perceived as embedded within a local community context, which provides socio-economic opportunities that influence the patriarch's perception of the need to engage individual members in migration.

Dependent Variable

Our dependent variable (Migration Type) is polytomous (non-migration = 0, rural–rural, rural–urban, and international migration), and indicates whether or not an individual usually resident in a village in the Kayes region in 1982 recorded at least one move, of any duration, to a rural, urban, or inter-national destination during the period 1982–9. Non-migrants are defined as persons who did not record any move during the period 1982–9. The sample included 1,012 migrants (35.3%) and 1,851 non-migrants (64.7%); 206 members of the sample population (7.2%) were rural–rural migrants, 125 (4.4%) rural–urban migrants, and 681 (23.8%) international migrants. Of the migrants, 441 (43.6%) were male, and 571 (56.4%) were female.

Evaluation of our main proposition is facilitated by the multinomial logistic regression model, which estimates a series of parameters for contrasts among different categories of a polytomous dependent variable. The functional form of the multinomial logistic regression equation is as follows:

$$ln(P_j/P_m) = \sum \beta_i X_i,$$

where

j represents migration type;

m represents the reference category (Non-migrant);

$ln(P_j / P_m)$ represents the log odds of an individual being in category j relative to category m of the dependent variable;

X_i is a vector of selected independent variables; and

β_i is a vector of estimated parameters representing the change in the log odds of choice j versus the reference category m for a unit change in X_i.

Independent variables

Subordination

On the basis of the central organizing principles of patriarchy, namely, gender, generation, and consanguinity, I derived the ordinal variable Subord, which ranks household members according to their level of subordination to the patriarch. In descending order of subordination, the variable includes the patriarch, eldest daughter, younger daughters, other female relatives, eldest son, other male relatives, younger son, junior wife, senior wife, and non-relatives. Primarily because of the need for parsimony in our multi-level model, I treat this variable as continuous.[3]

Females are the household sub-group most subordinate to the patriarch. Compared to their male counterparts, therefore, females offer the patriarch greater guarantees of returns from migration. I hypothesize that the positive rural–rural migration effect of subordination to the patriarch is enhanced among females.

The migration effects of subordination to the patriarch may also be subject to ethnic variation. The patriarch's authority is based upon his custodianship of the lineage's inputs into agriculture, including land, capital equipment, and livestock (see Meillasoux 1981). In the final analysis, the positive migration effect of subordination to the patriarch may be strongest among sedentary agriculturalists, among whom are the Khassonke, who constitute the largest group in our sample (Pollet and Winter 1971; Klaus 1976; Mazur 1984). I expect that the positive rural–rural migration effect of subordination to the patriarch will be enhanced among the Khassonke.

Rural development often involves the development of institutions such as schools, which challenge traditional values (Massey *et al.* 1988). We therefore hypothesize that village development inhibits the positive rural–rural migration effect of subordination to the patriarch.

Individual-Level Control Variables

Age-82 is a continuous variable measuring age in 1982. Migration is a life-cycle phenomenon (Connel *et al.* 1976; Goldstein 1978). Ages 15–34 are the productive years, when individuals are also eligible for either continuing education or marriage, factors which increase the likelihood of migration. On the other hand, increased family ties and personal capital at older ages reduce the likelihood of migration. I therefore expect a curvilinear relationship between age and migration, and this is the reason I have also included the age variable in a squared form.

Gend is a categorical variable (male = 0, female). Rural–rural marriage migration is central to the functioning of patriarchy; I therefore expect females to be more likely to migrate than males. On the other hand, the male bias in non-farm job opportunities leads us to expect males to be more likely to engage in rural–rural and international migration than females, an effect which is strongest for international migration.

Mari-82 is a categorical variable (never married = 0, currently married, formerly married) representing marital status in 1982. Migration is related to family formation (see Lee 1966; Connel *et al.* 1976; Goldstein 1978; Findley 1987) and therefore, irrespective of migration type, we expect the never-married to be more likely to engage in migration than either the currently or formerly married. However, the migration effect of marital status may be different for males and females. Because of women's child-rearing and domestic responsibilities, the migration-inhibiting effect of being either currently or formerly married may be stronger for females than for males.

Primig-82 is a categorical (no prior migration experience = 0, at least one prior move) and represents an individual's previous migration history. Individuals who have migrated in the past may have established employment contacts who can expedite the job-seeking process, as well as acquaintances who can assist with food and accommodation at destination (Fields 1975; Thomas and Byrnes 1976; Yap 1977). This reduces the financial costs of migration, as well as the waiting time for receipt of returns from migration. Therefore, compared to persons with no migration experience, members with migration experience may be more likely to engage in migration, with the effect being strongest for international migration.

Household-Level Control Variables: Social

Pbros-82 is a continuous variable which measures the number of the patriarch's brothers who were present at the beginning of the migration interval, and represents the strength of the patriarch's control over his household. In less-developed economies, horizontal household extension can be perceived as a function of the absence of adequate alternative sources of sustenance for the extendee (Robertson 1991). With the patriarch controlling vital resources, he may not need to fear household fission through out-migration. Horizontal household extension may therefore increase the likelihood of migration, irrespective of the destination of migration.

Soninke, Khassonke, and Others (Others = 0) are dummy variables representing the patriarch's ethnicity. As intimated earlier, I expect the Khassonke to be the ethnic group most likely to engage in migration, albeit more in rural–rural migration.

Household-Level Control Variables: Economic

Income-82 is a categorical variable (medium = 0, high, income missing) representing household income, measured in CFA. The 33rd and 66th percentiles provide the cut-off points for the low and medium income categories, respectively, while households whose income falls above the 66th percentile constitute the high income category. The income missing category comprises households (36) with no income recorded for 1982.[4] Household income is an important indicator of the need for supplementary income through migration. However, the migration effect of household income is not necessarily linear and negative. In fact, some studies have demonstrated a U-shaped relationship between household income and migration, with migrants more likely to originate in rich and poor households than in middle-income households (Connel *et al.* 1976; Findley 1987). This finding is explained by the fact that, while both lower- and upper-income households are risk-takers, middle-income households are risk-averse (Findley 1987). I therefore expect a curvilinear relationship between household income and migration.

Village-Level Control Variables

Ldev-82, Mdev-82, and Hdev-82 are dummy variables representing low, medium, and high levels of village development in 1982, respectively, with development determined by position on a composite measure of the availability of water sources and public and social services within the village. Ldev provides the ideal contrast category, since most villages are not expected to have significant levels of development.

Contrary to the commonly held assumption that people will stay if there is rural development, development may actually increase the likelihood of migration. If development involves the transmission and adoption of new agricultural technologies such as irrigation, patriarchs may re-locate some household members in extra-local labour markets in order to obtain the income to purchase the necessary inputs, including hybrid seeds and equipment (Findley 1987).

Similarly, if development involves the establishment of public and social service institutions, including agricultural extension, local government administration, schools, and clinics, these organizations may serve as a source of information about alternative labour markets. Schools in particular may actually prepare individuals for participation in these extra-local labour markets. The conjunction of the need for the inputs into improved agriculture and information diffusion may therefore increase the volume of rural out-migration. However, as Findley (1987) points out, the positive migration response to development may decline once rural development becomes self-sustaining. In conclusion, therefore, patriarchs in households located in villages with medium development may be more likely to engage household members in migration than patriarchs whose households are located in villages with either low or high development.

Poorer households are less likely than other households to have members with the educational qualifications compatible with modern-sector employment. The financial costs of migration are also relatively higher for poorer households. By increasing the availability of local off-farm work, village development may therefore inhibit migration by individuals in poorer households compared to individuals from richer or medium-income households. Irrespective of destination, village development may therefore reduce the stimulating migration effect of low level of household income.

Vacces-82 is a categorical variable (no road or rail access to an urban centre = 0, road or rail access to an urban centre). The accessibility of the village to market or urban-industrial centres increases the physical availability of the option of rural–urban migration (Harbison 1981). Accessibility to urban centres is also critical for international and rural–rural migration since these centres are often also transportation nodes. Irrespective of destination, compared to patriarchs in households located in villages that are not accessible to urban centres, patriarchs in households located in villages that are accessible to urban centres may therefore be more likely to engage household members in any migration.

Household Economic versus Household Social Dynamics

Household economic welfare is an important aspect of the function of household leadership. But in our patriarchal household model, achievement of the economic welfare of the household through migration depends upon the existence of a household authority structure which promotes migrant remittances and/or return migration. I therefore suggest that the migration effect of household social dynamics is stronger than the migration effect of household economic variables.

Results

Table 10.1 presents the results of my preferred multinomial regression model. This is the model in which non-significant parameter estimates have been removed.

Subordination to the Patriarch

The results provide support for my hypothesis that subordination has a positive effect on rural–rural migration. A one-level increase in subordination increased the log odds of rural–rural migration by slightly more than 26 per cent, at $p < 0.05$. On the other hand, instead of an enhanced positive rural–rural migration effect of subordination among females as expected, highly subordinate females were more likely to engage in international migration than their male counterparts. Nevertheless, this latter result is consistent with my hypothesis that the migration effects of social factors are stronger for females than for males.

Table 10.1. Parameter estimates for multinomial logistic regression model of migration from the Kayes region, of Mali, 1982–1989, with destination outcomes: preferred model, all (omitted category in parentheses)[a]

	Mali rural versus no migration	Mali urban versus no migration	International migration versus no migration
Constant	−5.7921**	−7.2384**	−2.3314**
Individual-level variables			
Age-82	0.1393**	0.1626**	0.0860**
Age-82^2	−0.0021**	−0.0021**	−0.0012**
Gend (Male)			
Female	1.8845*	−0.9937	−0.6061*
Mari-82 (Never)			
Currently married	−2.1473**	−0.9619*	−1.3461*
Formerly married	−1.9396*	−0.5185	−1.1136*
Primig-82 (None)			
At Least 1 Move	0.1244	−0.4131	0.6181**
Subord	0.2620*	0.0717	0.0345
Household-level variables			
Pbros-82	−0.2533	0.2127	−0.1314
Patriarch's ethnicity (Others)			
Soninke	0.5579*	0.8163*	−0.3495*
Khassonke	1.2367*	0.3320	−0.1304
Income-82 (Medium)			
Missing	0.7124*	0.0034	0.0805
Low	−0.3755	0.5617	−0.1144
High	0.1196	−0.0647	0.0108
Village-level variables			
Vedv-82 (Low)			
Medium	0.0278	0.8145*	0.4326*
High	−0.0533	0.6334	0.4760*
Vacces-82 (No)			
Yes	0.1039	1.6600	0.5567*
Interactions			
Medium Vdev & Low household income	0.2968	−1.4117*	−0.1201
Khassonke & Subord	−0.1688*	0.0723	−0.0283
Female & Subord	−0.0823	0.0211	0.1459*
Female & Pbros-82	0.0872	−0.6237*	−0.1364

[a] The results of a log likelihood ratio test for improvement between the pooled sample and the sample split by males and females were non-significant. My test for gender differentials in the multinominal model therefore involved inclusion of a dummy variable for gender.

* $p < 0.05$.
** $p < 0.01$.

Source: Estimates by the author.

Ethnicity also conditioned the link between subordination and rural–rural migration, though not in the expected direction. The positive rural–rural migration effect of subordination was reduced among the Khassonke group.

Individual-Level Control Variables

In general, the individual-level control variables behaved as expected, as expected age in 1982 was non-monotonically related to the likelihood of migration for all migration types. Females were less likely to engage in international migration than males, but more likely than males to engage in rural–rural migration. As expected, currently and formerly married individuals were less likely to engage in rural–rural and international migration than the never-married. However, the parameter estimate for rural–urban migration by the formerly married is non-significant. Also as expected, prior migration experience had no effect on rural–rural migration, but increased the likelihood of international migration. Contrary to my expectation, however, prior migration experience had no effect on the likelihood of rural–urban migration.

Household-Level Control Variables: Social

Co-residence by the patriarch's brothers did not behave as expected in the main effects model. However, the migration effect of co-residence was conditioned by gender. This interaction produced a negative relationship between co-residence and rural–urban migration by females, a result which is significant at $p < 0.05$.

As expected, the Soninke were more likely than other ethnic groups to engage in rural–rural and rural–urban migration. Surprisingly, however, the Soninke were less likely than other groups to engage in international migration. This latter result contradicts much of the literature, which shows the Soninke as being the most likely to engage in international migration to France (Pollett and Winter 1971). However, our definition of international migration also includes moves to other African countries, which may account for the anomaly.

Household-Level Controls: Economic

Level of household income did not behave as expected. The results suggest that individuals from households with low and high incomes were not more likely to engage in international migration than individuals from households with medium income. Interestingly, individuals from households with missing income data were more likely to engage in rural–rural migration than individuals from households with medium income. As expected, however, low levels of household income conditioned the migration effect of village development, although only in villages at medium development, and for rural–urban migration alone. The significant and negative coefficient for the interaction between medium village development and low household income indicates a reduction in the likelihood of rural–urban migration from poorer households at medium levels of development.

Interpretation of the interaction between medium village development and low household income is complicated by the poor quality of the income data. This proviso notwithstanding, the job opportunities which accompany rural development are most likely to attract the poor, who may either have insufficient funds to finance long-distance migration or lack the qualifications and skills for extra-local modern-sector employment.

Village-Level Control Variables

Contrary to expectation the curvilinear migration effect of village development was only obtained for rural–urban migration. Compared to the log odds of rural–urban migration from villages at low levels of development, the corresponding log odds for villages at medium levels of development were about 81 per cent higher. On the other hand, there were no significant differences in migration propensities from villages at low and high levels of development, respectively. In contrast, while village development had no effect on the likelihood of rural–rural migration, there was a monotonic relationship between level of village development and international migration.

The results support two apparently contradictory theories on the relationship between development and migration. On the one hand, the monotonic relationship between international migration and development is consistent with Massey's (1988) theory that development promotes internal and international migration through the labour displacement which accompanies capitalization, as well as through improvements in transportation which facilitate population movements between high- and low-income countries. On the other hand, the curvilinear relationship between rural–urban migration and village development is consistent with Findley's (1987) hypothesis that medium development stimulates migration as a household strategy to obtain the inputs necessary to derive benefits from local developments in agricultural technology.

Contrary to expectation, the positive migration effect of village accessibility was not independent of migration destination. Village accessibility had its strongest positive effect on international migration. A possible explanation for this result is that unlike rural–rural and rural–urban migration, transportation to international destinations is only obtainable over well-established routes.

Household Social versus Household Economic Factors

The results of likelihood-ratio and chi-square goodness-of-fit tests of our model are shown in Table 10.2. As Table 10.2 shows, the model has some pre-

Table 10.2. Goodness-of-fit tests for multinomial logistic regression model of migration from the Kayes region, Mali, 1982–1989, with destination outcomes

Model/Stage	-2 log likelihood	Pseudo-R^{2a}	Change from prior model			-2dLL	dDf	p	N
			Chi-square	Df	p				
Baseline (intercept only)	$-2,718.8157$								2,863
I. Age, Age^2, Gender, Education, Marital status, Prior migration experience	$-2,532.5976$		372.44	21	0.01	186.22	21	0.01	2,863
II. Household income, Young children, Current migrants	$-2,515.0548$		407.52	36	0.01	17.543	15	n.s.	2,863
III. Subordination to patriarch, Patriarch's brothers co-residing	$-2,493.8162$		450.00	42	0.01	21.239	6	0.01	2,863
IV. Patriarch's ethnicity	$-2,476.6345$		484.36	48	0.01	17.182	6	0.01	2,863
V. Village development	$-2,471.5687$		494.49	54	0.01	5.066	6	n.s.	2,863
VI. Village drought, Village access	$-2,466.868$	0.09	503.90	60	0.01	4.701	6	n.s.	2,863
VII. Interactions									
Medium Vdev & Low household income	$-2,462.2058$		513.22	63	0.01	4.662	3	n.s.	2,863
High Vdev & Low household income	$-2,461.2369$		515.16	66	0.01	0.969	3	n.s.	2,863
Medium Vdev & Subordination to patriarch	$-2,460.6951$		516.24	66	0.01	1.511	3	n.s.	2,863
High Vdev & Subordination to patriarch	$-2,461.7551$		514.12	66	0.01	0.451	3	n.s.	2,863
Soninke & Subordination to patriarch	$-2,459.9334$		517.76	66	0.01	2.272	3	n.s.	2,863
Khassonke & Subordination to patriarch	$-2,459.1844$		519.26	66	0.01	3.021	3	n.s.	2,863
Female & Subordination to patriarch	$-2,455.0085$		527.61	69	0.01	4.176	3	n.s.	2,863
Female & Patriarch's brothers co-residing	$-2,451.0717$		535.49	72	0.01	3.937	3	n.s.	2,863
Preferred model	$-2,457.4748$	0.10	522.68	60	0.01				2,863

n.s. = not significant.

[a] The pseudo-R^2 is the equivalent of the R^2 value obtained in ordinary least-squares regression. It is a measure of the proportion of variance in the dependent variable explained by the model.

Source: Estimates by the author.

dictive value (stage VI). The model chi-square value is highly significant at $p < 0.01$, and the pseudo-R^2 value is 0.09.

As the results show, individual-level characteristics (stage I) produce a highly significant change in the log likelihood ratio. However, addition of household economic characteristics (stage II) does not produce a statistically significant improvement in the explanatory value of the model. In contrast, household social characteristics (stage III) produce a highly significant change in the log likelihood ratio. Similarly, the household social control variable of ethnicity also produces a highly significant change in the log likelihood ratio. As with the household economic variables, the change of log likelihood ratio on addition of village contextual variables, and the interaction terms, are all non-significant.

We can also assess the relative utility of the different levels of context by comparing their model chi-square values when introduced into the baseline model. The results of these tests are presented in Table 10.3.

As Table 10.3 shows, individual characteristics were the strongest predictors of migration destination. The model chi-square value is highly significant at $p < 0.01$ and highest when the model contains only the intercept and these individual-level characteristics. Comparison of the chi-square values for the

Table 10.3. Goodness-of-fit tests for the utility of individual, household, and village-level characteristics in the multinomial logistic regression model of migration from the Kayes region, Mali, 1982–1989, with destination outcomes

Model/Stage	−2 log likelihood	Change from prior model			N
		Chi-square	Df	p	
Baseline (intercept only)	−2,718.8157				2,863
I. Age, Age^2, Gender, Education, Marital status, Prior migration experience	−2,532.5976	372.44	21	0.01	2,863
II. Subordination to the patriarch, Patriarch's brothers co-residing	−2,697.2792	43.07	6	0.01	2,863
III. Subordination to the patriarch, Patriarch's brothers co-residing, Patriarch's ethnicity	−2,676.6742	84.28	12	0.01	2,863
IV. Household income, Young children, Current migrants	−2,701.2186	35.19	15	0.05	2,863
V. Village development	−2,709.2145	19.20	6	0.05	2,863
VI. Village development, Drought, Accessibility	−2,706.2947	25.04	12	0.05	2,863

Source: Estimates by the author.

models containing only the intercept and our household social variables of interest with the models containing only the intercept and the household economic variables provides further support for the patriarchal household model of migration. The model chi-square value for the model containing the intercept only and the economic characteristics of the household, 35.19, is about 18 per cent smaller than the model chi-square value for the model containing the intercept only and household social characteristics, 43.07.

Addition of the household social control variable of ethnicity almost doubles the model chi-square value for the model containing only the constant and the household social characteristics, to 84.28. Similarly, the model chi-square values for village-level characteristics are smaller than the value for household social characteristics.

Summary, Conclusions, and Discussion

The generalizability of my findings is limited by conditions which are peculiar to Mali. The country is predominantly Muslim, and at the time of survey, Mali was the least urbanized nation in Sub-Saharan Africa, and one of the poorest. Educational levels in the Kayes study area itself were extremely low, with the majority of our sample having received little or no formal education. These are all factors which promote the resilience of patriarchy as a form of social organization. The results are nevertheless encouraging.

In the Kayes region of Mali during the interval 1982–9, subordination to the patriarch was an important consideration in the decision to migrate. Highly subordinate individuals were restricted to rural–rural migration. However, instead of an enhanced positive rural–rural migration effect of subordination among females as expected, highly subordinate females were more likely to engage in international migration than their male counterparts. Individual characteristics, including age, marital status, and prior migration experience, also had strong effects on the choice of migration type. In particular, prior migration experience and gender, those characteristics most likely to enhance opportunities at destination, were positively related to international migration.

The study also indicates that, while the explanatory value of household social factors is second only to individual-level characteristics, the economic characteristics of the household and village context do not improve the explanatory value of my model. However, this finding may be influenced by the poor quality of the household income data. In addition, village-level economic factors, including level of development and accessibility, were positively related to rural–urban and international migration. Nevertheless, the results are consistent with my general proposition that household social factors play a critical role in population distribution.

In the final analysis, the results provide some support for my contention that conventional household survival models are an inadequate conceptualization of the migration decision-making process. More specifically, they suggest the need to incorporate social system continuity among the motives attributed to male rural household heads in Africa. Further research in this area, in different contexts and with improved data, will further our understanding of the dynamics underlying the retention of rural population.

Notes

1. Here, patriarchy is associated with patrilineal-patrilocal societies, and is defined as a social system in which rights and obligations are distributed along the axes of generation, age, and gender (Ryder 1984; Dixon-Mueller 1989).
2. The survey was part of a larger longitudinal study of the *Enquête de migration dans la vallée du fleuve Sénégal* (CERPOD 1982) and the *Enquête renouvelée de migration dans la vallée du fleuve Sénégal* (CERPOD 1989).
3. The rationale behind this rank-ordering is as follows. We place the patriarch, because of his position as household head, at the apex of this hierarchy. Then, among females who are more proximately related to the patriarch, the giving of priority to migration by the eldest daughter allows the patriarch to retain younger daughters in the household labour pool and also reduces the waiting time for receipt of income from migration. After daughters and female relatives, the eldest son occupies the next closest relationship to the patriarch, because inheritance among the ethnic groups in Mali is by primogeniture. After the children and other relatives, junior wives occupy the next level of proximity and then come senior wives. The patriarch can engage junior wives in migration to diffuse conflict amongst his co-wives as well as obtain income; in contrast, the senior wife, because of her senior status, is less likely than junior wives to be separated from the economic and sexual services of the patriarch. Finally, the patriarch has the least control over non-relatives (see Pollet and Winter 1971; Klaus 1976; Mazur 1984; Findley and Diallo 1988).
4. The income missing category is included to prevent reduction in our sample size.

References

Abu-Lughod, Janet L. (1976), 'Development in North African Urbanization: The Process of Decolonization', in Brian J. Berry (ed.), *Urbanization and Counter-urbanization,* Beverly Hills, Calif.: Sage, 191–211.

Adams, Adrian (1977), *Le long voyage des gens du fleuve,* Paris: François Maspero.

Amin, Samir (1977), *Imperialism and Unequal Development,* New York: Monthly Review Press.

Andah, B. (1990), *African Anthropology*: Shaneson CI Ltd.

Barnum, H., and Sabot, R. (1977), 'Education, Employment Probability and Rural–Urban Migration in Tanzania', *Oxford Bulletin of Economics and Statistics,* 31: 109–26.

Becker, G. (1976), *A Treatise on the Family,* Cambridge, Mass.: Harvard University Press.

Becker, G. (1981), *A Treatise on the Family*, 2nd edn., Cambridge, Mass.: Harvard University Press.

Cain, Mead (1989), 'Family Structure, Women's Status and Fertility Change', paper presented to the International Population Conference, New Delhi.

Caldwell, John C. (1982), *Theory of Fertility Decline*, London: Academic Press.

CERPOD [Centre d'Études et de Recherche sur la Population pour le Développement] (1982), *Enquête de migration dans la vallée du fleuve Sénégal*, Dakar: CERPOD.

——(1989), *Enquête renouvelée de migration dans la vallée du fleuve Sénégal*, Dakar: CERPOD.

Connel, J. B., Dasgupta, Laishley, B., and Lipton, M. (1976), *Migration from Rural Areas: The Evidence from Village Studies*, Delhi: Oxford University Press.

Coulibaly, Sidiki, Gregory, Joel, and Piche, Victor (1980), *Les migrations voltaiques: Importance et ambivalence de la migration voltaique*, Montreal: Centre Voltaique de la Recherche Scientifique et Institut National de la Démographie, Canada.

DaVanzo, Julie (1981), 'Microeconomic Approaches to Studying Migration Decisions', in Gordon F. DeJong and Robert W. Gardner (eds.), *Migration Decision Making: Multidisciplinary Approaches to Microlevel Studies in Developed and Developing Countries*, New York: Pergamon Press, 90–129.

Dixon-Mueller, Ruth (1989), 'Patriarchy, Fertility and Women's Work in Rural Societies', paper presented at the International Population Conference, New Delhi.

Fields, Gary (1975), 'Rural–Urban Migration, Urban Unemployment and Underemployment, and Job Search Activity in LDCs', *Journal of Development Economics*, 2: 165–87.

Findley, Sally E. (1987), *Rural Development and Migration: A Study of Family Choices in the Philippines*, Boulder, Colo.: Westview Press.

——and Diallo, Assitan (1988), 'Foster Children: Links between Rural and Urban Families?', paper presented at the African Population Conference, Dakar, Senegal.

——and Ouedraogo, Dieudonné (1992), 'Africa versus France: Factors Affecting the Choice of Malian Migrants', paper presented at the Annual Meetings of the Population Association of America, Denver.

Firebaugh, Glen (1985), 'Core–Periphery Patterns of Urbanization', in Michael Timberlake (ed.), *Urbanization in the World Economy*, New York: Academic Press, 293–304.

Goldstein, Walter (1978), *Planning, Politics and the Public Interest*, New York: Columbia University Press.

Harbison, Sarah F. (1981), 'Family Structure and Family Strategy in Migration Decision Making', in Gordon F. DeJong and Robert W. Gardner (eds.), *Migration Decision Making: Multidisciplinary Approaches to Microlevel Studies in Developed and Developing Countries*, New York: Pergamon Press, 225–52.

Harris, J. R., and Todaro, Michael (1970), 'Migration, Unemployment and Development: A Two-Sector Analysis', *American Economic Review*, 60: 126–42.

Klaus, Ernst (1976), *Tradition and Progress in the African Village: Non-capitalist Transformation of Rural Communities in Mali*, New York: St Martin's Press.

Lee, Everett (1966), 'A Theory of Migration', *Demography*, 3: 253–64.

Massey, Douglas (1988), 'Economic Development and International Migration in Comparative Perspective', *Population and Development Review*, 14: 383–413.

——Alarcón, R., Durand, J., and González, H. (1988), 'Return to Aztlan: The Social

Process of International Migration from Western Mexico', *American Journal of Sociology*, 94: 449–51.

Mazur, Robert (1984), 'Rural Out-migration and Labour Allocation in Mali', in Calvin Goldscheider (ed.), *Rural Migration in Developing Nations*, Boulder, Colo.: Westview Press, 209–88.

Meillasoux, Claude (1972), 'From Reproduction to Production: A Marxist Approach to Economic Anthropology', *Economy and Society*, 1: 93–104.

—— (1981), *Maidens, Meals and Money: Capitalism and the Domestic Economy*, Cambridge: Cambridge University Press.

Minvielle, Jean-Paul (1985), *Paysans migrants du Fouta Toro: La vallée du Sénégal*, Paris: Éditions de l'Orstom.

Oppong, Christine (1983), *Parental Costs, Role Strain and Fertility Regulation: Some Ghanaian Evidence*, Geneva: International Labour Organization.

Pollet, Eric, and Winter, Grace (1971), *La société Soninke (Dyahunu, Mali)*, Études ethnologiques, Brussels: Université Libre de Bruxelles.

Portes, Alejandro, and Walton, John (1981), *Labor, Class, and the International System*, New York: Academic Press.

République du Mali (1991), *Recensement général de la population et de l'habitat au Mali: Principaux résultats d'analyse*, Bamako: Ministère du Plan et de la Coopération Internationale, Direction National de la Statistique et de L'informatique.

Robertson, A. F. (1991), *Beyond the Family: The Social Organization of Human Reproduction*, Berkeley: University of California Press.

Ryder, Norman (1984), 'Fertility and Family Structure', in United Nations (ed.), *Fertility and Family Structure: Proceedings of the Expert Group on Fertility and Family*, New York: Columbia University Press, 279–319.

Thomas, R. N., and Byrnes, Kevin F. (1976), 'Intervening Opportunities and the Migration Field of a Secondary Urban Center: The Case of Tunja, Colombia', in R. J. Tata (ed.), *Latin America: Search for Geographic Explanation*, Boca Raton, Fla.: 83–8.

Todaro, Michael P. (1969), 'A Model of Labour Migration and Urban Unemployment in Less Developed Countries', *American Economic Review*, 59: 138–48.

United Nations (1991), *World Population Monitoring Report 1989*, New York: United Nations.

World Bank (1986), *World Development Report 1990*, Oxford: Oxford University Press.

Yap, Lorene Y. L. (1977), 'The Attraction of Cities', *Journal of Development Economics*, 4: 239–64.

PART IV

Health Care Behaviour in the Context of Poverty

11 Poverty, Women's Status, and the Utilization of Health Services in Egypt

Pavalavalli Govindasamy

Introduction

According to the World Health Organization (1985), an estimated half a million women in developing countries die each year from pregnancy and pregnancy-related causes. In a concerted effort to study the determinants of maternal mortality and intervene to reduce its levels, a number of international organizations launched the Safe Motherhood Initiative in 1987 (Eschen 1992). This initiative, which is part of a broader strategy for alleviating poverty and raising women's status through improved education, employment, health, and nutritional status, aims to reduce by half the number of maternal deaths worldwide by the year 2000 (Koblinsky *et al.* 1992).

Several population-based studies have documented the high levels of maternal mortality in developing countries and carried out research identifying its causes (Bhatia 1985; Kwast *et al.* 1986; Boerma 1987; Fauveau *et al.* 1988). A review of the literature on the subject demonstrates the varied and often complex relationship between maternal mortality and morbidity and its determinants (Rosenfield and Maine 1985; Herz and Measham 1987; Basu 1990; Kane *et al.* 1992; Obermeyer 1993; Younis *et al.* 1993). The conceptual framework proposed by McCarthy and Maine (1992) for analysing the determinants of maternal mortality systematically lays out the wealth of research in this area. Their framework is organized around three stages with the underlying assumption that a woman is at risk of pregnancy and its consequences. The outcomes of interest are: the prevention of the likelihood of pregnancy; reducing the likelihood of complications due to pregnancy; and improving the health of women with pregnancy-related complications. These outcomes are most directly influenced by a set of proximate determinants. These can be classified into: the health status of the woman; her reproductive status; her access to health services; her health care behaviour, which includes her utilization of health services; and a set of other factors, the nature of which is unknown. These determinants are in turn influenced by socio-economic and cultural factors.

This chapter focuses on the determinants of the utilization of maternal health services, more specifically the use of pre-natal care (including tetanus toxoid coverage) and attendance at delivery and place of delivery in Egypt.

Several studies have demonstrated the importance of maternal health services in reducing maternal morbidity and mortality (Rosenfield and Maine 1985; Herz and Measham 1987). Others have shown that maternal mortality is closely correlated with the lack of ante-natal care (Janowitz *et al.* 1984; Royston and Ferguson 1985; Chattopadhyay *et al.* 1986). The lower mortality among women who had antenatal care is partly due to their greater awareness of the benefits of hospital care (Hartfield 1980). Pre-natal care enables women to establish contact with medical staff and facilities which can assist them during an emergency situation, and ensures that women, their families, and especially the person assisting during delivery recognize any signs of complications associated with labour and delivery (Koblinsky *et al.* 1992). According to Chowdhury (1986) complications during labour and delivery have an effect on service use, as do women's previous exposure to or experience with modern health services (Leslie and Gupta 1989). Attendance is also strongly related to access (Harrison and Rossiter 1985). Several other studies have analysed the causes of under-utilization of maternal health services and identified both the quality and cost of care as important influencing factors (Fortney *et al.* 1988; El-Kady *et al.* 1989). Maternal age and parity have also been found to be important determinants of health care use (Leslie and Gupta 1989; Adekunle *et al.* 1990). Attendance is also strongly correlated with better socio-economic status as measured by education (Janowitz *et al.* 1984; Kwast *et al.* 1986). While a number of studies have demonstrated the impact of mother's education on child survival, there is little information associating the effect of women's education on maternal mortality (Caldwell 1979; Cleland and van Ginneken 1989).

More recent studies have examined in greater detail the status of women as an important determinant of maternal morbidity and mortality. Women do not always have the authority over decision-making in the event of complications. The Safe Motherhood Initiative has therefore pointed out that any effort to improve maternal health services and women's general health status has to be tied to other social and political development efforts aimed at elevating the roles and status of women (Eschen 1992). Basu (1990) argues that the mere provision of health care services does not guarantee its utilization but that important cultural differences, foremost among them being the status of women, account for differences in the utilization of health care services. Gender disparities in the utilization of health services may also be evident through the percentage of income spent on women's health, with women more likely to put the health of their children and husbands ahead of their own (Naguib and Lloyd 1994). In her comparative assessment of maternal care utilization in Tunisia and Morocco, Obermeyer (1993) contends that assuming the low valuation of women as the root cause of lower utilization is a simplistic notion that fails to recognize the complex relations between women's position and other socio-economic features and infrastructure that influence access to health care.

The interest of this research is twofold. It aims to quantify, first, the simultaneous effects of women's socio-economic, demographic, and domestic position on the likelihood of utilizing maternal health services, and secondly, the differential impact of variables that are commonly used as proxies of women's autonomy from variables that more directly measure her position within the household.

Why Focus on Egypt?

Egypt presents an interesting case study for several reasons. The nature of women's position in Egyptian society is complex. The vast majority of Egyptians are Muslim, and Islam is often alleged to confer a low status on women by imposing several physical and social restrictions on them. Caldwell (1986), for example, points to the role of religion in seeking an understanding of society's attitude towards women, when explaining why 'poor health achievers' are predominantly Arabic and Muslim. Lower status is linked to restricted access to education and employment, the two major determinants of improved health (Mason 1984; Caldwell and Caldwell 1988). Obermeyer (1992) points out that there is an ambivalence toward women's status in the Arab world, and as such a monolithic explanation linking religion to low female status may not be valid. This is especially true in the case of Egypt, where, alongside increased female school enrolment and labour force participation, is the reversion to veiling brought about by the revival of Islamic fundamentalism.

Egypt is the most populous country in the Arab world and the second most populous country on the African continent, with an estimated population of 57 million in 1993 (El-Zanaty *et al.* 1993). The majority of Egypt's population (53 per cent) is rural, although the urban population has grown rapidly. Socio-economic differences are not only marked by urban/rural residence but also by region. Egypt is divided into 26 administrative divisions, which can be classified into four regions, from the most developed to the least: the Urban Governorates of Cairo, Alexandria, Port Said, and Suez; Lower Egypt, which consists of the nine governorates of the Nile Delta; Upper Egypt, which comprises the eight governorates of the Nile Valley; and five frontier governorates on the western and eastern boundaries.

Fertility levels have remained relatively high in Egypt, with a crude birth rate just below 30 per thousand population and a total fertility rate of 3.9 births per woman aged 15–49. The mean number of children ever born to women aged 40–49 is 5.7 births per woman (El-Zanaty *et al.* 1993). The mortality level has continued to fall since World War II and was around 7 per thousand in 1993, the majority of all deaths being represented by infant and child mortality. Estimates from the 1992 Egypt Demographic and Health Survey show that infant mortality has declined to 62 deaths per thousand births during 1988–92.

Maternal mortality continues to be a serious problem in Egypt. The World

Health Organization (1991) estimates from vital statistics place the maternal mortality rate for the whole of Egypt at 60 per 100,000 live births in 1987.[1] Several independent studies on maternal mortality have also been conducted in various parts of Egypt (Abdullah *et al.* 1985; Fortney *et al.* 1986; El-Kady *et al.* 1989; Younis *et al.* 1993), with maternal mortality rates varying widely by area of study and methodological approaches used.

Egypt was the first Arab country to address population issues at the national level. However, maternal health, which only recently became an active part of population policy, primarily focuses on child welfare and maternal mortality, with little or no attention paid to reproductive morbidity or other aspects of maternal health, like female circumcision (Naguib and Lloyd 1994). Physical distance has often been found to be a primary deterrent to the utilization of health services (Adekunle *et al.* 1990). However, this is not the case in Egypt, which is one of the few countries on the African continent with the greatest array of medical services located within a few kilometres from a village. Reproductive services for women are easily available through some 3,700 family planning service outlets set up and operated by the Ministry of Health, with about 89 per cent of them also offering pre-natal, post-natal, and delivery care (Naguib and Lloyd 1994). An analysis of data on service availability collected during the 1988 EDHS shows that virtually all rural women are less than a few kilometres from a health provider, with 73 per cent of them living less than one kilometre from a health facility or having a health facility located within their village. Ninety per cent of rural women can reach a health facility in under thirty minutes, with the majority using a motorized means of transport. The majority of rural women (more than 71 per cent) live within five kilometres of general, family planning, and maternal and child health services, and few women (6 per cent) have to travel fifteen kilometres or more for any of them (Wilkinson *et al.* 1993). Private physicians are also widely available; however, they are mostly used for family planning services (Naguib and Lloyd 1994).

However, in spite of their wide availability, utilization of maternal health services is relatively low. Findings from the 1992 EDHS (El-Zanaty *et al.* 1993) indicate that nearly one in two Egyptian mothers did not receive antenatal care, with less than one in four having made four or more visits (the minimum considered acceptable for a healthy delivery). For more than two-fifths of births mothers did not receive tetanus toxoid injections. Almost three-quarters of births occurred at home, with more than half of them attended by a traditional birth attendant or daya.

Several questions come to mind from the above description. In a country where availability is high and physical distance is not a barrier, why is utilization low? What are the determinants of maternal health care utilization in Egypt? Is it socio-economic factors, cultural influences on women's position, or religious factors that play a part in influencing utilization? What are the policy implications? These questions are addressed in this chapter.

Data for Analysis

Differentials in maternal health care utilization are examined using the second Egypt Demographic and Health Survey (EDHS), the latest in a series of national-level population and health surveys, conducted in 1992–3 (El-Zanaty *et al.* 1993). The survey successfully completed interviews of 9,864 ever-married women aged 15–49, and collected information on issues pertaining to fertility, family planning, and maternal and child health. Information on maternal and child health care is birth-based, that is, it is collected for each child born to respondents in the five years preceding the interview. Since the basic tenet of this research is to examine the determinants of maternal health care utilization, the sample is restricted to women who ever had a child. The analysis is further restricted to one child per woman, selected at random. This manner of selection ensures that the subsample does not over-represent women with higher fertility (which would be the case if all births were selected), who are more likely to be rural and less educated, and is not biased against children born earlier (should last births be selected), who are less likely to receive health care. Restricting the sample in this manner yielded 6,190 women[2] who had had at least one birth since January 1987.

Methodology

Four dichotomous dependent variables measure utilization of maternal health care: receipt of pre-natal care, receipt of tetanus toxoid, assistance at delivery, and place of delivery. Respondents who received pre-natal care or delivery care from a health professional (doctor, nurse, or midwife) were classified as having pre-natal or delivery care, and if they did not receive any care or received care from someone other than a health professional they were classified as not having received care. This definition might understate the level of utilization, especially in a setting where the majority of traditional birth attendants have received formal training. However, this is not the case in Egypt. Tetanus toxoid coverage was classified by separating women who received at least one dose of tetanus toxoid injection from women who received none. Place of delivery was categorized as institutional delivery if the birth took place in a public or private medical facility (hospital or clinic) and home delivery if it took place at home.

The explanatory variables thought to influence each dependent variable were carefully selected and categorized. Variables that measured the socio-economic status of respondents included region of residence (Urban Governorates, Lower Egypt, and Upper Egypt), place of residence (whether urban or rural), education (none, some primary, primary through secondary, and completed secondary/higher), participation in the labour market (not working, working but not earning cash, and working for cash), an index measuring social class based on the ownership of five consumer items (respondent's own dwelling, radio, black-and-white television, fan, and refrigerator; a woman was classified as high if she owned 4–5 items, medium if she owned 2–3 items, and low if she owned 0–1 item), religion (Muslim or Christian), and exposure to the media (newspaper, radio, and television). Demographic variables included age of respondents and parity. All the independent variables used in the analysis are categorical, with the exception of age and parity (continuous).

There were several questions in the 1992 EDHS that attempted to measure women's autonomy more directly. These questions focused on women's actual position within the household, and her perception of her position vis-à-vis her husband and other relatives. For theoretical and substantive reasons this analysis covers only those variables that were least speculative, most directly relevant to women's own lives, and of the greatest substantive interest within the context of Egypt. Through a careful process of testing, the following were selected and categorized into binary variables for inclusion in the model: direct measures of her position included her input into decision-making about whether to have a/another child; her freedom to go outside the household, either alone or accompanied by her children, to buy household items or visit relatives; and whether she was her husband's first cousin or other blood relative. Her perception of a woman's position within the household and hence her own were captured by her responses to questions on whether a wife should speak out or keep quiet when in disagreement with her husband; whether a wife should be able to do market work; who should have the last word on the family budget; and who should have the last word on the use of family planning.

In order to isolate the impact of the more direct measures for women's position from measures that have often been used as proxies for women's position, two separate models are run for each dependent dichotomous variable using logistic regression. The first controls for the influence of the socio-economic and demographic variables (residence, education, employment, social class, religion, exposure to the media, age, and parity) and the second adds to the first model those variables that measure more directly women's actual and perceived position within the household.

Results

The frequency distributions of the variables used in the statistical analysis are presented in Table 11.1. About two-fifths of the women live in Upper Egypt, the most backward of the three regions, and an additional two-fifths live in Lower Egypt, which is intermediate in socio-economic status. The majority of women reside in rural areas. About one in two women have no education and only about one-fifth of women have completed secondary school. Most Egyptian women do not participate in the labour market, and a small minor-

Table 11.1. Distribution of women who had at least one birth in the five years before the survey, by background characteristics, Egypt, 1992 (%)

Region	
Upper Egypt	38.4
Lower Egypt	40.9
Urban Governorates	20.7
Residence	
Rural	58.3
Urban	41.7
Education	
None	48.7
Some primary	20.6
Primary through secondary	10.3
Completed secondary/higher	20.5
Employment	
Not working	77.7
Working, not for cash	12.5
Working for cash	9.7
Social Class[a]	
Low	31.3
Medium	54.2
High	14.5
Religion	
Muslim	94.8
Christian	5.2
Exposure to media	
Reads newspaper	
No	77.0
Yes	23.0
Listens to radio	
No	37.4
Yes	62.6
Watches television	
No	20.2
Yes	79.8
Age	
15–24	21.6
25–34	51.3
35+	27.1
Parity	
1–2	34.0
3–5	41.1
6+	24.8

Table 11.1 (cont.)

Indicators of women's position	
Decision to have another child	
Wife/Husband and wife	59.9
Husband/Others	40.1
Freedom of movement	
Yes	87.2
No	12.8
Wife should be able to express her opinion	
Yes	56.3
No	43.7
Women should be able to work	
Yes	72.5
No	27.5
Last word on family budget	
Wife/Husband and wife	35.2
Husband/Others	64.8
Last word on use of family planning	
Wife/Husband and wife	63.9
Husband/Others	36.1
Husband is first cousin or other blood relative	
Yes	41.9
No	58.1
Utilization of maternity care services	
Antenatal care	
Health professional	55.7
Traditional birth attendants/Others	44.3
Tetanus toxoid	
Yes	53.3
No	46.7
Delivery care	43.7
Health professional	
Traditional birth attendants/Others	56.3
Place of delivery	
Hospital/Health unit/Clinic	29.2
Home	70.8
Number of women	6,190

[a]The index measuring social class is based on the ownership of five consumer items: respondents own dwelling, radio, black-and-white television, fan, and refrigerator. A woman was categorized as being low, medium, or high on the social-class ladder if she owned 0–1, 2–3, or 4–5 items, respectively.

Source: EDHS, 1992.

ity work for cash. The majority of women fall into the medium social class category. The vast majority of the women are Muslims, with about 5 per cent belonging to the Christian faith. Women are most likely to be exposed to television and least likely to read a newspaper. This is consistent with the fact that the majority of women have little or no education. More than one in two women in the age group 25–34 have had at least one child in the five years preceding the survey, and two out of five have between three and five children. Indicators of women's position show that three out of five women in Egypt have a say in the decision to have a/another child, and only slightly more than one in ten women do not have freedom of movement. Two out of five women are married to their first cousin or other blood relative. Slightly less than three-fifths of women believe that a woman should express her opinion when in disagreement with her husband. In spite of the fact that the vast majority of women do not participate in the labour market, a majority of women believe that women should be able to do market work. Egyptian women believe that they should have relatively less voice in the family budget and greater say in the use of family planning. More than one out of two women have received antenatal care from a health professional or received at least one dose of tetanus toxoid injection. In contrast to pre-natal care, the majority of women do not utilize delivery care. Less than a third of the women had an institutional delivery, while only two out of five women received assistance at delivery from a health professional.

The bi-variate relationships between the use of maternal health care services and socio-demographic variables (data not shown) indicate that overall, residing in the Urban Governorates, urban residence, education, employment, social class, and exposure to the media are all positively related to health care utilization, with the exception of tetanus toxoid. Background differences are muted in the case of tetanus toxoid, presumably because of a mass public campaign targeted at Lower Egypt and rural areas and especially at mothers who prefer home deliveries, which are predominantly rural. Although Christians are more likely than Muslims to use maternal health care, religious differences are minimal. Younger age is associated with greater utilization, as is lower parity. Simple cross-tabulations between utilization of maternity care services and indicators of women's position reveal a similar picture, with utilization varying positively with women's greater decision-making power within the household and freedom of movement, and among women who believe that men and women should share equal status. Health care utilization is also higher among women who are not married to a first cousin or blood relatives.

Cross-tabulations were also drawn between indicators of women's position and some selected socio-economic variables. Women who actually enjoy a more egalitarian relationship in terms of their greater participation in decision-making and freedom of movement, or who believe that men and women should have equal status, or who are not related to their husbands, are more likely to be Christian, to come from the Urban Governorates, to reside in urban areas, to have completed secondary education, to work for cash, and to belong to the highest social class.

The simultaneous effect of socio-economic and demographic variables and variables directly measuring women's position on the likelihood of receiving maternity care services is shown in Tables 11.2 and 11.3. When only the socio-demographic variables are controlled, residence, education, age, and parity emerge as significant and strong predictors of the likelihood of receiving tetanus toxoid (Table 11.2). This likelihood remains much higher in Lower Egypt (odds ratio is 1.49), which is socio-economically more advanced than Upper Egypt. However, contrary to expectations, women residing in the Urban Governorates, the most developed of the three regions, are significantly less likely to receive tetanus toxoid than women residing in Upper Egypt. Residential differences are muted, presumably because of the mass public campaign to increase tetanus toxoid coverage between 1988 and 1992. In fact, there was a fivefold increase in the percentage of mothers who had received tetanus toxoid between the two Egypt Demographic and Health Surveys, with coverage increasing from 11 per cent in 1988 to 58 per cent in 1992 in the rural areas, and by 51 per cent between the two surveys in Upper Egypt (Sayed *et al.* 1989; El-Zanaty *et al.* 1993). Education is the strongest predictor of the likelihood of receiving tetanus toxoid injections, with mothers who have completed secondary school 1.6 times more likely to be immunized against tetanus than mothers with no education. Mothers who are participating in the labour market but not for cash are less likely than non-working mothers to receive tetanus toxoid injections. However, the significance of this relationship is not strong. Age and parity are highly significant and negatively correlated with the odds of receiving tetanus toxoid coverage. Social class, religion, and exposure to the media did not significantly affect the receipt of tetanus toxoid injections. Including variables that measured women's position did not significantly contribute to the understanding of the influence of these variables on the likelihood of receiving tetanus toxoid, with the exception of the variable that measured women's perception of who should have the last word on family planning. Women who believed that they alone, or together with their husbands, should have the last word were slightly more likely (odds ratio is equal to 1.1) than women who believed that their husbands or others should have the last word.

Pre-natal care by health professionals (doctor, nurse/midwife) is significantly and largely affected by socio-demographic variables. The odds ratio of receiving pre-natal care is shown in the last two columns of Table 11.2. The most powerful predictor of the likelihood of receiving pre-natal care from a health professional is education, whose effect does not wane even with the introduction of more direct measures of women's position. While living in urban areas does increase the odds of receiving pre-natal care, region of residence is less significant. In fact, residing in Lower Egypt is not significant at all as a predictor of receiving pre-natal care. Unpaid work is negatively and less significantly correlated with the likelihood of receiving pre-natal care than is not working. Where one is located in the social class ladder significantly affects the type of personnel seen for pre-natal care. Women who come from the highest social class are nearly one and a half times more likely than women from the lowest social class to receive pre-natal care from a health professional. Religion is not a significant predictor of women's use of pre-natal care. Age and parity are highly significant predictors of women's use of pre-natal services. The older a woman is or the more children she has, the less likely she is to use pre-natal care services. Exposure to the media, and especially a newspaper, influences women's health-seeking behaviour more positively, with women who read a newspaper almost twice as likely as women who do not to seek pre-natal care from a health professional. Exposure to the radio is also positive but slightly less significant. Introducing indicators measuring women's position does not significantly alter the explanatory strength of the socio-demographic variables. However, variables that measure women's position are slightly more influential in the case of use of pre-natal care as compared to the receipt of tetanus toxoid injections, even if only three of the seven indicators of women's position are important. A woman who believes that a wife should be able to express her opinion if she disagrees with her husband has a 20 per cent greater chance of receiving pre-natal care from a health professional than a woman who does not believe in expressing her own opinion. Similarly, women who believe that they alone, or together with their husbands, should have the last word on the use of family planning are more likely to use pre-natal care services than women who do not have input into this matter. Being married to a blood relative negatively affects women's utilization of health care.

Table 11.3 presents the simultaneous effects of background variables on the likelihood of utilizing delivery care, with the first two columns showing the odds ratios of background variables on the likelihood of delivering in a health facility, and the last two columns showing the likelihood of being attended by a health professional at delivery. Two separate logistic regressions are run for each of these two dependent variables, once again to gauge the contributory effects of direct measures of women's position. Socio-demographic variables emerge as strong predictors of the likelihood of delivering in a health facility as opposed to one's home, with education the most significant predictor. Mothers who have completed at least secondary school are over three and a half times as likely to have a hospital delivery than mothers who have no education. Place of residence is another strong predictor, with urban women and those residing in the Urban Governorates about twice as likely as rural women and women living in Upper Egypt to have an institutional delivery. Working for cash affects utilization of delivery services, though it is not highly significant. Institutional deliveries are significantly more prevalent among women who belong to the middle social class than among women from the lower social class, although it is not clear why the former is a more significant predictor

Table 11.2. Logistic regression analysis of pre-natal care showing odds ratios for the probability of receiving tetanus toxoid and pre-natal care from a health professional, Egypt, 1992 (reference category in parentheses)

Variable	Tetanus toxoid		Pre-natal care from a health professional	
	Restricted model[a]	Full model[b]	Restricted model[a]	Full model[b]
Region (Upper Egypt)				
Lower Egypt	1.49**	1.43***	1.00	0.92
Urban Governorates	0.66***	0.64***	1.35**	1.24*
Residence (Rural)	1.15	1.13	1.54***	1.47***
Education (None)				
Some primary	1.12	1.10	1.28***	1.22
Primary through secondary	1.36**	1.32**	1.61***	1.51***
Completed secondary/higher	1.61***	1.54***	2.74***	2.41***
Employment (Not working)				
Working, not for cash	0.83*	0.82*	0.80*	0.79**
Working for cash	0.91	0.91	0.98	0.96
Social class (Low)				
Medium	0.87	0.87*	1.24**	1.23**
High	0.95	0.95	1.38***	1.37**
Exposure to media				
Reads newspaper (No)	0.96	0.93	1.87***	1.78***
Listens to radio (No)	1.12	1.12	1.18**	1.17*
Watches television (No)	1.16	1.14	1.03	1.00

Religion (Christian)	0.80	0.81	1.18	1.22
Age	0.95***	0.95***	0.99***	0.99**
Parity	0.82***	0.82***	0.73***	0.74***
Indicators of women's position				
Decision to have another child (Husband/Others)		1.03		1.02
Freedom of movement (No)		1.11		1.05
Husband a blood relative (No)		0.98		0.89*
Wife should be able to express her opinion (No)		1.04		1.19**
Women should be able to work (No)		0.97		1.08
Last word on family budget (Husband/Others)		1.01		1.13
Last word on use of family planning (Husband/Others)		1.15*		1.16*
–2 log likelihood	8,164.26	8,153.20	7,419.20	7,385.20
Number of women	6,190	6,190	6,190	6,190

* $p < 0.05$
** $p < 0.01$
*** $p < 0.001$ for two-tailed test.

Source: Estimates by the author.

Notes: a. Only socio-demographic variables are controlled.
b. Includes variables that measure women's position.

Table 11.3. Logistic regression analysis of delivery care showing odds ratios for the probability of having an institutional delivery and receiving delivery care from a health professional, Egypt, 1992 (reference category in parentheses)

Variable	Institutional delivery		Delivery care from a health professional	
	Restricted model[a]	Full model[b]	Restricted model[a]	Full model[b]
Region (Upper Egypt)				
Lower Egypt	1.15	1.08	1.48***	1.41***
Urban Governorates	1.94***	1.80***	1.88***	1.75***
Residence (Rural)	2.29***	2.14***	1.78***	1.70***
Education (None)				
Some primary	1.35***	1.27**	1.61***	1.52***
Primary through secondary	1.68***	1.53***	2.22***	2.04***
Completed secondary/higher	3.63***	3.14***	4.56***	3.95***
Employment (Not working)				
Working, not for cash	0.94	0.94	0.91	0.92
Working for cash	1.12*	1.11	1.17*	1.16*
Social class (Low)				
Medium	1.38***	1.35***	1.38***	1.34***
High	1.16	1.15	1.45***	1.41***
Exposure to media				
Reads newspaper (No)	1.30**	1.24*	1.66***	1.56***
Listens to radio (No)	0.97	0.96	0.98	0.97
Watches television (No)	1.06	1.03	1.18	1.16

Religion (Christian)	1.34*	1.38*	1.12	1.15
Age	1.02**	1.02**	1.01**	1.01**
Parity	0.74***	0.75***	0.74***	0.74***
Indicators of women's position				
Decision to have another child (Husband/Others)		1.18*		1.09
Freedom of movement (No)		1.05		0.91
Husband a blood relative (No)		0.82**		0.91
Wife should be able to express her opinion (No)		1.20*		1.20**
Women should be able to work (No)		0.91		0.91
Last word on family budget (Husband/Others)		1.18*		1.27***
Last word on use of family planning (Husband/Others)		1.08		1.16*
−2 log likelihood	6,084.95	6,049.32	6,806.13	6,763.10
Number of women	6,190	6,190	6,190	6,190

* $p < 0.05$
** $p < 0.01$
*** $p < 0.001$ for two-tailed test.

Source: Estimates by the author.

Notes: a. Only socio-demographic variables are controlled.
b. Includes variables that measure women's position.

than the latter. Among the variables that measure exposure to the media, women who read a newspaper are significantly more likely to deliver in a health facility than women who do not. Listening to the radio or watching television are not significant predictors, presumably because almost all households own a radio or a black-and-white television and thus there is not much socio-economic distinction between women who are exposed to these two forms of media and women who are not. Muslims are slightly more likely to seek institutional deliveries than Christians. Unlike the case of pre-natal care, age is positively related to the likelihood of an institutional delivery. On the other hand, parity is negatively correlated with the odds of an institutional delivery. Introducing indicators of women's position into the model reduces, though slightly, the explanatory power of the socio-demographic variables. The strongest of these variables is relationship to one's husband. Women who are married to their blood relative are significantly less likely to have an institutional delivery.

Factors that significantly influence delivery care by a health professional are somewhat similar to the pattern seen for institutional deliveries, with a few exceptions (Table 11.3, last two columns). Residence is highly significant, including residence in Lower Egypt, which increases the likelihood of being attended at delivery by a health professional (odds ratio is 1.48). Being high on the social-class ladder is a stronger predictor than being at the middle. However, both categories of women are significantly more likely to have a birth assisted by a health professional than women from a low social class. Exposure to the print media positively influences women's health-seeking behaviour in terms of delivery care. The introduction of the more direct measures of women's position reduces somewhat the explanatory power of the socio-demographic variables, especially in the case of women who have completed secondary school, but does not reduce their significance. This category predicted a likelihood of being attended at delivery by a health professional which was four and a half times that of women with no education when not controlling for women's position, decreasing to under four times with the added variables. Much of this difference is absorbed by the predictive value of the variable that measures women's say in the household budget, a 25 per cent increase over women who have no say. Relationship to one's husband does not affect assistance at delivery, but having a say in the use of family planning does so positively.

Discussion

Socio-economic and demographic variables are highly significant and consistent predictors of women's health-seeking behaviour in Egypt. The strongest influence is exerted by education. Women who have some education are more likely to utilize maternal health services than women who have none, and women who have completed secondary school are about two to four times as likely as women with no education to utilize these services. This study reinforces the importance of education as an important determinant of health care use and supports the findings of other research (Caldwell 1986; Obermeyer 1993). Residing in urban areas and especially in the Urban Governorates enhances the likelihood of using maternity care services (with the exception of tetanus toxoid coverage). However, low utilization in rural areas and in the least developed of the three regions cannot be attributed to lack of available facilities, since most women in rural areas have a public health facility offering these services within five kilometres of their place of residence (Wilkinson *et al.* 1993).

Participation in the labour market has a mixed effect on health care use. Separating active women into those earning cash and those who do not helps to clarify some of the mixed results often found in studies that examine the role of labour market participation per se on maternal and child health and women's autonomy. The above analysis shows that women who work for cash are more likely to utilize delivery care services than women who are not involved in the labour market. However, working women who do not earn cash are less likely than the latter to utilize delivery care. Earning cash may perhaps give women greater control over its use or perhaps give the household greater flexibility over its use and hence encourage women to seek health care and bear its costs. On the other hand, women who do market work but are not paid in cash may be selectively drawn from the lower socio-economic strata and hence less likely to afford the time or money for modern health care. A recent study found that Egyptian women believe that market work is legitimate for economic reasons (Nawar *et al.* 1994), as women from wealthier homes do not do market work. In the case of Egypt, most women who work for cash are employed by the government sector (Nawar *et al.* 1994) and hence enjoy the many perquisites associated with civil service employment, including maternity care services, that could possibly explain why women who work for cash are more likely to utilize health care services. As in previous studies, women's economic status significantly influences health care use, albeit to a lesser extent (Stewart and Sommerfelt 1991).

Being exposed to the print media is significantly more important as a predictor of health care use than the influence of other forms of media. Given the fact that the majority of Egyptian women have never been to school, those able to read a newspaper are in the minority and most likely to be reasonably well educated. Exposure to the print media is more educational. As such, it is possible that the print media have greater coverage of the benefits of modern health care services and related issues, which encourages women who read a newspaper to utilize modern maternity services. In contrast, the majority of women are exposed to radio and television, which tends to be more entertaining, and government-sponsored messages generally tend to emphasize family planning (El-Zanaty *et al.* 1993). On the whole, religion per se was not found to be a significant predictor of utilization of health care services, contrary to what has been suggested by some studies (Caldwell 1986).

Age and parity are highly significant predictors of health care utilization. However, the direction of the effect of age is mixed, depending on the type of care. Age is negatively related to the utilization of pre-natal care, with older women less likely than younger women to receive pre-natal care from a health professional or to obtain at least one dose of tetanus toxoid, a finding that is consistent with other research in this area (Wong *et al.* 1987; Leslie and Gupta 1989). On the other hand, older women are more likely to deliver in a health facility or be assisted by a health professional at delivery, in line with what was found by Stewart and Sommerfelt (1991). Parity has a significant and consistently negative relationship with women's health-seeking behaviour, which confirms the findings of several other studies (Stewart and Sommerfelt 1991; Obermeyer 1993). Some of the negative effects of age and parity on health utilization may be attributed to the confidence that comes with age and with prior experience associated with a pregnancy or the pressures of child care (Adekunle *et al.* 1990).

Direct measures of women's position did exert a positive influence on health care utilization (with the exception of being married to one's blood relative), although their impact was much less significant, and introducing them into the model for the most part did not reduce the explanatory power of socio-demographic variables. Among the three variables that measured women's position in the household, being married to one's relative was the most important. This chapter supports the finding of other research that marriage to a relative restricts women's autonomy and reinforces traditional patterns of health care use (Dyson and Moore 1983; Obermeyer 1992; Nawar *et al.* 1994). Among variables that measure a woman's perception of her position in the household, having a say in the household budget is significantly related to her use of delivery care, perhaps because it implies a certain amount of control over spending and because a woman is able to pay for the assistance of a medical professional without having to ask her husband for the money. Similarly, women who believe that they should be able to participate in reproductive decision-making may have greater freedom to seek health care from professionals. A woman who believes that a wife should be able to express her opinion is also generally more likely to utilize modern health care services, perhaps because she is less likely to succumb to pressure from others in the household, especially her mother-in-law, who may have greater confidence in the use of traditional health care. The vast majority of women were free to move (87 per cent) but surprisingly, having the freedom to go out of the house did not significantly affect utilization of health care, perhaps because freedom of movement by itself did not grant women greater autonomy. Moreover, earlier regression analysis has shown that much of the impact of this variable is absorbed by place of residence and women's work status, which have been found to be highly significant predictors of a woman's freedom to move (Govindasamy and Malhotra 1994).

Conclusion

On the one hand, this research confirms that Egyptian women who are in a socio-economically advantageous position are much more likely to utilize maternal health care services than are younger and low-parity women. Thus, programmes aimed at improving women's access to education and paid employment, at increasing women's access to and use of family planning, and at improving the general living conditions in rural and less-developed regions should work in the right direction to reduce maternal mortality and morbidity. However, direct interventions targeted at specific disadvantaged groups can also have a positive impact on the use of maternity services, as was seen in the effectiveness of the mass public campaign to increase tetanus toxoid coverage in Egypt. This research supports the argument that women experiencing pregnancy-related complications are more likely to seek emergency treatment if they are already in contact with modern medical services. While pre-natal care identifies a small percentage of women at risk, it fails to capture the majority of women who may need access to emergency services in the event of obstetric complications (Maine 1990). Therefore, in order to reduce maternal mortality, programmes need to address the question whether access to hospitals with equipment needed to treat complicated deliveries is as uniform as access to primary health care services in Egypt.

On the other hand, the statistical analysis in their chapter does not explain why, given that Egypt's formal health structure is superior to that of many developing countries, utilization of modern maternity services is so low. Religion, and specifically Islam, was not found to be a significant factor restricting utilization. However, this could be due to the small number of non Muslims. The question whether religion acts to lower the status of women and hence impose restrictions on health care utilization needs to be further explored. Another issue that needs to be addressed is whether there is something about Egyptian cultural traditions which Christians and Muslims share regarding the nature of childbirth that may affect health care utilization. Although the 1992 EDHS did not include questions that specifically addressed religious practices on health care utilization, it did contain questions on women's position. The statistical analysis carried out in this research does support the conclusion that some direct measures of women's autonomy exert an independent and strong influence on their health-seeking behaviour when the influence of socioeconomic and demographic factors are controlled.

A woman's position within her household and her perception of her status is strongly and significantly correlated with her socio-economic status (data not shown) and hence serve as good proxies for measuring her status. However, where direct measures of her position are available, ignoring their impact may tend to underrate their relative importance as explanatory variables and hence fail to inform planners seeking to provide services responsive to and centred round women's reproductive needs. However, although the bi-variate analysis does show that Muslims are less likely to enjoy a higher status in the household and less likely to believe in equality between men and women, the logistic regressions do not confirm this conclusion.

Perhaps the explanation for the low utilization of maternal health services lies in the cultural factors inherent in Egyptian society, which transcend socio-economic, demographic, and religious factors. Studies have shown that there continues to be a deep commitment among Egyptian women to utilizing traditional practitioners within certain domains, foremost among them being childbirth, which is believed to be a natural phenomenon needing the experienced services of a traditional birth attendant or *daya* (El Messiri Nadim 1980). The advice of medical professionals is sought only in the case of complications. In contrast to the old and trusted *daya*, dispensers of modern maternity services are newly qualified and often young doctors who lack clinical experience, and tend to be biased against poor and uneducated women (Naguib and Lloyd 1994). Moreover, the unfamiliarity associated with delivering in a hospital environment, without the presence of friends and family and attended by medical professionals who continue to be predominantly male, discourages women from seeking obstetric and gynaecological care. More research needs to be done on existing cultural practices inhibiting women's use of maternity care services in a clinical environment.

Under these circumstances, what strategies can programmers adopt to increase the utilization of health services in Egypt? One possibility is a targeted attempt to encourage the use of pre-natal care (which is often offered in a less formal environment than a hospital and typically by a female nurse/midwife), to promote rapport between women and medical professionals as well as confidence in modern maternal services and to link women to such services, and to monitor complicated pregnancies, which would encourage more women to deliver in hospital. Another strategy is to make a concerted effort to train *dayas* in the use and practice of modern medicine and integrate them gradually into the circle of qualified medical professionals, encouraging them to administer care within a clinical environment under the auspices of trained medical professionals. Yet another strategy is to overcome the gender barrier associated with lack of utilization by encouraging more women to become doctors, and to promote women's medical practice, especially in rural and less-developed areas.

Notes

The valuable assistance provided by Elisabeth Sommerfelt of DHS/Macro International Inc. throughout my research is acknowledged.

1. Underestimation of maternal mortality is common even in countries with excellent vital registration systems. Even though registration of deaths of women in the repro-

ductive ages is virtually complete in Egypt, misclassification of causes of deaths is a common problem. For example, when causes of deaths were matched from vital statistics and a population-based study of women in the reproductive age group in the Menoufia Governorate, maternal deaths were found to have been misclassified or under-reported by as much as 70% (Kane *et al.* 1992).

2. This excludes 17 women with missing information for selected variables.

References

Abdullah, S. A., Fathalla, M. F., and Aleem, A. M. A. (1985), 'Maternal Mortality in Upper Egypt', paper presented at the WHO Interregional Meeting on Prevention of Maternal Mortality, Geneva.

Adekunle, C., Filippi, V., Graham, W., Onyemunwa, P., and Udjo, E. (1990), 'Patterns of Maternity Care among Women in Ondo State, Nigeria', in Alan G. Hill (ed.), *Determinants of Health and Mortality in Africa*, Columbia, Md.: Demographic and Health Surveys, 1–45.

Basu, A. M. (1990), 'Cultural Influences on Health Care Use: Two Regional Groups in India', *Studies in Family Planning*, 21: 275–86.

Bhatia, J. C. (1985), 'Maternal Mortality in Anantapur District, India: Preliminary Findings of a Study', paper presented at the WHO Interregional Meeting on Prevention of Maternal Mortality, Geneva.

Boerma, J. T. (1987), 'Maternal Mortality in Sub-Saharan Africa: Levels, Causes and Interventions', paper presented at the IUSSP Seminar on Mortality and Society in Sub-Saharan Africa, Yaounde, Cameroon.

Caldwell, J. C. (1979), 'Education as a Factor in Mortality Decline: An Examination of Nigerian Data', *Population Studies*, 33: 395–413.

——(1986), 'Routes to Low Mortality in Poor Countries', *Population and Development Review*, 12: 171–220.

Caldwell, P., and Caldwell, J. C. (1988), 'Kinship Forms, Female Autonomy, and Fertility: What are the Connections?', paper presented to the Rockefeller Foundation Workshop on the Status of Women in Relation to Fertility and Mortality, Bellagio, Italy.

Chattopadhyay, S. K., Sengupta, B. S., Chattopadhyay, C., Zaidi, Z., and Showail, H. (1986), 'Maternal Mortality in Riyadh, Saudi Arabia', *British Journal of Obstetrics and Gynaecology*, 90: 809–14.

Chowdhury, S. (1986), 'Determinants of Health Care Utilization in Rural Bangladesh', Johns Hopkins University Ph.D. thesis.

Cleland, J., and van Ginneken, J. (1989), 'Maternal Schooling and Childhood Mortality', *Journal of Biosocial Science*, 10: 13–34.

Dyson, T., and Moore, M. (1983), 'On Kinship Structure, Female Autonomy, and Demographic Behaviour in India', *Population and Development Review*, 9: 35–60.

El-Kady, A. A., Saleh, S., and Gadalla, S. (1989), 'Obstetric Deaths in Menoufia Governorate, Egypt', *British Journal of Obstetrics and Gynaecology*, 96: 301–6.

El-Messiri Nadim, N. (1980), *Rural Health Care in Egypt*, Ottawa: International Development Research Centre.

El-Zanaty, H. F., Sayed, H. A. A., Zaky, H. H. M., and Way, A. A. (1993), *Egypt*

Demographic and Health Survey 1992, Cairo: National Population Council; Calverton, Md.: DHS/Macro International.

Eschen, A. (1992), *Acting to Save Women's Lives: Report of the Meeting of Partners for Safe Motherhood*, Washington, DC: World Bank.

Faveau, V. M., Koenig, M. A., Chakraborty, J., and Chowdhury, A. I. (1988), 'Causes of Maternal Mortality in Rural Bangladesh 1976–1985', *Bulletin of the World Health Organization*, 66: 643–52.

Fortney, J. A., Susanti, I., Gadalla, S., Saleh, S., Rogers, S. M., and Potts, M. (1986), 'Reproductive Mortality in Two Developing Countries', *American Journal of Public Health*, 76: 134–8.

————————— Feldblum, P. J., and Potts, M. (1988), 'Maternal Mortality in Indonesia and Egypt', *International Journal of Gynaecology and Obstetrics*, 26: 21–32.

Govindasamy, P., and Malhotra, A. (1994), 'Aspects of Female Autonomy in Egypt: What can we Learn from DHS Data?', paper presented at the Annual Meetings of the Population Association of America, Miami.

Harrison, K. A., and Rossiter, L. A. (1985), 'Childbearing, Health and Social Priorities: A Survey of 22,774 Consecutive Hospital Births in Zaria, Northern Nigeria', *British Journal of Obstetrics and Gynaecology*, 92: 3–13.

Hartfield, V. J. (1980), 'Maternal Mortality in Nigeria compared with Earlier International Experience', *International Journal of Obstetrics and Gynaecology*, 18: 70–5.

Herz, B., and Measham, A. (1987), *The Safe Motherhood Initiative: Proposals for Action*, Washington, DC: World Bank.

Janowitz, B., Lewis, J., Burton, N., Lamptey, P. (1984), *Reproductive Health in Africa: Issues and Options*, Research Triangle Park, NC: Family Health International.

Kane, T., El-Kady, A. A., Saleh, S., Hage, M., Stanback, J., and Potter, L. (1992), 'Maternal Mortality in Giza, Egypt: Magnitude, Causes, and Prevention', *Studies in Family Planning*, 23: 45–57.

Koblinsky, M. A., Rooney, C., Griffiths, M., Hugue, Z., Leighton, C., Kwast, B., and Tinker, A. (1992), *Programming for Safe Motherhood: Draft Prepared for the World Bank*, Washington, DC: World Bank.

Kwast, B. E., Rochat, R. W., and Kidane-Mariam, W. (1986), 'Maternal Mortality in Addis Ababa, Ethiopia', *Studies in Family Planning*, 17: 288–301.

Leslie, J., and Gupta, G. R. (1989), *Utilization of Formal Services for Maternal Nutrition and Health Care in the Third World*, Washington, DC: International Services for Research on Women.

McCarthy, J., and Maine, D. (1992), 'A Framework for Analyzing the Determinants of Maternal Mortality', *Studies in Family Planning*, 23: 23–33.

Maine, Deborah (1990), *Safe Motherhood Programs: Options and Issues*, New York: Center for Population and Family Health, Columbia University.

Mason, Karen O. (1984), *The Status of Women: A Review of its Relationships to Fertility and Mortality*, New York: Rockefeller Foundation.

Naguib, N. G., and Lloyd, C. B. (1994), *Gender Inequalities and Demographic Behaviour: Egypt*, New York: Population Council.

Nawar, L., Lloyd, C. B., and Ibrahim, B. (1994), 'Women's Autonomy and Gender Roles in Egyptian Families', paper presented at the Population Council Symposium on Family, Gender, and Population Policy: International Debates and Middle Eastern Realities, Cairo.

Obermeyer, C. M. (1992), 'Islam, Women, and Politics: The Demography of Arab Countries', *Population and Development Review*, 18: 33–57.

——(1993), 'Culture, Maternal Health Care, and Women's Status: A Comparison of Morocco and Tunisia', *Studies in Family Planning*, 24: 354–65.

Rosenfield, A., and Maine, D. (1985), 'Maternal Mortality: a Neglected Tragedy. Where is the M in MCH?', *The Lancet*, 13: 83–5.

Royston, E., and Ferguson, J. (1985), 'The Coverage of Maternity Care: A Critical Review of Available Information', *World Health Statistics Quarterly*, 38(3): 27–88.

Sayed, H. A. A., Osman, M. I., El-Zanaty, F., and Way, A. A. (1989), *Egypt Demographic and Health Survey 1988*, Cairo: Egypt National Population Council; Columbia, Md.: IRD/Macro Systems.

Stewart, K., and Sommerfelt, E. (1991), 'Utilization of Maternity Care Services: A Comparative Study Using DHS Data', in *Proceedings of the Demographic and Health Surveys World Conference, Washington, DC. Volume III*, Columbia, Md.: IRD/Macro International.

Wilkinson, M. I., Njogu, W., and Abderrahim, N. (1993), *The Availability of Family Planning and Maternal and Child Health Services*, Columbia, Md.: Macro International.

Wong, E., Popkin, B., Guilkey, D., and Akin, J. (1987), 'Accessibility, Quality of Care and Prenatal Care Use in the Philippines', *Social Science and Medicine*, 24: 927–44.

World Health Organization (1985), *Prevention of Maternal Mortality: Report of WHO Interregional Meeting, Geneva, 11–15 November*, Geneva: World Health Organization.

——(1991), *Maternal Mortality: A Global Fact Book*, Geneva: World Health Organization.

Younis, N., Khattab, H., Zurayk, H., El-Mouelhy, M., Amin, M. F., and Farag, A. M. (1993), 'A Community Study of Gynaecological and Related Morbidities in Rural Egypt', *Studies in Family Planning*, 24: 175–86.

12 Maternal Education and Child Health: Evidence and Ideology

Sonalde Desai

Introduction

Research on women's status and demographic change has traditionally argued that lower fertility and mortality can be achieved by improvements in such indicators of women's status as education, employment opportunities, and control over resources (Mason 1984). The empirical support for some of these claims is stronger than for others, but none the less it is generally believed that policies which affirm women will lead to desirable demographic outcomes. A great deal of this research has been conducted by feminist scholars, genuinely interested in the potential for improving women's status vis-à-vis that of men and seeing positive demographic outcomes as a bonus accompanying such socially desirable policies as improvements in women's education.

Recently, however, advocacy for investing in women by improving their educational status or providing them with home-based income-earning opportunities has gained currency in more traditional institutions such as the World Bank (World Bank 1993). Investment in women's education also forms one of the major cornerstones of the policy recommendations emerging out of the 1994 International Population and Development Conference recently held in Cairo. Frequently this is seen as a positive change, since it leads to the incorporation of women's concerns into mainstream development planning. However, this change has also been seen as a co-option of feminist terminology by development agencies, particularly since this change has occurred concurrently with a variety of other macro-economic changes which have a strong adverse effect on women's lives (Sen and Grown 1987; Heyzer 1992).

Research on the link between maternal education and child health provides an interesting example of the complex interplay between empirical evidence, ideologically driven interpretation of this evidence, and public policy. The belief that increased maternal education results in improvements in child health and survival has provided a strong impetus to the advocacy for investment in women's education. Although there can be little doubt regarding the importance of women's education for the economy, society, and women themselves, whether investment in women's education should form a central core of health policies in developing countries is far from clear. Indeed, by vesting the responsibility for maintaining child health in mothers, this approach may even result in increasing the burden on women, particularly since the importance of individual health behaviour may be used to justify reductions in public health expenditure.

In this chapter, I evaluate some of the empirical evidence linking maternal education and child health and then discuss the implications of these findings for health policies in developing countries. I argue that: (1) research on the links between maternal education and child survival is inconclusive regarding the causal impact of maternal education on child survival; and (2) recent public policy discussions emphasizing the role of the mother in enhancing child survival make unrealistic demands on mothers and result in increasing burdens on women.

Empirical Evidence

By now, the close link between increases in maternal education on the one hand and improvements in child health and survival on the other has been widely acknowledged throughout the demographic community, governments in developing countries, and international donor agencies.[1]

This acknowledgement is primarily based on two types of evidence. At the macro-level, countries with high female education or literacy rates experience low infant and child mortality (Caldwell and Caldwell 1985) and this inverse relationship is very strong. At the micro-level, children of mothers who are educated tend to have a lower probability of dying, higher nutritional status, and a higher probability of being immunized than those of uneducated mothers. As numerous empirical studies have demonstrated (Hobcraft, McDonald and Rutstein 1984; Bicego and Boerma 1991; Boerma, Sommerfelt, and Rutstein 1991), this bi-variate relationship is quite strong.

However, advocating investment in women's education as an important health policy measure moves beyond this simple correlation to assume implicitly that: (1) improvements in maternal education have a *causal* effect on child health and survival; and (2) this effect is *large* and consequently any changes in maternal education can be expected to bring about substantial improvements in child health. This chapter argues that the literature in this area, while extensive in quantity, simply does not examine these two issues in sufficient depth to support these two assumptions.

Maternal Education as a Proxy for other Factors

It is widely recognized that educated women tend to come from families that have higher income and status in the community than less-educated women. Additionally, they also tend to marry men with higher education and income. Consequently, women's education may often act as a proxy for family income and status. Moreover, educated women also tend to live in areas that are more developed and have both schools and hospitals. Hence, maternal education may also act as a proxy for the characteristics of the community. Thus, it is important to control for a number of individual and community characteristics—primarily income, social status of the family, access to high-quality health services, and access to adequate water and sanitation facilities—before we can judge whether any observed correlation between maternal education and child survival is indeed causal.

Empirical research in this area is ambiguous at best. Surprisingly few studies control for family income. Studies based on the Demographic and Health Surveys (DHS) and the World Fertility Survey (WFS) cannot control for family income since these data were not collected in either the WFS or the DHS. Inclusion of such simple controls as father's education, income, and quality of housing reduces the effect of maternal education substantially, although the residual effect remains positive and is significantly different from zero in some countries but not in others (Hobcraft, McDonald, and Rutstein 1984; Hobcraft 1993). Even in-depth qualitative studies like the one by LeVine *et al.* (1991) often rely on such indirect measures of socio-economic status as an index composed of husband's education, occupation, access to water, drainage, and latrine, and appliance ownership. The few studies which control for family income show mixed results. Some studies show that maternal education has a large and statistically significant effect on indicators of child health after controlling for income (Davanzo, Butz, and Habicht 1983; Thomas and Strauss 1992); others show that inclusion of controls for family income, husband's education, and other household-level variables substantially attenuates the impact of maternal education (Victora *et al.* 1986; Alderman 1990).[2]

In addition to having a higher family income, educated women are also likely to be from higher-status families and may be better able to manipulate the health delivery system. Thus, educated women's ability to obtain better health care for their children may not be due to their increased knowledge of the health delivery system but rather to a more favourable response to the health needs of high-status educated women by health service providers. Family social status is difficult to measure at best, and so far as I know, only one study has controlled for unobserved family factors. Behrman and Wolfe, in two related papers (Behrman and Wolfe 1987 and Wolfe and Behrman 1987), examine child anthropometric measures and infant mortality (as well as female health) for adult sisters in Nicaragua who differ in educational levels and find that without controlling for family effects, maternal education has widespread positive health and nutrition effects, but after controlling for unobserved characteristics of family of origin, education effects are substantially smaller in size and are not statistically significant.

Additionally, women's education frequently serves as a proxy for the nature of communities in comparisons both across and within countries. In cross-national comparisons, countries with high levels of female education (or literacy) also tend to have higher incomes and higher male education levels. More-over, as Palloni (1981: 643) has pointed out,

the extent of illiteracy in a society reflects not only the limitations of individuals but, more importantly, the capacity of a system to organize and mobilize to fulfill societal necessities. From this point of view, the proportion illiterate in a population is less an indication of the fraction of mothers with inadequate knowledge to treat and feed a sick child or to challenge the authority of elders than a reflection of the degree of social and political maturity of the system above and beyond the amounts of wealth at its disposal and the degree of equality of its distribution.[3]

At sub-national level, this issue is even more relevant. Generally, educated women live in areas with schools. Given the geographical disparities in many developing societies, areas with schools also tend to be areas with sufficient political power to obtain medical services, better health coverage, higher incomes, and better water and sanitation systems. Indeed, results from the Demographic and Health Surveys show substantial intra-country disparities in health outcomes (Hobcraft 1994). Unfortunately, these community-level factors are rarely measured adequately in large-sample surveys like the Demographic and Health Surveys and the World Fertility Surveys. Hence, the maternal education variable in DHS- or WFS-based analyses is quite likely to reflect unobserved community characteristics such as ethnic composition of the community, distance from a metropolitan area, and location of the com-munity within the political power structure of the country.

Relatively few studies using data from large national surveys have controlled for these community characteristics; indeed, given the paucity of research in this area, it is not readily apparent which factors should be considered. Hence it is difficult to determine the extent to which education may be a proxy for the conditions prevalent in the local community. The studies that have looked at the effect of maternal education while controlling for the effect of community characteristics have found conflicting results. For example, after controlling for some of the community characteristics, a reduced but still significant effect of maternal education on children's anthropometric outcomes and/or mortality has been found for Brazil and Côte d'Ivoire (Strauss 1990; Thomas and Strauss 1992) but not for Ghana (Alderman 1990; Lavy *et al.* 1993). Methodologies in these studies vary and the community charac-teristics that are considered also vary. In contrast to explicit control of com-munity characteristics, Desai and Alva (1995) examine the differences in child health by maternal education within different communities covered under the Demographic and Health Surveys. This study finds considerable attenuation in the effect of maternal education on child health in models where community characteristics are controlled using a fixed-effects framework.

Examination of the findings from studies analysing the role of individual and community characteristics in affecting child health suggests that the present state of knowledge does not permit us to conclude that maternal education is causally linked to improved child health. Moreover, this relationship appears to vary through time and across countries. Using data from the Demographic and Health Surveys, Hobcraft (1993) finds that the link between maternal education and child health is substantially weaker in Sub-Saharan Africa than in other parts of the world. Similarly, Preston and Haines (1991) find very little relationship between maternal education and child survival in the United States at the turn of the century. These observations suggest that instead of advocating a simple causal relationship between maternal education and child health, it may be more important to examine the pathways through which maternal education may affect child health, and then examine the conditions under which improved education may or may not translate into child health improvements.

Research on pathways linking maternal education to child health is recent in origin and is limited to a small number of qualitative studies of health behaviour (Lindenbaum 1990; Levine *et al.* 1991) and to some summary measures of health behaviour abstracted from the Demographic and Health Surveys (Boerma *et al.* 1990; Boerma, Sommerfelt, and Rutstein 1991). Two important pathways have been hypothesized (Caldwell and Caldwell 1993): (1) educated mothers may find it easier to use medical facilities and as a result may be more likely to use pre-natal care, immunize children, and seek treatment for sick children and follow the treatment prescribed; and (2) educated mothers may be more likely to engage in child care practices that enhance child health.

Evaluating this literature in a recent review of women's education, child welfare, and child survival, Hobcraft (1993: 161) concludes, 'Despite a decade of attention to pathways, the evidence is still not clear about which pathways are important where, and even leaves room for doubt as to whether the strong associations of child survival and access to health care with levels of women's education are causal.'

Moreover, the links between these intermediate behavioural factors and actual health outcomes remain far from clear. For example, it has been argued that educated mothers are more likely to use antenatal services. Pre-natal examination is expected to result in better monitoring of high-risk pregnancies, resulting in high-risk women being sent to hospitals for delivery, thereby reducing stillbirths and neonatal deaths. However, studies show that risk-based screening of difficult pregnancies is not as simple as it appears and a large number of difficult deliveries and resulting maternal and neonatal mortality is experienced by women with low-risk pregnancies. In this situation, access to emergency obstetric care is more important than the risk screening which takes place during pre-natal visits to a trained birth attendant. If this argument is valid, then reduction in neonatal and maternal mortality associated with utilization of antenatal services may be relatively modest (Freedman and Maine 1992).

From Individual Variation to Societal Change

I have argued above that the research on the link between maternal educa-tion and child health and survival at an individual level is inconclusive. A majority of studies in this area show a positive, albeit weak, relationship between maternal education and child health; however, it is difficult to con-clude from these studies that this relationship is causal.

An examination of mortality decline in developing countries adds to this note of caution. In the second half of the twentieth century, mortality has declined all over the world, and this decline has taken place in all strata of society. Compositional analysis by Cleland (1991) provides interesting docu-mentation. His results show that between the mid-1970s (when the WFS surveys were conducted) and the mid-1980s (when the DHS surveys were con-ducted), female education increased and infant mortality decreased in the twelve countries for which comparative data exist. However, this decline occurred in all educational groups, with the result that child mortality differences by maternal education remained more or less constant. Moreover, only a modest percentage of the decline in child mortality is attributable to increasing educational levels, as reflected in the compositional change. The direct effect of increasing education is 10 per cent or less in seven of the twelve countries studied.

Maternal Education and Child Health: the Making of a Field

As the literature reviewed above suggests, although the bi-variate relationship between maternal education and child health is strong, we do not know the causal pathways through which it operates, nor have we been entirely suc-cessful in controlling for a variety of socio-economic differences between edu-cated and uneducated women. Moreover, in many societies, only a modest percentage of mortality improvements over time can be attributed to rising female education rates (Cleland 1990; Florez and Hogan 1990). This suggests a need for caution and more research before we can confidently say that maternal education results in higher infant and child survival and better health.

This caution, suggested by a small group of researchers (Hobcraft 1993; Ewbank 1994), is not reflected in public perception, the public policy com-munity, or the general field of demography. The opinion of this wider com-munity is more congruent with the following passages from the 1993 World Development Report, which focused on investment in health:

What people do with their lives and those of their children affects their health far more than anything that governments do. What they can do is determined, to a great extent, by their income and knowledge—factors that are not completely within their control.

In every society, moreover, the capabilities, income and status of women exert a powerful influence on health. . . . Policies to expand educational opportunities, particularly for girls, help households achieve healthier lives by increasing their access to information and their ability to make good use of it. (World Bank 1993: 37–8)

Education greatly strengthens women's ability to perform their vital role in creating healthy households. It increases their ability to benefit from health information and to make good use of health services; it increases their access to income and enables them to live healthier lives. It is not surprising, therefore, that a child's health is affected much more by the mother's schooling than by the father's schooling. . . . Demographic and Health Surveys in twenty-five developing countries show that, all else being equal, even one to three years of maternal schooling reduced child mortality by 10 per cent. (World Bank 1993: 42)

Interestingly, the preceding passage cites a 1993 paper by John Hobcraft as empirical support, while ignoring Hobcraft's contention in the same paper that:

as has been stressed throughout this paper, we can still not be sure that the associations of all these key factors in child health with maternal education are causal. Associations are often attenuated by control for a limited range of other factors. Control for key unmeasured factors might reduce these associations with mother's education to negligible levels. (Hobcraft 1993: 173)

Sociologically, perhaps a more interesting question is what has led to such divergence in interpretation of the same results. In order to examine this, we must reflect on the historical context surrounding the emergence of advocacy within the field of demography for increased investment in women's education. Focus on women's education first emerged in the context of fertility decline. In the context of the debate between 'development' and 'family planning' approaches to fertility decline, advocates of the development camp identified women's education as a key determinant of fertility. It was argued that increased education changes the demand for children by reducing the benefits of large families and also by increasing the cost of children. Moreover, educational improvements and associated changes in women's position in the family increase women's ability to carry out their fertility preferences through contraceptive use. Thus, governments were urged to focus on changing the climate within which reproductive choices were made and acted upon, instead of focusing excessively on provision of family planning services.

Following this lead, public health researchers also began to focus on maternal education as a key determinant of child health and survival. However, in transporting arguments surrounding fertility to a study of mortality, very little attention was paid to the differences in the nature of the phenomena being studied. Education is expected to affect fertility through: (1) change in the value of children—via changes in the cost of raising children, reliance on children for old-age support, and household power structures; and (2) the ability to carry out reproductive preference through efficient use of contraception. But it is difficult to make analogous arguments for mortality.

It is also difficult to argue with complete conviction that educated mothers value the lives of their children more than uneducated women do. It is possible to argue that maternal education leads to changes in the power structure within families, resulting in a greater quantity of resources being directed towards children. However, this mechanism operates only if mothers value the lives of their children more than fathers or grandmothers do—an assumption with relatively little empirical support as yet. The one instance in which education can plausibly reduce child mortality is in the context of discrimination against female children in food or health expenditure. However, even within this situation, the link between maternal education and sex differentials in mortality is not uniform. At least one study in India finds that educated mothers seem to discriminate more efficiently against female children (Das Gupta 1987), another (also conducted in India) finds that the benefits of education in reducing discrimination against female children are limited to landed families (Clark and Sreeniwas 1994). Moreover, with the exception of South Asia, few countries demonstrate a high degree of gender-based discrimination in food allocation (Haddad *et al.* 1994). A brief review of this literature is enough to suggest that the value of children's health and life is unlikely to differ substantially by maternal education levels.

It can plausibly be argued that education increases women's ability to carry out their preferences for improved child survival, just as it is hypothesized to increase their ability to carry out their fertility preferences. However, individual control over mortality is significantly weaker than individual control over fertility. At present, a wide range of effective contraceptives allow substantial individual control over fertility. In contrast, mortality is a function of a variety of factors—immunization rates in the community, water and sanitation systems, the prevalence of such infectious diseases as tuberculosis, the availability of food, the health care system, and parental care and knowledge. Thus, the link between education and mortality can reasonably be expected to be weaker than the link between education and fertility.[4]

Political and Policy Implications

Although the empirical support for a link between maternal education and child health is relatively weak, the importance of this relationship has been widely accepted because it results in a highly desirable public policy prescription—increase in investment in girls' schooling. Gender-based disparities in education vary across the world but are substantial in many developing countries (United Nations 1990). Advocacy groups for increased investment in girls' schooling—consisting of many liberal social scientists as well as feminist scholars and activists—seized upon this apparent correlation as an increased incentive for policy makers and the international donor community to focus on women's education.

There can be little opposition to improving women's access to education and reducing gender inequalities in education. However, over-emphasizing the link between maternal education and child health and survival has a variety of negative implications, particularly for poor women. In order to examine these potentially negative implications, it is important to focus on the changes in the practice of public health in the present climate of privatization prevalent in a majority of the developing world.

Over the past decade and a half, the field of population and development has increasingly moved its focus from social responsibility toward individual action and responsibility. Whereas the traditional public health package of the 1970s emphasized both disease prevention and cure, public investments in disease prevention have been increasingly de-emphasized in favour of curative services (Pebley 1993). For example, oral rehydration therapy has frequently been favoured over improvements in water and sanitation, and targeted nutritional supplementation has been advocated instead of generalized food subsidies (Okun 1987; United Nations 1990). This reduction in public responsibility for disease prevention has been accompanied by a renewed emphasis on encouraging health-seeking behaviour on the part of individuals. This focus on individual responsibilities takes many forms, which include: advocating improvements in education, particularly women's education, to facilitate health-seeking behaviour; increased reliance on user fees in the provision of health services; and community participation in the organization of health services.

Privatization of the health sector is part of a global trend towards privatization of such diverse sectors as education and agriculture. A number of factors have contributed to this trend:

1. To some extent privatization is a reaction to the policies of the 1970s whereby many developing countries over-committed their resources to a large number of social welfare programmes. With stagnant or even negative economic growth in many developing countries in the 1980s and early 1990s, these commitments were difficult to sustain. As a result, countries have started trimming their expenses in the social sectors. Some of these changes are the result of structural adjustment policies recommended by the International Monetary Fund, while others stem from internal political decisions. As already noted, the health sector has been severely affected by these retrenchments (Cornia, Jolly, and Stewart 1987).

2. Certain welfare policies, particularly those affecting social sectors and food subsidies, were rationalized as being redistributive in nature. However, sometimes these subsidies benefit groups belonging to higher socio-economic strata, who have greater power to influence resource allocation in their favour (Griffin 1992). In India, for example, the richer states of Maharashtra and Gujarat have 1.5 and 1.2 hospital beds per 1,000 population respectively, while the poorer states of Bihar and Madhya Pradesh have only 0.3 and 0.4 beds respectively (World Bank 1993). Similarly, higher education, which mainly

benefits urban residents, frequently consumes a disproportionate share of public funds while primary education lags behind.

This failure of redistributive policies has been used to justify the transition from state-supported welfare programmes to market-based systems in such areas as health, education, food pricing, and public utilities.

3. It is argued that structural adjustment policies, by decreasing public expenditure, will allow governments to trim their budget deficits and thus promote economic growth. As average incomes rise, fewer people live in poverty and health status improves. Data on changes in child mortality for the period 1960–88 show that although child health has been improving everywhere, the gains are much less rapid in countries with slow economic growth (World Bank 1993).

Although the above-mentioned factors have led to a reconsideration of social welfare policies, this has not come about without considerable opposition. For example, UNICEF-led advocacy has focused on the potentially negative impact of structural adjustment policies on the health of poor children and has sought to soften these policies by advocating 'adjustment with a human face' (Cornia, Jolly, and Richard 1987). It is in this political context that the presumed association between maternal education and child health has emerged as a significant policy instrument.

If child health is largely a function of family behaviour and investment in maternal education is crucial to improved child health, then it follows that educated mothers can find ways of dealing with less than optimal structural conditions by changing their own behaviour. For example, reduction in food subsidies can be counterbalanced by providing nutritional education for women so that they may switch from expensive to inexpensive food grains by substituting millet for rice (Behrman 1988), or potential negative health consequences due to the privatization of water and sanitation systems may be overcome by educating women to administer oral rehydration therapy to children dehydrated by diarrhoea (World Bank 1993).

This chapter argues that this stress on individual behaviour tends to make unrealistic demands on individuals, particularly mothers. Mothers are seen as all-powerful actors determining their children's survival, with the implication that somehow, uneducated women are failing in their responsibilities. This approach seems to assume that households—particularly mothers—can achieve better health for their children, if only they were willing and more knowledgeable. Thus, the focus seems to have shifted from the social conditions that lead to the disease to the characteristics of those who are affected and the medical responses (Kent 1991).

The increased focus on individual action provides a rationale for the withdrawal of public involvement from a variety of sectors, as discussed above. However, little attention has been directed towards the fact that in so doing, these policies unduly burden women, particularly poor women. Research on diarrhoeal diseases and public policies targeted at reducing mortality associated with diarrhoea provide an interesting example.

Although the links between the quality and quantity of water supply and the prevalence of diarrhoeal diseases are well known (World Bank 1992), it is increasingly being argued that government expenditure on water provision is unnecessary since mortality associated with diarrhoeal diseases can be reduced through administration of oral rehydration therapy.[5] Families, particularly mothers, need to learn that a child with diarrhoea is likely to die of dehydration unless rehydration therapy is administered. The use of oral rehydration therapy is frequently linked to women's education, and a search of the POPLINE bibliographic data-base conducted in Spring 1993 revealed that of the 1,985 entries on diarrhoea, 38 per cent mention oral rehydration therapy and 22 per cent mention education (usually in conjunction with each other), but only 5 per cent mention water supply, 8 per cent mention sanitation, and a mere 2 per cent mention income.

However, very little attention is directed to the fact that oral rehydration therapy, marketed aggressively by such international agencies as UNICEF, is particularly demanding of women's time because it requires constant feeding of very small amounts of solution over a long period. A study conducted in Honduras documents the fact that in some situations mothers administer very little of the solution to children (Kendell, Foote, and Martorell 1984), perhaps because they grow impatient with the therapy. A related problem is that the solution may not meet parents' felt needs. While the solution prevents dehydration, it does not actually stop diarrhoea. Mothers, on the other hand, may be looking for a medicine that stops diarrhoea immediately, thus saving them valuable time (Bolton *et al.* 1989). Given the high demands on women's time in many parts of the world, focusing on women's education in order to reduce deaths associated with diarrhoeal diseases serves to add to the already heavy burden carried by poor women.[6] And when advocated in conjunction with recommendations for withdrawing public investment in water distribution systems (World Bank 1993), this focus on women's education serves to shift the burden of dealing with diarrhoeal diseases from society as a whole to women in poor households.

Women's Status and Child Health: Refocusing the Discussion

In this chapter, I have argued that the link between maternal education and child health is not as established as is generally believed. Moreover, this focus on women as procurers of family health has a variety of negative consequences for women. In particular, the overstatement of maternal importance in determining child health tends to be used as evidence to justify reductions in state responsibilities for the provision of public health and such basic elements of the infrastructure as water and sanitation. These two observations suggest a need for re-evaluation of the discussion in this arena.

Much of the research on women's status vis-à-vis child health has implicitly focused on mothers as agents working on behalf of their children to seek improvements in child health and has consequently suggested that the more power and knowledge that mothers have, the better it is for their children. There can be little opposition to this statement. However, our discussion of what constitutes women's power needs to be broadened. At present, much of the discussion on women's empowerment seems centred largely on factors that affect women themselves, while leaving social institutions around them unchanged. Some of these factors, such as female seclusion, gender hierarchies in the family, and lack of educational opportunities, have been mentioned by other chapters in this volume. However, the transformation of the institutional structure is an integral part of women's empowerment. Poverty and lack of state support for child health care disempowers women as much as, if not more than, lack of education or lack of power in the household. While these factors affect both men and women given the gender division of the household, the decline in state resources devoted to such areas as the provision of water, sanitation, and health services particularly disadvantages women.

I suggest that a restructuring of the distribution of responsibility between mothers and the state in influencing child health outcomes—as well as other demographic outcomes—should be placed at the core of future discussion in this arena. Women, both as mothers and in their own right, cannot be empowered until some of the responsibilities that are currently devolved to the level of the family are transferred to society as a whole. Of particular interest to this restructuring are factors that affect child health, such as the provision of health services and better water and sanitation services, and factors that affect women's domestic responsibility, such as the availability of child care and the preservation of such common-property resources as water and firewood (Desai and Jain 1994).

Notes

This chapter is a revised version of a paper presented at the IUSSP Seminar on Women, Poverty and Demographic Change, Oaxaca, Mexico. This chapter benefited from extensive comments by Karen Mason, Susheela Singh, Joan Kahn, and participants in the seminar. Needless to say, the views presented in this chapter are the sole responsibility of the author.

1. For example, nearly half the studies reported at a conference in Canberra on health transitions focused on maternal education (Caldwell *et al.* 1990).
2. Income is treated as an exogenous variable in some studies, as an endogenous variable in others.
3. The much-celebrated cases of Kerala and Sri Lanka can be viewed in the light of

political maturity just as easily as they can be viewed in the light of increased female education.

4. Ironically, several comparative studies of the relationship between maternal education and fertility have also argued that the impact of education on reproductive behaviour is modest: fertility preferences vary little by education (Lightbourne 1985), and the relationship between education and fertility appears to depend on the level of socio-economic development and is curvilinear, with primary schooling sometimes resulting in fertility increase (Jejeebhoy 1993).

5. Ironically, research based on the Demographic and Health Surveys shows negligible differences by maternal education levels in the incidence of diarrhoea.

6. This is another instance in which a simplistic model of the links between knowledge, behaviour, and health outcomes has been assumed. Studies of the effectiveness of oral rehydration therapy in reducing diarrhoeal deaths are more cautious (Victora *et al.* 1993).

References

Alderman, Harold (1990), *Nutritional Status in Ghana and its Determinants: Social Dimensions of Adjustment in Sub-Saharan Africa*, Working Paper No. 3, Washington, DC: World Bank.

Behrman, Jere (1988), 'The Impact of Economic Adjustment Programs', in David E. Bell and Michael E. Rich (eds.), *Health, Nutrition and Economic Crises: Approaches to Policy in the Third World*, Dover, Mass.: Auburn House Publishing, 189–265.

—— and Wolfe, Barbara L. (1987), 'How Does Mother's Schooling Affect Family Health, Nutrition, Medical Care Usage, and Household Sanitation?', *Journal of Econometrics*, 36: 185–204.

Bicego, George T., and Boerma, J. Ties (1991), 'Maternal Education and Child Survival: A Comparative Analysis of DHS Data', in *Proceedings of the Demographic and Health Surveys World Conference, Washington, D.C. Vol. 1*, Columbia, Md.: IRD/Macro International, 177–204.

Boerma, J. Ties, Sommerfelt, A. E., Rutstein, S. O., and Rojas, G. (1990), *Immunization: Levels, Trends and Differentials*, Columbia, Md.: IRD/Macro International.

———— (1991), *Child Morbidity and Treatment Patterns*, Columbia, Md.: IRD/Macro International.

Bolton, Pamela, Kendall, Carl, Leontsini, Elli, and Whitaker, Corinne (1989), 'Health Technologies and Women of the Third World', in Rita S. Gallin, Marilyn Aronoff, and Anne Ferguson (eds.), *The Women and International Development Annual*, Boulder, Colo.: Westview Press, 105–37.

Caldwell, John C. (1979), 'Education as a Factor in Mortality Decline: An Examination of Nigerian Data', *Population Studies*, 33: 395–413.

—— and Caldwell, Pat (1985), 'Education and Literacy as Factors in Health', in Halstead, Walsh, and Warren (1993), 181–5.

———— (1993), 'Women's Position and Child Mortality and Morbidity in Less Developed Countries', in Nora Frederici, Karen Oppenheim Mason, and Solvi Sogner (eds.), *Women's Position and Demographic Change*, Oxford: Clarendon Press, 122–39.

—— Findley, S., Caldwell, P., Santow, G., Braid, J., and Broers-Freeman, D. (eds.) (1990),

What We Know about the Health Transition: The Cultural, Social and Behavioural Determinants of Health, Canberra: Health Transition Centre, Australian National University.

Clark, Alice, and Sreeniwas, Sudha (1994), 'Class, Maternal Education and Excess Female Child Mortality in Gujarat State', paper presented at the 1994 Annual Meetings of the Population Association of America, Miami.

Cleland, John (1990), 'Maternal Education and Child Survival: Further Evidence and Explanations', in Caldwell *et al.* (1990), 400–19.

——(1991), 'Socio-economic Inequalities in Childhood Mortality: The 1970's Compared with the 1980's', in *Proceedings of the Demographic and Health Surveys World Conference, Washington DC. Vol. 1*, Columbia, Md.: IRD/Macro International, 135–54.

Cornia, Giovanni Andrea, Jolly, Richard, and Stewart, Frances (1987), *Adjustment with a Human Face: Protecting the Vulnerable and Promoting Growth*, 2 vols., Oxford: Clarendon Press.

Das Gupta, Monica (1987), 'Selective Discrimination against Female Children in Rural Punjab', *Population and Development Review*, 13: 77–100.

Davanzo, Julie, Butz, W. P., and Habicht, J.-P. (1983), 'How Biological and Behavioural Influences on Mortality in Malaysia Vary during the First Year of Life', *Population Studies*, 37: 381–402.

Desai, Sonalde, and Alva, Sumya (1995), 'Maternal Education and Child Health: How Strong is the Relationship?', unpub. MS.

——and Jain, Devaki (1994), 'Maternal Employment and Changes in Family Dynamics: The Social Context of Women's Work in Rural South India', *Population and Development Review*, 20: 115–36.

Ewbank, Douglas C. (1994), 'Maternal Education and Theories of Health Behaviour: A Cautionary Note', *Health Transition Review*, 4: 215–23.

Florez, C. Elisa, and Hogan, Dennis P. (1990), 'Women's Status and Infant Mortality in Rural Colombia', *Social Biology*, 37: 188–203.

Freedman, L. P., and Maine, D. (1992), 'Women's Mortality: A Legacy of Neglect', in M. A. Koblinsky, J. Timyan, and J. Gay (eds.), *Women's Health: A Global Perspective*, Boulder, Colo.: Westview Press, 147–70.

Griffin, Charles (1992), *Health Care in Asia: A Comparative Study of Cost and Financing*, Washington, DC: World Bank.

Haddad, Lawrence, Pena, Christine, and Slack, Alison (1994), *Poverty and Nutrition within Households: Review and New Evidence*, Washington, DC: International Food Policy Research Institute.

Halstead, S. B., Walsh, J. A., and Warren, K. (eds.) (1985), *Good Health at Low Cost*, New York: Rockefeller Foundation.

Heyzer, N. (1992), 'Gender, Economic Growth and Poverty', *Development*, 1: 50–3.

Hobcraft, John (1993), 'Women's Education, Child Welfare and Child Survival: A Review of the Evidence', *Health Transition Review*, 3: 159–75.

——(1994), *The Health Rationale for Family Planning: Timing of Births and Child Survival*, New York: United Nations.

——McDonald, J. W., and Rutstein, S. O. (1984), 'Socioeconomic Factors in Infant and Child Mortality: A Cross-National Comparison', *Population Studies*, 38: 193–223.

Jejeebhoy, Shireen (1993), 'How Education Influences Women's Autonomy: Channels to Fertility and its Proximate Determinants', paper presented at the Workshop on Female Education, Autonomy and Fertility in South Asia, New Delhi.

Kendell, Carl, Foote, Dennis, and Martorell, Reynaldo (1984), 'Ethnomedicine and Oral Rehydration Therapy: A Case Study of Ethnomedical Investigation and Program Planning', *Social Science and Medicine*, 19: 253–60.

Kent, George (1991), *The Politics of Children's Survival*, New York: Praeger Press.

Kleinman, Joel C., Fingerhut, Lois A., Prager, Kate, and Kessel, Samuel S. (1992), 'Relationship of Sociodemographic Characteristics to Infant Mortality in the United States', in *Proceedings of the International Collaborative Effort on Perinatal and Infant Mortality. Vol. 3*, Hyattsville, Md.: National Center for Health Statistics, 133–43.

Lavy, Victor, Strauss, John, Thomas, Duncan, and de Vreyer, Philippe (1993), 'Quality of Health Care, Survival and Health Outcomes in Ghana', unpub. MS.

LeVine, R. A., LeVine, S. E., Richman, A., Uribe, F. M. T., Correa, C. S., and Miller, P. M. (1991), 'Women's Schooling and Child Care in the Demographic Transition: A Mexican Case Study', *Population and Development Review*, 17: 459–96.

Lightbourne, R. E. (1985), 'Individual Preferences and Fertility Behaviour', in J. Cleland and J. Hobcraft (eds.), *Reproductive Change in Developing Countries*, London: Oxford University Press, 165–98.

Lindenbaum, S. (1990), 'Maternal Education and Child Care Processes in Bangladesh: The Health and Hygiene of the Middle Classes', in Caldwell *et al.* (1990), 425–40.

Mason, Karen Oppenheim (1984), *The Status of Women: A Review of its Relationship to Fertility and Mortality*, New York: Rockefeller Foundation.

Mensch, B., Lentzner, H., and Preston, S. H. (1985), *Socioeconomic Differentials in Child Mortality in Developing Countries*, New York: Department of International Economic and Social Affairs, United Nations.

Okun, D. (1987), *The Value of Water Supply and Sanitation in Development: An Assessment of Health-Related Interventions*, Washington, DC: US Agency for International Development, Bureau of Science and Technology.

Palloni, Alberto (1981), 'Mortality in Latin America: Emerging Patterns', *Population and Development Review*, 7: 623–49.

Pebley, Anne R. (1993), 'Goals of the World Summit for Children and their Implications for Health Policy', in James N. Gribbles and Samuel H. Preston (eds.), *The Epidemiological Transition: Policy and Planning Implications for Developing Countries*, Washington, DC: National Academy Press, 170–96.

Preston, S., and Haines, M. (1991), *Fatal Years: Child Mortality in Nineteenth-Century America*, Princeton: Princeton University Press.

Sen, Gita, and Grown, Caren (1987), *Development, Crises and Alternative Visions: Third World Women's Perspectives*, New York: Monthly Review Press.

Strauss, John (1990), 'Households, Communities and Preschool Children's Nutrition Outcomes: Evidence from Rural Côte d'Ivoire', *Economic Development and Cultural Change*, 38: 231–61.

Thomas, Duncan, and Strauss, John (1992), 'Prices, Infrastructure, Household Characteristics and Child Height', *Journal of Development Economics*, 39: 301–31.

United Nations (1990), *Human Development Report*, New York: United Nations Development Programme.

Victora, Cesar G., Vaughan, J. Patrick, Kirkwood, Betty R., Martines, Jose Carlos, and Barcelos, Lucio B. (1986), 'Risk Factors for Malnutrition in Brazilian Children: The Role of Social and Environmental Variables', *Bulletin of World Health Organization*, 64: 299–309.

—— Huttly, S. R., Fuchs, S. C., Barros, F. C., Garenne, M., Leroy, O., Fontaine, O., Beau, J. P., Fauveau, V., and Chowdhury, H. R. (1993), 'International Differences in Clinincal Patterns of Diarrhoeal Deaths: A Comparison of Children form Brazil, Senegal, Bangladesh, and India', *Journal of Diarrhoeal Disease Research*, 11: 25–9.

Wolfe, Barbara L., and Behrman, Jere R. (1987), 'Women's Schooling and Children's Health: Are the Effects Robust with Adult Sibling Control for Women's Childhood Background?', *Journal of Health Economics*, 6: 239–54.

World Bank (1992), *World Development Report 1992: Development and Environment*, New York: Oxford University Press.

—— (1993), *World Development Report 1993: Investing in Health*, New York: Oxford University Press.

Index